A MAP OF
BOHEMIA
From the Explora
GELETT BURGE
THE SEA OF CARE
of Peace
RCADY
LICE
Forest of Arden
M I A
of
Fame
VITIA

Berkeley Bohemia

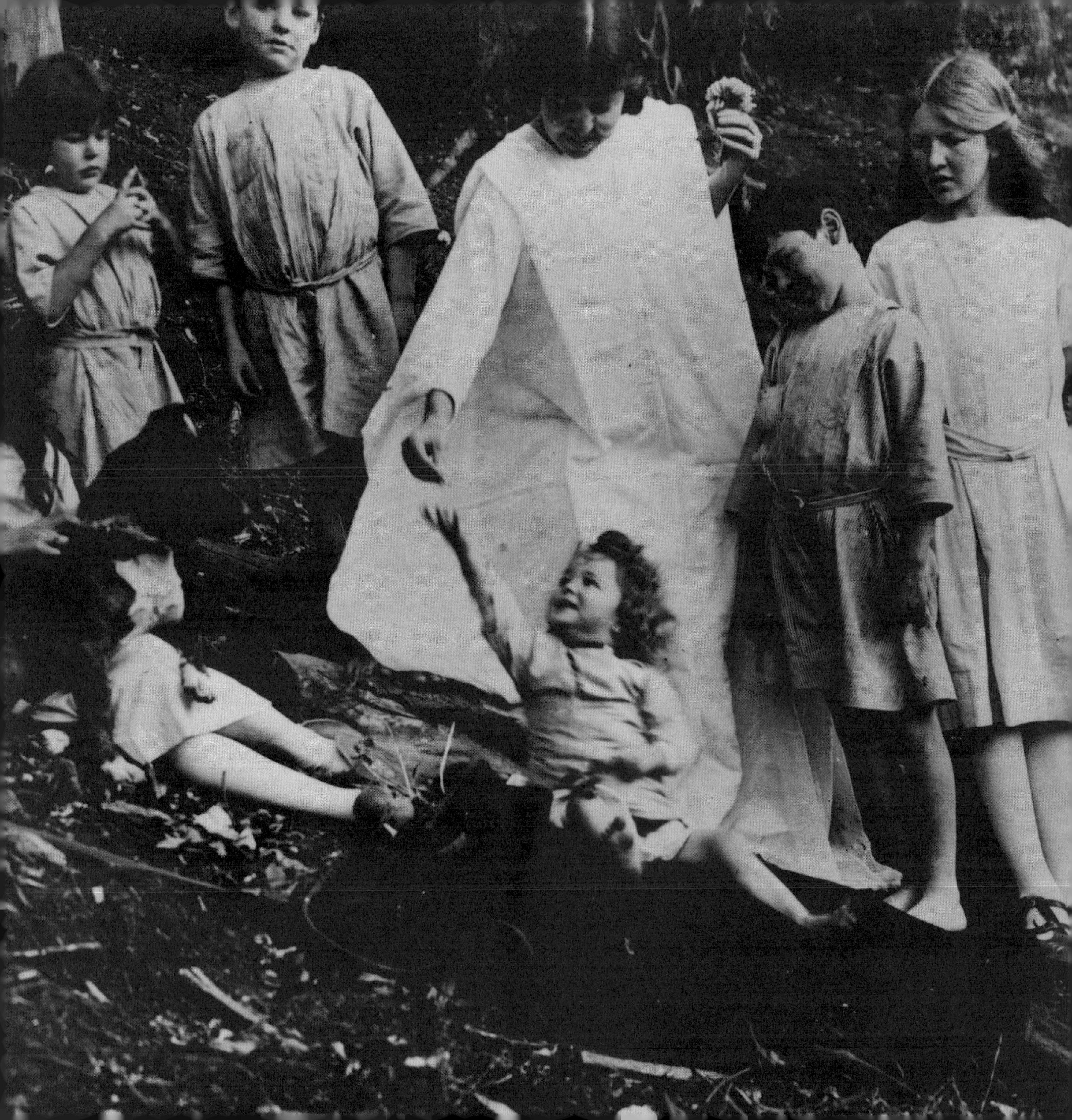

berkeley bohemia

ARTISTS AND VISIONARIES OF THE EARLY 20TH CENTURY

ED HERNY

SHELLEY RIDEOUT

KATIE WADELL

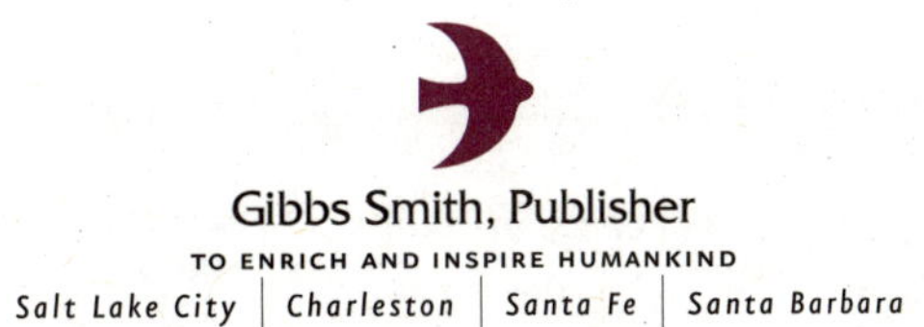

Gibbs Smith, Publisher
TO ENRICH AND INSPIRE HUMANKIND
Salt Lake City | Charleston | Santa Fe | Santa Barbara

First Edition
12 11 10 09 08   5 4 3 2 1

Text © 2008 Ed Herny, Shelley Rideout and Katie Wadell
Photos credited on page 197

Published by
Gibbs Smith, Publisher
P.O. Box 667
Layton, Utah 84041

Orders: 1.800.835.4993
www.gibbs-smith.com

Designed by Kathleen Tandy
Printed and bound in Canada

Library of Congress Cataloging-in-Publication Data
Herny, Ed.
  Berkeley bohemia : artists and visionaries of the early 20th century / Ed Herny, Shelley Rideout, and Katie Wadell. — 1st ed.
      p. cm.
  ISBN-13: 978-1-4236-0085-5
  ISBN-10: 1-4236-0085-1
  1. Arts, American—California—Berkeley—20th century. I. Rideout, Shelley. II. Wadell, Katie. III. Title.
  NX511.B47H47 2008
  700.9794'67—dc22
                              2007033842

For Bernyce, who inspired me to write this book
—ED HERNY

For Aunt Jenny Ruth, a true bohemian
—SHELLEY RIDEOUT

For my parents, who encouraged me to explore
—KATIE WADELL

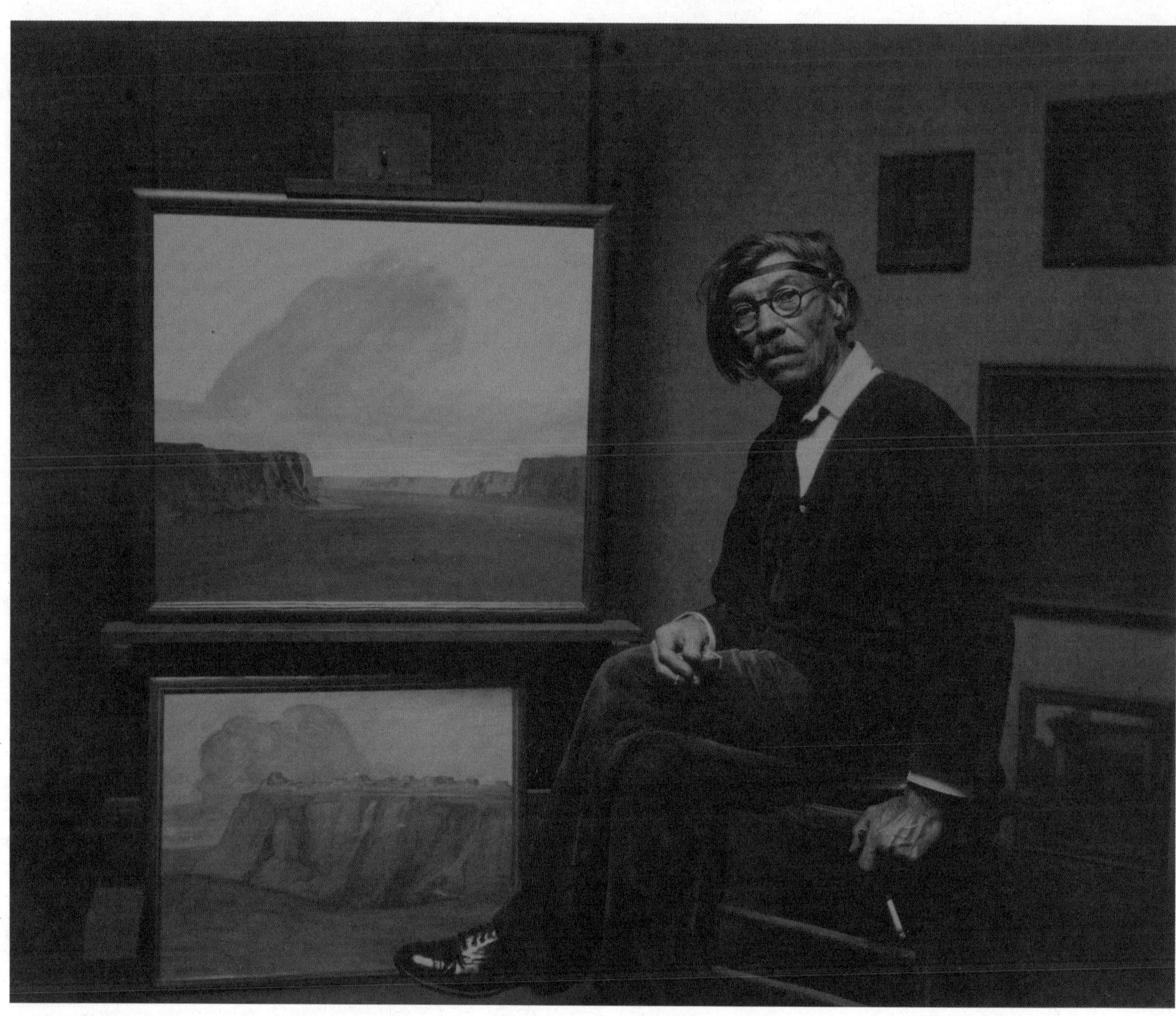

Xavier Martinez
in his studio.

contents

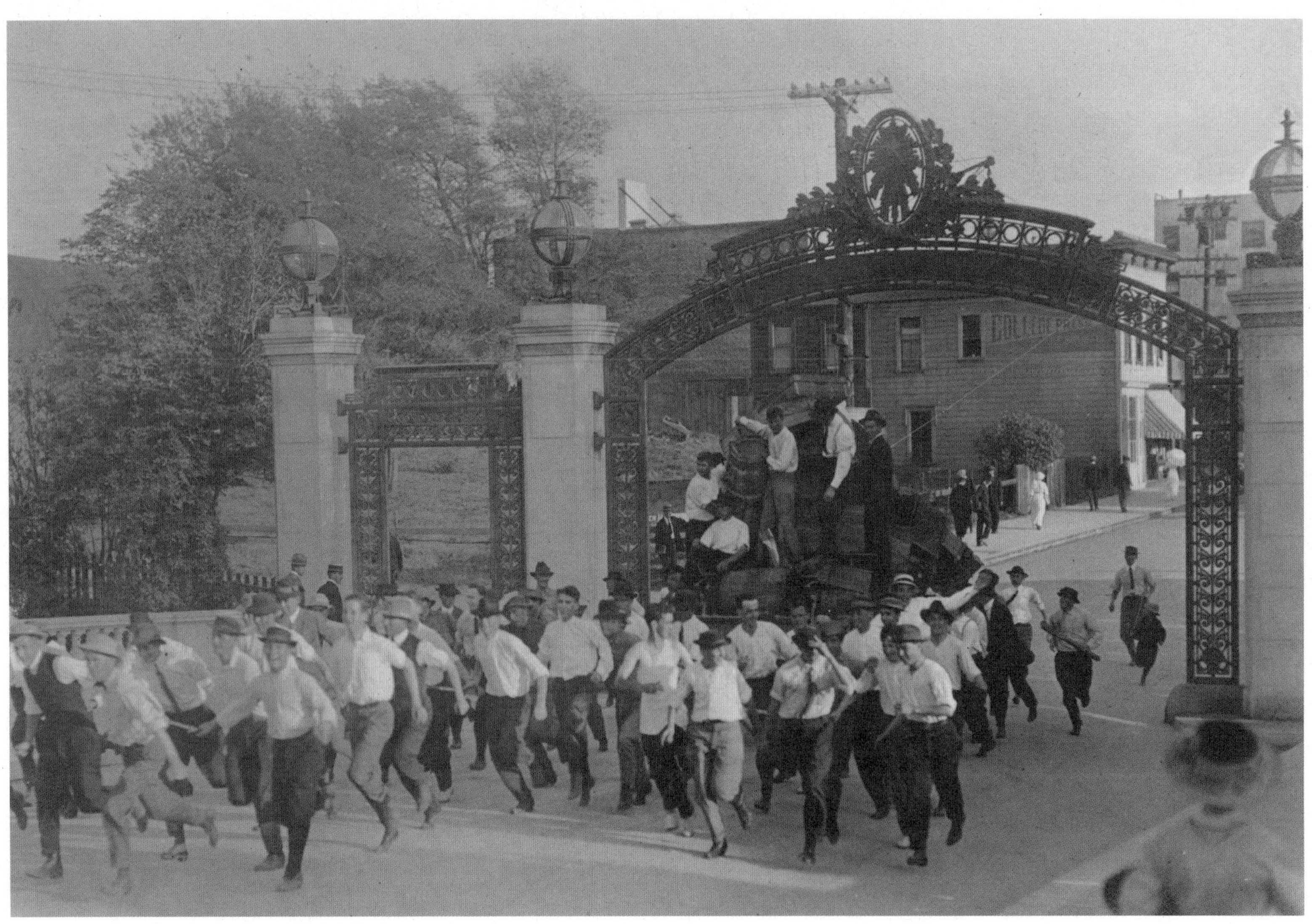

Exuberant university freshman wearing distinctive hats rally at Sather Gate on the south side of the campus.

acknowledgments

We would like to thank the board of directors of the Berkeley Historical Society for supporting a 2004 exhibition and 2005 publication that featured early versions of some of the material in this book. We also owe thanks to the following individuals from the Historical Society who contributed time, knowledge and expertise: John Aronovici, for sharing family photos and memories; Sue Austin, for fact checking; Steve Finacom for pointing out valuable source material; Kenneth Cardwell, BHS Archivist, and Therese Pipe, oral history specialist, for assistance with research; Mark Peters for help with scanning; Allen Stross, Master of Photography, for taking photos specifically for the project; and the late John Stansfield for his encouraging words.

Anthony Bruce and the Berkeley Architectural Heritage Association provided photographs and much valuable assistance. The staff of the Bancroft Library patiently located files and photographs, as did Tricia Rouch of the San Francisco Performing Arts Library and Museum and Steven Lavoie and Martha Bergmann of the Oakland Public Library. Drew Johnson, curator of photography at the Oakland Museum of California, was very generous with his time and helpful advice. Janice Woo at the California College of the Arts Library located photos and sources. Reference librarians at the Berkeley Public Library, the San Francisco Public Library, the Newberry Library, the California Historical Society and Northwestern University Library helped focus our research on Berkeley's early history. Staff at the University of California, Los Angeles Library tirelessly provided photocopies of letters and papers. Harvard University Library generously allowed us to reproduce photographs from its collection.

Mary Bucher and Lee Palsak were extraordinarily generous with family photographs, memories and stories, thus providing living links to past bohemians. Thanks are also due to Tim Hansen and Alan Thomsen for contributing background material on the Keelers and to Harold Wright for his help with research.

Thanks to our editor, Katie Newbold, who juggled dealing with three authors and still kept smiling and to Gibbs Smith, who shared our vision of illuminating the lives of early Berkeley bohemians and made it a reality.

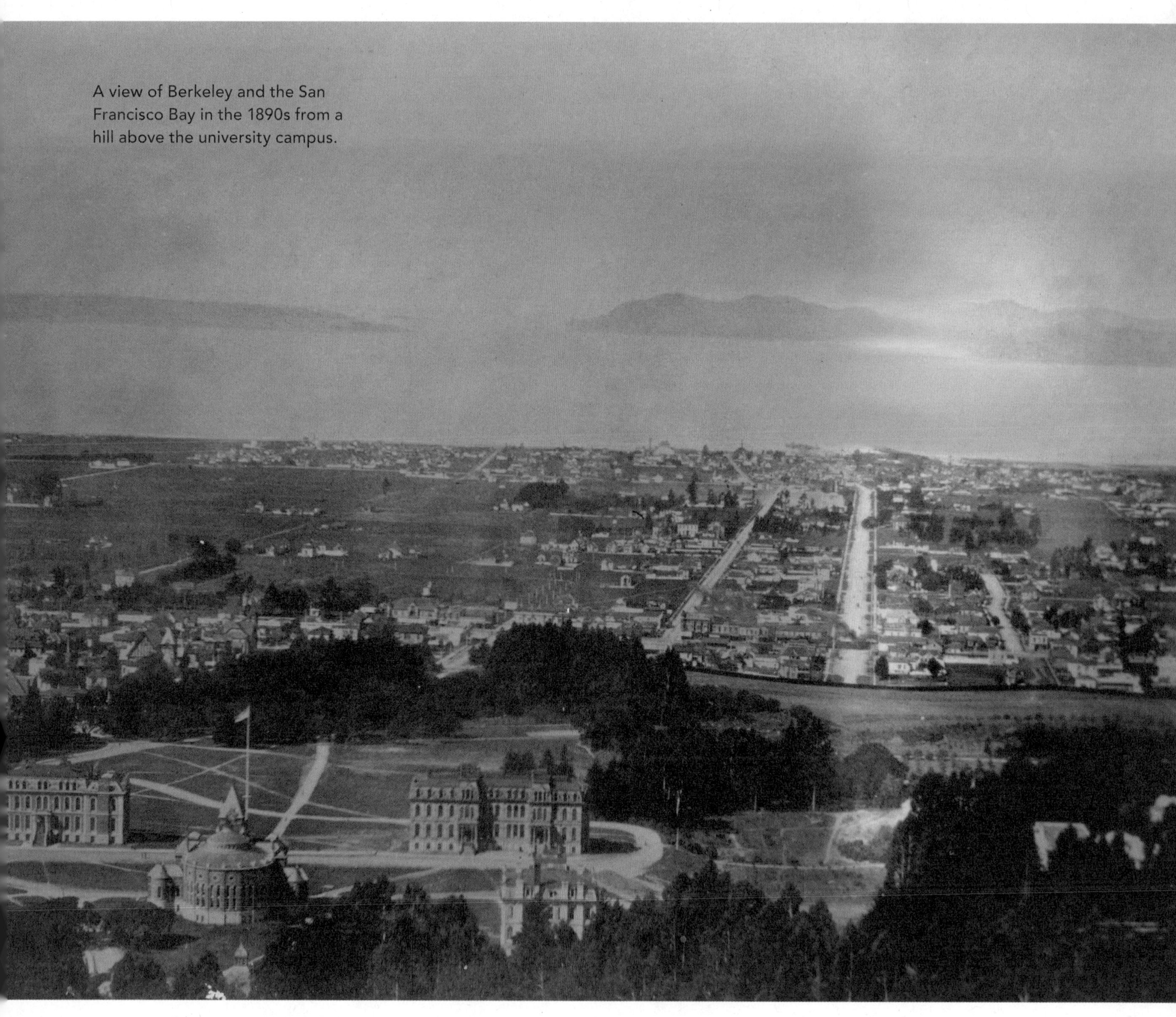

A view of Berkeley and the San
Francisco Bay in the 1890s from a
hill above the university campus.

introduction

The concept of Bohemia was certainly not unique to Berkeley. Nineteenth-century industrialization, with its attendant ills and the rise of a rapacious capitalism, provoked many people around the world to either political or artistic reaction. Inspired by ideals stemming back to Rousseau, fed by the British Arts and Crafts movement and crystallized, in one aspect at least by Henri Murger's 1845 novel *Scenes de la Vie Boheme*, famous bohemian enclaves sprang up in Paris and New York's Greenwich Village.

More bucolic bohemias existed in the English countryside, in Carmel, California, and, later, in Santa Fe and Taos, New Mexico. In California, particularly in the East Bay and Berkeley, a unique combination of ingredients provided fertile ground for individuality, eccentricity and creative expression. Three factors were dominant: topography and climate, the presence of the University of California, and the Gold Rush mentality that drew people from all over the world to the region.

Berkeley featured the San Francisco Bay on the west side and rolling hills on the east, with creeks that flowed from the hills to the bay. The location offered natural beauty and scenic views, a temperate climate and a close proximity to the financial and trading center of San Francisco. The bay led to the ocean and to transportation waterways all across the Pacific and beyond.

The university, founded as the College of California in 1855 in Oakland, bought land and established a site in Berkeley in 1860. Its presence and growth helped transform what could have become merely a pretty suburb of Oakland or a bedroom community of San Francisco into a town bubbling with ideas and open to experimentation. Scholars from all points east were attracted to the educational and teaching opportunities offered by the growing school.

In his book *History of Berkeley*, George Pettitt points out that the university provided employment to educated men who had fought in or worked for the Confederate Army, who might not have been considered employable elsewhere in the United States. Among

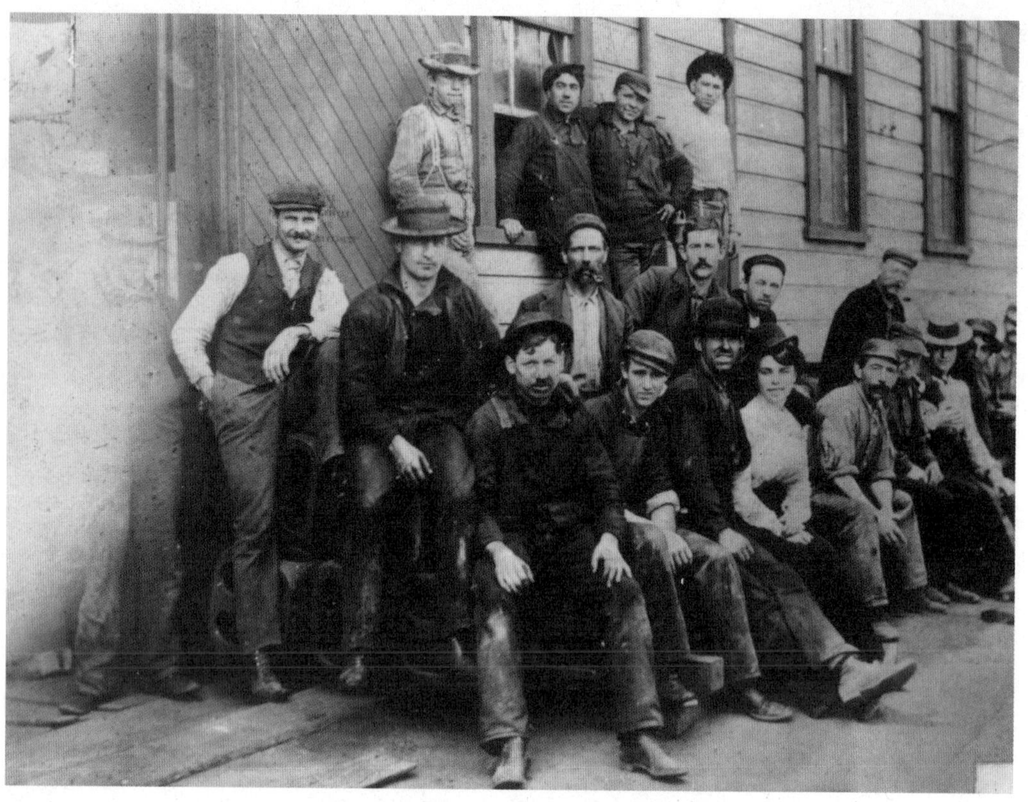

farmland. A commercial and residential district had grown up around the campus, which was situated on Strawberry Creek and backed up to the hills. Substantial homes were built on lots in the College Homestead Tract, land previously owned by the university and sold to fund the growth of the campus. The residents were primarily caucasian, Protestant and in some way affiliated with the university. Rooming houses, restaurants and small businesses serving the campus community lined Telegraph Avenue, the main transportation route into Oakland.

Two miles to the west lay the community of Ocean View, an industrial town on the bay. Founded in the 1850s, Ocean View was home to factories, lumberyards and farms. Its population was working class and ethnically diverse, including Italians, Finns, Swedes, Mexicans, Germans and Chinese. Antagonism and rivalries between the two communities marked the early years of both towns' histories, but in 1878, pressured by the fear of being swallowed up by the larger city of Oakland, just to the south, Ocean View and Berkeley incorporated as the city of Berkeley.

Incorporation did not ensure cooperation. In 1873, prompted by stories of students staggering home drunk from bars in Ocean View, the State of California had imposed the University Liquor Law, prohibiting the sale of alcohol within two miles of the university campus. This caused the owners of more than two dozen bars and saloons in Ocean View to howl in protest, claiming that the elite professors of the university

these were the LeConte brothers, John and Joseph, who were influential in the growth of the university and the town.

California drew others in the 1860s and 1870s: men and women running from the past or wishing to invent a new one, people who felt constrained by the older cities of the East Coast or intrigued by wide open space and a wide open society. Fortune seekers, charlatans, adventurers and refugees from poverty and persecution flocked to the San Francisco Bay Area, coming overland by wagon, around Cape Horn by ship or, after 1869, across the vast continent by train. By the 1870s, what we know today as Berkeley was two small communities separated by could serve wine in their homes but an honest working man could not buy a drink after a hard day's labor. In 1876, the two-mile law was reduced to one mile, but in 1899, the Town Trustees passed an anti-saloon ordinance, further inflaming the situation.

East Berkeley and West Berkeley had separate transportation routes into Oakland, with those in the area around the campus taking a horse car along Telegraph Avenue and those in Ocean View traveling along San Pablo Avenue. It was not until 1891 that a horsecar line running across University Avenue connected the two communities.

The mistrust between the two very different communities that composed Berkeley extended to an inability to agree on a site for the Town Hall. After renting temporary locations that rotated between East and West for several years, a wooden hall was built at the corner of University Avenue and Sacramento Street, a location convenient to none of the residents.

In the meantime, enterprising businessmen Francis Kittredge Shattuck and J. L. Barker were intent on a plan to lure the Southern Pacific Railroad to Berkeley. In 1876, they donated land they owned just west of the campus for a railway station. This became Shattuck Square, and the station built there became a transit hub. Soon the train lines extended to Vine Street, aiding and promoting commercial and residential development north of the campus.

After nearly ten years, the residents of East Berkeley were able to persuade those of West Berkeley to move the town hall to a location closer to the UC campus and the developing transit hub on Shattuck Avenue. This project literally required moving the existing structure, as the change in location carried the proviso that no money be spent on the construction of a new building. In 1899, the wooden hall was moved, with the aid of one horse, to a location at Grove Street and Center Street at a cost of $999. It very shortly burned to the ground; the origin of the fire was never established. Since then, however, city hall has remained within a few blocks of the campus and the downtown area.

Annexation of outlying areas and the development of residential tracts continued as real estate agents touted the area's beauty and convenience. Berkeley grew in population. Peralta Park was developed as an area of fine homes to the north, and the Lorin district, a prosperous little community

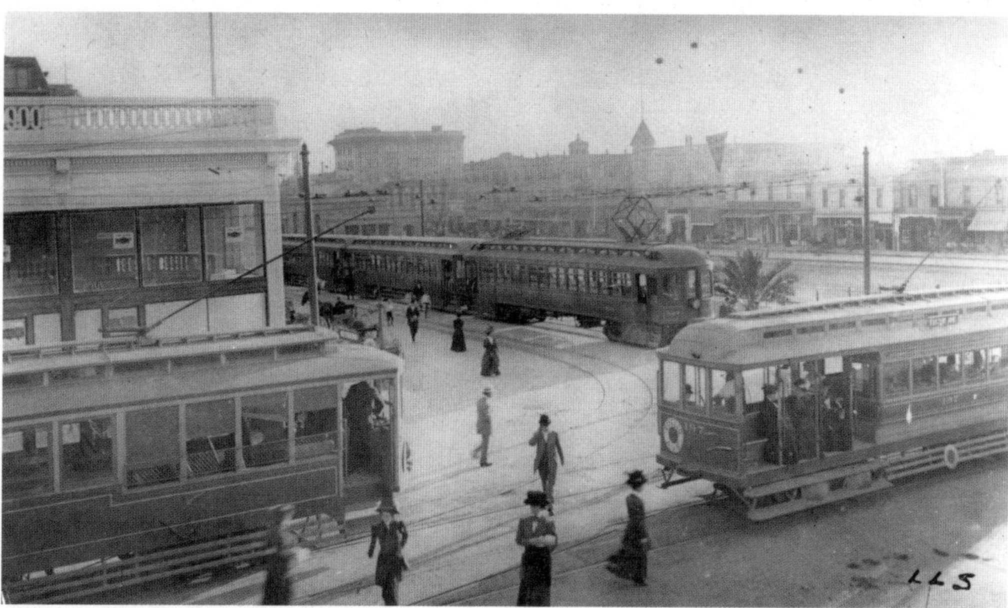

All trains met at the downtown Berkeley transit hub in Shattuck Square.

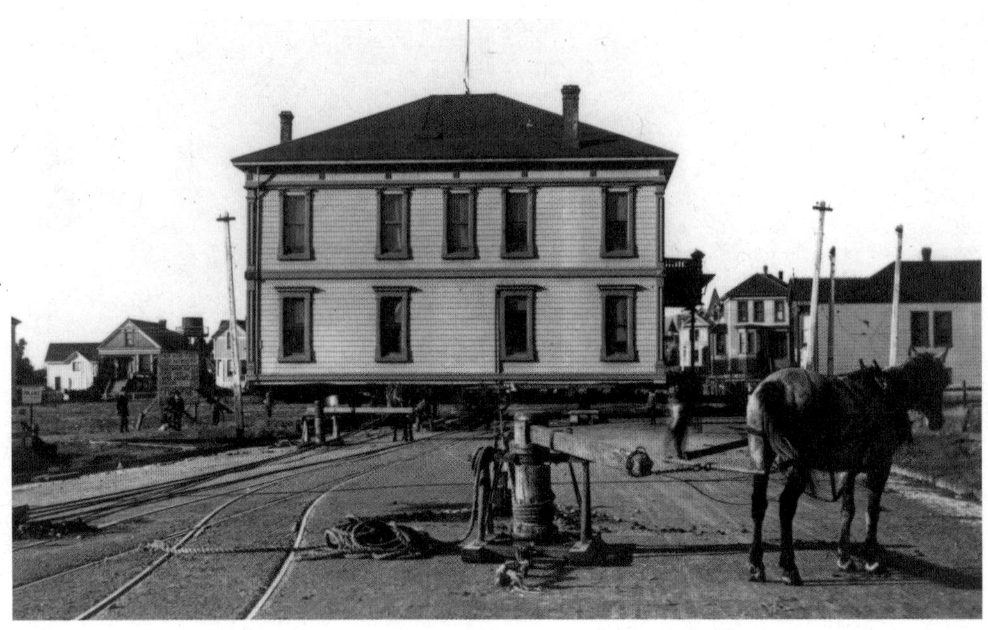

In 1899 the town hall was moved to Grove and Center Streets.

close to the Oakland border, was annexed to Berkeley in 1902.

By 1903, the Key System network of electric trains feeding to the ferry terminal enabled Berkeley residents to travel from the downtown Berkeley station to San Francisco in thirty-six minutes. The electric trains eventually extended to Northbrae and Thousand Oaks, where lots were sold and housing tracts were developed, as well as up Claremont Avenue to the grand Claremont Hotel, built in 1915. The population, which had been only 2,000 at the time of incorporation, had grown to 13,000 by 1900. At this point, Berkeley still retained a pastoral air. Small farms and pastures occupied much of the open space, and trees, planted by the thousands, created the appearance of a forest on the previously bare, rolling grassland.

In the decade between 1900 and 1910, the population more than tripled, swelling to 56,000 by 1920. The 1906 Earthquake and Fire in San Francisco sent thousands of refugees to the East Bay and many of them remained. The growing prestige of the university, as it became known as one of the country's most distinguished research institutions, drew scholars from around the country and, increasingly, from around the world. The city became more urban but still retained its distinctive charm.

In this setting, then moral in tone, naturally beautiful and increasingly beautified by civic efforts, and close to the city of San Francisco, the "Paris of the West," Berkeley imagined itself as the "Athens of the West." It was a city of scholars, a crossroad of cultures and a magnet for visionaries. It was also a city where ordinary men and women struggled to make a living, raise their families and dream their dreams. The artists, writers and thinkers who populated the area were profoundly influenced by the natural setting and by the idea of community.

Here, life went to a gentler pace,
And dreams and dreamers found
    a place.[1]

This poem, from the 1926 novel *Love in Greenwich Village* by Floyd Dell, might have been written with Berkeley in mind. The dreamers who inhabited early Berkeley are those whose lives we will explore here, the sort of person Merriam Webster's dictionary defines as bohemian: "a person (as a writer or artist) living an unconventional life, usually in a colony with others."

prologue

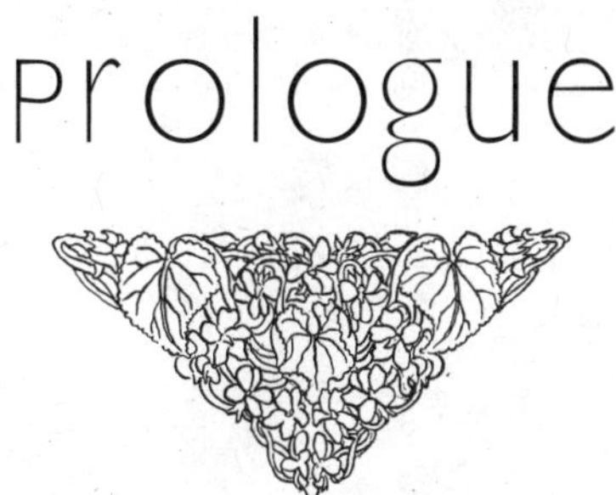

Walking down Fulton Street in a quiet tree-lined area just south of the university campus in contemporary Berkeley, California, it is possible to go back in time. On a spring evening all is still as the setting sun slides towards San Francisco Bay. The fragrance of jasmine and roses emerges from the yards of brown-shingled houses. A sleek black-and-white cat stretches from his cushion on a front porch and saunters down the steps, disappearing around the side of the house through the hydrangeas.

From the open window of a large yellow Queen Anne house a block farther down the street, a piano concerto slides through the lace curtains as the sound of children's voices float from a backyard. Crossing the street slowly between one curb and another, the walker is in the Berkeley of the 1920s for a brief moment. For that split second, the events, struggles, ideas and people of Berkeley Bohemia are as vital as today's news, and the past is alive.

Walk with us for a little way and see if you too can hear its echoes.

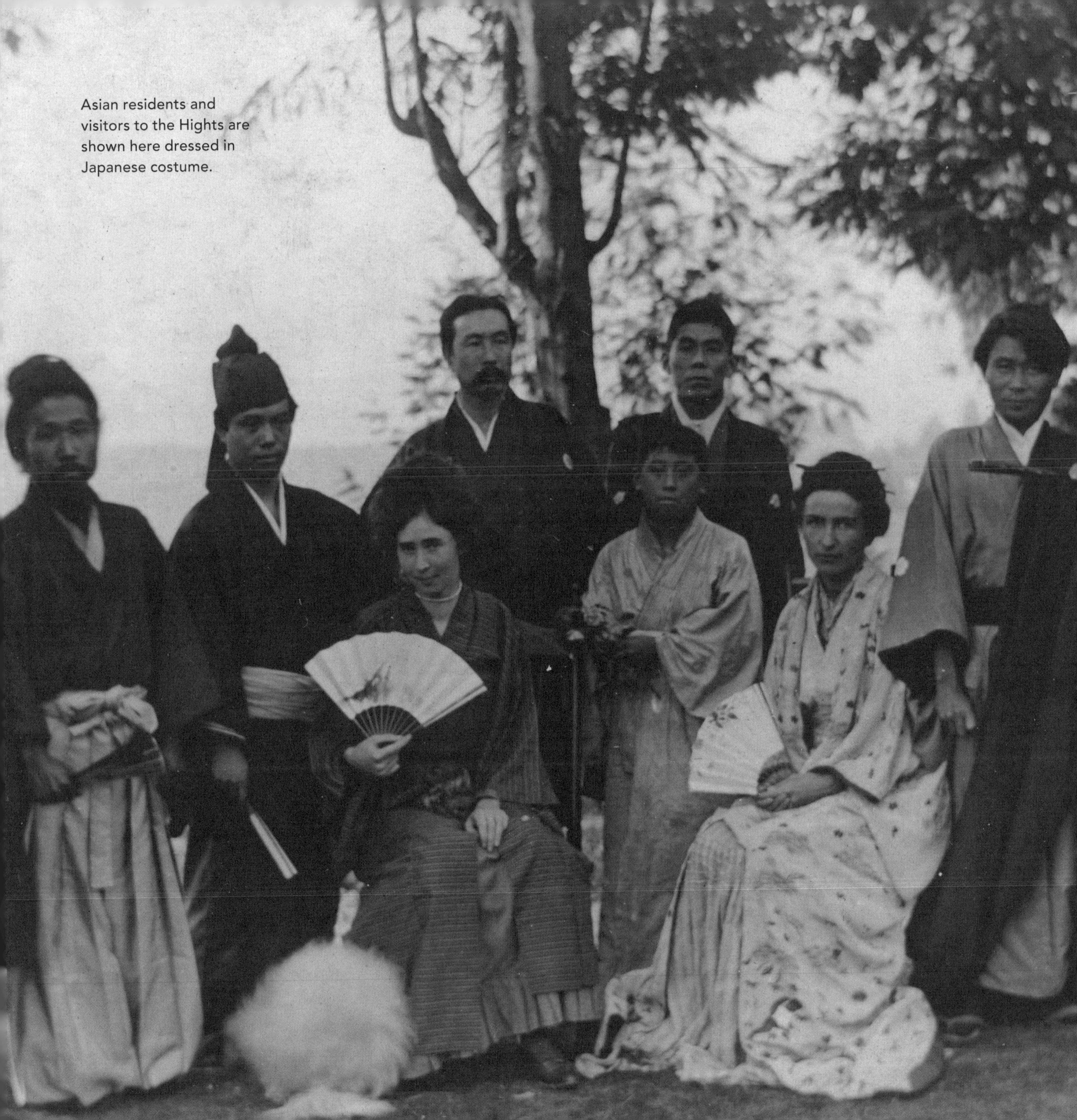

Asian residents and
visitors to the Hights are
shown here dressed in
Japanese costume.

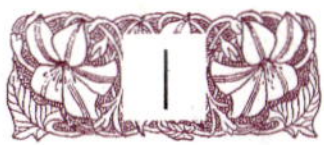

pioneers and passersby

"Upon the heights beyond my reach,
You drink from Art's immortal spring,
And vision dreams denied my speech,
And paint the songs I may not sing."
—Ina Coolbrith,
"To William Keith, Artist"

WILLIAM KEITH

In the 1890s, there were many visitors to a pleasant house at 2207 Atherton Street, just south of the university campus. This was the home of renowned artist William Keith and his second wife, Mary McHenry Keith. By this time Keith was one of the old guards of the Bay Area artistic community. A native of Scotland, he had immigrated to New York as a teenager, along with his sisters and widowed mother. After an early apprenticeship in New York with engraver William Robert to learn the "art, trade and mystery of Engraving on Wood illustrations for Books,"[1] Keith made his way to San Francisco. There he found work as an engraver but quickly turned his attention to sketching and painting in watercolors.

Encouraging notices from art critics for his watercolors of Mount Tamalpais, Yosemite, the Russian River and other northern California landmarks prompted Keith to begin experimenting with oils. A reviewer in the August 1868 *Overland Monthly* commented, "William Keith, a Scotchman by birth, a good wood engraver and one of our best watercolorists in landscapes, has lately given evidence of astonishing capacity in oils. . . . His atmospheres are luminous. His woods have depth and richness. His coloring is full of the finest feeling. He imbues his pictures with poetry."[2]

It was the habit of California landscape artists to spend part of the year on sketching trips. On a trip to Yosemite in October 1872, Keith went with a letter of introduction from a mutual friend to naturalist John Muir. When Muir led Keith and his party to a view of Mt. Lyell, in the

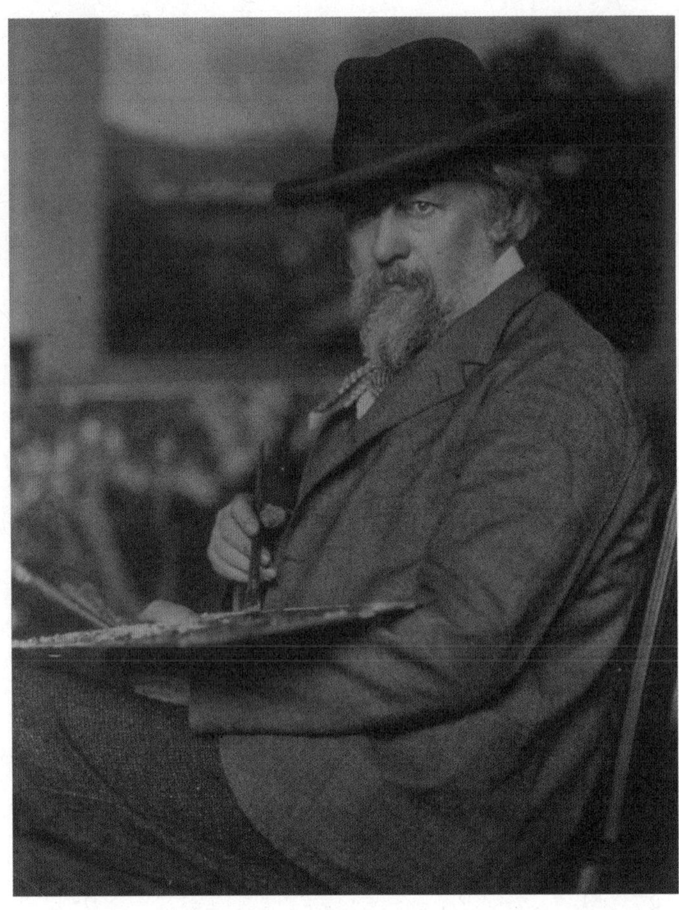

This portrait of William Keith at his easel shows him as a rather romantic figure.

Tuolumne River area, Muir reported that Keith was so struck by the sight that he "dashed forward, shouting and gesticulating and waving his arms like a madman."[3] The two Scotsmen, born in the same year, became fast friends, a friendship that endured for forty years until Keith's death in 1911.

In search of even more spectacular scenery to paint, Keith went on an 1873 expedition to the Rocky Mountains with photographer C. E. Watkins. The travelers chartered two railroad cars for the journey, taking horses and wagons, with hay and feed in one wagon. Watkins's photographs of western scenery were popular in the East. Some of them were made into slides for stereoscope, thus enabling a family in a New England parlor to experience, in a small way at least, the remarkable scenery of the western frontier.

William Keith's friend John Muir was perhaps the person most responsible for bringing a new awareness of the natural world to the American public. Earlier artists and writers had romanticized nature, but Muir hiked the West for over forty years, writing eloquently about what he saw and experienced. Muir's numerous books and articles created a vivid impression of the vast grandeur of the mountains, rivers and forests of the West. He first excited popular imagination about the potential of the remote mountain places and then worked to preserve them from development. When President Theodore Roosevelt visited Yosemite in 1903, Muir took him on a camping trip. In a note to Keith, Muir wrote, "Dear Willie: All went well according to the President's own plan. We camped alone in the Mariposa grove, back of Glacier Point, and at foot of Valley. Had glorious time."[4] This experience eventually encouraged Roosevelt and Congress to transfer all of Yosemite into the National Park system.

What Muir did with words, his friend William Keith did with his canvases. Some of his paintings were done expressly for the purpose of being reproduced as chromolithographs, such as a view of Mount Baker from Vancouver Island, commissioned in 1869 by the Currier and Winter store at 211 Kearny Street in San Francisco. This picture was advertised as being for sale "here and in the East,"[5] thus enabling it to be seen by a much wider audience than could attend a showing at a gallery or museum.

Keith's career was flourishing and his paintings began to command better and better prices. Cincinnati publisher O. J. Wilson, who had met Keith and Muir in the Sierras, commissioned a painting from Keith in 1875 and paid him $2,500 for "Morning on the Upper Merced." Reviewer J. W. Gally commented on seeing one of Keith's Merced paintings, "He has it. This man has more water in his puddle than the rest of them. This picture was never painted in a studio."[6]

After the death of his first wife, Elizabeth, in 1882, Keith was a widower with two teenaged children and, by all accounts, in very low spirits. The Reverend Joseph Worcester, of the San Francisco Swedenborgian Church, introduced Keith to the lively Mary McHenry, daughter of a prominent San Francisco judge and the first female graduate of Hastings College of the Law. During the summer of 1882, Mary McHenry took an art class from Keith and participated in a sketching trip with the class to the Santa Cruz Mountains. The following spring of 1883 found Keith sketching in Berkeley and Piedmont, and on June 2, 1883, several local newspapers reported the Keith-McHenry wedding, held in Mary's Berkeley home. Though an active and ardent supporter of women' rights, Mary McHenry gave up her fledgling law practice to marry the widower eighteen years her senior.

After a honeymoon in San Diego, the newly married couple went to Munich for two years, where Keith took up figure painting. He seems to have mastered this as quickly as he had mastered oils and was soon turning out impressive portraits. Mary, who was an accomplished linguist, acted as interpreter, though in letters to her family that winter she complained of the cold and of living very frugally.

While in Munich, the Keiths had received a letter from their friend Catherine Hittell of San Francisco, who advised them to buy antiques, household ornaments and furnishings in Europe, as interesting things could be had so much more cheaply there. She also advised them to tell the U.S. Customs agents that these were used

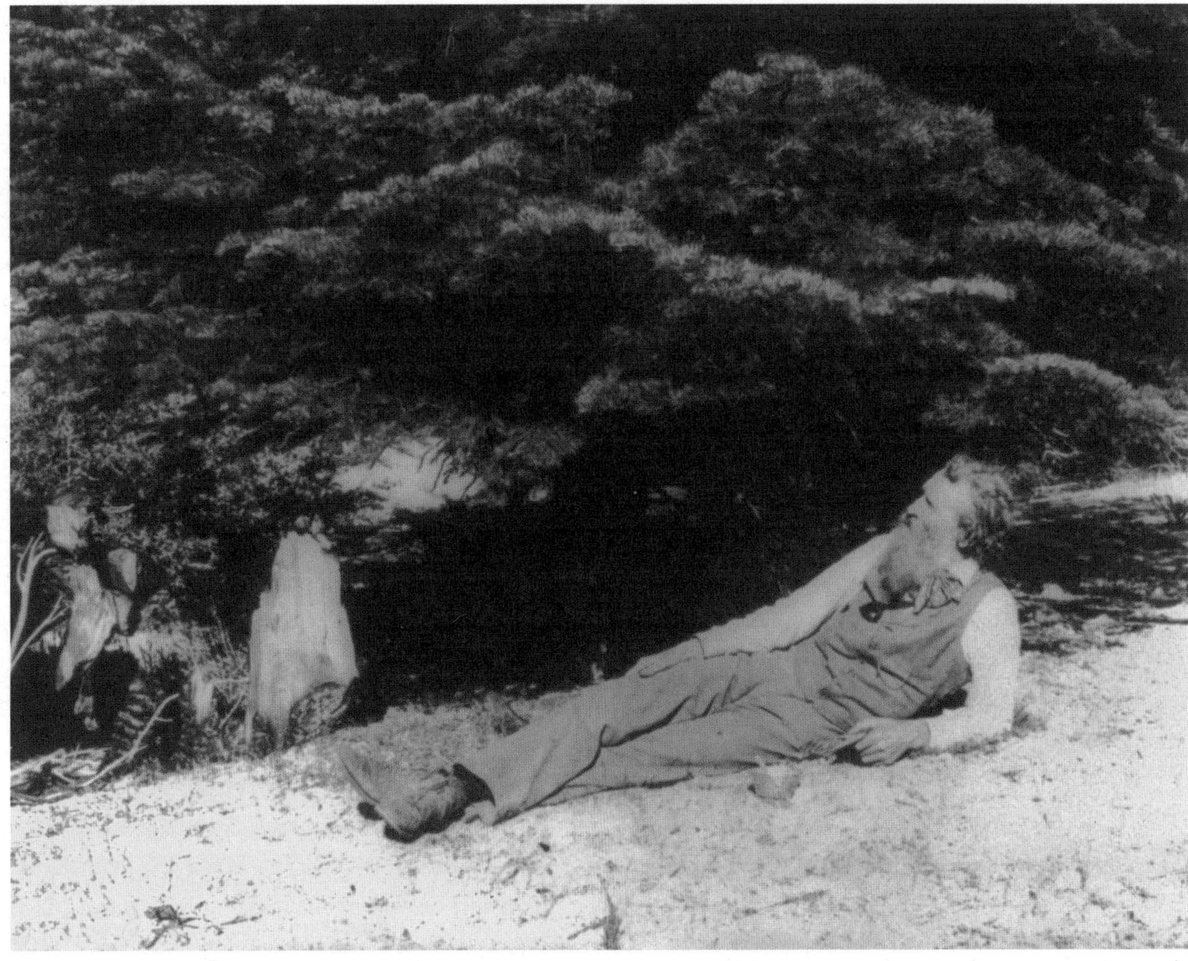

John Muir reclines on a hillside, always 'most at home in the outdoors.

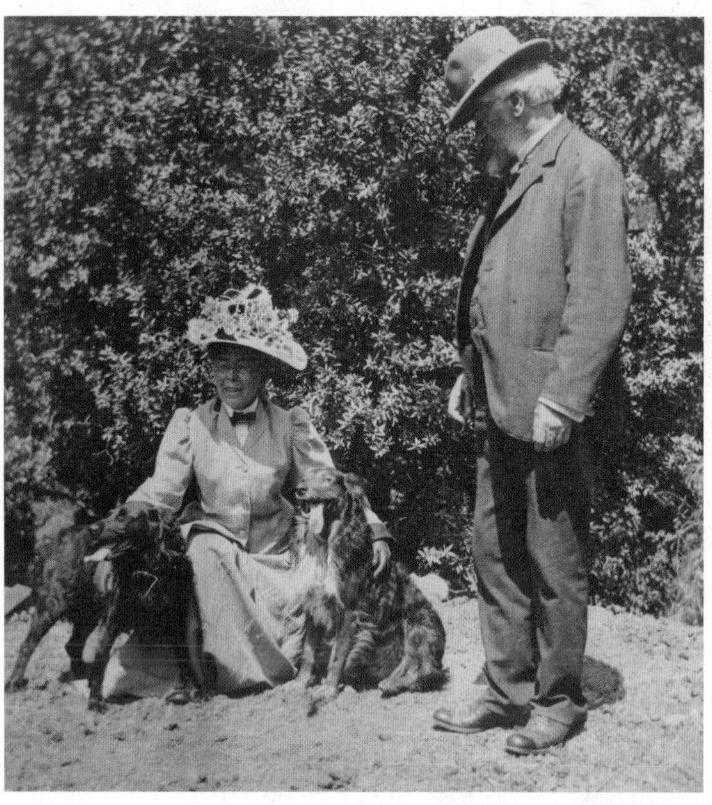

An aging William Keith with his wife, Mary, and their dogs Brownie and Hazel, ca. 1909.

household goods, thus avoiding paying duty upon returning to the United States.

When the Keiths returned from Europe, they set to work with the aid of architect W. W. Goodrich to design and build a house on the Atherton Street lot they had acquired before they left. A local newspaper noted the features of this "artistic residence," which was styled a "quaint old colonial Knickerbocker."[7] The article detailed the cement and bronze panels decorating the façade and described the laborsaving appliances, including petroleum-burning fireplaces and kitchen range, as well as built-in hot water heaters.

A fine painting studio was part of the house, though Keith retained his studio in San Francisco and still traveled there by ferry almost every day. Both the Keith studio in San Francisco and the Keith home in Berkeley were gathering places for the community of artists and writers. Keith also belonged to the Bohemian Club in San Francisco, a men's club established in 1872 as a private club for professional artists, actors and writers. Keith's friend Ina Coolbrith was made an honorary member of the club in recognition of her importance as a poet and to the social network of the Bohemians.

⬙ INA ⬙ COOLBRITH

By the time Coolbrith actually became a Berkeley resident, she was a very old woman crippled with arthritis. During Coolbrith's long life, she had struggled against societal prejudice, financial difficulties, family burdens and ill health. In the process she had reinvented herself over and over, becoming the literary icon photographed by Ansel Adams in 1926: a sad but stately figure seated in a chair, the fluffy white cat at her feet a foil for the exquisite lace scarf that covered her hair.

Though not a Berkeley resident until the last five years of her life, Coolbrith had lived for many years in Oakland, and she had a network of friends and acquaintances stretching across the entire Bay Area and beyond.

Named California's first Poet Laureate in 1915, Coolbrith began life as Josephine Donna Smith, born to a Mormon family in Nauvoo, Illinois, in 1841. Her father, Don Carlos Smith, was the younger brother of Joseph Smith, Jr., founder of the Mormon religion, but a few months after Ina was born her father died of pneumonia. After Joseph Smith was killed during a mob attack, and the other inhabitants of the surrounding area began to force the Mormons out, her mother remarried a non-Mormon and moved the family to California, erasing all trace of her controversial past. After spending time in northern California and San Francisco, the family moved to Los Angeles. Coolbrith began writing poetry as a girl, publishing her first pieces in the *Los Angeles Star* in 1856. She went through a brief marriage to Robert Carsley, which ended scandalously when her husband accused her of infidelities and threatened to kill her, dragging her down the main street for all the inhabitants of the town of Los Angeles to see. After divorcing, she moved with her mother, stepfather and half brothers to San Francisco in 1862. Taking her nickname Ina and her mother's maiden name Coolbrith, she was determined to put the scandal and heartbreak of her married life behind and to make her way as a writer in the bustling and colorful city. As an already published poet, she gradually became friends with a group of writers who were defining the western experience through their prose and poetry. It may be difficult for modern readers to imagine the excitement generated by the appearance of a new issue of a magazine or the gallery showing of an artist's new paintings, but in the nineteenth century these served the role that other entertainments such as the opening of a blockbuster movie or the release of a new Harry Potter book do today.

One of the few women in the group, Coolbrith contributed a steady stream of poetry to the *Overland Monthly*, the new literary journal edited by Bret Harte. Also, along with Charles Warren Stoddard, she served as an unofficial editorial consultant, helping choose the articles, stories and poems that would appear in the magazine.

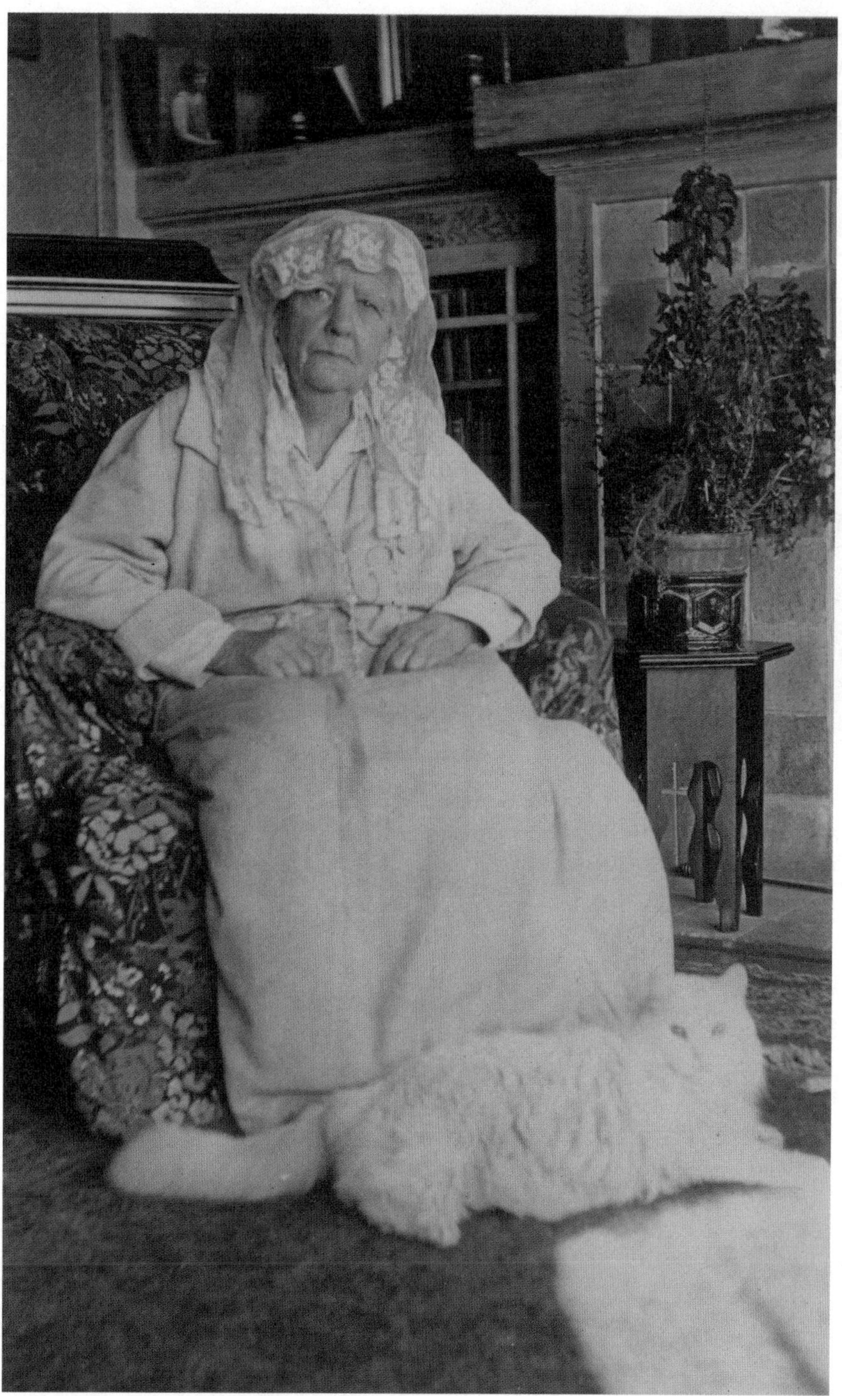

Ina Coolbrith had a succession of white Persian cats throughout her life.

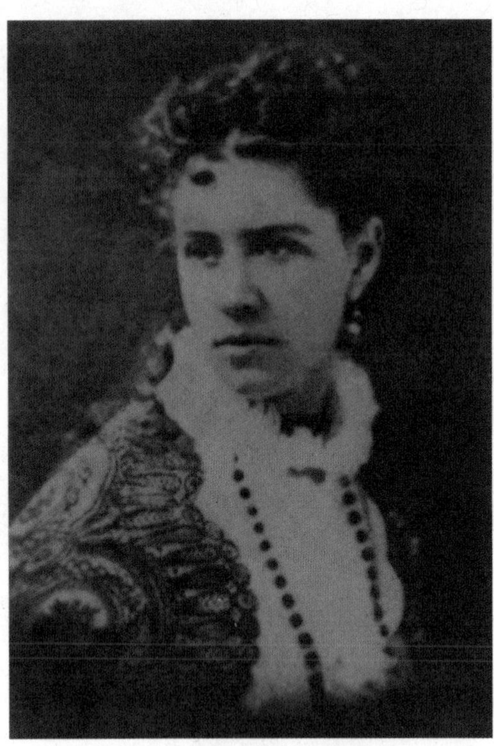

Ina Coolbrith at about age thirty was described by all who knew her as beautiful but very serious.

Poetry did not pay very much, however, and she worked as a grammar school teacher to help contribute to the family expenses.

The *Monthly* was founded with the intention of demonstrating that good literature could be created even in the raw, new western states. The journal succeeded in this task, but Coolbrith was unable to capitalize on her increasing fame. While her friends Samuel Clemens, Bret Harte, Charles Warren Stoddard and others departed the Bay Area for prestigious editing jobs and profitable lecture tours, Coolbrith remained behind. The death of her widowed sister Agnes in 1874 left Coolbrith with the responsibility of providing for her orphaned niece and nephew as well as her mother. Then, as now, women writers and artists were often forced to put domestic responsibilities before their art. Coolbrith set aside her ideas of pursuing a literary career and took a job as the first librarian of the Oakland Free Library. She moved her family to Oakland and was soon working ten-hour days, six days a week. She continued to write poetry and to sporadically publish, but her library work and home duties consumed much of her energy for the next eighteen years.

Coolbrith's extended family eventually included Calle Shasta, the half-Indian daughter of her friend Joaquin Miller.

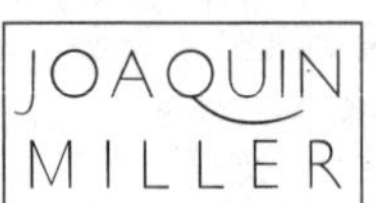

Miller's story is a colorful one also involving a name change. He was born on a farm in Indiana and christened Cincinnatus Hiner Miller in 1837. His family slowly made its way west over the next few years, winding up in Oregon. Gold miner, horse thief, Indian fighter and Pony Express rider were only some of the occupations that Miller claimed. He had little formal education but had a great love of tales and stories that he heard from the old-timers around the campfire. Like many of the pioneers of the nineteenth century, he read voraciously and acquired knowledge where and when he could. He served as editor of two pro-slavery newspapers in Oregon, not because he believed in slavery, but because he felt that the Confederacy was the underdog in the Civil War. In 1862, Miller married Theresa Dyer, another budding poet whose pen name was Minnie Myrtle.

Miller self-published his first two books of poems, *Specimens* and *Joaquin et al.*, in 1868. Even before that he had filled his newspaper columns with his own poetry. Miller's career in Oregon ended with his serving as a Grant County judge for three years. Then, after a divorce that his wife instigated, he left for San Francisco and the larger world, hoping to find a publisher for his poetry and recognition as a poet.

In 1870, Miller arrived in San Francisco, en route to New York and England, where he hoped to find a more appreciative audience than he had in the American press. Ina Coolbrith was instructed by her friend Charles Warren Stoddard, whom Miller had written to in advance of his arrival, to squire the stranger around and introduce him to members of the literary colony. Coolbrith later described Miller as tall, blond and good-looking. He, in turn, quoted Tennyson to describe the twenty-nine-year-old Ina as "Divinely tall and most divinely fair."[8]

They must have made a handsome couple. Harr Wagner, Miller's friend and author of the 1926 biography *Joaquin Miller and His Other Self*, is of the opinion that Miller's and Coolbrith's forty-three-year friendship was based on the "affinity of genius."[9] Coolbrith was a more accomplished poet than Miller, but he far surpassed her in a flair for showmanship and self-promotion.

Miller planned to visit Lord Byron's gravesite in Nottingham, England. He and Ina Coolbrith took the ferry to Sausalito and gathered laurel branches that she fashioned into a wreath to be placed on the grave. Her poem "With a Wreath of Laurel" was derived from this occasion. Coolbrith later claimed that it was she who suggested Miller's name change from Cincinnatus to Joaquin, after the famous bandit Joaquin Murrieta, who had been the subject of Miller's poem. Supposedly she also suggested that he adopt more flamboyant clothing to enhance his credentials in Europe as a "western" poet. Miller was already known for his eccentric dress (he arrived in San Francisco wearing a sombrero and beaded moccasins), but he certainly continued in this vein, startling and delighting British society with his shoulder-length hair, open-necked shirt, flowing sash and bearskin cape. He became a media star and his popularity in Europe helped promote his work in the United States.

After Miller's travels in England and Europe, he returned to live in New York and Washington, D.C., for many years. Harr Wagner states that Miller did not dare return to live in the West because of the "coarse and unscrupulous"[10] newspaper publicity about his marriage to Theresa Dyer, the two children he was supposed to have abandoned and wildly contradictory tales about his life among the Indians. The East Coast also provided employment, and Miller published poems, stories and plays, achieving notoriety and a moderate amount of financial success. He also married again, making Abbie Leland the second or perhaps third Mrs. Miller, if one counts Paquita, the Indian woman who bore his daughter, Calle Shasta.

Miller returned to California in 1885 to a writing job on the staff of the *Golden Era*, a San Francisco literary magazine edited by Harr Wagner. He also bought a large tract of bare land in the hills above Oakland. Here he erected some small cabins and began planting trees and flowers. His idea was to start an artist's colony, and he named his home the "Hights," an eccentric spelling he insisted on.

To the Hights came many visitors and both long- and short-term lodgers. One of these was young Japanese poet Yone Noguchi. The eighteen-year-old Noguchi had moved to San Francisco in 1893, eager to learn more of the United States after a lifetime studying English. Hungry and homeless for the first time in his life, Noguchi started working as a houseboy, one of the few jobs open to young Japanese men in California. But he disliked

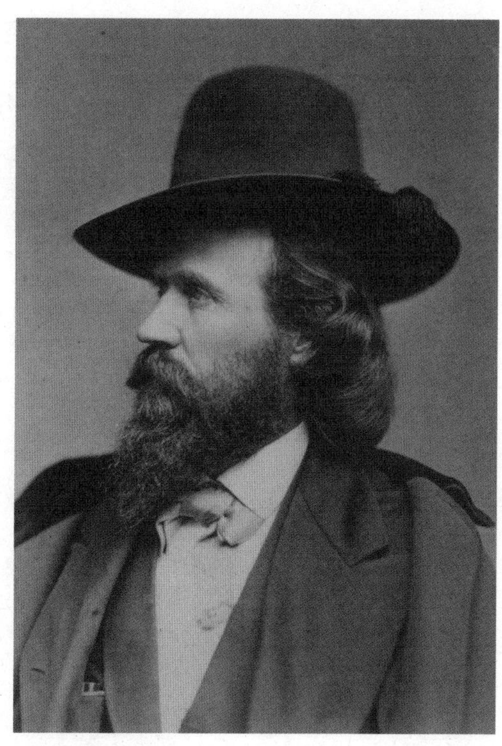

An 1876 photograph of Joaquin Miller shows him as the handsome gentleman that Ina Coolbrith first met.

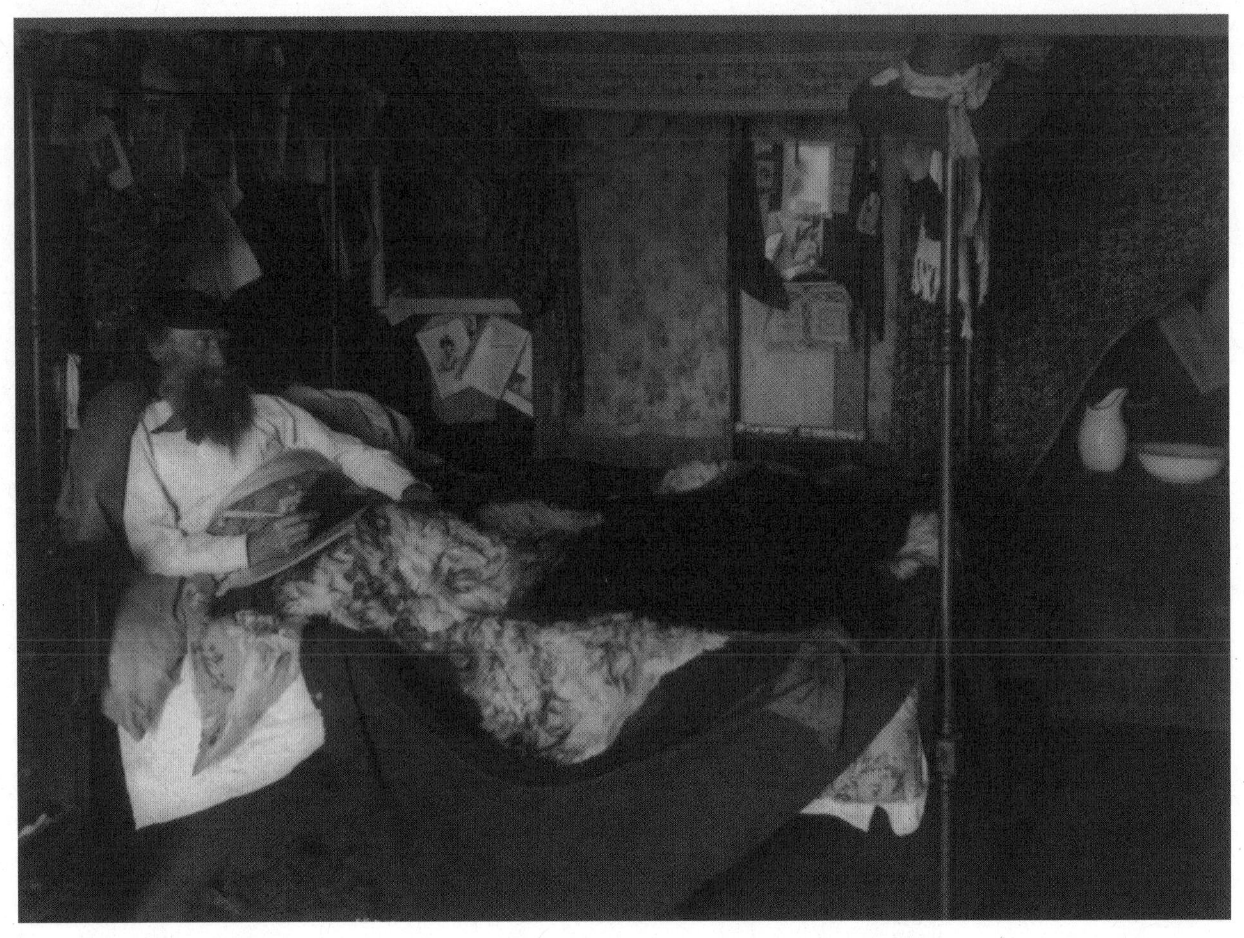

Joaquin Miller at work in bed on Christmas Day, 1896. Miller did most of his writing in bed.

where the journalists got the better end of the deal. Noguchi and the other workers slept on piles of newsprint on the premises of the paper. When Noguchi got sleepy after his bedtime reading of the *Encyclopedia Britannica*, he set the volume down on his pallet and used it as a pillow.

Soon the young writer heard of a famous local poet who lived like a Japanese hermit on a mountaintop across the bay. Joaquin Miller was well respected by the local Japanese emigrants, and Noguchi, who loved American poetry, sold all his books except a volume of Edgar Allan Poe's poems to pay for the ferry to Oakland. The afternoon that he arrived, Miller was lying in bed, where he did most of his writing, dressed in one of his outrageous outfits. Noguchi described this as a silk skullcap, a corduroy suit with a red sash, a bearskin thrown around his shoulders and a huge diamond ring on his hand.

Inviting the young man to dinner at his mother's cabin, the giant poet "picked abundantly the roses red or white, which he scattered over the large dinner table, exclaiming 'God bless you.'"[11]

the menial labor and found work on a leftist Japanese language newspaper called *Soko Shimbun*, the *San Francisco News*. It was run by an organization of exiled Japanese radicals called Aikoku Domei, the Patriotic Union, and it advocated the overthrow of the current Japanese government.

Life on the newspaper was hard, although Noguchi managed to make it seem romantic and adventurous in his autobiography, full of rumbles with the employees of a rival leftist Japanese-language paper and barters at the local Chinese restaurants,

Noguchi moved to the Hights, becoming one of a colony of Japanese and Chinese artists whom Miller invited to live on his property. Miller referred to Noguchi as his student, but other visitors called him Miller's houseboy. Though Miller never insisted that his students work, Noguchi cooked and cleaned. He recalls planting and cutting trees, tending the rosebushes and harvesting plums, all for nothing but food, lodging and (once) a gift of two pairs of wool socks. While grateful for Miller's mentorship, Noguchi hints in his autobiography that he would have liked to sully the relationship with a little exchange of cash. Whenever he wanted to go to the San Francisco library, he had to hike five or six miles in order to borrow the fare from a friend, a fellow Japanese emigrant who washed dishes at a downtown Oakland hotel.

Life in "God's garden" was hard, but Noguchi did have the advantage of meeting the dozens of literary visitors who made the pilgrimage to the Hights. He reportedly had a sexual relationship with Charles Warren Stoddard, and he also came to the attention of journals that began publishing his poetry.

Harr Wagner states emphatically, "There were no wild parties staged at the Hights. Joaquin objected to noise. He loved the silences, parties of two in the moonlight, or wandering over his hills and down in the deep shadows like unto midnight in the canyon."[12] Wild parties or not, Miller was known for keeping a jug of whiskey under his bed, and there certainly were many unconventional gatherings at the Hights.

Elsie Whitaker Martinez, who, as a girl, tagged along with her father, Herman Whitaker, on his fortnightly visits to socialize (and drink) with Miller, remembered the Japanese-style barbeques with kebabs of meat and onions grilled over an open fire, as well as raw fish and soy sauce, which she pronounced "delicious."[13]

Miller loved practical jokes and one of his most famous was the Song of the Rain Bear. After inviting his guests to gather inside a small dimly lit cabin with a great buffalo robe on the floor, he would chant the Song of the Rain Bear in the Modoc language. Soon the visitors would hear the sound of rain pattering on the roof, though it had been sunny a few moments before. This was the result of either a hose held by one of his Japanese students or a hidden faucet that Miller manipulated in the darkness (stories vary).

While the older generation of bohemians was settling into middle age, and fame had either found them or passed them by, there was a fresh crop coming up, eager to break new ground with their artistic endeavors. Passing through Berkeley and environs for a short time, but leaving a lasting impression, were several young men who would later become famous.

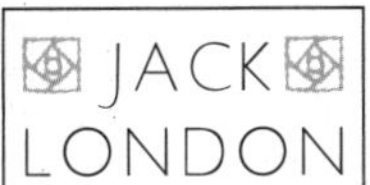

Jack London made a brief appearance on the University of California campus in Berkeley, attending UC for about six months in 1897–98. Berkeley was just over the border from Oakland, where he had lived most of his life, but it was a world away from London's life experiences. In the introduction to London's most auto-biographical novel, *Martin Eden*, Andrew Sinclair paints London at this period as "grasping at knowledge with the despera-tion of a drowning man and the arrogance of the self taught."[14] London had left school after the eighth grade, needing to work to help support his family. He was a regular visitor at the Oakland Free Library, where librarian Ina Coolbrith encouraged and guided his reading. Several years later, he managed to complete high school and then took the entrance exams for the university. However, when his stepfather became ill, London's contributions to the family coffers were necessary, and his formal education ceased. Eleven years later, when London was a famous author, he wrote of his hero Martin Eden, also from working-class roots, becoming involved with an intellectual Berkeley family. Befriended by her brother, Eden falls in love with Ruth, the daughter of the family. He strives to educate himself, to become someone who can fit in with a girl of her class, but eventually becomes embit-tered and scornful of the people who know life only through books.

FRANK NORRIS Another aspiring author attended Berkeley in the 1890s. Frank Norris's stay at the university was a longer and happier one than London's had been, but he, too, found the academic environment lacking. Norris's family had money, and when he entered

UC as a twenty-year-old freshman, it was after spending two years at the prestigious Academie Julian in Paris. He had hoped to become a painter but found that he was better at imagining artworks and critiquing the art scene than he was at producing the required paintings.

Norris hoped that his classes at the uni-versity would give him practical training as a writer, but this was not the case. His classes in the English Department were theoretical; the students were not trained to write cre-atively but to analyze and discuss. Norris did not feel that he received any encourage-ment or guidance for his own writing from his professors. In spite of this, Norris wrote and illustrated stories for student publi-cations and sold stories to the *Overland Monthly*, the *Argonaut* and the *Wave*. He brought a painter's eye for detail and color to his writing, as evidenced in this selection from "The Santa Cruz Venetian Carnival," published in the June 27, 1896, issue of the *Wave*:

There was a glare of sunshine, and the air had a different taste that sug-gested the sea immediately. The plat-form was crowded, mostly with people from the hotels, come down to meet the train, girls in cool, white skirts and straw sailors, and young men in ducks and flannels, some of them carrying tennis rackets. It was quite a different world at once, and you felt as if things had been happening in it, and certain phases of life lived out, in which you had neither part nor lot. You in your overcoat and gritty business suit and black hat, were out of your element; as yet you were not part of that world where so many people knew each other and dressed in white clothes, and you bundled yourself hurriedly into the corner of the hotel bus before you should see anybody you knew.[15]

In 1891, Frank Norris expanded his social horizons by pledging Phi Gamma Delta and becoming a "Fiji." He was remembered by one of his fellow fraternity members as "a likeable fellow of patrician blood, living in a Continental rather than an American atmosphere, Bohemian in social inclinations, responsive to the beautiful and imaginative in art and life yet disorderly and unsystematic in personal habits and mental attitude. He was restless and bored with the routine of college discipline."[16]

He moved into the Fiji House on Dana Street, near Bancroft Way, where he became a popular member of the fraternity. His room was described as a "curiosity," its walls hung with souvenirs of his art-school days in Paris. One evening Norris returned very late from a trip to San Francisco and went straight to his room. His fellow Fijis reported hearing strange noises coming from Norris's room during the night. When they opened the door in the morning, Norris lay sound asleep on the bed. All the wall decorations were in a heap on the floor and in their midst sat a monkey, which he had somehow acquired.

Norris's most lasting contribution to Phi Gamma Delta was his creation of the Pig Dinner, an affair held on the evening before the big game with Stanford. Norris wrote a mock ceremonial and introduction for the suckling pig that was then consumed by the brothers of the fraternity. Norris withdrew from the university in 1894 just before graduation. He had failed the mathematics examination and did not want to put in the additional study time necessary to pass it. In spite of his lack of a degree, Norris, like Jack London, became a well-known and successful author. He remembered his days as a Fiji fondly and, in 1900, sent a poem titled "The Exiles Toast" from his home in New Jersey. This was read at the now-annual pre-game Fiji dinner.

THE LARK

Crossing paths with Norris at Berkeley in the early 1890s was Gelett Burgess, a young Bostonian who was an instructor in topographical drawing. Burgess's employment at the university was brief. One evening, while on a drinking expedition to San Francisco with several similarly high-spirited friends,

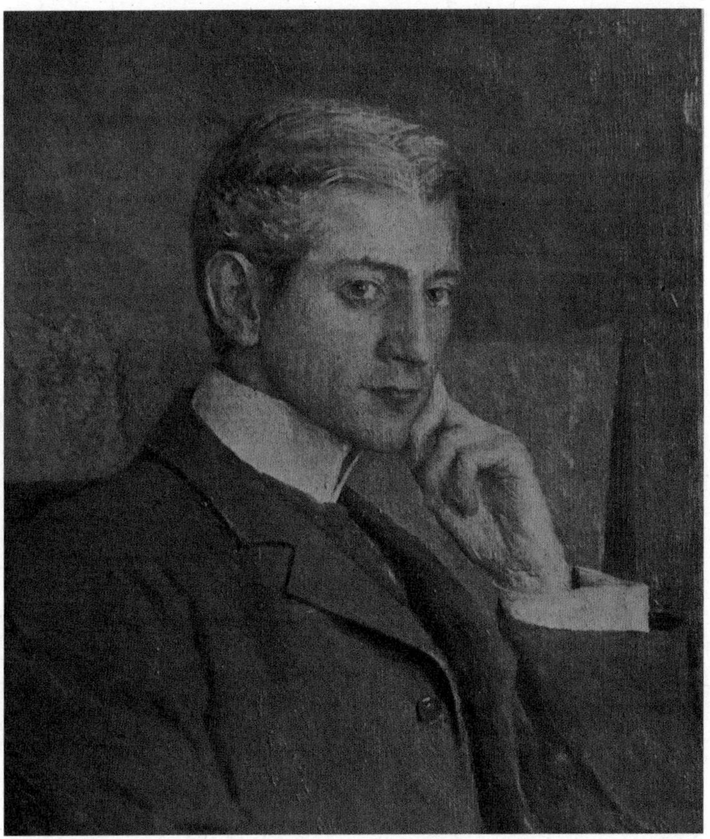

Ernest Peixotto, a friend of Frank Norris from the days they attended art school together in San Francisco, did the painting that this magazine illustration is based on.

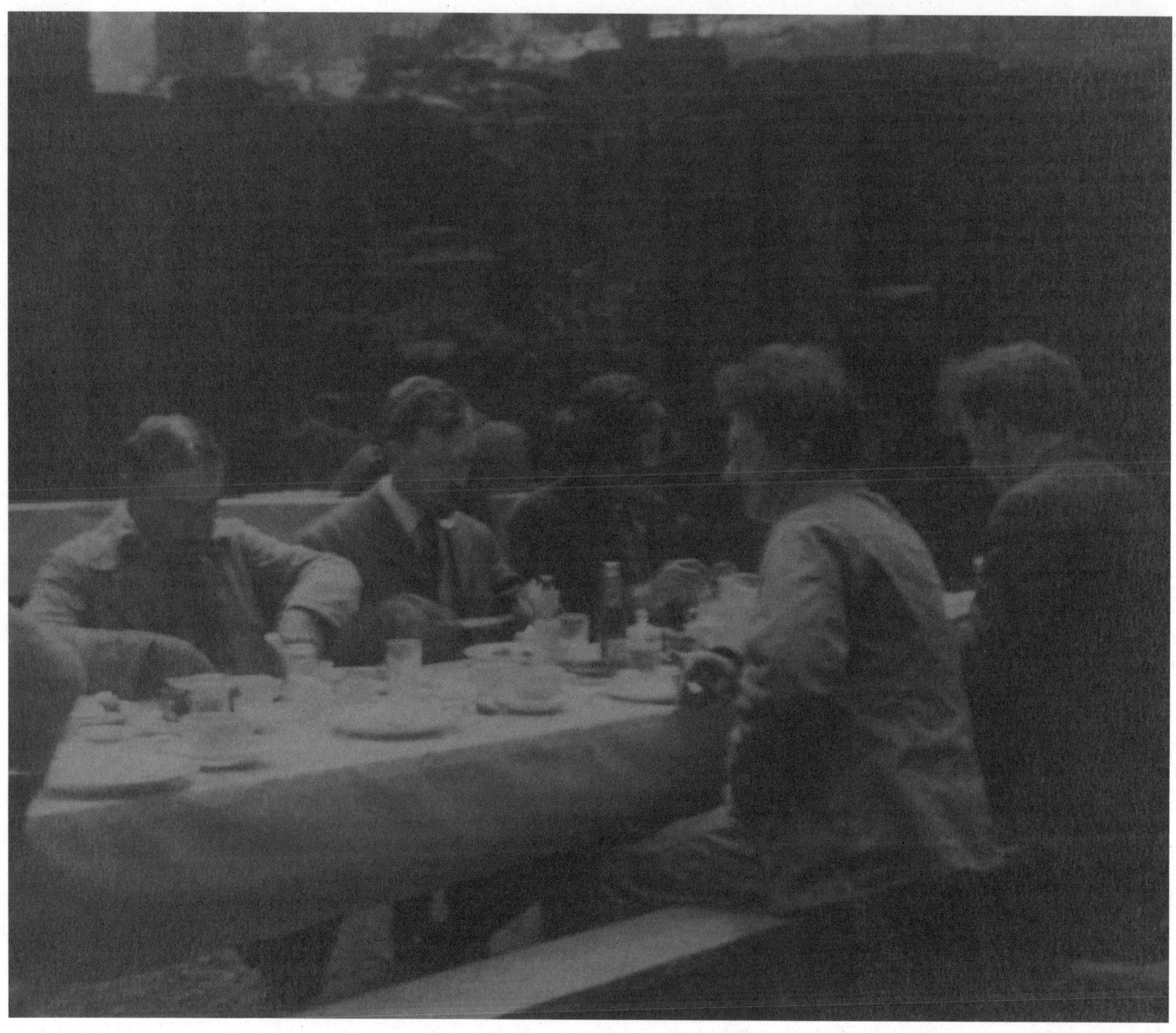

Gelett Burgess and Porter Garnett sit side
by side (left to right) with Xavier Martinez
sitting across from them at dinner.

they pulled down a statue of prohibition-ist Dr. Henry Cogswell, at the corner of Market and California Streets. This led to Burgess's dismissal from the university, but he soon put his joking to good use. Moving back to San Francisco, Burgess launched a brave new publication called the *Lark*. Published for only two years, from 1895 to 1897, it created a sensation. If the original *Overland Monthly* had first brought literary San Francisco to the attention of East Coast readers, the *Lark* put it firmly on the map.

Printed on the cheapest paper the editor could find, bamboo paper purchased by the bale in Chinatown, the little journal strove to amuse, shock and delight. Burgess illustrated it with zany cartoons, featuring elongated figures called "Goops." Poetry, stories, satires, mock advertisements and artwork by a group of innovative young people filled the pages.

It was the *Lark* that first published the poems of Yone Noguchi. Titled "The Night Reveries of an Exile," Burgess's introduction to the poems describes Noguchi:

An exile from his native land, a stranger in a new civilization,—a mystic by temperament, race, and religion,—these lines which I have rephrased, setting his own words in a more intelligible order, are his attempts to voice the indefinable thoughts that came to him on many lonely nights, the journal of his soul,—nocturnes set to words of a half-learned, foreign tongue; in form vague as his vague dreams.[17]

Noguchi's poetry is indeed strange and dreamy, but what really caused a sensation was the juxtaposition of his wistful lyrics in the same publication as Burgess's most infamous ditty:

I never saw a Purple Cow,
I never hope to see one,
But I can tell you Anyhow
I'd rather see than be one. [18]

Also contributing to the *Lark* at various times were Porter Garnett, Willis Polk, Florence Lundborg, Bruce Porter, Carolyn Wells, Juliet Wilbor Tompkins and artist Ernest Peixotto, a boyhood friend of Frank Norris's. The group was referred to as "les Jeunes." Even the venerable William Keith submitted an illustration for one issue. Each issue featured quotations and plays on words about larks. When they decided to end the publication in the spring of 1897, Bruce Porter wrote, "Looking back, the enthusiasm that made the *Lark* smacks of a youth we have already passed—yet we shall pray to retain it till Death comes rapping at the door, and we step out into the dark."[19]

INA COOLBRITH, HER LATER YEARS

While the *Lark* was rising up, the older generation of poets and artists was dealing with the waxing and waning fortunes of middle life and old age. Ina Coolbrith's job as Oakland's librarian came to an abrupt end in 1892, when the library board of directors replaced her with her

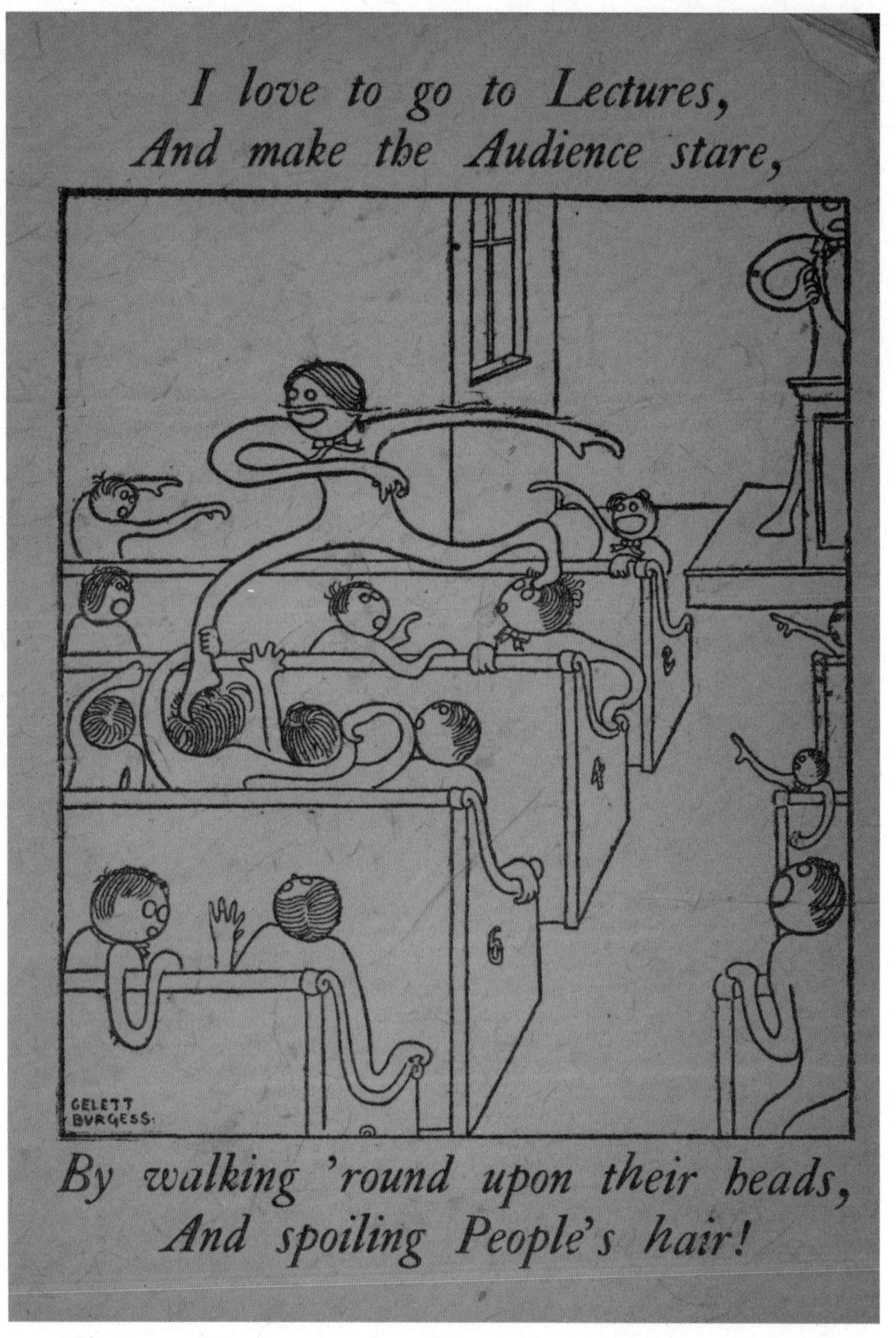

One of Gelett Burgess's Goop cartoons in *the Lark*.

nephew Henry Frank Peterson. Stunned by this betrayal, which was widely covered in the local press, her friends rallied round and found her a position as the librarian of the Bohemian Club. Coolbrith moved back to San Francisco. With her part-time duties at the Bohemian Club less time-consuming than her previous job had been, Coolbrith was finally free, as far as her limited finances would allow, to write, to travel and to participate in a number of literary gatherings. In 1895, her book *Songs from the Golden Gate*, with illustrations by William Keith, was published. It did not bring her much money, but her reputation as a poet was growing.

Her old circle of friends came to her aid once more after the great San Francisco earthquake and fire of 1906. Running from her Russian Hill home, with only her two cats and the clothes on her back, Ina Coolbrith and her companion, Josie Zeller, wound up at Fort Mason, along with thousands of others made homeless by the catastrophe. There Joaquin Miller's friend Harr Wagner found her three days later. He told her that Miller had rushed down from the Hights and tried to reach her but had not been allowed to enter San Francisco because he did not have a pass. Her home and all its contents, including her nearly completed manuscript of the history of California literature, were lost to the fire. Her student border, Robert Norman, had managed to return to the residence and rescue one of her scrapbooks and a small box of letters. Everything else was gone.

Donations of money, clothing and books came from all those who had known her over the years. Benefits and raffles were held in her honor and various schemes were proposed for a fund to build her a new home. Coolbrith was a proud woman and found some of this attention irritating, though at the same time, at the age of sixty-five, and with increasingly ill health, she could hardly afford to turn it down. In a letter to William Keith, dated July 18, 1907, she hoped to visit him as soon as her rheumatism would allow. "Also, I wanted to bring back to you your kind offering through Charlie Keeler, which I cannot accept, remembering all you have done for me in the past."[20]

Despite poverty and ill health, Ina Coolbrith kept on, driven by the pioneer toughness that had brought her across the country in a covered wagon as a child. At the age of seventy-five, she organized a Congress of Authors and Journalists for the 1915 Panama-Pacific International Exposition. There, University of California President Benjamin Ide Wheeler presented her with a laurel wreath and the title "loved, laurel-crowned poet of California," an honor later confirmed by the state legislature. She spent several winters in New York City, once again discreetly subsidized by her Bohemian Club friends. There she wrote, in four winters, more poetry than she had written in the previous twenty-five years.

Having outlived most of her contemporaries and all of her good friends, she died in her niece's home in Berkeley in 1928, hav-ing declined to write an autobiography of her long and colorful life. "Were I to write what I know, the book would be too sensational to print; but if I were to write what I think proper, it would be too dull to read."[21]

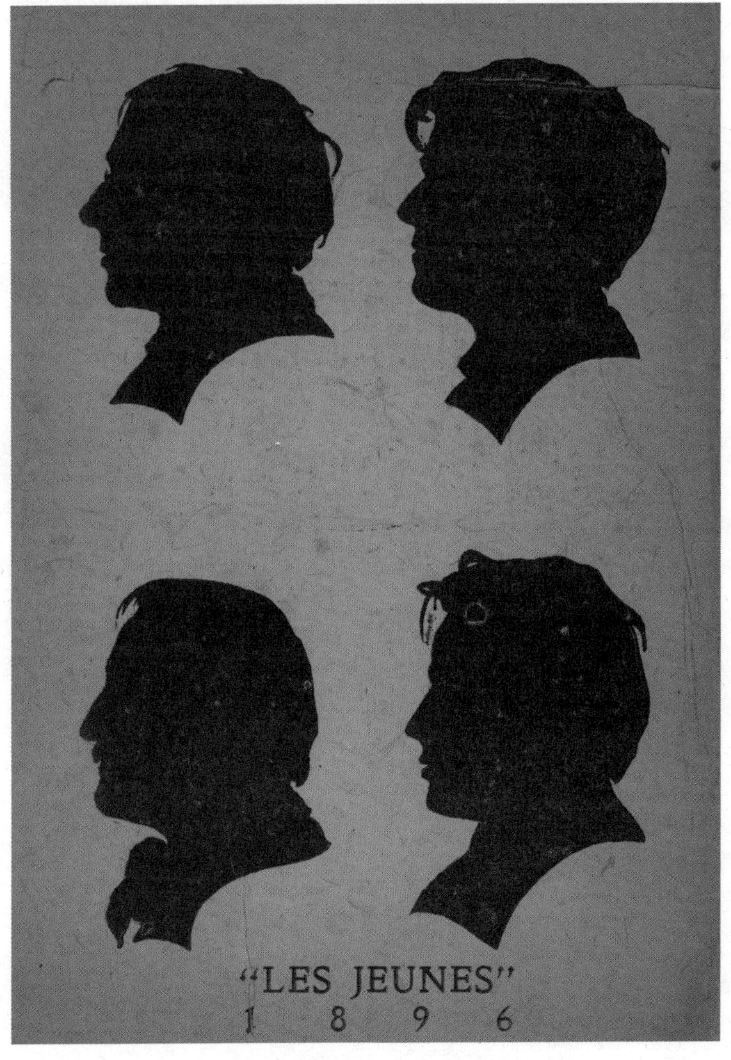

Les Jeunes in 1896, from an issue of *the Lark*. Clockwise from top left are Gelett Burgess, Ernest Peixotto, Willis Polk and Bruce Porter.

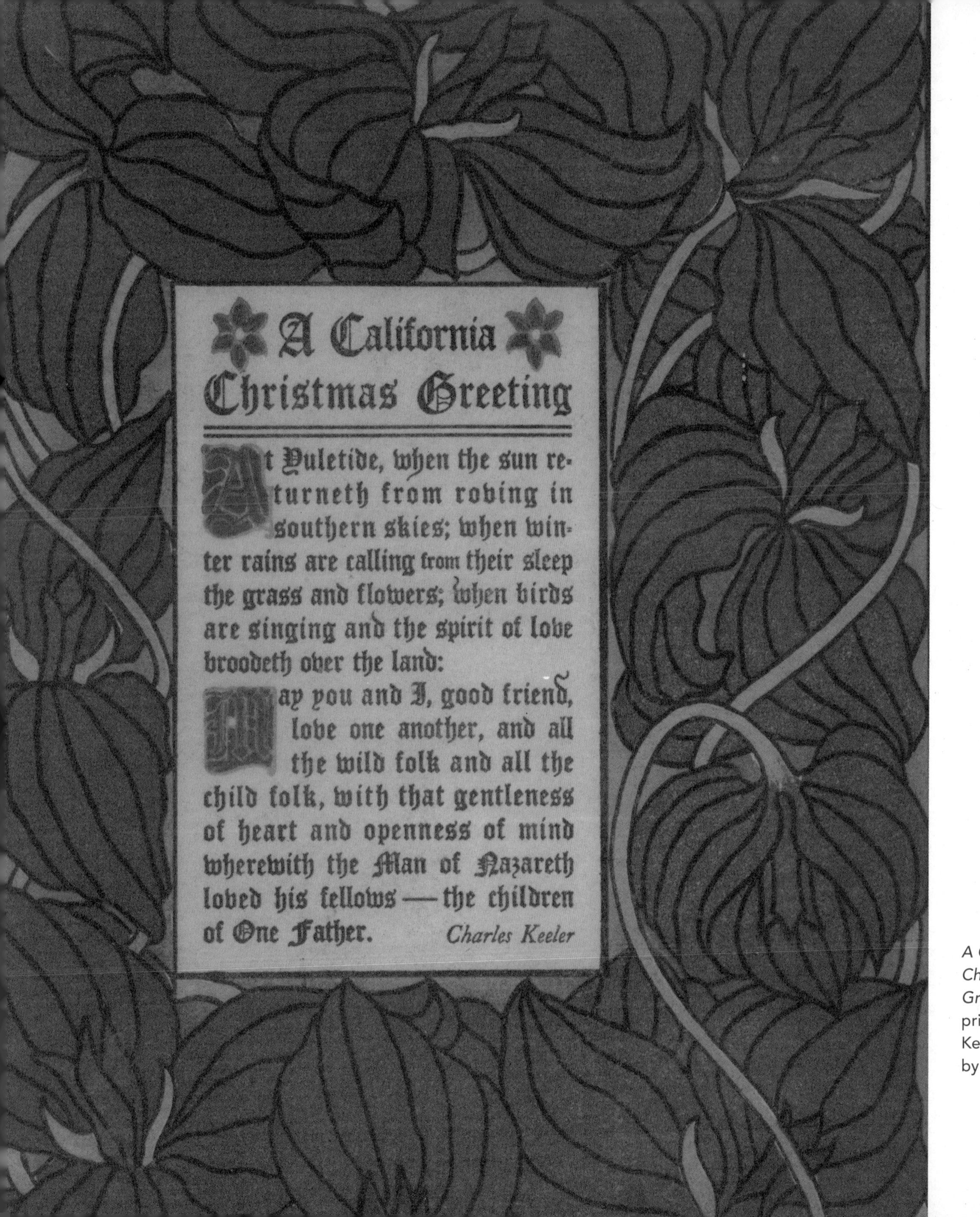

A California Christmas Greeting—block print by Louise Keeler, with text by Charles Keeler.

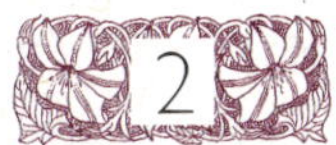

charles and Louise keeler

C harles and Louise Keeler are the leading contenders for the title of "Ultimate Berkeley Bohemian Couple." They deserve this posthumous distinction for many reasons, but most assuredly for the central role they played in weaving the web of Berkeley's artistic community.

Just as Berkeley's early bohemian middle-class lifestyle did not quite fit the stereotype of their Parisian contemporaries, neither did the scope of their creative pursuits. The serendipitous circumstance of having a great university in a comparatively unpretentious small-town setting made it possible for the creative life in Berkeley to transcend the schism between the arts and the sciences that was typical in America's eastern cities and those of Europe. Charles Keeler was both a product and a producer of this fortunate combination.

While none of Berkeley's bohemians led a typical life, even of their milieu, the Keeler's rich and varied artistic output is illustrative of how broad and fruitful one couple's contribution could be.

Charles Augustus Keeler arrived in Berkeley with his family at the age of sixteen in 1887. At an early age he began to develop a great appreciation for nature, especially wild birds. He spent a great deal of time in the outdoors, studying the habits of the wildlife. At the same time, thanks to the influence of his cultured stepfather, he acquired a taste for art, music, poetry and literature. At eighteen, he arranged to leave Berkeley High School some months before graduation without compromising his standing to enter the University of California the following fall. This enabled him to accept a temporary position with the U.S. Biological Survey to study and

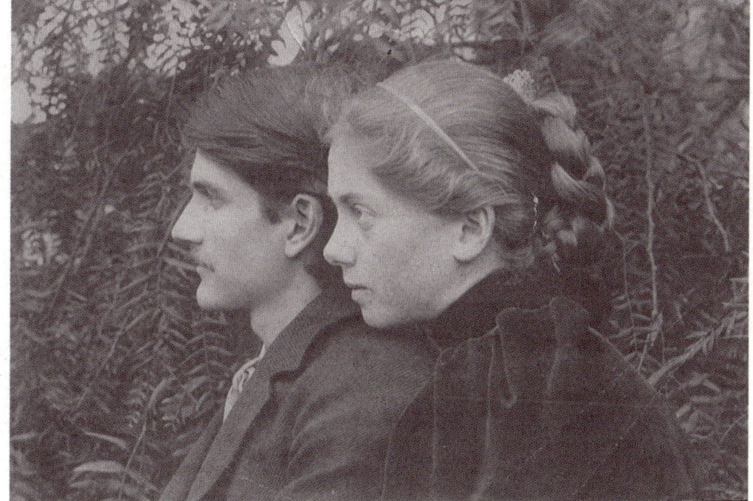

Charles and Louise Keeler, ca. 1895.

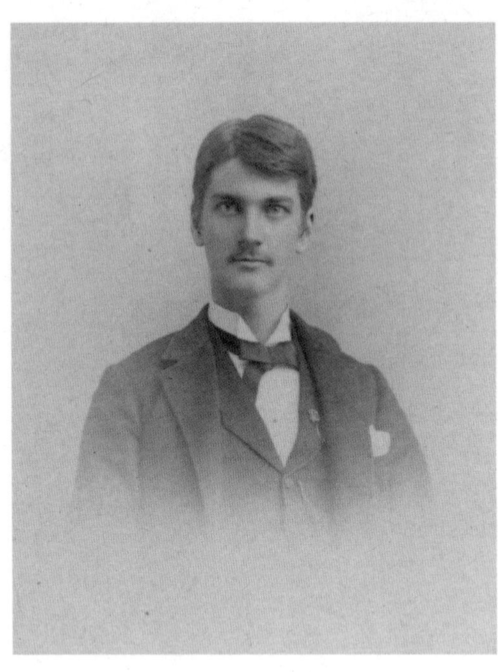

Portrait of a young Charles Keeler on a carte-de-visite photograph.

report on the bird and animal life in northern Nevada.

After returning, he entered the university in 1889 but had to withdraw after only two months to care for his ailing stepfather. When his stepfather passed away, he returned to the university but was compelled to cease his college studies yet again when his mother died in April 1891. During Keeler's short college career, he organized the Berkeley Evolution Club. This group achieved a great following but aroused the moral indignation of the city's religious community because of the inherent contradictions between the theory of evolution and the teachings of the Bible. Soon after leaving college, he secured a position at the California Academy of Sciences. While working there, he drew upon his wildlife fieldwork and study of evolution to complete his first book, *Evolution of the Colors of North American Land Birds*, in 1893.

At this time, along with studying and writing on ornithology, his love of literature, music and art led him to write poems and attend concerts, operas and art exhibitions. He soon purchased his first painting, one by William Keith, and was introduced to the artist. This began a great friendship that lasted until the artist's death. He also befriended several professors at the university who had organized the Philosophical Union. These included John Le Conte, the physicist; Le Conte's brother Joseph, the geologist; and George Holmes Howison, the philosopher. Keeler, the young poet and scientist, attended the Philosophical Union's meetings regularly. This was the genesis of a great change in his life. Professor Howison was a brilliant exponent of the philosophy of idealism and, for a time, Keeler sought to refute this doctrine from a scientific viewpoint. But ultimately, the artistic side of his nature transcended the scientific side, and soon he came to embrace the idealistic philosophy that he had opposed.

One day in 1892, a neighbor introduced Keeler to Louise Mapes Bunnell. Her interests were uncannily parallel to his. She was a student of entomology and art and was also interested in poetry and philosophy. The common ground of their curiously varied inclinations was inescapable, and they soon became close friends and fell in love. Sadly, they were both in frail health. Though they believed they were destined for each other, they decided that they ought not to marry due to their health problems. To avoid temptation, Louise traveled to New York. But after completing his bird book, Charles determined that he could not be apart from Louise any longer. He then booked passage on a sailing ship via Cape Horn to New York. When, before embarking, he sought his physician's advice about his frail health, he must have been both amazed and delighted when the man, with no knowledge of Charles's plans, recommended a prolonged sea voyage. The thread of this love tale took yet another twist when, upon arriving in New York, Charles was informed that Louise had a short time before returned to California. Staying only two days in New York, he set out for home.

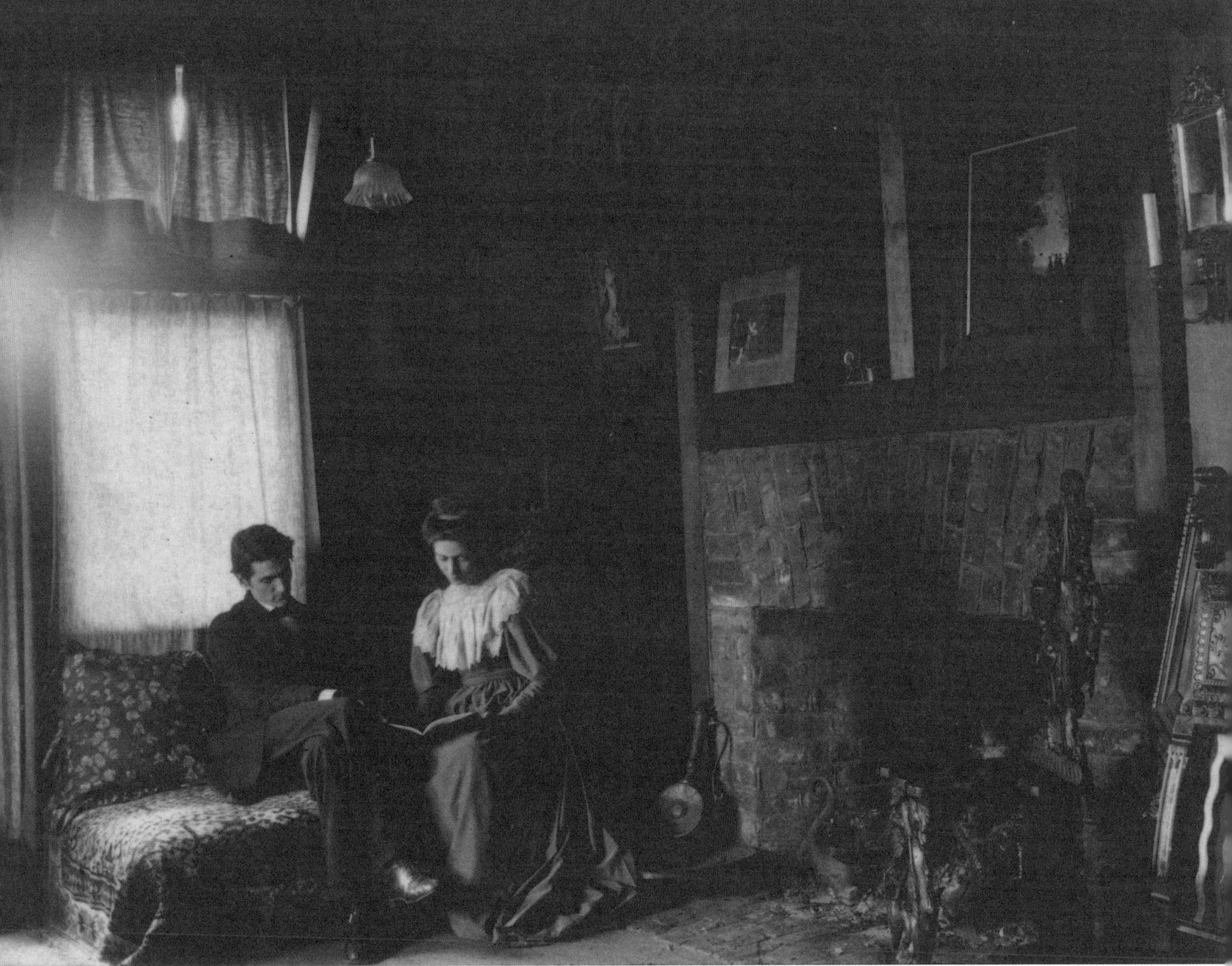

Charles and Louise in their
Maybeck home on Highland Place
in North Berkeley.

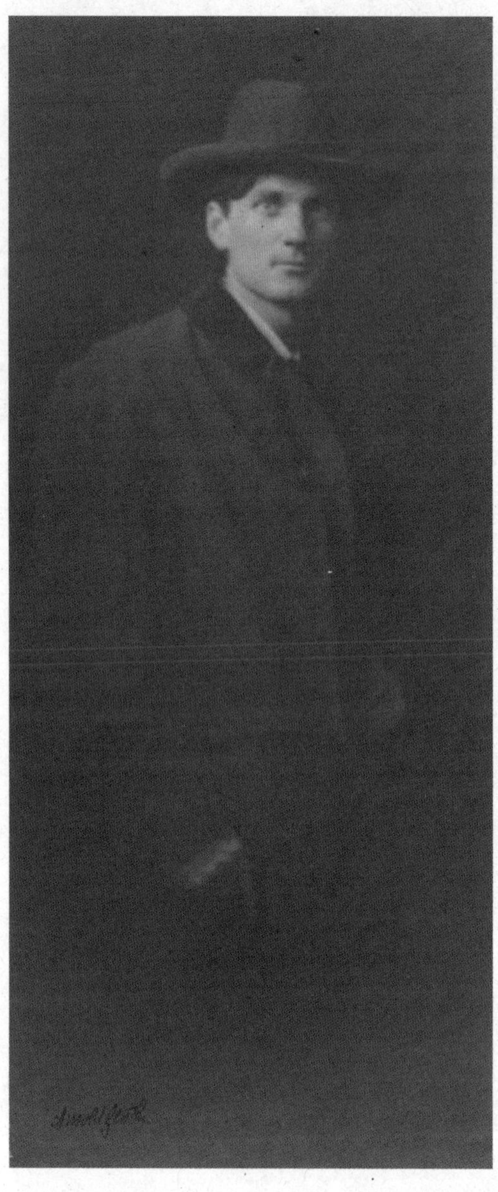

ABOVE: **Portrait of Charles Keeler by Arnold Genthe.**

FACING PAGE: **Handbill for Charles Keeler's book** *Elfin Songs of Sunland.*

This time, he traveled by train and managed to attend the 1893 World's Fair in Chicago on the way. When at last they were reunited in California, they decided, though both were still in poor health, to marry. As they were both doomed to die anyway, their feeling was they might as well die married. They shared an extended honeymoon at a ranch in a remote area of northern California, during which time their mutual love for art, literature and each other blossomed, and this unfolding uplifted, widened and deepened their creative vision.

S oon after their return to Berkeley in 1894, their first collaboration was published—Charles's first book of verse, *A Light through the Storm*, illustrated with drawings by Louise. The following year, when they learned they were expecting their first child, their friend—architect Bernard Maybeck—insisted on designing a new home for them. Unconstrained by the usual demands of clients, Maybeck was free to create a new style of home. For the next twelve years, the Keelers lived in and received their friends in this home in the hills of North Berkeley and Maybeck was soon designing "simple homes" for many of them. Charles became the leading proponent for this style, and in 1898, he helped to organize the Hillside Club to promote Maybeck's ideas of simple artistic homes and beautiful neighborhoods. Though it was a women's club at first, its members later decided to admit men as well, and Keeler served as its president from 1903 to 1905.

During this time, Charles was in charge of the Berkeley Unitarian Church Sunday school and began a revolutionary approach to teaching. He introduced the teaching of nature, history and comparative religion as a preparation for Bible study. He also organized a church orchestra and gave lectures on art to the school.

In 1896, Charles published a poem entitled "The Promise of the Ages" in book format. This work was the first to embody his personal philosophy and illustrated the conflict between idealism and materialism. Keeler named his first child Merodine, born shortly after the poem's publication, after one of its characters.

He gave a public reading of the poem before an audience that included most of the faculty of the university. Accompanied by classical music, it was well received; in later years, he would return to public performances of his poetry as a much-needed source of additional income.

Charles's health took a very bad turn in 1897, and he spent most of the year convalescing, with Louise at his side, at the homes of friends in the Sierras and in Southern California. These were tough times for the Keelers, but later that year their fortunes improved when they were hired to produce a promotional pamphlet on southern California for the Santa Fe Railway. This work represented the second published collaboration for the couple. It was published in 1898, and Charles's text and Louise's drawings were both highly praised. Five years later, their Southern California illustrated narrative was integrated into a larger work, *To California and Back* by C. A. Higgins, that included all of California and five other western states. Also in 1898, the Women's Auxiliary of the First Unitarian Church of Berkeley published a book entitled *A Berkeley Year—A Sheaf of Nature Essays*. It included one chapter by Charles, "A Glimpse of the Birds of Berkeley," and decorations for the entire volume by Louise. Her woodcut ornamental chapter initials, deeply impressed in red ink, are quite striking. In 1899, the Keelers produced two books. The first, *Bird Notes Afield*, contained little decoration and no mention of Louise. The second was arguably their finest book collaboration. *A Season's Sowing* contains nearly one hundred quatrains by Charles, in the style of Omar Khayam's *Rubaiyat*. What really elevates this work, however, are Louise's drawings. Done in the medieval woodcut style of William Morris's Kelmscott Press, they represent her most sumptuous contribution to book illustration. Indeed, the dedication of this book eloquently sums up, not merely their partnership in this work, but surely their lives' collaboration:

> Together have we toiled for beauty's
> sake,
> And all our labor has not been in vain,
> Since in our hearts this token did awake:
> Love's blessing falls on those who
> share life's pain.[1]

Also, in that apparently very busy year of 1899, Charles was a participant in a major scientific expedition. E. H. Harriman of the Union Pacific Railroad personally conceived, financed and accompanied this project. Known as the Harriman Alaska Expedition, its small staff included many of the leading scientists, authors and artists of its day. The group included John Muir, John Burroughs, C. Hart Merriam, George Bird Grinnell, William H. Brewer, Louis Agassiz Fuertes and Edward S. Curtis. During the months of June and July, this group on board the ship *George W. Elder* traveled from Seattle to Alaska, exploring the Alaskan coast from the south up to the Bering Sea. The group made scientific observations and recordings and documented the landscape, wildlife and human inhabitants in words, photographs and paintings. Keeler's assignment was as both poet and birdwatcher. The final report of the expedition includes his essay on the birds of Alaska. On board the Elder, he shared a cabin with John Muir. The two spent much time together, exploring and

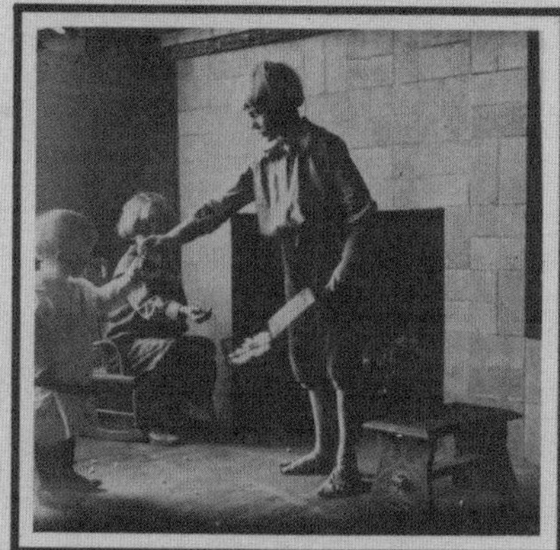

POPPING CORN

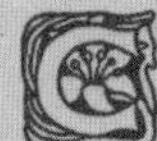COME, you merry little fellows,
Poke the coals and blow the bellows;
Here's the popper, shell the corn,
And let it pop this winter morn.

Pop-a-tee-pop-pop-pop!
See the kernels skip and hop,
See them puff out full and white,
Hear them crackle in affright.

Now shake, shake, shake,
Till your hands and faces bake;
Tip it, turn it,
Or you'll burn it,
And a dreadful muss you'll make.

Now it's done we'll have a feast;
Smallest hands must take the least!
Hot and crisp and white and sweet,—
Isn't this a jolly treat!

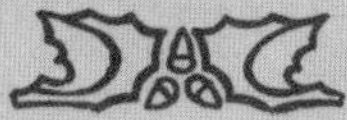

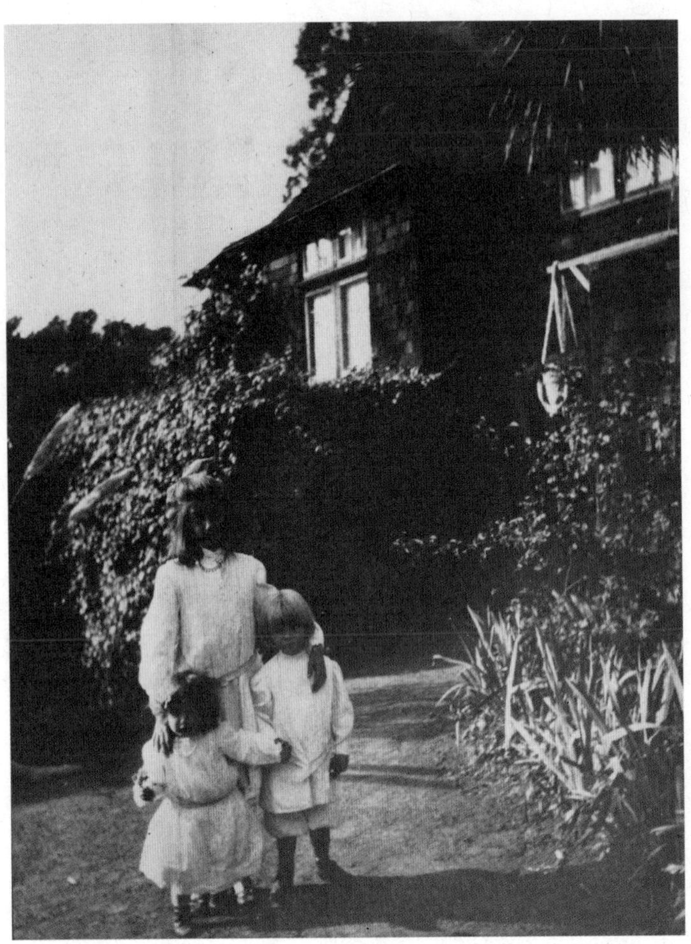

Merodine, Eloise and Leonarde Keeler in front of their home on Highland Place in Berkeley.

observing, and became lifelong friends.

In 1900, Charles published a book of poems, *The Idylls of El Dorado*, with beautiful California wildflower illustrations drawn by Louise. Later that year, Charles and Louise were offered a trip to Tahiti to write and sketch their observations for the Oceanic Steamship Company. At first Charles feared he would have to decline this offer as Louise was very ill at the time. However, after further consideration, they decided the trip might actually improve Louise's health, and they set sail for the South Seas with their five-year-old daughter, Merodine. Their decision was proved right, and Louise's health was nearly completely recovered by the time they reached Tahiti.

The trip proved an artistic success as well. Charles and Louise sent back narratives and sketches that were used for magazine articles and a pamphlet entitled *Tahiti the Golden*, which was published in 1902. In fact, the Keelers were so successful that the trip was extended from the original six weeks to a year and went on from Tahiti to the Cook Islands, New Zealand and Australia. A small volume of poetry, *A Wanderer's Songs of the Sea*, with the cover designed by Louise, also appearing in 1902, completed their South Pacific work.

Shortly after their return to California, Charles wrote *San Francisco and Thereabout*. With cover and decorations drawn by Louise, this simple and brief guidebook to the San Francisco Bay Area proved to be their best-selling book.

In 1904, Charles wrote his first book for children, *Elfin Songs of Sunland*. It was a book of children's poems with decorations by Louise. It was very popular and had been published in four editions by 1920. Charles even had composer Charles H. McCurrie set some of the poems to music, and he published a booklet of these songs in 1909. Much later, Charles produced a phonograph record on which he recited some of its rhymes.

In 1904, Charles produced his most significant book, *The Simple Home*. In this work he eloquently preaches the Arts and Crafts ideals of honesty and simplicity in home design, construction, furnishing and even garden layout. Written while he was president of the Hillside Club, this book had a great impact on home building not only in Berkeley, but extending to all of California and the nation. His architectural ideas echo those of his friend and mentor Bernard Maybeck, but the idealism is all Charles Keeler:

The ideal home is one in which the family may be most completely sheltered to develop in love, graciousness and individuality, and which is at the same time most accessible to friends, toward whom hospitality is as unconscious and spontaneous as it is abundant.

Gradually the dweller in the simple home will come to ponder upon the meaning of art, and will awaken to that illuminating insight that all art is a form of service inspired by love.

Charles's last publishing effort in 1904 was a play in verse form called *The Triumph of Light—A California Midwinter Sun Mystery*. In this allegorical "masque," Mortality, represented by a sick old man who has led an inauthentic life, is gradually brought "into the light" by the intervention of Mother Nature, her nature spirits and the King of Day. In the final scene, Mortality is given the "torch of truth" and curtains are thrown back from a covered canopy to reveal the "mystery of life"—the sleeping child, Love—who, with a kiss, gives him immortality. The play was performed early in 1905 to a packed house at the Berkeley Unitarian Church. At this event, as in many of his dramatic presentations, Charles sought to "exalt the drama as of old to a religious rite instead of an entertaining exhibition."[3]

In this production, we see some of the first evidence of Charles's genius as artistic web weaver. His highest achievement lay not in authoring the work, but in inspiring a broad spectrum of his community, including a judge and two professors, to actively participate in its staging.

Late in 1903, Charles and Louise's only son, Leonarde, was born. He was named after Leonardo da Vinci and achieved a measure of fame later in life for his work on improving the lie detector. In the spring of 1905, their second daughter, Eloise, was born. She would later achieve success as a writer and actress.

The great San Francisco earthquake struck on April 18, and the fire that followed lasted for several days. The Keeler family played a significant part in this drama, and ultimately suffered a great loss. Louise's father was stricken with apoplexy while visiting them and died in their home three days later, exactly a week before the earthquake. Charles's rescue efforts at the time of the quake began in his own home. Sensing the danger from the swaying chimney, he pulled both Leonarde and Merodine from their beds and placed them in a safer spot, just seconds before the chimney fell where they had been sleeping.

As soon as his family was secure, Charles was on the ferry to San Francisco. One of his first goals was to try and save the paintings of his friend, artist William Keith. However, upon

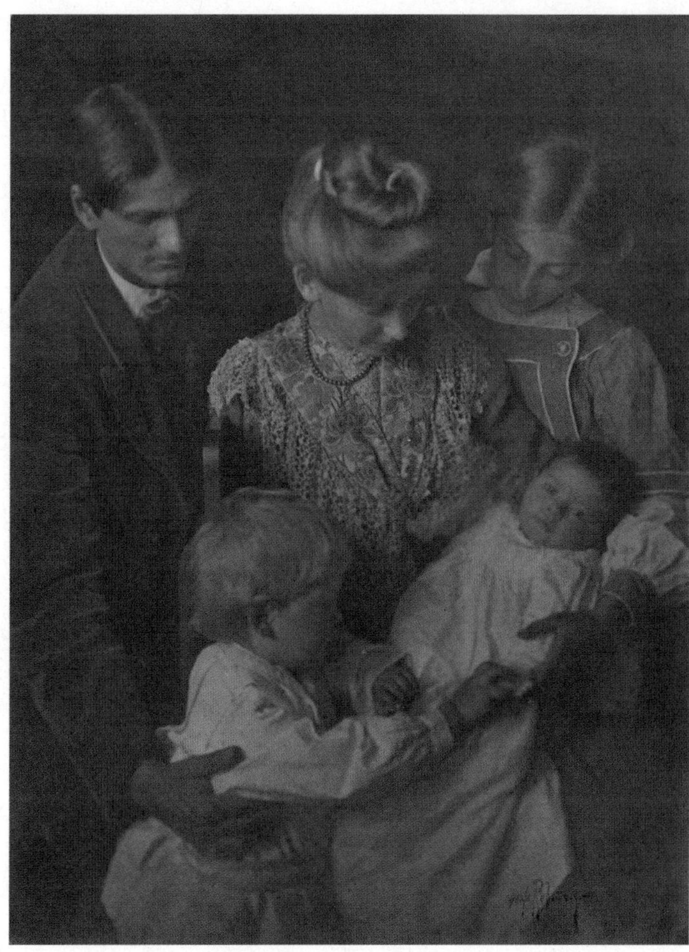

Charles, Louise, Merodine, Leonarde and Eloise Keeler in a portrait by Hana Robison.

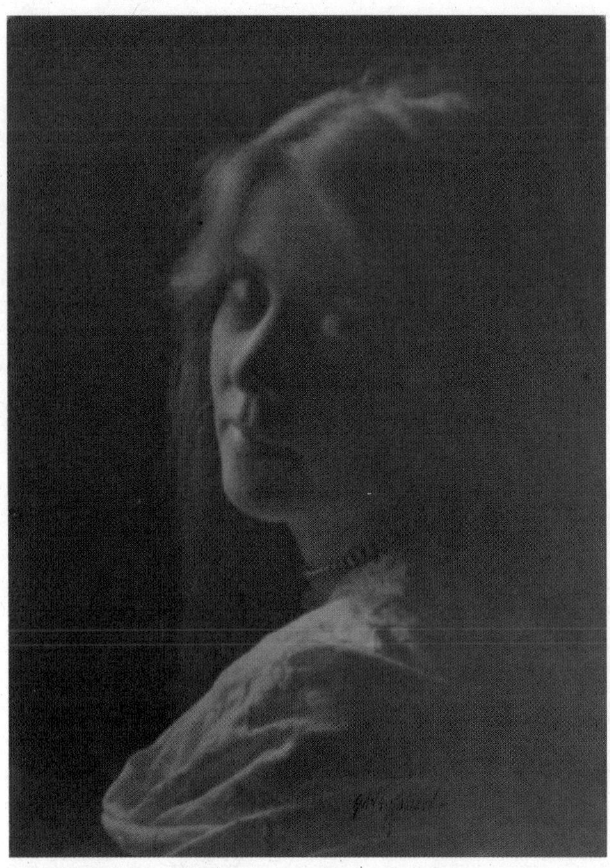

Portrait of Louise Keeler
by Hana Robison.

reaching the city, he grasped the scale of the disaster and the overwhelming needs of the rescue effort, and his focus quickly shifted to more humanitarian concerns. At first he was assigned to traverse the city in an automobile, notifying those who had been appointed to the relief committee. This proved no easy task amid the fire and chaos. Later, on the third day of the fire, he was part of a group of volunteers who helped the firemen halt the fire at Van Ness Avenue. After the fire was extinguished, he helped distribute clothing, tents and blankets to the refugees. But what of the fate of William Keith's paintings?

On the first day of the fire, a group of Keith's friends succeeded in moving nearly two thousand of his canvases in an express wagon from his studio to a home on California Street. Unfortunately, the next day the fire reached this location and burned all but twenty-six of them. Keith, upon learning of the loss, immediately bought new painting supplies and began painting, resolving "that his life-work should be done over, better than before."[4]

Charles recorded his observations and participations in the great disaster in a book called *San Francisco Through Earthquake and Fire*.

After four days of valiant effort, Charles returned to Berkeley. There he found Louise already engaged in relief work herself. She helped to organize and direct the distribution of clothing and medical supplies for the victims and refugees.

However, the strain and trauma of the disaster proved too much for her frail health. Louise collapsed and was hospitalized, and after a long courageous fight for her life, she passed away in February 1907. Charles never completely recovered from the loss of Louise, the great love of his life and artistic collaborator. He spent the next summer with his children living in Yosemite, drawing what solace he could from the grandeur of the Sierra wilderness. A small hint of the loving inner nature of Charles and Louise and their family can be gleaned by examining a sensitive series of their portraits created by Berkeley photographer Hana Robison.

U pon returning to Berkeley, the children moved into their grandmother's large house on Dwight Way. Charles continued with his creative projects, and in 1908, he was elected president of the newly organized Studio Club of Berkeley. He wrote two plays for this organization, whose membership was composed "entirely of those who have accomplished something, either as artists, writers or composers. It is considered the nucleus of the art movement in Berkeley."[5] From this description, it would seem to be the Berkeley analogue of the Bohemian Club of San Francisco. The two plays, *Love or Art* and *The Will o' the Wisp*, were presented at the Hillside Club in March 1908 on a stage specially built

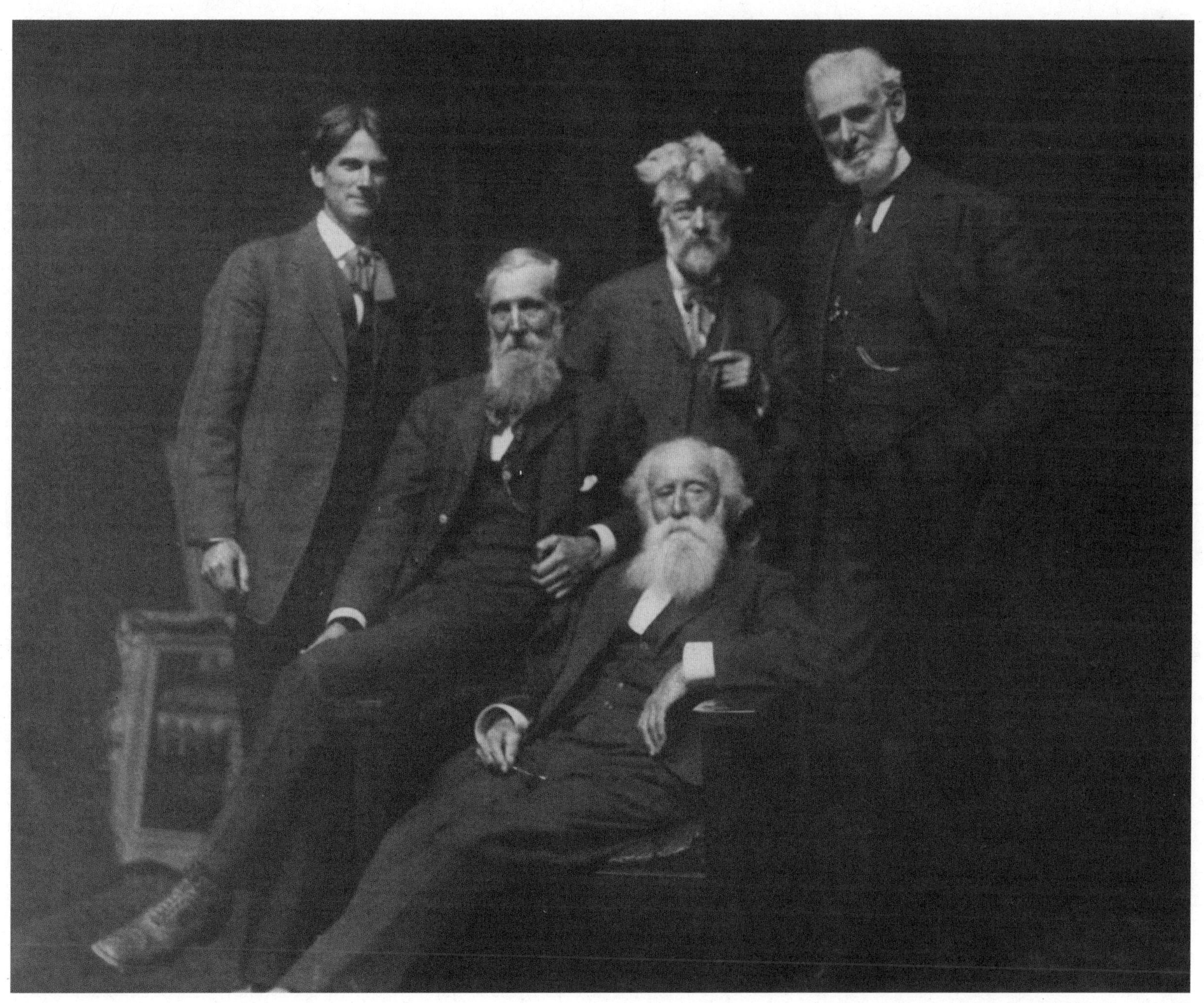

Charles Keeler, John Muir,
William Keith, Francis Brown
and John Burroughs (seated)
at Keith's San Francisco studio,
May 1909.

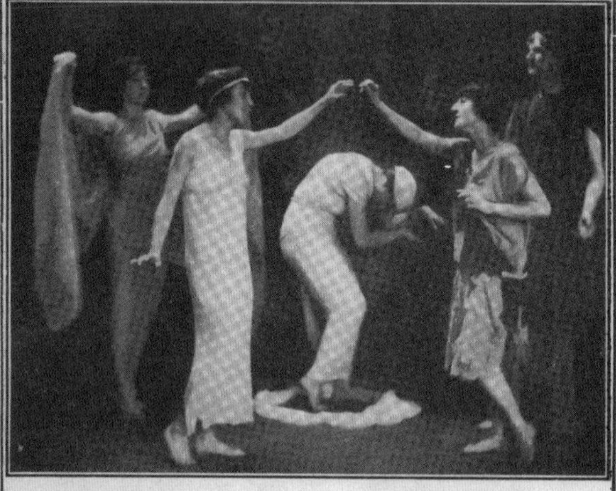

for these productions. They achieved such notable artistic success that the club was compelled to schedule a repeat performance a week later to meet the demand for tickets. Appearing among the Studio Club members was photographer Anne Brigman playing Sybil of Nepenthe.

It is clear from contemporary accounts that Charles was not simply the author of these works but the chief organizer and instigator of their production. Going beyond his personal creativity to being the artistic web weaver, he was at his best in his success at bringing together other artists for a common purpose and inspiring them to create outside their usual spheres.

In May of the following year, William Keith invited naturalist John Burroughs, who was visiting California, to view some of his new paintings at his studio. This seemingly minor artistic event produced a significant legacy. Several of the invited guests gathered around Keith to pose for a photograph. The result was one of the most interesting group portraits of its era, combining the likes of Charles Keeler, John Muir, John Burroughs, Francis Brown and William Keith.

In August 1911, Charles embarked on a world tour. This trip gave him the opportunity to give poetical performances to new audiences and to broaden his knowledge of the world and its peoples. His itinerary included Hawaii, India, Japan and much of Europe. His appearances were well received, and he made use of the opportunity to meet many of his fellow poets in these distant lands.

In 1912, Charles returned to America but decided to live in New York City rather than Berkeley. He brought his children there and enrolled them in boarding schools. While at first glance it may seem strange that Charles, the poet-naturalist, should choose to live in such an urban setting, it was probably economic necessity that dictated his choice. New York City was then the hub of literary and publishing activity and, therefore, a natural choice for a place to further his career. And of course, the great city boasted its own and much older Bohemia in Greenwich Village. Charles recited his poems and helped to stage dramatic presentations in some of the big hotels and salons of New York's wealthy patrons of the arts. One of his more noteworthy productions was a mystical dance-poem called "The Enchanted Forest," in which his poetry reading was accompanied by musicians and dancers. The work was performed at the Waldorf-Astoria Hotel under the auspices of a group of Metropolitan Opera House players as one of their series of "moments musicales."

One Easter vacation, Charles took the children with him upstate to the small town of Wyoming, New York, to stage one of his plays, *After the Great Spirit—A Play of the Seneca Indians*. At the invitation of Mrs. Cooley Ward, the Keelers and thirty other visiting artists stayed at her home while teaching and performing their arts for the local townspeople at a kind of informal summer school provided by their hostess.

Charles stayed in New York until 1917, although he sent his daughters back to Berkeley in 1915 in time to visit the Panama-Pacific International Exposition held in San Francisco that year. During his East Coast sojourn, he did manage to get one book of his poems published, *The Victory*, in 1916.

Upon his return to Berkeley, Charles was unsure in which direction to steer his life. The world was at war and most people were consumed with extreme patriotism and war fever. It was becoming clear to him that in this context, there was little demand for his poems of love and peace. Although his finances were low, he moved into a little studio cottage he had built in the Claremont neighborhood in the Berkeley Hills. On the hillside adjacent to it, he built a small outdoor amphitheater that seated about three hundred people.

Here, every Sunday, he would produce theatre parties for soldiers and sailors. From local churches and civic groups, one hundred and fifty young women would volunteer as "dates" for a like number of enlisted men. They would sit together in the hillside theatre, consume the donated "double lunches" and

enjoy the presentations provided by Keeler, the YMCA and other local groups. This lasted for a year and a half, until the war was over.

In 1919, in a somewhat more peaceful time, Charles published *Sequoia Sonnets*. This small volume of poems, whose principal theme was love, would prove to be his final book-length published work. Merodine, his eldest daughter, following in her mother's artistic footsteps, supplied the illustrations. She had studied art at the College of Arts and Crafts in Berkeley under Xavier Martinez, who had high praise for her "conception of color and feeling for design."[6]

In 1921, the leaders of Berkeley's business community hired Charles as managing director of the Berkeley Chamber of Commerce. It is doubtful that this group knew quite what they were getting themselves into in giving this position to Berkeley's visionary community arts networker. In his first year in this position, he succeeded in having the chamber sponsor a week-long Manufacturers' and Merchants' Fair in a

ABOVE: Brochure promoting Charles Keeler's poetry recitals in New York, 1916.

FACING PAGE: Handbill from performance of *The Enchanted Forest* at the Waldorf-Astoria Hotel in New York in 1915.

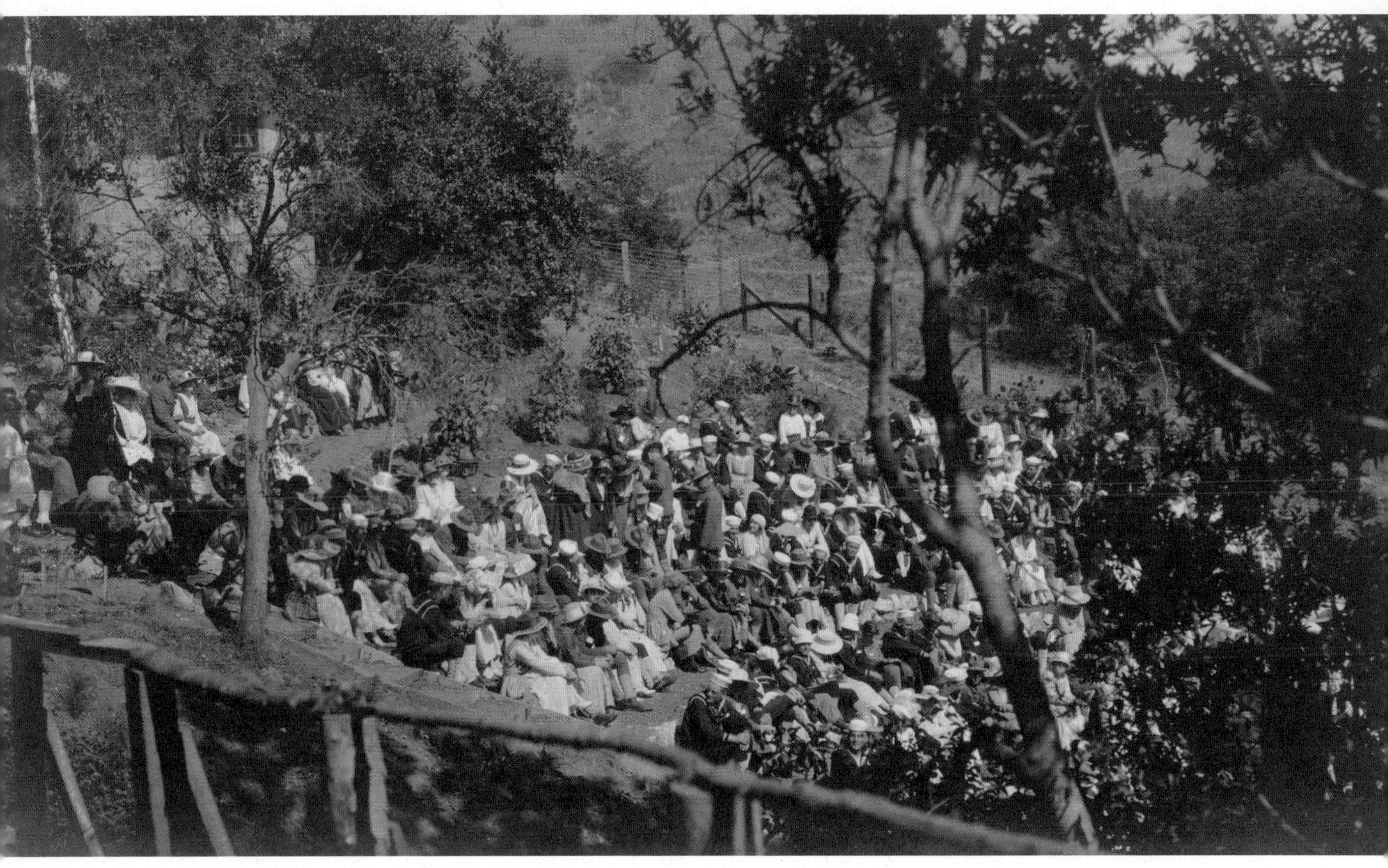

ABOVE: Audience composed of World War I soldiers accompanied by young women from Berkeley, watching a performance at the amphitheatre adjacent to Keeler's Claremont studio.

huge tent across from City Hall and a three-day Music Festival in the Greek Theatre. While the former delighted and benefited the business community, Charles personally directed and delighted in the latter. Local composers, musicians and choral groups were featured. The Berkeley Music Festival opened with chimes master Henry Safford King playing on the Campanile bells followed by a concert of the music of California composer Charles Wakefield Cadman. But perhaps the most memorable portion of the festival was the Saturday matinee concert given by the pupils of the Berkeley schools.

Under the direction of Miss Victorine Hartley, the program included a chorus of two thousand voices, a massed school band of one hundred fifty pieces and a kindergarten orchestra led by five-and-a-half-year-old conductor Irving Rosedale. A reporter noted that Rosedale "keeps a strict eye on his performers and a wrong note brings his frown."[7]

Charles attempted to build upon the great success of the music festival by announcing later that year that the Chamber of Commerce had plans to establish Berkeley as a literary and art center. He wrote:

With such names as Edward Rowland Sill, John Muir, Joaquin Miller, Jack London, Frank Norris and Herman Whittaker among the dead writers associated with Berkeley and Oakland; with Edwin Markham, Ina Coolbrith, Peter B. Kyne and others among those who resided here in the past, but have now left us, it seems to the Berkeley Chamber of Commerce an opportune time at this holiday season to recall our literary background, to take an interest in the writers still with us and to encourage others to make their home here."[8]

And this was just one part of a larger vision he set out in a tentative program for the chamber. In this comprehensive document he outlined his ideas on water development, city planning, industrial development, labor issues, transportation, commerce, automobile access, residential beautification, business, historical awareness and cultural development. In that final category he proposed:

Making Berkeley an art center: (a) Building a building and loan company for building artists' studios; (b) Building an art gallery for Berkeley; (c) Building a theatre for a good stock company to present good legitimate

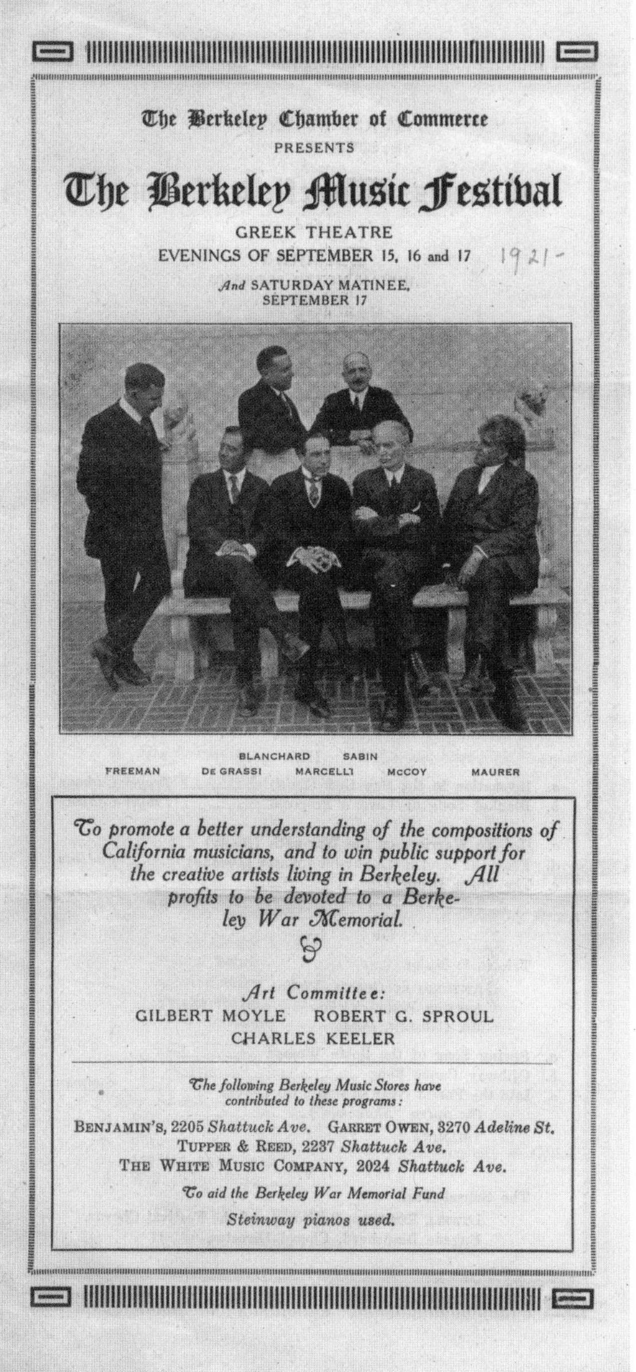

Program cover from the Berkeley Music Festival of 1921.

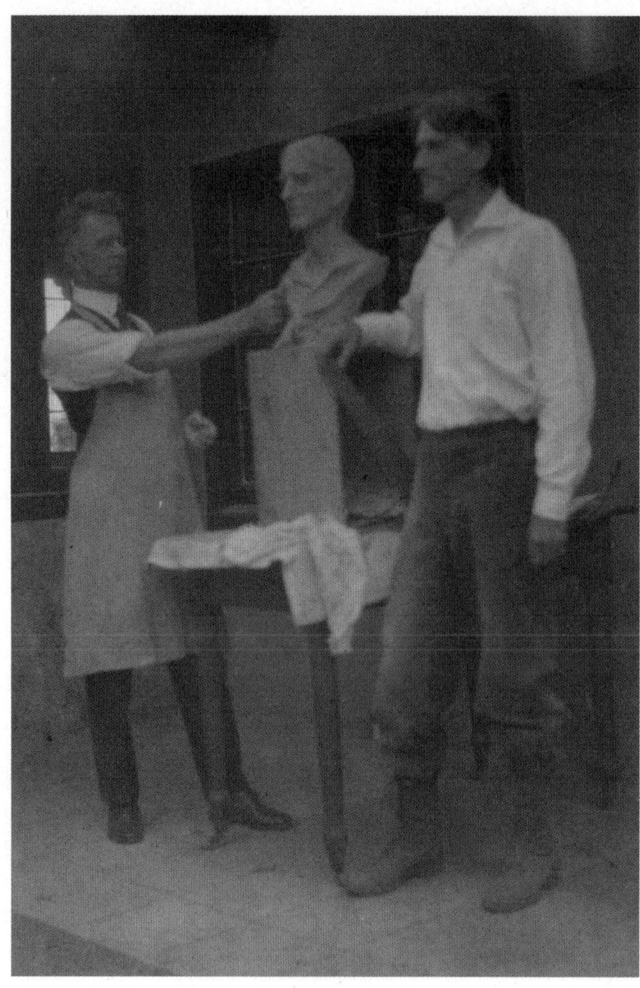

Sculptor Roger Burnham
at work on a bust of
Charles Keeler.

drama; (d) Supporting resident artists in their creative work; (e) Inducing painters, composers, sculptors, poets and playwrights to come to Berkeley to live; (f) Holding music festival featuring resident composers, art exhibitions, poetry readings, etc."[9]

Charles succeeded in persuading the chamber to form an arts-and-crafts committee to further these goals. This committee opened an arts-and-crafts shop in November of 1922 featuring needlework, textiles, paintings and tooled leather and tiles, among other things. They had at least one success in attracting artistic talent to come to Berkeley. Roger Noble Burnham (the noted sculptor) and his wife (founder of the Lanai Players of Honolulu) moved to Berkeley from Hawaii after being courted by Charles and the chamber. Mr. Burnham established a sculpture studio, and Mrs. Burnham organized a community theatre group. Mr. Burnham's first production in Berkeley was, appropriately, a bust of Charles.

At about the same time Charles was beginning his new chamber position, he also became the beneficiary of a unique business venture. A group of his literary and business friends formed a corporation called the Live Oak Publishing Company. In exchange for taking the publishing and production rights to his literary works, the corporation would sell up to $75,000 worth of stock, and he would receive the proceeds of the stock sales. The local papers were quick to spin this arrangement with headlines such as, "Poet Keeler's Brain Listed for $75,000 in Contract."[10]

One of its first productions was a series of seventeen soirees presented at Berkeley's College Women's Club. The series was touted as "the first time that the public has been privileged to hear from an artist his complete message, the reading of his own poems and plays, his aims, ideals and visions. Such readings and addresses have heretofore been given by another after the death of the author."[11]

Charles' choice of topics for these presentations ranged from his own life story to his ideas on such subjects as "The Road to Happiness," "Shall the World Deny Beauty?" and "Art and Its Relation to Bolshevism." He devoted the last of the series to the art of his dear friend William Keith, who had passed away ten years previously. The series was so successful that a second round was planned. This time an even broader field was covered, including "a discussion of psychic research and the evidences for a belief in personal survival after death, and discourses on Bolshevism, Socialism and democracy."[12]

It was also at this time that Charles began teaching English at the "A to Zed School" in

Berkeley. While there, he met poet Ormeida Curtis Harrison, who was an assistant principal at the school, and the two were married in 1921. Their common interests went beyond poetry to the study of psychic phenomena. Charles and Ormeida both joined the California Writers Club, and Charles was its president from 1921 to 1923.

In addition to (and transcending) his ability to write poetry, Charles Keeler possessed the soul of a poet. An idealist and spiritual seeker all his life, he finally integrated and published his ideas for a new religion in 1925. In *An Epitome of Cosmic Religion*, he sets forth an outline of this new religion. In its opening paragraph, he writes,

> Civilization is now on trial. If the people of the world, drawn ever closer together by fast steamers, express trains, air craft swifter than the storm winds, and broadcasting of speech to far lands in a trice, cannot acquire the habit of tolerance and learn to understand one another, there is grave danger for the future security of mankind.[13]

In the pages that follow, he gives the framework for a new "Cosmic" religion that at once honors and respects the teachings of the old religions and finds their common ground, but is nonetheless not beholden to any of them. His vision for a new trinity is one composed of love, truth and beauty. He ends his brief religious treatise with this salutation:

> If such a religion will boldly face the living problems of the modern world, knowing and treasuring those things that are precious in the past but emancipated from the tyranny of traditions and conventions, what may it not accomplish! With resolute good will to all peoples, with patience and tolerance, with a rediscovery of beauty and a sense of awe in the presence of holy things, Cosmic religion may call back the spirit from materialism to idealism, and heal the wounds of a war-distracted world.[14]

In the hope of realizing his vision, he founded the First Berkeley Cosmic Society in 1925. His hillside amphitheatre served as a ready-made outdoor chapel at which to hold its meetings. The group achieved some limited success in attracting members but never achieved the widespread success he had hoped for. Interest soon waned, and by 1930, the new religion ceased meeting.

While Charles found little of value in many aspects of modern culture, such as modern poetry and modern art, this did not preclude him from embracing parts of modern technology. In the late 1920s and early 1930s, he wrote many successful scripts for radio serials, including *Skipper Brown's Yarns* and *The O'Flanagan Family*.

In the mid-1930s, Charles attempted to illuminate the contributions of the great men of art and ideas who had helped to shape and inspire his own life. He did this by composing biographical sketches of sixteen of

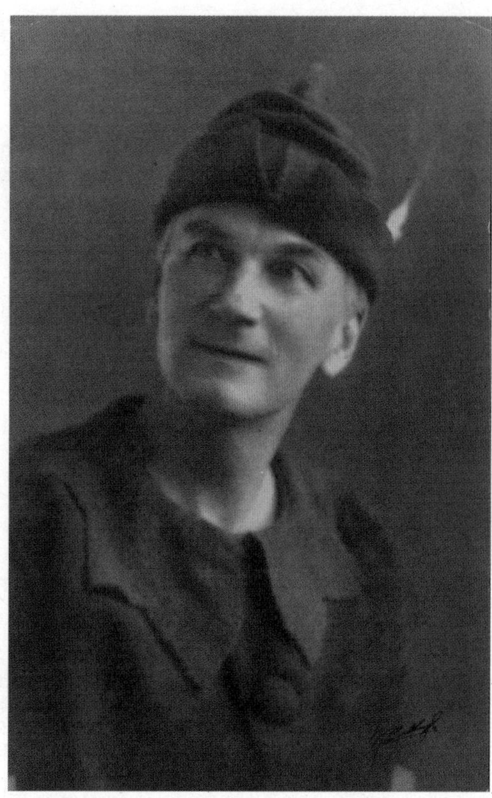

Charles Keeler in "elf" attire for a costume recital of his poems at the Berkeley Women's City Club in 1921.

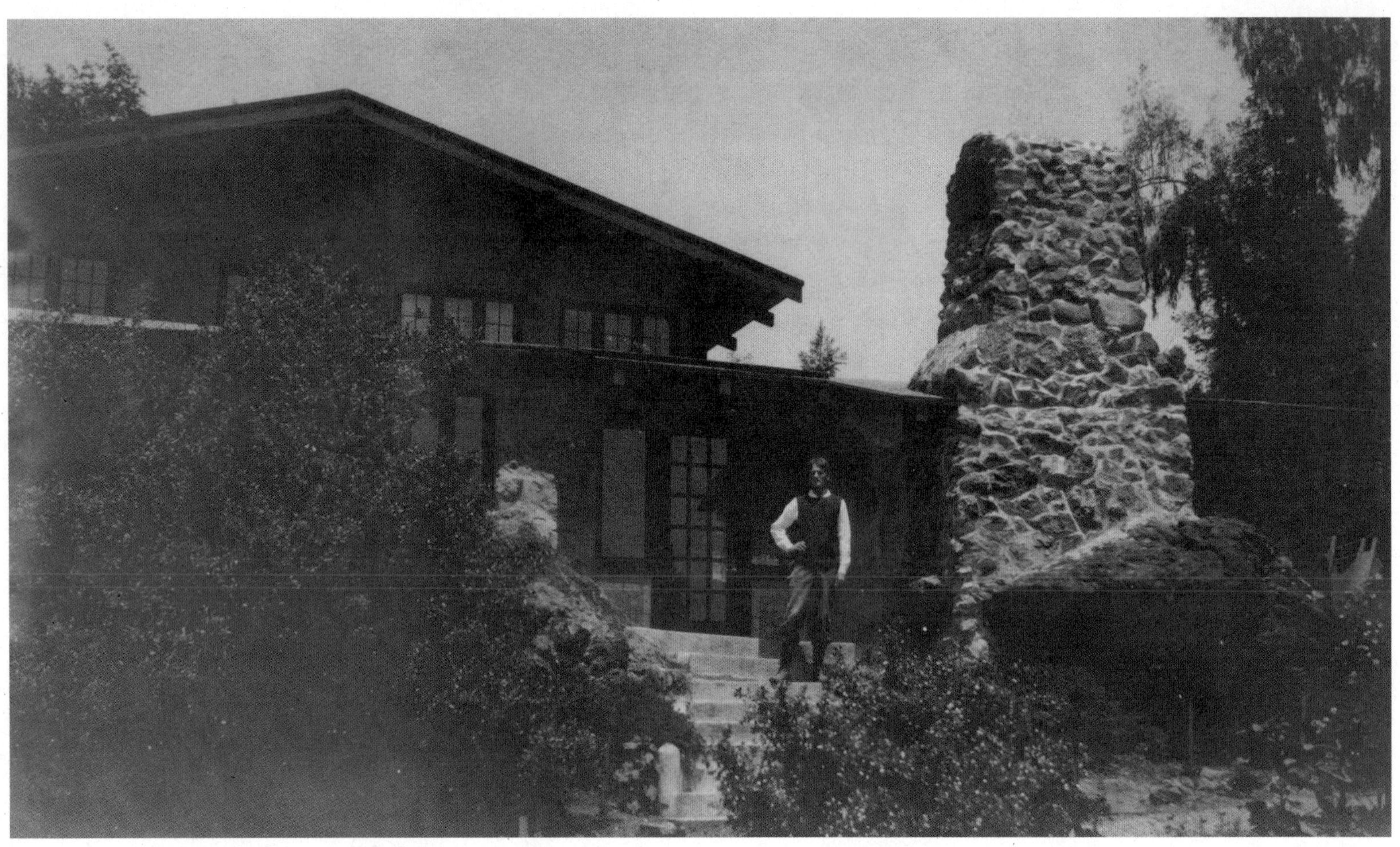

them, thereby creating his only unpublished manuscript: *Friends Bearing Torches—A Company of Great-Hearted Californians.* Charles felt particularly blessed to have lived his life in a time and place in which he could share the friendship of a "cluster of illustrious men,"[15] whom he believed were analogous to those of Athens in its golden age and Europe in the Renaissance. This group of mentors and friends includes, in part, William Keith, John Muir, Ina Coolbrith, Edwin Markham, Joaquin Miller, Charles F. Lummis and Bernard Maybeck. Written largely from personal experience, these short monographs are rich in anecdotes and associations otherwise unrecorded. The lack of success in finding a publisher for his "tribute of love to a company of great souls"[16] was frustrating and saddening for Charles, and hopefully this situation may yet be remedied.

Charles Keeler died at home on July 31, 1937, underappreciated and nearly forgotten by his contemporaries. His contributions in previous decades were no longer at the forefront of public awareness in a Depression-era world preparing for war. It was not until the 1970s and the resurgence of interest in the Arts and Crafts movement that Charles's accomplishments would again be remembered and valued. Although art would continue to flourish in Berkeley, for the next two decades bohemianism itself was in a kind of hibernation that would last until its sleeping seeds would begin to sprout in the form of a new generation.

It is no simple matter to distill from the rich artistic lives of Charles and Louise Keeler the essence of their contribution to Berkeley Bohemia. While a case could be made for the entirety of their creative output being their legacy, it is the effect of the interaction of their lives on their contemporaries that would seem to be most significant.

From 1895 to 1907, their home on Highland Place was a mecca for bohemianism, Berkeley-style. Countless visits were made by a plethora of artists, writers, poets, photographers, naturalists and dancers who were friends of the Keelers. And along with these, even more of their "ordinary" Berkeley neighbors paid calls. There was always something interesting going on at the Keelers.

After Louise's passing, and, later, with Ormeida, Charles carried on the role of instigating, inspiring, coordinating and encouraging participation in the arts.

From their church and neighborhood productions in the early years to the community-wide efforts with the Chamber of Commerce later on, a pattern emerges of an ever-widening scope of influence as they successfully fostered artistic involvement among Berkeley's residents. It is in the creation of this artistic web that their enduring legacy resides and, indeed, continues to this day.

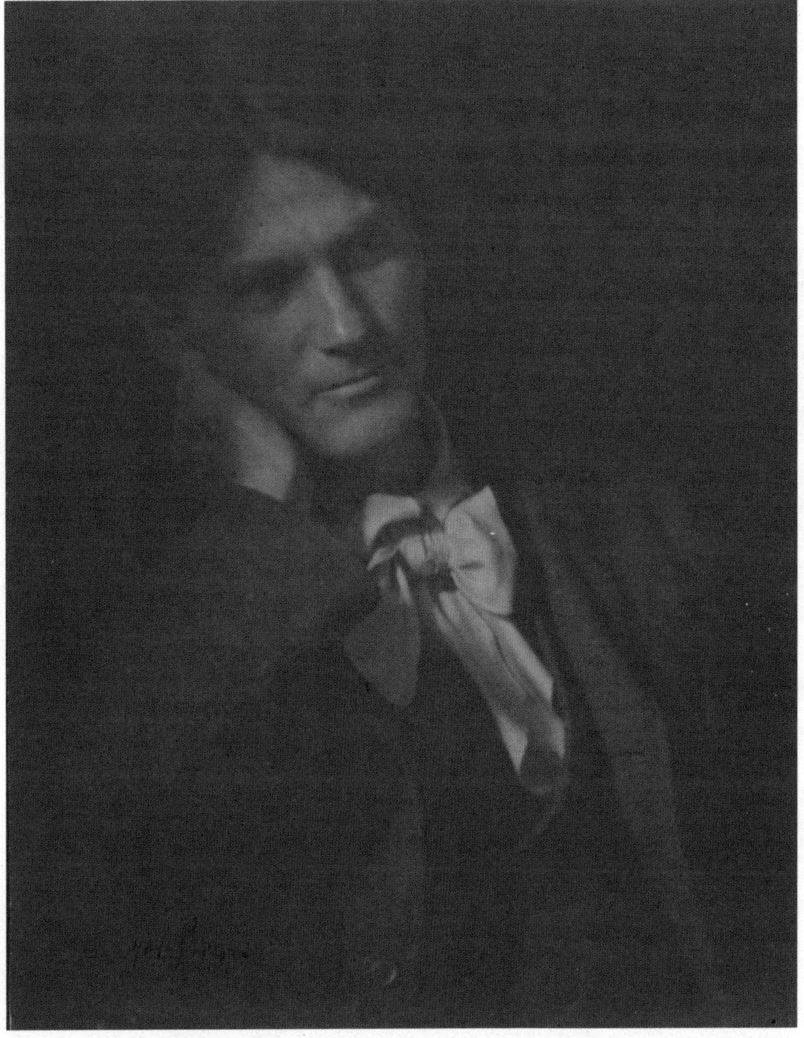

Portrait of Charles Keeler by Hana Robison.

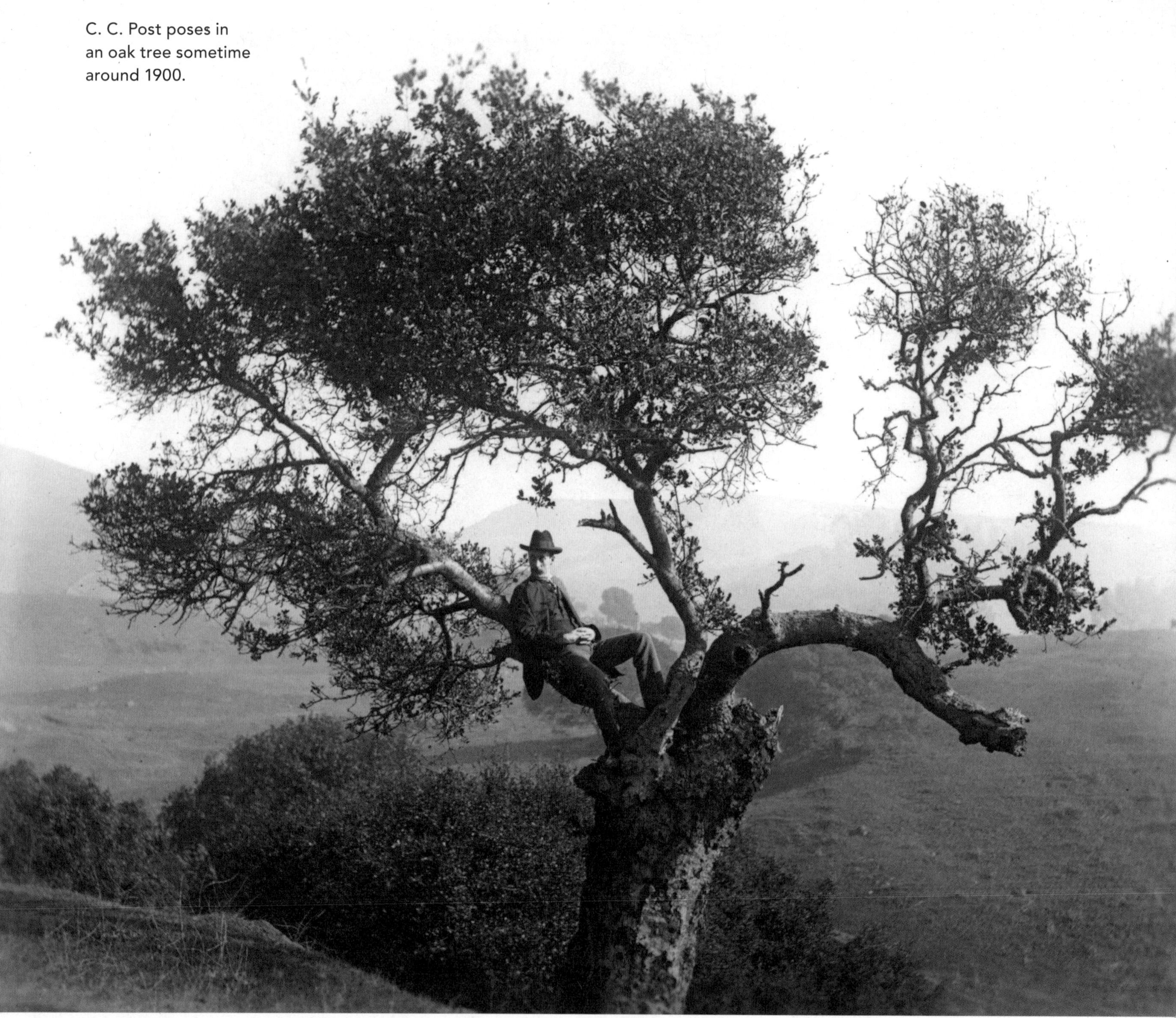

C. C. Post poses in
an oak tree sometime
around 1900.

LIVING WITH NATURE

"I set right off from our little house, which was one of the last before
the empty Berkeley Hills began, and I walked all over the tops of
the mountains for about four hours with perfect security, in spite
of the fact that it was not considered the thing to do, I discovered
afterwards, by respectable Berkeleyans."[1]
—Charles Seeger

If Charles Seeger remembered that hiking was not seen as "the thing to do" by the more conservative elements of Berkeley life, he was certainly not alone in his love of the hills and gardens of Berkeley. If you were a nature lover in Berkeley in the 1920s, you might have picked up a slim volume of poetry called *Twigs from the Berkeley Branch*. It was a suitable name for a book that was created by Berkeley Club women and sent as tribute to the National League at Washington, with its play on the word "branch." But the title, and the book, also perfectly showed how widespread the love of nature was among Berkeley's cultured classes. The book was filled with odes to geraniums and dahlias, flowers that appeared in many Berkeley yards.

Two of the book's most dramatic entries showed how, in Berkeley's mind, these garden blooms were far more significant than mere decoration. They represented a way of life, as demonstrated in a pair of verses by Mary Bird Clayes, who dabbled in Berkeley's writer's scene and was a member of the California Writer's Club. "Evening in Berkeley" was a description of her city's natural bounty. In Berkeley, the poet sees "magenta bands" in the west "arch[ing] the sapphire bay." Turning around to face east, she finds an equally exquisite view. "Above the eastern hills . . . the great moon shone with silver light."[2] In the contrasting poem, "Evening in the City," San Francisco became a grim shadow of the bright jewel-like colors of Berkeley. In the city, evening is the only time that nature can enter the harshness of city life; a single "still enchanted hour" among the "hard and rough" commercial world. Most of the time, Clayes's

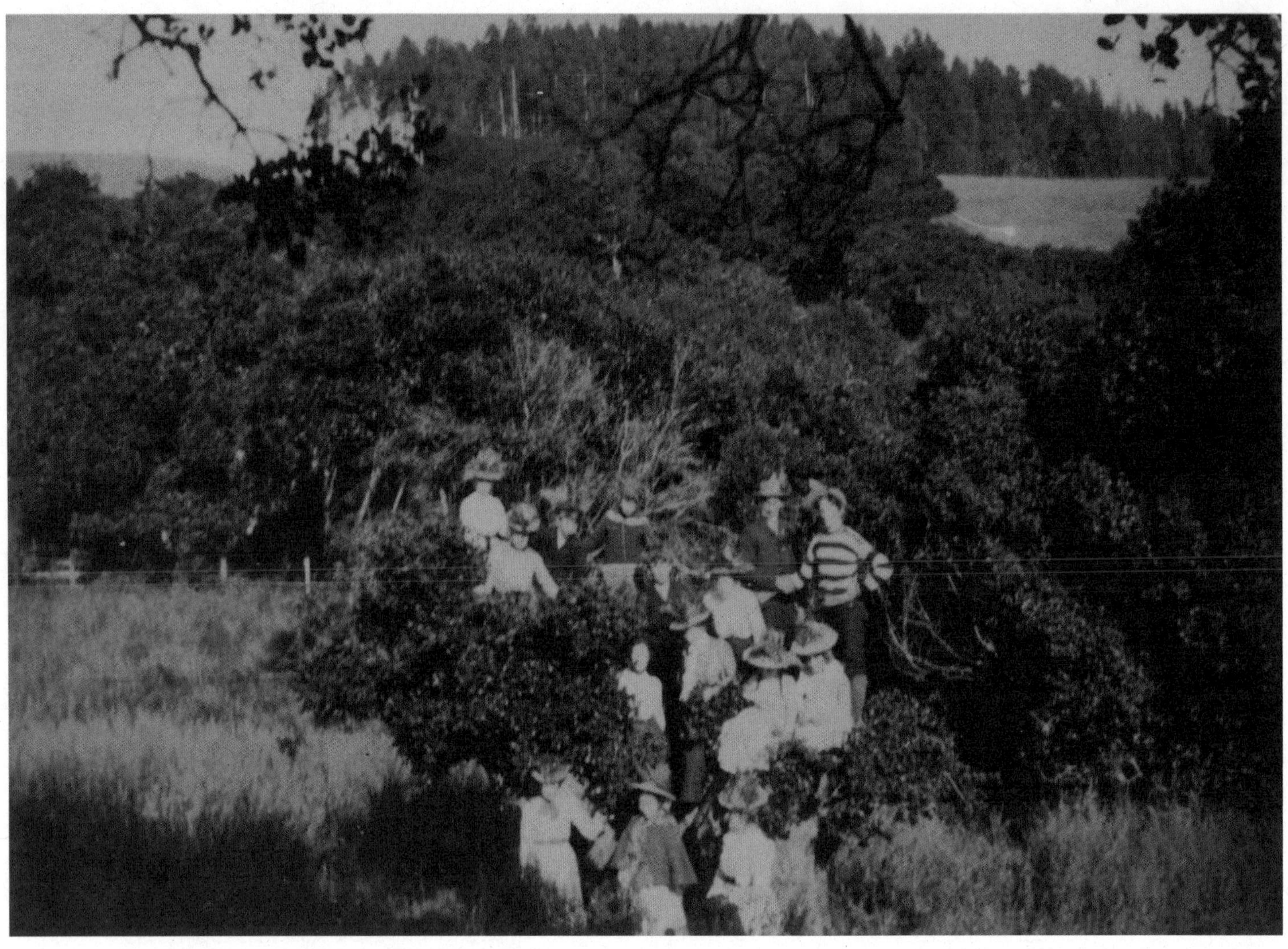

Picnickers on a 1903 trip to Wildcat Canyon, an undeveloped part of Contra Costa County.

poem said that the city was full of nothing but "iron, and stone, and cruel Power." Clayes, like most of her contemporaries, believed that society was rejecting nature in favor of power and that Berkeley offered a better way.[3]

Starting when ruddy-cheeked, sophisticated architect Bernard Maybeck came to the city in 1890, America was becoming increasingly urban (and suburban, as in the case of Berkeley). The same changes that were driving people (including Berkeleyans) to the cities were also making them uncomfortable with the mechanization of their time and eager to bring the contemplative and rejuvenating aspects of nature into daily life—into their schools, homes and architecture.

Maybeck and his clients exemplified Berkeley's utopian way of looking at nature. Their ideas divided into two streams of thought, each connected by new ideas that trickled from many points to merge like the creeks that once ran through the East Bay Hills. One stream was domestic, interested in "natural" homes, "natural" schools and "simple" living, however these ideas might be defined. Freedom from excessive decoration and formality, they thought, was the best way to obtain health, happiness and harmony. The other stream was grand and romantic as the rivers that flowed from the Sierra Nevadan snowmelt. Through living in a purely natural setting, one could come closer to God. Nearly all Berkeley bohemians subscribed to both beliefs, which shared a faith in the goodness of a nature that was not fierce but not quite tame either.

THE INFLUENCE OF THE ARTS AND CRAFTS MOVEMENT

These streams were fed by rivulets in many different places. Bernard Maybeck drew his influences from the English Arts and Crafts movement, which was started by English artist and thinker William Morris in the 1870s. Morris, like thousands after him, was inspired by reading the works of John Ruskin, a slightly older art critic who criticized the mechanization and over-decoration of the Victorian age—and who eventually was honored by a philosophy club in the Berkeley Hills, the Ruskin Club. Morris and Ruskin's concerns were not so much with man's disconnect from nature, but with his disconnect from the simplicity and honesty of rural work. The mechanization of production, Ruskin claimed, made the artisan just another machine. Against the bright colors and machine-made clutter that the Victorians so loved, Ruskin and Morris advocated handmade arts, celebrating the materials and hand skills that made a building, a pot, a rug or a piece of furniture.[4]

Another influence was nearby. John Muir, the leader of California's ecology movement, was a close friend of many Berkeley residents. His books, letters and lectures told Berkeley residents about the spiritual benefits of travel through the Sierra vistas that were only a few days' ride from their homes. Even closer than Muir was a third influence, right in their own city. Between 1900 and 1910, Berkeley's landscape was visibly changing.

The city's most striking geographical features are the East Bay Hills, the steep boundary between urban Alameda and rural Contra Costa counties—wetter and more forestlike on the Berkeley/Oakland side, dryer and covered with low bushes on the Contra Costa side. The sides of the hills are dotted with native live oak and imported eucalyptus. In 1905, painter Ernest Peixotto wrote in *Romantic California*, "These Piedmont Hills are little known except to a few persistent lovers of nature and to some painters like William Keith, who draws many of his motifs from among their live oaks, and the lamented Arthur Atkins, who so well interpreted their russet slopes . . . [and] groves of Eucalypti whose madder leaves form pungent carpets upon the ground." He added, "You will be surprised by the suddenness of the

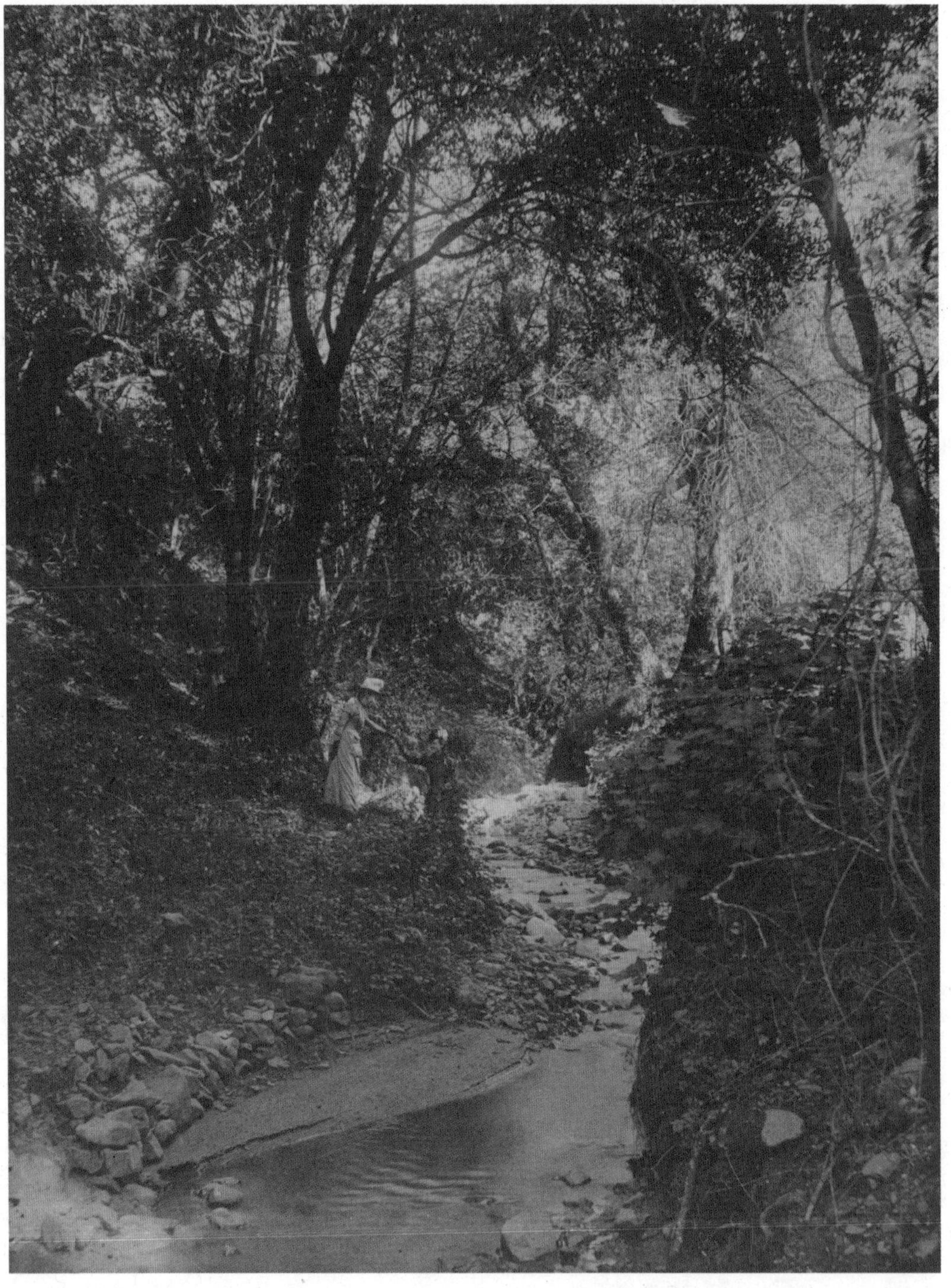

Nell and Blanch Morse enjoy Strawberry Creek in the late 1890s.

transition from populous city street and suburban avenue to quiet deserted hillside."[5]

Just as Peixotto was writing about the unknown and unappreciated hills, he worried that his beloved hills were "being divided into building lots" by developers. Oakland writer Herman Whitaker likewise recognized the changes and sarcastically wrote that "it would be too much to hope that Berkeley should escape the aegis of the Building Contractor."[6] The city of hills was now proclaiming itself the "City of Homes."

THE HILLSIDE CLUB

In response, the Bohemians started the Hillside Club. Beverly Lacy Hodghead, a mayoral candidate, was one of the speakers in 1909. In his speech to the club members, he used the plain language of the businessman and the candidate to claim that "the club was organized . . . for the purpose of providing a place where the people of this section of the city could congregate and consider questions which relate to the upbuilding of this community in particular and Berkeley in general."[7]

Hodghead's speech probably did not win him any votes from the Hillside Club members, as he was completely wrong about the reason why the club was started. In fact, a group of Berkeley women started the club to stop the city's "upbuilding." They wanted "to protect the hills of Berkeley from unsightly grading and the building of unsuitable and disfiguring houses."[8]

Margaret "Madge" Robinson had the idea first. In 1896, she and her extended

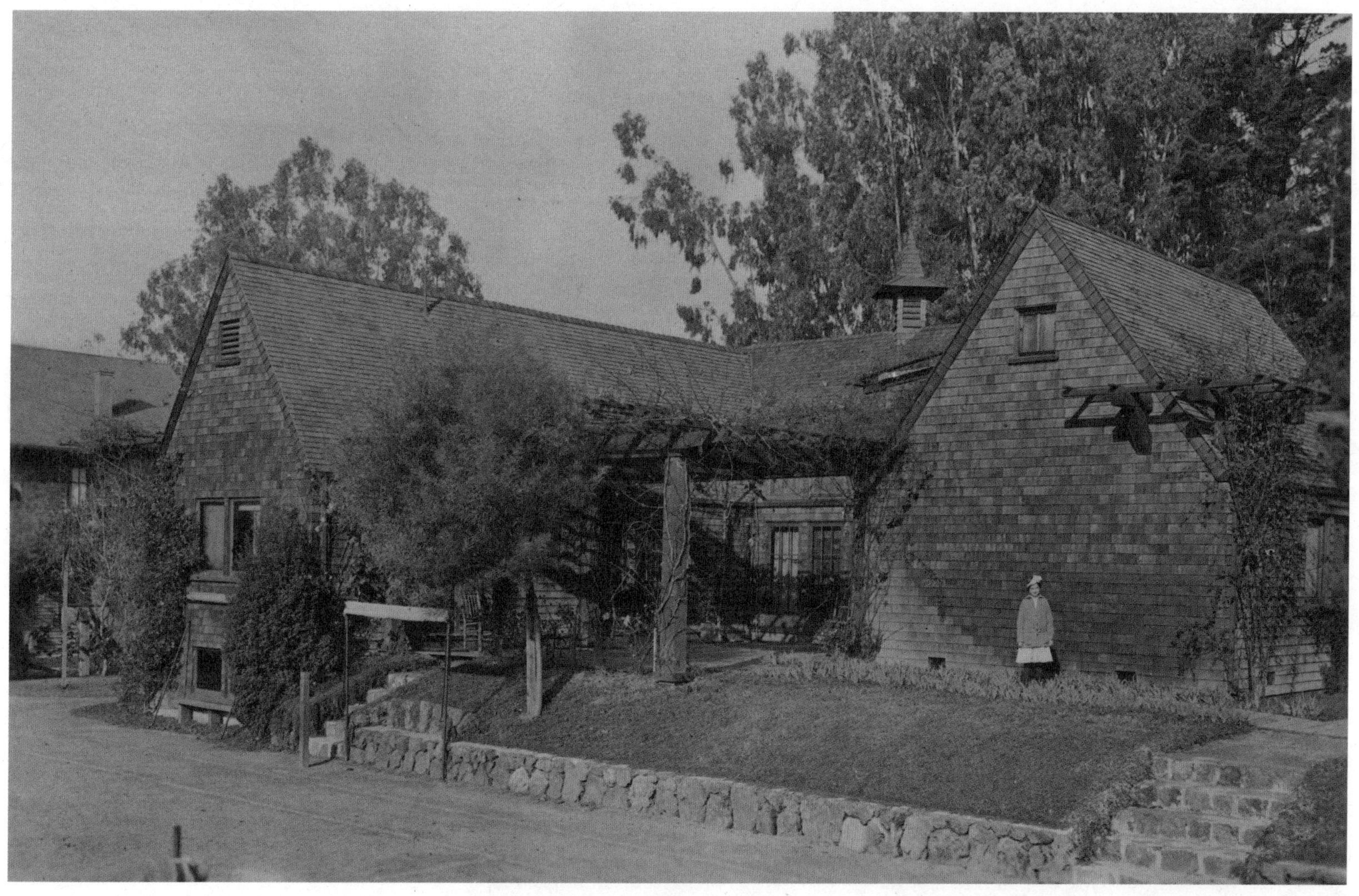

family moved from Oakland to Berkeley, where her stepfather planned to retire in a custom-designed home. Along with her older sister, May R. Gray, Robinson founded the Hillside Club to help "the nature-lover, the home-lover, [and] the peace-lover" who could never find peace while "God's hills [are] scarred with such unhealthy growths, such freaks of houses."[9]

The ideas of building to adapt to the natural setting had been floating around Berkeley for several years, especially at the Ruskin Club, a local philosophy club that debated the Arts and Crafts movement. However, Robinson was also probably influenced by the magazines that were springing up all over the country in the 1800s and 1890s, like the *Craftsman* from Syracuse, New York, *Ladies Home Journal* in Philadelphia and *House Beautiful* from Chicago. She wrote for the last of these in 1899, explaining the architectural goals of the Hillside Club.

The Randolph School's building combined the Hillside Club's ideas of harmonious building materials, such as natural shingles, with classroom gardens that encouraged children to spend time outdoors.

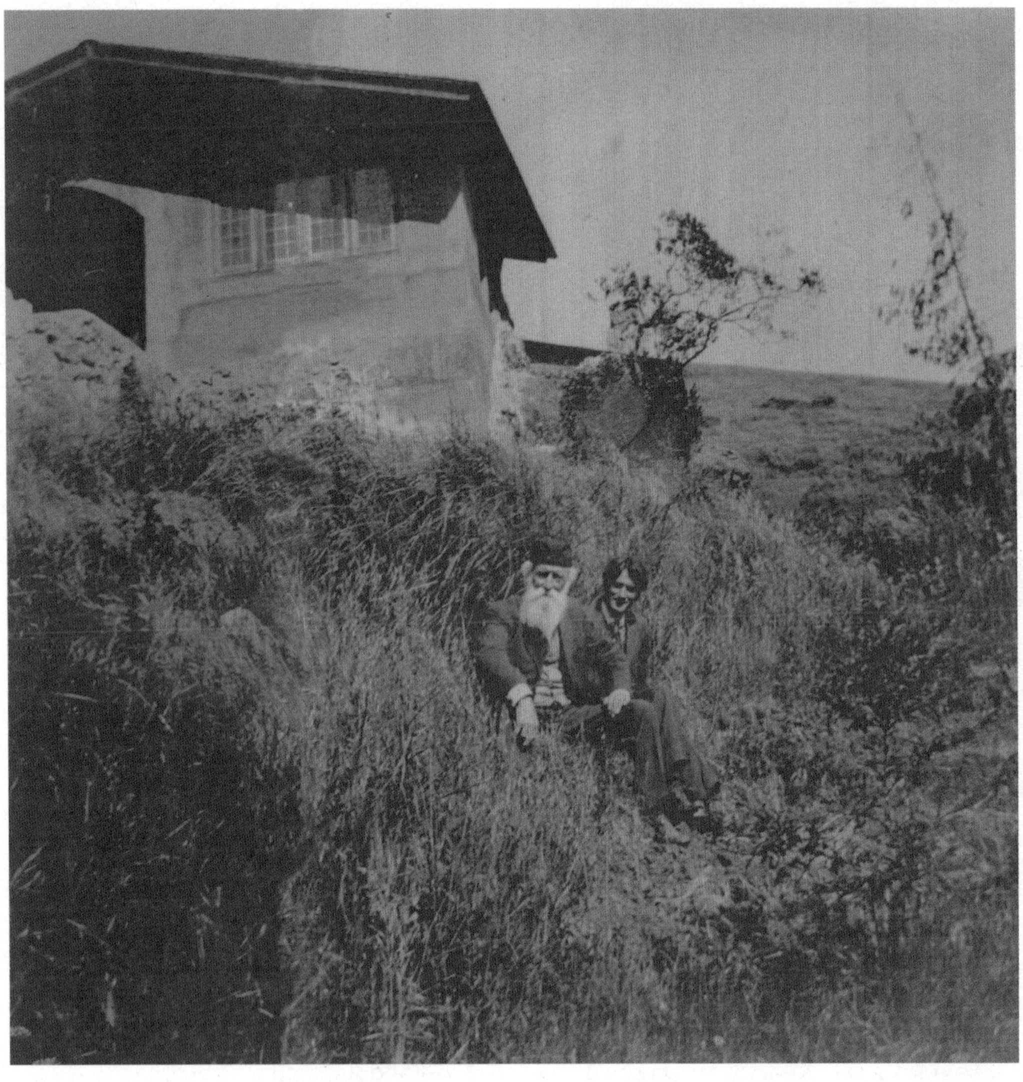

Bernard Maybeck and Charles Keeler both worked on the McGrew home in 1900, imbuing the house with the ideals that would come to epitomize *The Simple Home.*

Originally, the club was only open to women. The club's first act was to assert aesthetic control over a new elementary school that the city wanted to build in the center of their growing neighborhood. They convinced the city that a natural school—one that embodied all their ideas of beauty—could be built as cheaply as a traditional boxy schoolhouse. But the men soon made

an impact on the club's activities, especially because the club's efforts at lobbying city hall were limited by the fact that none of the women members could vote.

Once they joined, men dominated the club's leadership. Indeed, the club ruled that, although women were the founding members, only men could ever serve as president. The ever-active Charles Keeler stepped into the presidential role from 1903 to 1905. He soon published a plan for growth: *Hillside Club Suggestions for Berkeley Homes.* The club soon included a cross section of Berkeley types: professors and professionals, businesswomen and housewives, artists and art collectors. They gathered in the evenings for debate, theatrical performances (often written and performed by club members) and lots of talk about how to best live in harmony with nature. For some, like Annie Maybeck, the Hillside Club was all they needed in terms of social life.

Keeler's *Suggestions* were the culmination of these discussions. The hillside dwellers wanted their homes to demonstrate "simplicity" and "genuineness," without "insincere ornament."[10] The house, ideally, should blend into the landscape, as if it had grown there. In the suggestions, Keeler molded the ideas of the English Arts and Crafts movement to fit the California environment.

Nothing epitomized insincerity as much as paint, which Keeler called "hard," "characterless" and even unsafe (whether to the spirit, the health of the inhabitants or the look of the street was unclear).[11] Instead of painting a house, he said, one should build it of unpainted wood, dull stone and shingles. If the owner could not afford fine natural materials, a flowering vine might add some color and style. On the inside, the house should be paneled with wood and ornamented only with a large fireplace and maybe a few especially well-made pieces of molding or carving. To contrast with the dark wood-heavy interiors of the home, Keeler advocated lots of open-air rooms. Each house should have some enclosed gardens, some porches shaded with vines, some south-facing patios. To Keeler, one of Berkeley's best features was the weather, which meant that one might "sit out of doors two thirds of the year" in comfort and elegance.[12]

But the *Suggestions* went beyond the style of individual houses to dictate how each house should relate to its neighbors. Streets should wind around streams and oak trees, not slice the countryside in a rectangular grid. Houses should be placed on lots to allow as much open space as possible—four houses, for example, should each be built on corners of their lots, leaving the center as "in effect like one garden."[13] The gardens that connected these buildings contained "fairy-tale forests" of eucalyptus trees, acacia, begonias, geraniums and Monterey cypress.[14]

Keeler was only expressing the ideas of his friend and mentor, Bernard Maybeck. Maybeck, one of Northern California's greatest architects, was born to a German emigrant father in Greenwich Village, New York. At sixteen, young Bernard went to Paris to apprentice as a furniture designer but ended up studying at the top architecture school, the École des Beaux-Arts. In 1890, after stopping in New York and Kansas City, he joined a small intellectual community in Berkeley. There, he met Joseph Worchester, a Swedenborgian minister of the Piedmont hills, whose intellectual gatherings introduced Maybeck to the "simplicity" advocated by English philosophers and artists like Morris and Ruskin. His first residential commission was Keeler's house in 1894, and new house commissions came almost every year for the next several years. In times when Maybeck's jobs were slow, his wife, Annie Maybeck, managed the buying, selling, and leasing of the family real estate, managing to keep the Maybecks in middle-class style.

The simple style was not limited to architecture, but spread into the other arts. Keeler expanded his ideas into a book called *The Simple Home*, which was published by Paul Elder of San Francisco. Elder used natural designs and woodcuts in his books, and

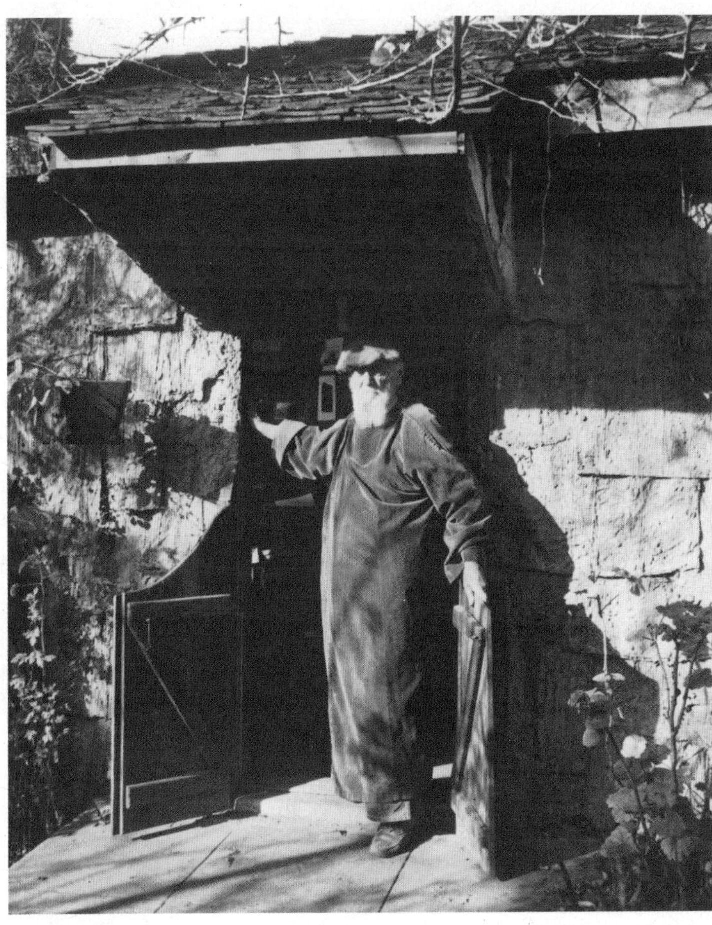

This photo of Bernard Maybeck was taken by Lionel Berryhill. Maybeck wore custom-tailored suits to meet clients, but put on red velvet robes of his own design when he was at home.

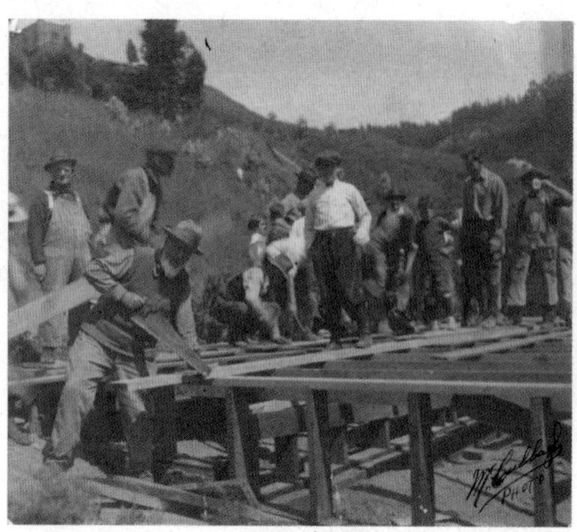

Bernard Maybeck (with saw) joins a community effort to build the Codornices Clubhouse, probably just before the city's Codornices Park was opened in 1915.

then sold them through Maybeck-designed bookstores. Certainly, the Simple Home was not necessarily a humble home. Many homes in the Hillside Club's area included libraries, performance spaces, many bedrooms and servants' quarters. Photos of the Keeler and Maybeck homes show that they were lined with dark wood, built-in bookcases and Japanese screens, and dotted with small furniture. One picture shows Maybeck's toddler granddaughters sitting next to the unscreened fire in a fireplace three times their size. A tiny picture of a Renaissance gentleman hangs on the wall behind them, watching their play.

According to Maybeck's daughter-in-law Jacomena, "the big Maybeck house was a glamorous place" when she first saw it in 1921, with "a sleeping porch for each bedroom, two fireplaces, a raised dining room" and two living rooms.[15] The Maybecks pushed their beds through French doors in summer so they could sleep outdoors on their porches. Two years later in 1923, the house burned in a wildfire, and the Maybecks moved in with Annie's mother. The Maybecks' son, Wallen, sick of living like a refugee in his grandmother's house and used to sleeping outdoors since his childhood, set up a sleeping bag on the foundation of his family's burnt home. The rest of the family followed him back to the site and lived in a series of always-changing buildings, with a large studio to dance or draw in, a series of bedrooms, bathrooms and sleeping porches added on, and a "half-outdoors" kitchen. Maybeck blended "house and garden [into] a single entity," sitting barefoot under the trees while drawing in his notebook.[16]

Maybeck's home was unusual but not nearly as unique as was one of his most famous (and for him, one of his most frustrating) collaborations. Annie Maybeck, doing her job to keep the family fed, sold a chunk of land to a new family who wanted to live life completely according to natural terms. Dancer Florence Boynton, her husband, Charles, and their seven children wanted to move from their conventional house in Alameda, two towns over, to a wild temple in Berkeley. They asked Maybeck to design a house in the Berkeley Hills that fit with Mrs. Boynton's profession as a dance teacher in the Isadora Duncan style. Since Duncan-style dancers wore ancient Greek robes, the dance teacher wanted a Greek temple to live in. (Apparently, the ideas were all Florence's, and Charles was happy just to go along for the ride.)

Florence Boynton had very precise ideas about the Temple of Wings, as she called her house. After much arguing with Maybeck, and after switching architects partway through the project, she got her wish. The end result was two huge domes for a roof, held up by thirty-two Corinthian columns that reached the equivalent of two stories above the hard floor. No walls enclosed the living spaces, leaving the family in communion with the outdoors at all times. It was as if the sleeping porches had taken over the entire house.

Canvas curtains hung between each column, ready to be let down during rainstorms, while tall eucalyptus trees and low bushes protected the family's privacy. Inside, the house was decorated with Greek-influenced furniture. Copies of ancient Greek statues dotted the rooms, some missing arms and legs, as if they had just been dug out of an archaeological site. The massive domes were painted blue and decorated with images of "heavenly bodies" to reflect the night sky.[17]

The Temple of Wings was Berkeley's most unique home for nine years, until it, too, burned in the 1923 wildfire. Only the elaborate concrete columns survived, looking "antique, historic, and picturesque as all get-out."[18] Two of the Boynton children married in the ruins of their family home that year, to the sound of Greek singing and cymbals. But with the Boynton children grown, the family needed a different kind of house. Mrs. Boynton rebuilt around the surviving columns, creating a house that was divided into two conventionally walled living spaces surrounding a courtyard. The fire-ravaged columns decorated both the outside and the inside of the new house, re-creating the Grecian temple effect.

In the nine years that it stood, Florence Boynton's house was the strictest interpretation of natural living that the city had known. But to Berkeley's bohemians, natural living meant more than just how one built a house. The ideals of natural living infused through all the main activities of the homemaker,

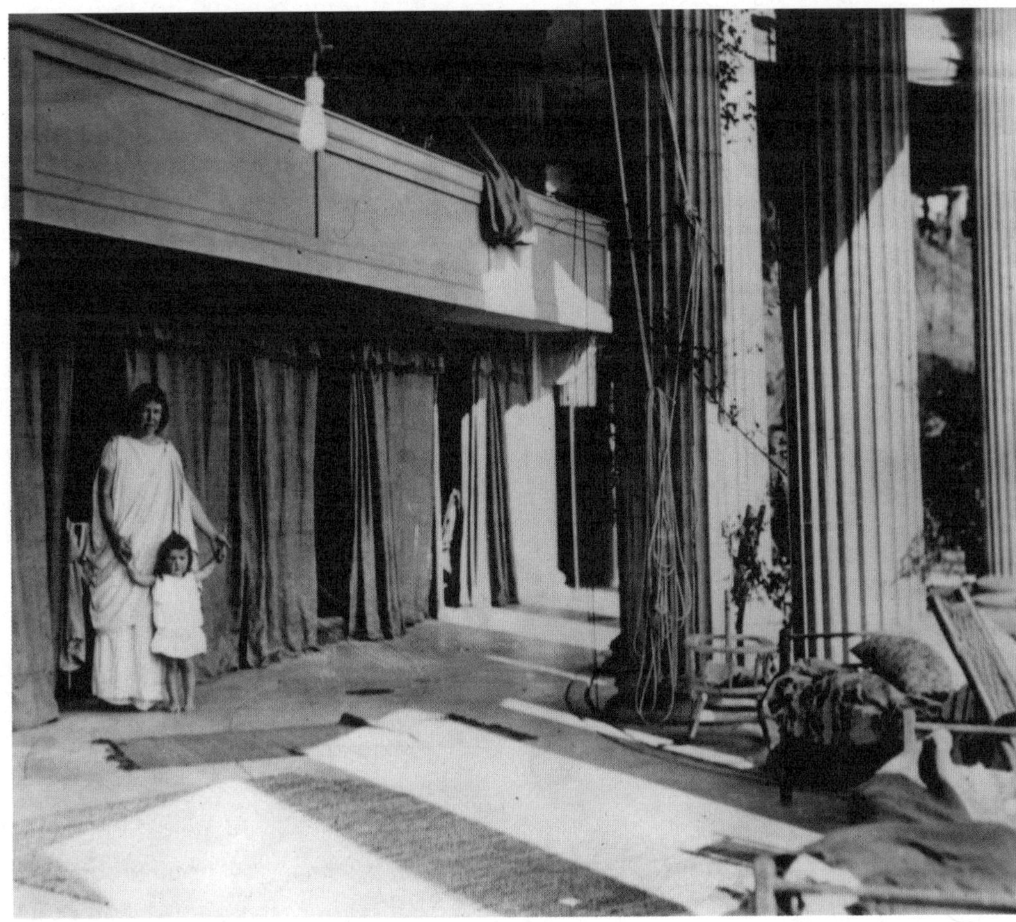

including childbirth, dress, food, bathing and education.

Again, Florence Boynton led the pack. After bearing five daughters in the customary indoor way, she decided to give birth to her first son among the flowers of her Alameda garden. She believed that natural birth was the most painless and wanted to be sure to get as much nature as possible into the experience. Her beloved garden surroundings would not only calm her, she most likely thought, but would also be a happy beginning for the baby, lessening the

Charles and Florence Boynton raised their children in the open air of the Temple of the Wings. Heavy canvas curtains covered the more private rooms of the house.

shock of his trip out of the womb. Screens were set up to stop people watching from the neighboring yards, and the doctor was stationed among the arbors.

That same year, she started a program to teach her ideas of natural child rearing to the local mothers. She soon had the support of the Berkeley Parent Teacher Association, at that time a radical group composed mostly of bohemians from the hills. The five-step program that Boynton taught was a dramatic break from the home economics courses that the mothers might have taken as young girls.

Florence Boynton taught the course on clothing. She argued that conventional clothing, especially stiff woolen garments, restricted people and were especially bad for growing limbs. The Boynton children wore tunics and bare feet around the house, allowing them plenty of freedom of movement and lots of contact with the invigorating outdoors. It seems that her neighbors took her suggestions to heart. Annie Maybeck favored the pale shifts that her husband designed, even while her husband encouraged their son to buy expensive suits. That same year, 1910, Charles Keeler told his children's caretakers to give them "rub-downs with rock salt and corn-meal, followed by an ice-cold shower," presumably to keep them healthy and in touch with natural materials rather than processed soap.[19]

A Mrs. Boone of the Berkeley Parent Teacher Association led a study group on food and advocated a completely raw food diet. The idea was that, just as the crafts-man should not be distanced from the work by machines, so should the eater not be separated from the food by cooking. Children should eat fresh fruits and nuts and drink "whole milk fresh from the cow," without even the intervention of skimming off the cream.[20]

Naturally, one could not eat a raw diet without being a vegetarian, and Berkeley vegetarian cuisine of the 1910s was very simple, possibly to the point of being boring. Winona, a student at the university, "ate only nuts and fruits and carrots," according to memoirist Florence Jury, who said that Winona was "different."[21] Mary Hoexter remembers that her uncle Lazar Blochman ate simply "a pound of yellow cheese" for dinner, bringing the cheese with him when he dined at other people's houses.[22] Annie Maybeck, on the other hand, ate no dairy. She spread mashed avocado on her bread instead of butter.[23]

The Boyntons served their guests and children a day-to-day monotony of unleavened bread, honey, nuts, milk and fresh fruit. Their custom home was completely without a kitchen, as the only food they prepared were peanuts roasted over a central brazier. Although the food was in abundance—one neighborhood girl remembered "garbage-can sized containers" of nuts—the Boynton children apparently craved more conventional food.[24] Other neighbors reported that they would trade their school lunches for their classmates' bologna sandwiches.

The Boyntons were not the only ones who rebelled. Annie and Bernard Maybeck were some of the most dedicated followers of natural child rearing and had at least one disagreement with their children over it. According to their daughter-in-law Jacomena, they decided to cut loose from conventional structures and call their son "Boy" until he was old enough to choose his own name. Unfortunately, "Boy" chose a name that his parents hated. When he was about five, he decided to dub himself "Wollenburg," after Charles Wollenburg—a kindly neighbor who gave the child candy. His parents finally compromised by calling him Wallen.[25]

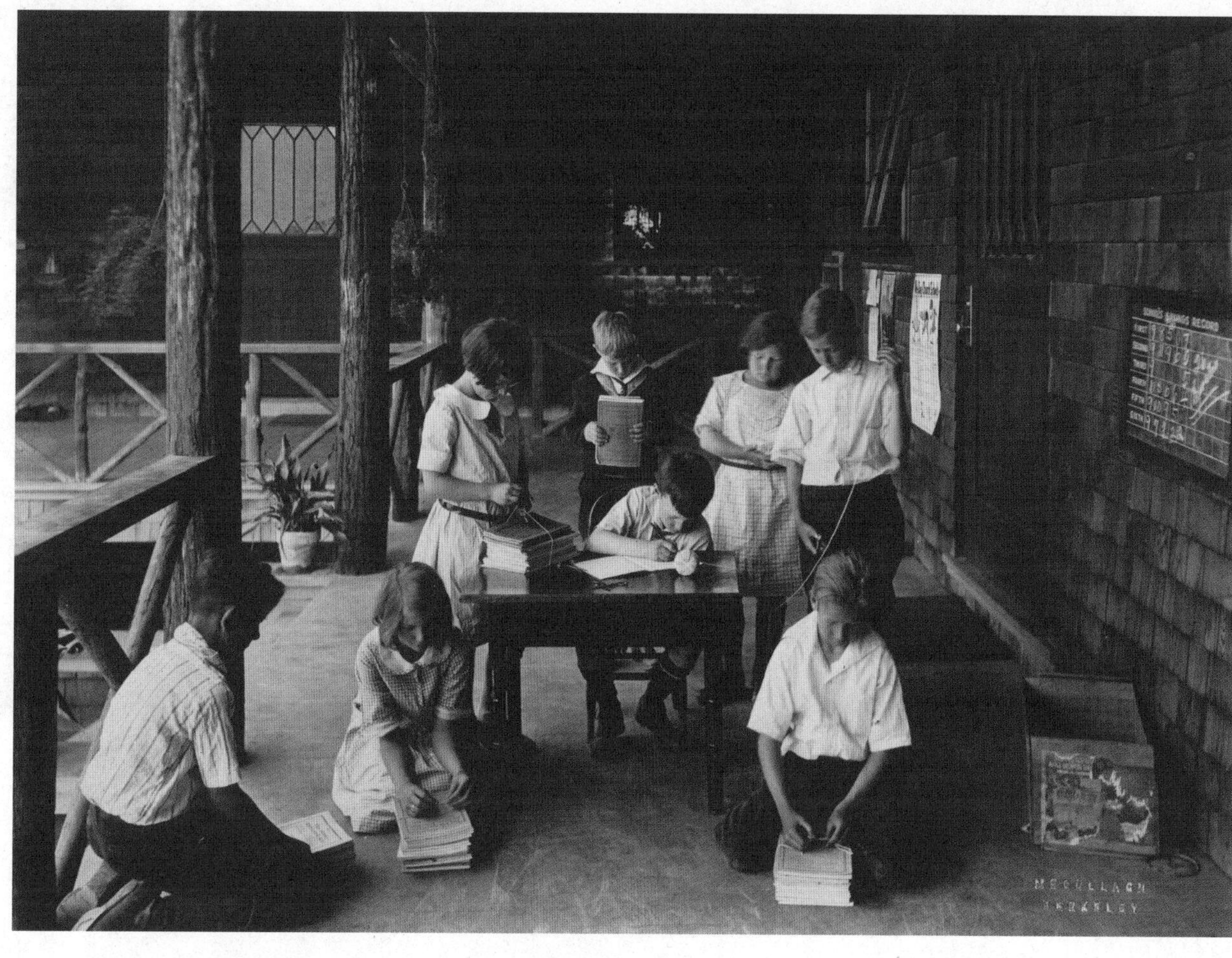

<table>
<tr><td>SCHOOLING ✦ IN THE ✦ BERKELEY HILLS</td></tr>
</table>

With this kind of preschool life, was it any surprise that the bohemians wanted their children to learn in schools that freed them from the mechanization of textbooks and the stiff discipline of traditional schoolrooms? Some Bay Area bohemians simply kept their children out of school or let them stop attending when school became too much for them.

Wanda Muir, daughter of naturalist John Muir, never went to school until she needed a short remedial course in order to get into the University of California. She was sent away to board at Northern California's preeminent school for young ladies, the Anna Head School in Berkeley. Her parents made sure that old friends like the Keelers introduced young Wanda to the artistic social circle of her new city.

Others had even less schooling. Henry Cowell was taken out of school after "six

The Hillside School's "little wooden schoolhouse," built with the encouragement of the women of the Hillside Club, offered outdoor verandas where classes could meet on warm days in Berkeley.

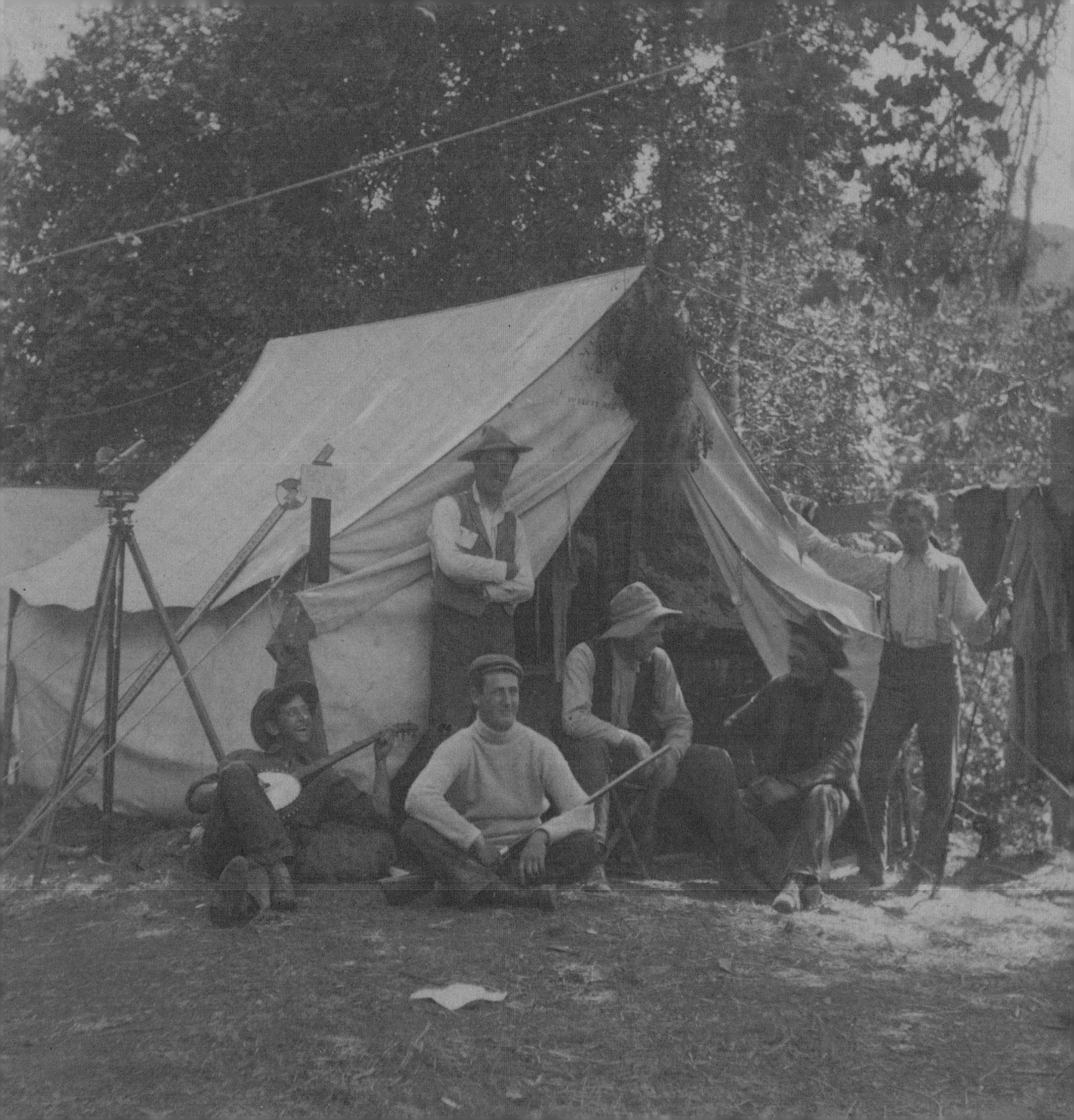

weeks in the first grade," but still managed to get into the University of California after a pair of professors discovered his musical talents. His impoverished parents were talented but passed their "dilettante" attitudes on to their son. They never taught him any conventional subjects, instead encouraging him to learn only what he wanted. He never even learned to take baths before attending the university. Some of the women students couldn't stand his smell and locked him in a bathroom until he agreed to wash himself.[26]

Wanda and Henry were the extremes of natural child rearing, although they were not alone. Other parents reacted, not by taking the child out of school, but by remaking the entire education system to fit their ideals of natural living. Their result was the Hillside School House, one of the earliest projects of Madge Robinson's Hillside Club. A grammar school for hill children, it emphasized freedom of expression and contact with nature. Children studied and played outside on the school's large verandas for much of the year. When bad weather forced them indoors, they enjoyed redwood classrooms with hanging plants and hammered-iron hardware.

After the Hillside daughters graduated from grammar school, Berkeley offered boarding opportunities and natural education at the Snell Academy. The school advertised that it offered "admirable opportunities for Nature study" and "endless possibilities of outdoor life." Botany and geology classes frequently left the classroom to hike the canyons of Berkeley, observing plants and rocks where they lay.

Once the girls graduated from high school, they might attend the University of California. There, they could join students like the girl known as "Winona," a sort of loner vegetarian who thought nothing of walking to Yosemite or some other distant place when the spirit moved her," according to her coworker Florence Jury, a friend of Jacomena Maybeck. "I had never met anyone like her" before going to the university, Jury said. Even the more conventional young women of the 1920s embraced natural living during their student days. Jury, for example, lived in a boarding house with a sleeping porch that ran the length of the house, where she and the other women would sleep in rows outside and move inside only to change or study. At least one other women's boarding house in the 1920s had a similar arrangement, with canvas privacy curtains like those on the Temple of Wings.[27]

For their brothers who also attended the university, a trip to the Sierras was almost a part of the curriculum, especially for young men studying the natural sciences or anthropology. Student Charles Palache's experience was typical. In 1889, he took a six-week-long summer trip to the Sierras with professor Joseph "Little Joe" LeConte and a group of other students, ostensibly to observe glacial activity and other geological formations. The young men rode horseback from Berkeley to Yosemite, traveling about twenty miles a day. LeConte taught them to make camp coffee and bread and to supplement their food supplies by hunting doves and rattlesnakes and picking raspberries.

FACING PAGE: **Students relax at the "Dew Drop Inn," base camp for an 1898 trip to the Sierras with the university's Summer School of Surveying.**

Much of Palache's trip was taken up in hanging out in camp, swimming and scribbling in his diary. Only occasionally did he discuss geology with the "prof."

The group reached Yosemite by the middle of July and was overwhelmed by its beauty. On July 17, Palache wrote, "Charlie Merrill (alias the Dude, alias the Snake-Charmer), Morgan (alias Rosie, alias the Buck) and self (alias Whiskers, alias the Late Mr. Palache, alias the great Unwashed) rose and ate breakfast at 2:30 a.m. (it consisted of coffee and cold flap-jacks), and rode down the valley by the light of the waning moon, this being our only chance of seeing the moonlight effect in *Yo Semite* [*sic*]."[28]

Palache always seemed to be the one young man who, in a group picture, would have a crushed hat and a crooked tie. His mind was on more studious things than his appearance, as he was later a member of the Harriman expedition (along with Charles Keeler) and professor of geology at Harvard. The "prof" who inspired him, Joseph LeConte, would soon become one of the founding members of a new organization devoted to preserving Yosemite and encouraging Californians to experience nature. This new pioneering group was called the Sierra Club.

THE SIERRA CLUB

John Muir began discussing the possibility of starting a group to save Yosemite in about 1886. Sierra lovers first gathered to chat at the studio of William Keith in San Francisco, but eventually, the group overflowed Keith's busy studio. They then started gathering in the San Francisco offices of Warren Olney, a lawyer who would eventually become the mayor of Oakland. The group eventually set up a formal meeting in June 1892, at which Olney officially drew up the charter for the Sierra Club and all the members signed on. They unanimously elected Muir as their president and chose Olney as vice president, which was courteous considering that they continued to meet at his office for another year.

Although the founding officers of the Sierra Club were men, women joined the club from its earliest days. Many signed up because they wanted to preserve the California environment. (Indeed, one of the oldest environmental groups in California, the Save the Redwoods League, was started by the San Jose Women's Club. It was originally called the Sempervirens Club, after the coast redwood or California redwood, *Sequoia sempervirens*).[29] Many more joined because they, too, wanted to enjoy mountaineering trips through the Sierras. Pictures from early Sierra Club camping trips show women sitting in camp, hiking and eating by the light of Japanese lanterns. One photo shows trouser-clad mountain climbers with heavy boots and pickaxes, including one climber whose large-brimmed hat looks like it came from the fashion plates of a ladies' magazine.

These camping trips were the brainchild of another young man who first encountered the Sierras on a student trip, William Colby. Colby's timing for the camping trips was perfect. The same year that he started the trip, 1901, was the beginning of San Franciscans' love of the outdoor vacation. Newspaperman John P. Young, the managing editor of the *San Francisco Chronicle*, discovered this trend when he decided to commemorate the paper's anniversary by doggedly researching through the paper's back files. He found that "a marked increase of the disposition of San Franciscans to indulge in summer outings" appeared between 1901 and 1906, with a multiplicity of "country resorts" that drew people to the beach, the hills and the "noble forests."[30]

Only ten years after the advertisements for country resorts started appearing in the *Chronicle, California for the Sportsman*, a publication of the Southern Pacific Railroad, included two pages of resorts in the Tahoe area alone, each listed with the nearby fishing lakes and streams, all organized in "the regular order of the steamer trip, which starts from the Tahoe Tavern Wharf and ties up with the railroad, so that one can leave San Francisco overnight and reach the lake at Tahoe Tavern for a trout breakfast of some other fellow's catching."[31] More and more San Franciscans were joining the Sierra Club pioneers on their trips through the mountains.

Colby's timing was less impeccable on another idea. He thought that he was saving the Sierra Club from obsolescence, as its environmental activism was almost finished. As Colby put it, the club's goal was "protecting the irreplaceable value of the Sierras

from the ravages of the greed which unfortunately accompanies the advance of civilization," and in 1901, he was certain that the Sierras were soon to be protected forever.[32]

Colby's optimism, while admirable, came far too soon. Only five years later, he realized how much more work the club needed to do to preserve the Sierras from development. That year, San Francisco applied to dam Hetch Hetchy Valley, a Sierra valley that was as dramatic as Yosemite.

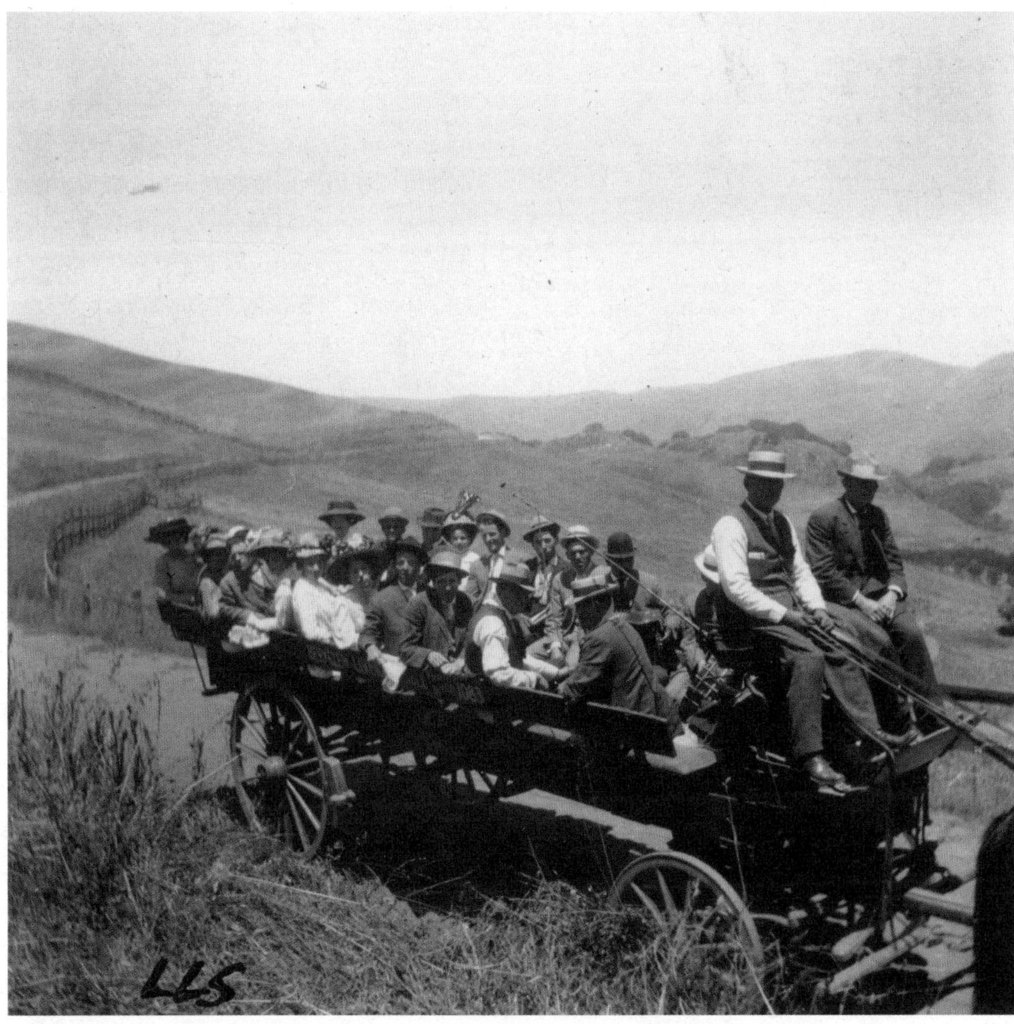

Members of the Native Sons of the Golden West, a club that celebrated California's gold rush heritage, ride to a picnic in the hills between Alameda and Contra Costa counties.

Some Sierra Club members supported the damming (most prominently, Warren Olney, the mayor of Oakland) as necessary for economic growth. Many ecologically minded Californians agreed, arguing that planned harvesting of trees and water were the best way to support the state's growth. Mrs. Robert J. Burdette, president of the California Federation of Women's Clubs, told her membership to advocate for forests "not only for their beauty . . . but from the stronger reason that under their shadows live springs of water."[33]

Other Sierra Club members insisted that preserving the Sierras untouched was worth any sacrifice. In 1908, Colby wrote to the editor of *Collier's* magazine, saying, "My life and my business interests are interwoven with those of San Francisco, and no one has her welfare more at heart than I, and yet I know that this precedent of entering national parks is wrong in principle and unnecessary in fact."[34] The club was torn apart by the tensions.

But in Berkeley, where natural living was rarely compromised no matter how large the stake, most members followed John Muir in condemning the dam as inexcusable. They reveled in being what their supporter Horace Bradley called "sentimentalists" and "inexact dreamers"[35] instead of hard-hearted businessmen, willing to destroy the landscape for what one poet called the "Sweatshop" of San Francisco.[36] Like Muir, they believed that the pure Sierra landscape, with its cathedral-like splendor, was "a holy land, if ever there was one."[37] Ansel Adams, the famous nature photographer, gently chided his best friend, Cedric Wright, for taking this attitude too far. Wright, firmly ensconced in the Berkeley bohemian world, thought that anyone could be reformed by exposure to the "humanizing powers of the mountains." "He wanted to invite Joseph Stalin on a Sierra Club outing!" laughed Adams.[38]

Irrepressible jokesters like Ansel Adams teased and disagreed with the Berkeley school. (Adams especially disagreed with their vegetarianism. He ate everything that he could, according to Albert Stern, who said that Adams liked "dates, coffee, hangerger sandwitches [*sic*], also Club and Monte Carlo, French pastry, chicken salad, cinnamon toast, coffee, waffles, all kinds of soup, pound cake, chocolate cake, butterscotch sundaes . . . " and thirty-eight other foods, from potato chips to caviar.)[39] Still, Berkeley residents kept their convictions that the natural life was the best way to promote health, happiness and beauty. Whether in the "cathedral" of the mountains or in the simplicity of the unpainted home, natural living was an antidote to the pressures of urban life and a way to counteract the loss of Berkeley's hills to development.

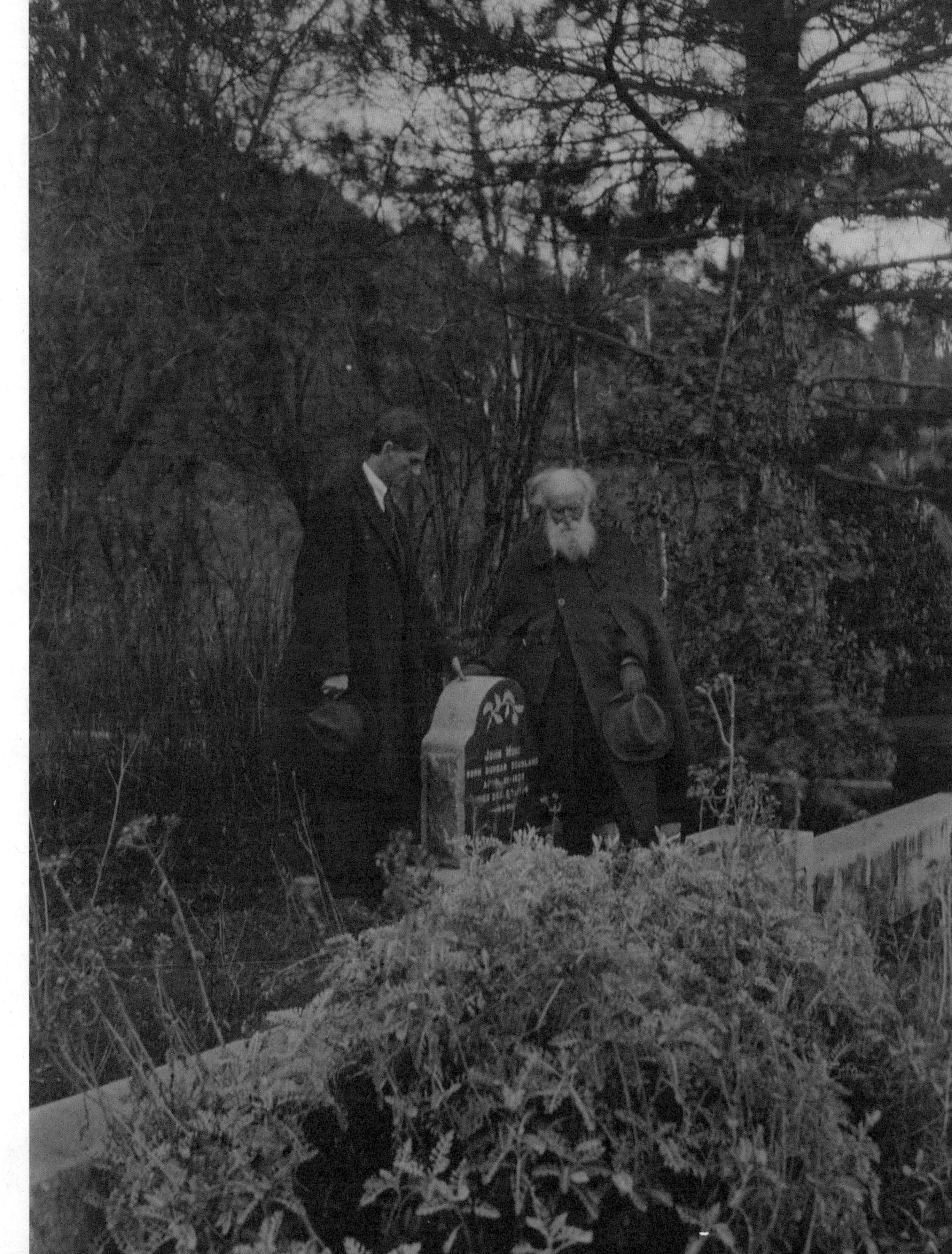

Sometime between 1914 and 1921, Charles Keeler and naturalist John Burroughs pay homage to John Muir, a fellow member of the 1889 Harriman Expedition to Alaska. Muir was buried near his Martinez home, in a grave lined with the boughs of the *Sequoia gigantea* tree (giant sequoia) that he made famous.

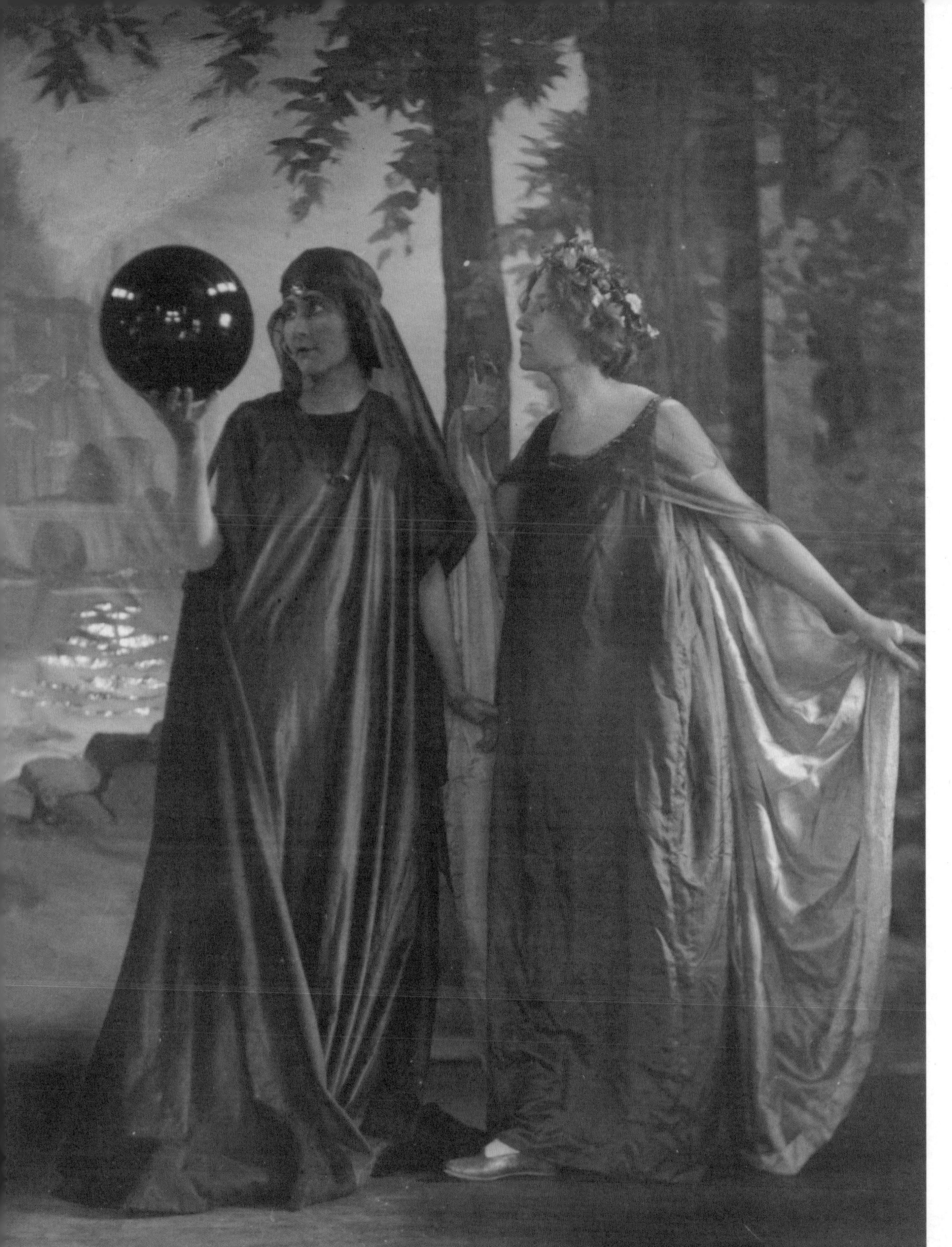

Portrait of Anne
Brigman and
Adelaide Hanscom,
attributed to
Adelaide Hanscom.

Pictorial Photography Arises, Flourishes and Fades in the East Bay

In the first half of the nineteenth century, photographers were primarily concerned with documenting reality. The novelty of being able to record man and nature in minute detail was so captivating that most early photographers saw little need to alter or obscure the reality they could now reproduce. Then, in the late 1880s, a new and more artistic approach to photography emerged, soon christened *pictorialism*. Factors contributing to this new approach included the availability of simpler cameras and the creation of amateur camera clubs that followed.

Most of these clubs soon admitted professional photographers as well and engendered a spirit of competition wherein photographers were inspired to create images for other photographers. Since such photographs were not primarily produced to be sold, their makers enjoyed a greater freedom to indulge their artistic natures and to have as their goal instead the composition of beautiful images.

The pictorialists used various methods to create their vision of life through a romantic haze. The simplest was to intentionally have the lens slightly out of focus. Soon special lenses were available that embodied a "softening" effect. A variety of gadgets, substances and methods were employed, all with the goal of producing more artistic images.

Choice and composition of subjects were also important in this process. Portraits, especially of women and children, were favored. Often, elaborate costumes and play-acting were employed, sometimes requiring the photographer to also be a director.

The amateur camera clubs and, particularly, their publications were an endless source of information for the photographers. In the San Francisco Bay Area, the preeminent periodical was *Camera Craft*, official organ of the California Camera Club. This club began publishing the magazine in 1900, and in their first year they claimed to be the largest camera club in the world. Using the recently invented printing process known as halftone, *Camera Craft* was able to inexpensively reproduce photographs on its pages.

The California Camera Club accomplished its mission of helping its members learn from each other through many different avenues. It organized social events and weekend outings that provided entertainment in addition to photo opportunities. Its downtown San Francisco headquarters were well outfitted with rooms for reading, exhibiting, developing pictures and socializing. Competitive photographic exhibitions called "salons" were held at the headquarters and in other venues.

In 1901, 1902 and 1903, the First, Second and Third San Francisco Photographic Salons were held at the Mark Hopkins Institute of Art. These photo exhibitions, staged side by side with exhibitions of California paintings, gave the public an opportunity to see the connection between the work of some of the tonalist painters (Arthur Mathews, Xavier Martinez and Charles Rollo Peters) and the pictorialist photographers. In 1906, San Francisco's earthquake and fire destroyed not only the California Camera Club's headquarters, but also the studios and work of many of its members. Those whose studios were located in Berkeley and Oakland, and thereby spared by the conflagration, had the good fortune to not lose their precious prints and negatives. In the aftermath of the disaster, the California Camera Club eventually found new quarters, and its members found ways to continue on with their photographic pursuits.

In 1915, two of the club's leading members were chosen to organize the photographic department of the Panama-Pacific International Exposition in San Francisco. During this event, members were also encouraged to exhibit prints at their club's quarters so that visitors to the fair would have the opportunity to see an even greater selection of their work. In 1917, the club held its last salon at the Palace Hotel. By this time, the center of gravity of the pictorialist movement was beginning to shift to Southern California. In the 1920s, the pictorialist style continued to be pursued by photographers throughout the state, but their themes and subject matter were shifting toward modernism and "straight" photography. By the early 1930s, pictorial photography was over in California. Perhaps the event most symbolic of its demise and replacement was the founding of Group f/64 in 1932 by several local photographers. The group, which included Ansel Adams, was dedicated to sharp focus photography, though all of them had previously embraced pictorialism.

Adelaide Hanscom was born in Empire City, Oregon, in 1876. By the time she was five, her family had moved to Berkeley to a large house on Walnut Street. Her father found employment with a local lumber company, became Berkeley's town clerk in 1897 and soon thereafter advanced to town auditor.

At age fifteen, Adelaide left school. A free spirit from an early age, Adelaide enjoyed hiking in the Berkeley Hills and later on, camping with her Sierra Club friends. In 1892, she began studies at the Mark Hopkins Institute of Art in San Francisco. While studying painting, she was also immersed in the milieu of other aspiring bohemians, including Laura Adams, Emily Pitchford and Xavier Martinez. She specialized in portrait painting, and she later was a drawing instructor at this school as well as in the Berkeley public schools.

Sometime before 1900, Adelaide took up photography and set up a darkroom in her family home on Walnut Street. Pictorial photography soon prevailed over painting as the best medium for expressing her artistic talent. In 1901, the Channing Club of Berkeley, associated with the First Unitarian Church, held a photographic exhibition of 227 prints, and Adelaide won second prize for portraiture. At this exhibition, one of the judges was Mary L. Bisbee, who had a photographic studio in downtown Berkeley from 1899 to 1905 and produced an exceptional portrait of Anne Brigman.

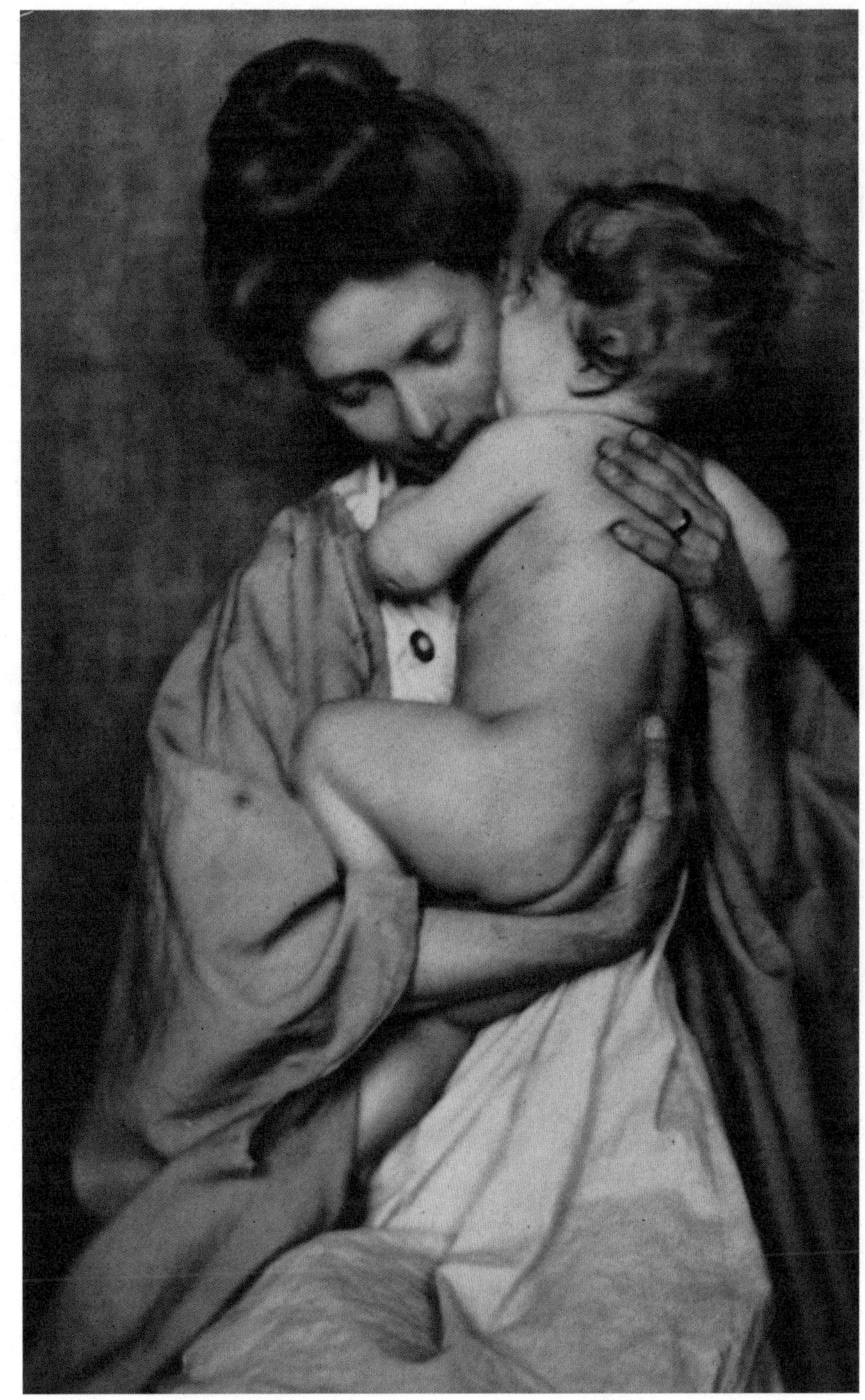

Mother and Child, portrait of Louise Keeler and her son, Leonarde Keeler, by Adelaide Hanscom.

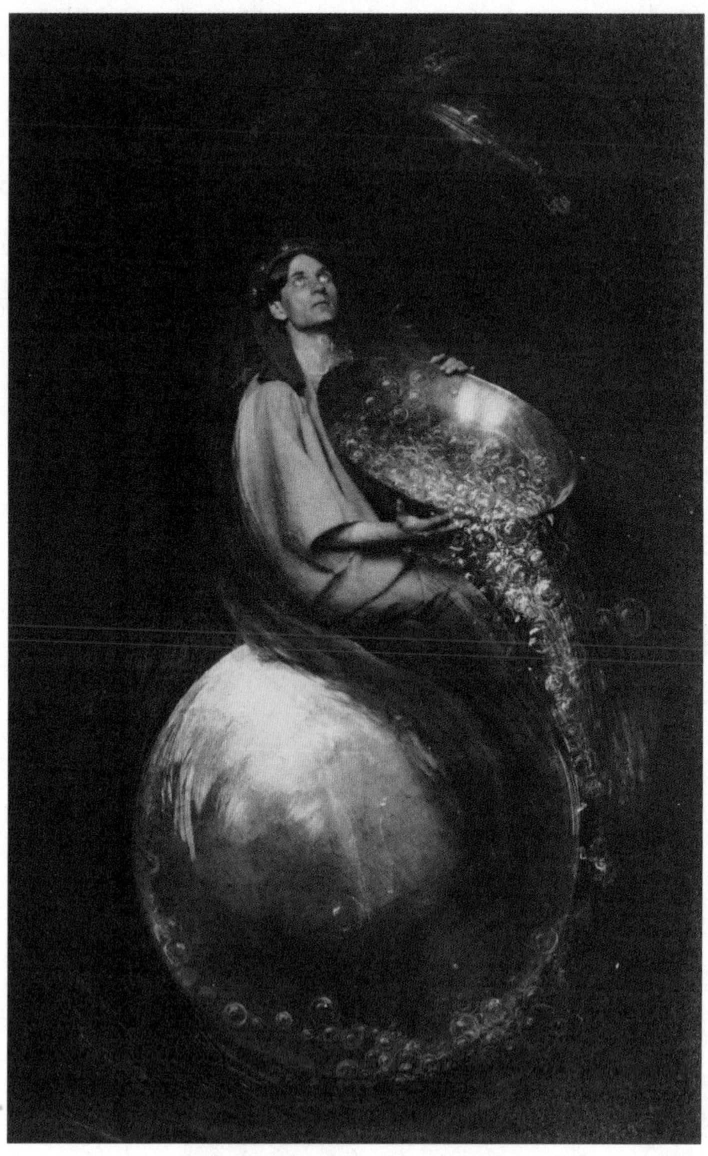

A heavily retouched photo of Charles Keeler by Adelaide Hanscom, from her illustrated edition of *The Rubaiyat*, 1905.

The following year when Adelaide's friend Laura Adams gave up her studio in the prestigious Flood Building in San Francisco, Adelaide moved in. At the Third Photographic Salon in San Francisco in 1903, she exhibited five prints, including a study called *Mother and Child*, a portrait of Louise Keeler and her baby son, Leonarde. This print was highly acclaimed and helped establish her reputation as a pictorialist photographer.

Later in 1903, she embarked on what would become her most successful creative work—photo illustrations for *The Rubaiyat*. For this work, Adelaide convinced local writers to dress in classical Persian garb and pose for photographs illustrating the quatrains of Omar Khayam's immortal poem. In an interview in the *Oakland Tribune* she revealed something of her method:

I think of all the people I know and do not know to fill the part. After I had selected the models came the task of costuming them. I studied my tone values very closely to get certain effects that would otherwise have been impossible. I studied the lines and composition before I made a direct photograph, and in many instances worked my plate to the limit of the law. I get my effects by any hook or crook that I can devise. I searched up and down the whole creation to find the face, figure, and temperament to fit the part. In many cases it was difficult to find the right model.[1]

In the finished work, those chosen included Joaquin Miller, George Sterling, George Wharton James, Charles Keeler and several artistically posed semi-nude unidentified women. The book was published in 1905, and in its first edition, the images were produced as photogravures on fine tissue paper. Her innovative approach and technical mastery brought the book national acclaim. Also in 1905, she photographed the only performance of Charles Keeler's play *The Triumph of Light* at the Berkeley Unitarian Church and her pictures were later published in the *Overland Monthly*.

The next year proved to be a tragic one. The San Francisco earthquake and fire destroyed her studio in the Flood Building, and her lifelong collection of negatives, including those from *The Rubaiyat*, were lost. Adelaide was, like any serious artist, devastated by the loss of her work. In September, she moved to Seattle and opened a photographic studio specializing in portraits of Seattle's society people. A contemporary Berkeley newspaper account mentions that she was already working on her next great project.

The new project, inspired by the great success of her *Rubaiyat*, would be a series of illustrations for Elizabeth Barrett Browning's *Sonnets from the Portuguese*. However, the changing circumstances of her life would delay the completion of this work for many years.

While still residing in Seattle, she exhibited prints of her *Rubaiyat* illustrations at the Arts & Crafts Exhibition in Idora Park in Oakland.

In 1908, she married a British mining engineer named Gerald Leeson. Her marriage was a happy one, but it was difficult for her to continue her photographic work as her husband's career required traveling to small mining towns in Alaska and Idaho. She did manage to again show her *Rubaiyat* prints at an exhibition of the Berkeley Art Association at the First Congregational Church in November 1908. For the next three years, the family shuttled between Berkeley and Seattle until they finally settled in Danville, California, in 1911, where Gerald took up chicken ranching and Adelaide finally had her own darkroom again to do her photographic work.

In 1916, after she completed her pictorialist photogravure illustrations, *Sonnets from the Portuguese* was published by the Dodge Publishing Company. This work, while beautifully crafted, did not receive the same acclaim as her *Rubaiyat*.

Soon after, her husband, Gerald, enlisted in the Canadian Army and was shipped out to France. He was killed in action in October 1916, when he fell on a grenade to save his comrades. Her husband's death was a shock from which Adelaide never fully recovered, and she produced no significant artistic work after that. In 1932, she was struck and killed by a hit-and-run driver in Pasadena.

Though Adelaide Hanscom's productive photographic career was brief, in her unique vision of *The Rubaiyat* and in her prolific body of sensitive portraiture, she has left us a lasting legacy of her artistry.

EMILY H. PITCHFORD

Emily Pitchford was born in Gold Hill, Nevada, in 1878. Her family later moved to San Francisco, where, in the 1890s, she attended the Mark Hopkins Art Institute. It was here, during this period, that she befriended Laura Adams and Adelaide Hanscom, and all three ultimately became pictorialist photographers. When Laura Adams opened her portrait studio in San Francisco's Flood Building in 1899, both Emily and Adelaide were able to work there as well. In 1902, Laura Adams gave up her Flood Building studio and moved to Berkeley, where she established another studio in her home. Emily shared this space with her for several years.

In March 1905, Emily exhibited five photographs at the Starr King Fraternity Exhibition in Oakland. In a review of the show, photographer Anne Brigman described one of Emily's pictures, *Woman*

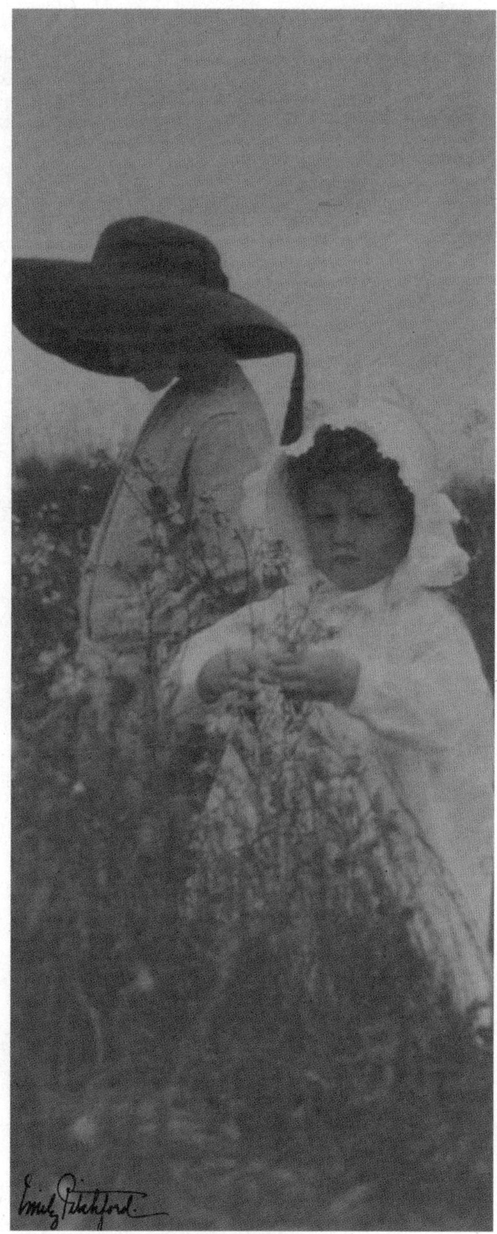

Portrait of woman and child by Emily Pitchford.

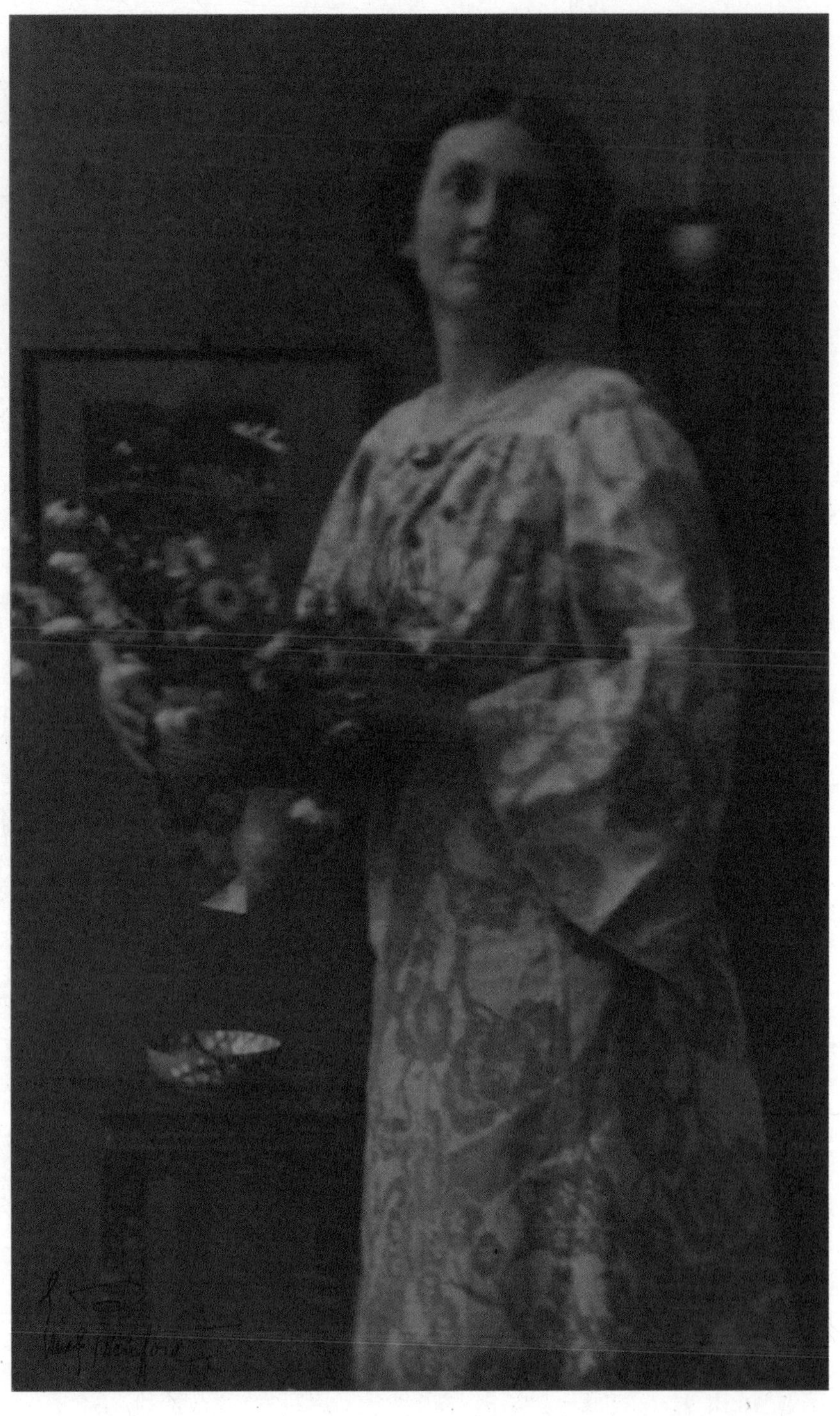

Portrait of Anne Brigman
by Emily Pitchford.

Glancing Over Her Shoulder, "as having the peculiar elusive quality that we call soul."[2] By 1906, Emily had established her own commercial photo studio in downtown Berkeley. The following year, three of her photographs were published in *Camera Craft* and two were hung at the Worcester (Massachusetts) Art Museum exhibit. In May 1908, Emily and her colleague Annie Brigman provided an "exceptionally fine" monthly exhibit of pictures for the California Camera Club in San Francisco.

In October 1908, an exhibit was produced that seemed a culmination of all the previous events showcasing pictorialist photography in Berkeley's vicinity. Billed as the Arts and Crafts Exhibition, it was held in Idora Park, North Oakland, a kind of urban family resort that boasted, among its other attractions, a theatre, skating rink, zoo, outdoor swimming pool and numerous rides. The Arts and Crafts Exhibition was contained in the skating rink building that had been extensively modified for this show. "Old Nuremberg" was chosen as the background theme, and a crew of carpenters and painters created a scenic reproduction of a street in that old German city. Situated in these stage-set miniature buildings were the booths of the exhibitors. Although apparently conceived at the last minute, this ambitious plan seems to have been executed surprisingly well. Many of the exhibitors included demonstrations of their crafts along with the items for sale. The arts and crafts represented included painting, photography, sculpture, needlework, jewelry making, metalsmithing, woodworking and furniture making, leatherwork, ceramic arts and many more.

Photography was disproportionately well represented, and in the Berkeley area especially so. A contemporary newspaper account includes a review of all five of the pictorialist photographers outlined in this chapter: "Anne W. Brigman presents a most elaborate series of photos, among the series being the famous picture 'The Spider's Web,' and 'The Witch Tree.' Oscar Maurer presents a series of scenes from Old Mexico and Miss Emily Pitchford presents an excellent series of child studies. Mrs. Laura Adams Armer offers a number of studies with a picture entitled 'Carmel' as one of the best. Miss Adelaide Hanscom exhibits her remarkable collection of Rubaiyat pictures."[3]

Annie Brigman wrote a review of the show that appeared in the December 1908 issue of *Camera Craft*, in which she offered much praise for her pictorialist colleagues and in particular referred to Emily Pitchford's work as possessing a "spirited delicacy."

The following month, it was Berkeley's turn and the Second Annual Exhibition of the Berkeley Art Association was held at the First Congregational Church. Although it was a substantial and well organized show, it must have been difficult for Berkeley not to feel upstaged by the much larger Idora Park extravaganza that had so recently concluded in Oakland. The exhibitors included many of the leading painters, photographers, sculptors and craftsmen of the Pacific coast. Among the participant pho-

tographers were Adelaide Hanscom, Oscar Maurer and Emily Pitchford. Emily was also in charge of the photography department.

For the next two years, Emily continued her career as a photographer in her Berkeley studio. In 1911, she married William Leo Hussey and moved to South Africa with him, where they lived for ten years. Emily continued making and exhibiting photographs while abroad. In 1921, they returned to Berkeley, where they remained for the rest of their years. Emily passed away in 1956, leaving a rich legacy of her very artistic portraiture, including many sensitive images of her colleagues and their families.

OSCAR MAURER

Oscar Maurer was born in 1871 (the same year as Charles Keeler) in New York City. His family moved to San Francisco in 1886. For at least two generations before Maurer's birth, both sides of his family had produced an impressive number of painters and lithographic artists. On the eve of his departure from New York, one of these gentlemen decided to determine if young Maurer had inherited his share of the family talent. To this end, he asked the lad to demonstrate his skill in several freehand drawing exercises to see how he might best express himself in art. Upon viewing the results, it was suggested that Maurer should experiment with photography. He took this advice and embarked on a lifelong artistic odyssey in photography.

Maurer found San Francisco and the Bay Area artistically stimulating. In his later

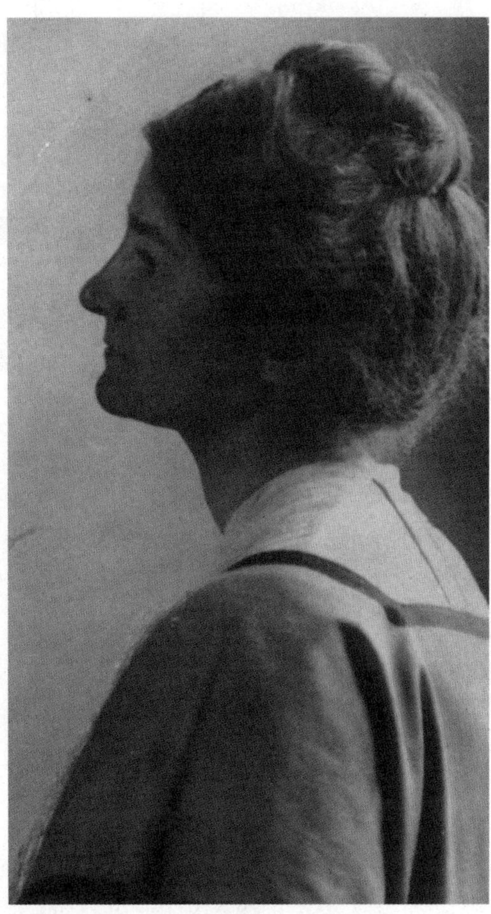

Portrait of Adelaide Hanscom by Emily Pitchford.

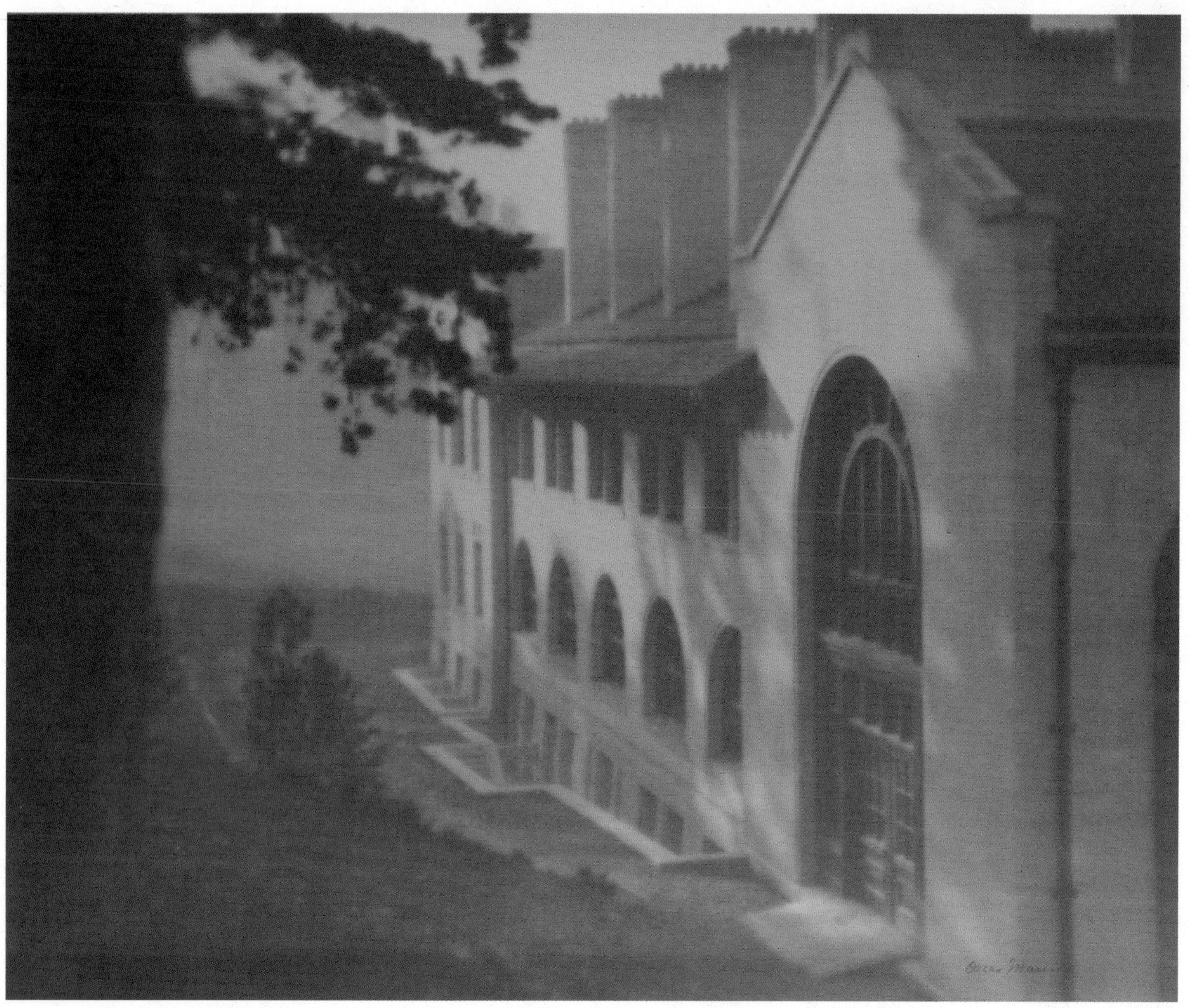

Pictorialist study of the Hearst Memorial
Mining Building at the University of
California, Berkeley, by Oscar Maurer.

years he recalled, "With my 4 x 5 camera on a tripod and my homemade drop shutter on the lens, and, of course, glass plates, I made photographs of Chinatown, Golden Gate Park, the waterfront, the ferryboats and cloud effects. On a rainy day, with a cheap little camera called a Bull's Eye special, I secured pictures of people walking the wet sidewalks with umbrellas up. The reflections from the pavement were perfect. A row of eight of these pictures was shown in Hirsch and Kaiser's [photographer's supply store] window on Kearney Street."[4]

In 1896 he helped organize the San Francisco Amateur Photographic Association. Before this group was even in operation, they were invited to merge into the California Camera Club and did. Maurer soon became an influential member and went on to serve as its director. Early on, he had embraced the pictorialist style so popular in the club. In an article for *Camera Craft* magazine in 1900, he wrote, "Not until the present day has the camera been recognized as a legitimate means for the production of pictures that may be termed works of art. . . . My own observation convinces me that among the vast amount of good material that professional and amateur photographers have produced on this Coast, enough may be secured to make a very creditable display at the Hopkins Art Institute should that body deem it advisable to take that step."[5]

By the very next year, the Mark Hopkins Institute of Art held its first San Francisco Photographic Salon. Maurer had his prints

exhibited at this and subsequent salons.

In 1901, he also exhibited in the photographic section of the Industrial Arts Exhibition at the Mechanics Pavilion in San Francisco.

In 1899, the Southern Pacific Company employed him to take photographs in Mexico to be published in *Sunset* magazine. He later entered several of the excellent pictures from this trip in various salons and exhibitions. One of them, *The Storm,* won several prizes.

Maurer married Margaret Robinson, founder of the Hillside Club, in 1903, and in 1905, the couple moved into her family's substantial home on Le Roy Avenue in Berkeley. The home was famous for its charm and design and was known as Weltevreden.

In 1905, four of his prints were accepted for exhibit at the First American Photographic Salon at the Palace Hotel. He continued to work in San Francisco where he shared a studio with Arnold Genthe. He eventually got his own studio in the Academy of Sciences building on Market Street, the same edifice that housed the California Camera Club. Unfortunately, this building burned in the 1906 earthquake and fire, and Maurer lost all his existing negatives. After the fire, Maurer moved his studio to Berkeley, first in his home and later into

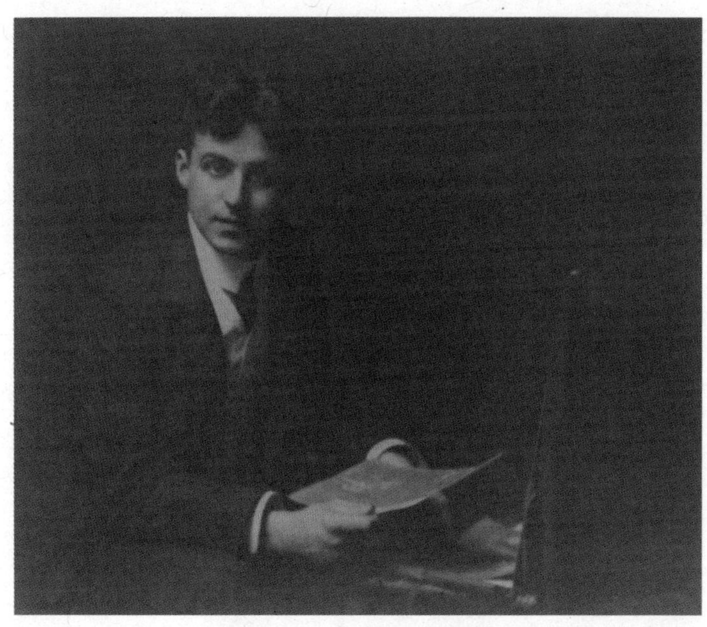

Portrait of Oscar Maurer by Arnold Genthe.

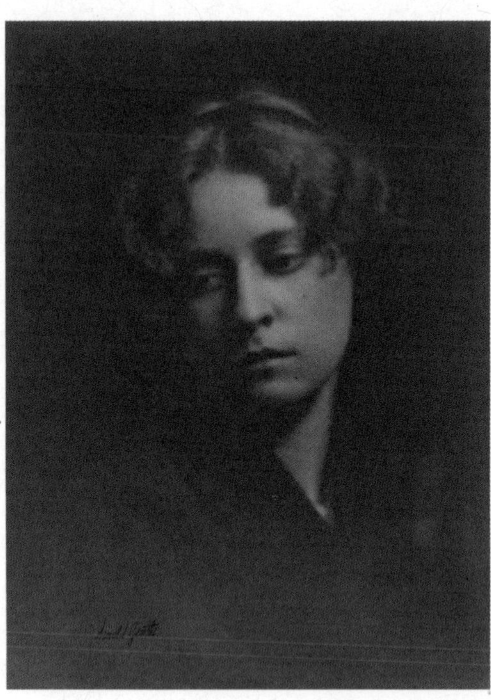

Portrait of Laura Adams Armer
by Arnold Genthe.

a small nearby building specially designed for him by his friend Bernard Maybeck.

At the 1908 Arts and Crafts Exhibition in Idora Park in Oakland, one of the pictures from his Mexican trip, entitled *Mexican Doorways*, was highly praised.

A few years later, Maurer and his wife moved to Del Mar near San Diego. They remained there for several years and then parted in a friendly divorce. He was soon remarried to Elizabeth Baker Robinson, and the couple remained together for thirty-five years until her death. For much of that time, they were back on Le Roy Street at Weltevreden.

Maurer continued to live in Berkeley until his death in 1965.

LAURA ADAMS ARMER

Laura May Adams was born in Sacramento in 1874. She was educated in the public schools of San Francisco and entered the Mark Hopkins Institute of Art in 1893. For the next five years, she studied painting and drawing under Arthur Mathews, the school's director. During this time she was active in the Sketch Club, a San Francisco club for women artists founded in 1887 that survives to this day as San Francisco Women Artists. Although talented, she was not successful as an artist, and in a scenario reminiscent of that of Oscar Maurer, a relative suggested she take up photography. As would seem only natural for one who had made the transition from painting to photography, she chose pictorialism.

In 1899, she opened a photography studio in San Francisco's Flood Building. Specializing in portraits of California's high society people, her artistic style brought her success. She was fortunate at this time to have Arnold Genthe, arguably the most talented of San Francisco's artistic portrait photographers, as her friend and mentor. Laura learned much from his natural style and ability to put his subjects at ease and to be able to snap the shutter at the perfect, yet unexpected, moment. Something of her philosophy of pictorial photography can be gleaned from her article "The Picture Possibilities of Photography," published in the September 1900 issue of the *Overland Monthly*:

This age does not chase elusive shadows, but it chains the sunbeams, using them as a medium for soul expression; for what we call soul in a picture is but another name for symmetry, harmony—the perfect blending of idea and expression. The painter may attain it; why not the photographer? . . . In portraiture especially the photographer has a wide field. He can approach the painter on almost common ground. Each should be in sympathy with his model, and each should be a keen observer of character, and by using the artistic intelligence each may produce pictures that will live.

In 1901, Laura exhibited ten pictures and won second prize for her portrait of Arthur Mathews in the First San Francisco

Photographic Salon. She also participated in the Second and Third San Francisco Portrait Salons in 1902 and 1903. A review of the 1902 salon in *Camera Craft* magazine stated of her work: "This year the pictures accepted from her form one of the strongest series of portraits in the exhibition. Indeed, the portrait of Miss Henschel . . . is the strongest and most charming portrait on the walls."[6]

She married artist Sidney Armer in 1902, moved to Berkeley, gave up her studio in the Flood Building and opened one in her new home.

The Starr King Fraternity, a Unitarian Church group, held its fifth annual art exhibit at Maple Hall in Oakland in March 1905 with the goal of creating a permanent Art Fund for Oakland. The exhibit included paintings, sculpture and photography by local artists.

Laura exhibited six photographic prints and two designs for bookplates. In April, the First American Photographic Salon was held in San Francisco and one of the pictures that Laura exhibited at the Oakland show, called *The Laurels*, was accepted and hung there. She also participated in the Arts and Crafts Exhibition at Idora Park in Oakland in 1908, where her photographs were described as "painter-like in quality and composition."[7]

At the Berkeley Art Association exhibition in 1908, Laura entered three pictures, including a portrait of Charles Keeler.

A further indication of her success can be taken from the words of Robert H. Fletcher, Director of the San Francisco Art Association, who stated in 1915, "Mrs.

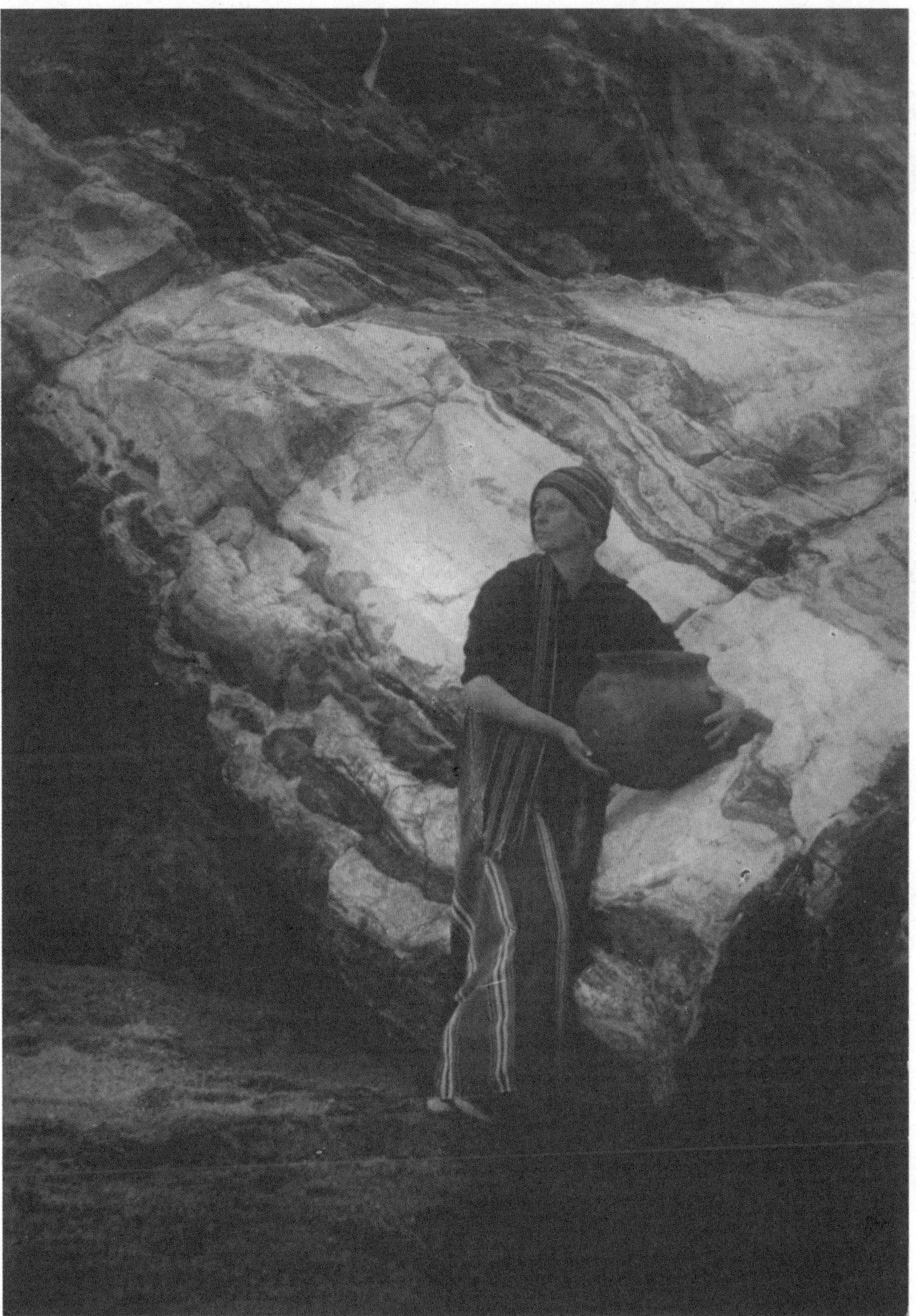

Portrait by Laura Adams Armer.

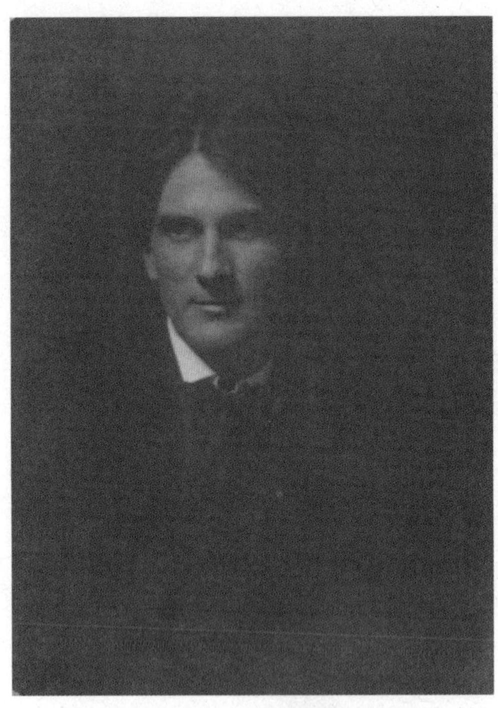

Portrait of Mr. Charles Keeler, exhibited at the Second Exhibition of the Berkeley Art Association in 1908 by Laura Adams Armer.

Laura Adams Armer is principally engaged in placing photographs upon the plane of art, at which work she has received medals and honors at every salon held in the U.S. and England."[8]

In the 1920s, she developed a strong interest in Native American subjects and began spending several months each year with the Navajo and Hopi in Arizona, where she painted, photographed and wrote about their way of life and beliefs. In 1928, she produced *The Mountain Chant*, the first Native American motion picture that was spoken in an Indian language. The film depicted a nine-day Navajo healing ceremony.

In 1931, she published her first book, *Waterless Mountain*, a children's book on Native American culture illustrated with her photographs. The book won two awards, and she published several more in the following years.

In 1938, Laura and her husband moved from Berkeley to Crescent City, California. A few years later, they moved to Fortuna, California, where she spent the remaining years of her life. She passed away in 1963, having led a remarkably rich, productive and fulfilling life.

ANNE BRIGMAN

Anne Wardrope Nott was born near Honolulu, Hawaii, in 1869. Growing up surrounded by such a wild and beautiful tropical landscape had a profound and lasting influence in her life. When she was sixteen, she moved with her family to Los Gatos, California. In her new environment, though the latitude was more temperate, there was an abundance of nearby wilderness and natural beauty in which she could continue to find inspiration.

In 1894, she married Martin Brigman, a sea captain from San Francisco, and the couple moved to Oakland. Annie accompanied her husband on some of his voyages to the South Seas, but during others, she remained at home, free to pursue her artistic endeavors. From childhood, her artistic temperament had found expression in painting landscapes and in writing poems, plays, short stories and magazine articles.

She began making photographs in 1901. To say that she was a natural at photography would greatly understate the innate talent that led to her almost immediate success.

Perhaps, like many of her contemporaries, her training in painting gave her an advantage. By the very next year, she had joined the California Camera Club and had five of her photographs selected for exhibit at the Second San Francisco Photographic Salon. One of these, *Portrait of Mr. Morrow*, was praised in *Camera Craft* as "one of the best portraits in the exhibition."[9] Her pictures were created in the pictorialist style, and she accomplished this by making major modifications to her negatives. When critics wrote disapprovingly of her extensive retouching methods, she replied: "There are those who cry 'faked' when other means are used with it, but are we not living in an age in which we are free reasonably so to do as we please? Who is going to limit himself to one tool when two or more will make his workmanship more beautiful? I claim the right to run the gamut from a lens to a shoe-brush to gain the desired effect."[10]

Later that year, when Alfred Stieglitz published his first issue of *Camera Work*, Annie wrote to him, praising the photographs reproduced in it. By 1903, Stieglitz had accepted her as an associate member of his photography group—the Photo-Secession—an honor conferred on only one other West Coast resident, Oscar Maurer.

By 1905, Annie had found a way to integrate her photographic skill, her inspiration from wild nature and her philosophy of freedom in artistic expression into a synthesis that would bring her both her greatest acclaim and her harshest criticism. This took the form of photographic landscapes incorporating female nude figures.

Many of them were posed on her frequent summer camping trips in the Sierra Nevada Mountains of California. Often, her models would be placed in the branches or hollow trunks of pine and juniper trees. She never used professional models, preferring instead friends and even herself.

This approach was a daring departure for a woman photographer in the barely post-Victorian time in which she lived. But Annie simply didn't believe in succumbing to fear. Her belief was that "fear is the great chain which binds women and prevents their development. Cast fear out of minds of women and they can and will take their place in the scheme of mankind and in the plan of the universe as the absolute equal of man."[11]

Annie went on to successfully exhibit her photographs in many shows and salons, locally, nationally and even in Europe. In 1905, the Starr King Fraternity Exhibition in Oakland that featured local photographers, including her friends Laura Adams Armer and Emily Pitchford, accepted thirteen of her prints. Annie wrote a review of this exhibit for *Camera Craft* in which she spoke favorably of their pictures. The following year Stieglitz raised her standing in the Photo-Secession from associate member to that of "fellow."

In 1908, she demonstrated her dramatic talents when she played the part of the Sibyl of Nepenthe in a play called *Will-O'-The-Wisp* by Charles Keeler, presented by the Studio Club at the Hillside Club House in Berkeley. Her friend Laura Adams Armer designed the costumes for this production. Later that year, she won a prize for her photograph *The Kodak: A Decorative Study*, and it appeared on the cover of the 1908 Kodak catalogue.

In October of that year, she once again joined her friends and colleagues Laura, Emily, Adelaide and Oscar in displaying her photographs at the Arts and Crafts Exhibition at Idora Park in Oakland, California. In a review of this event for Camera Craft, she wrote glowingly of their work, and of her own work she mused, "They are the partially realized fancies that flourished in the golden or thunderous days of two months in a wild part of the Sierras where gnomes and elves and spirits of the rocks and trees reveal themselves under certain mystical incantations."[12]

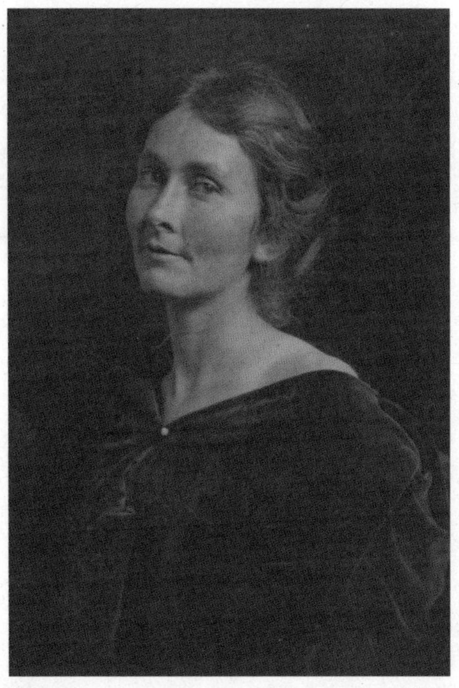

Portrait of Anne Brigman
by Mary L. Bisbee.

Anne Brigman's prizewinning photo, *The Kodak: A Decorative Study*, was chosen to appear on the cover of the 1908 Kodak catalogue.

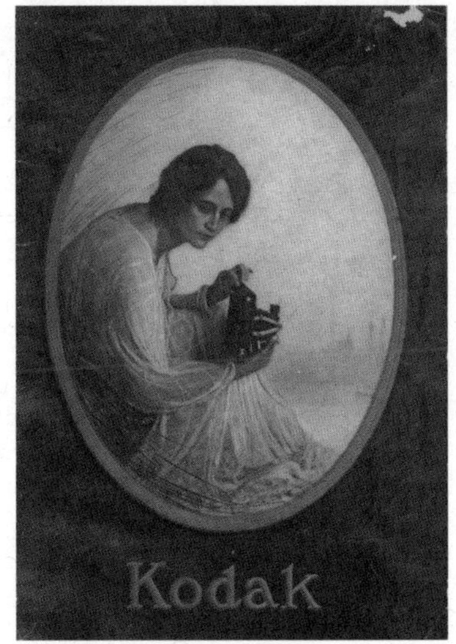

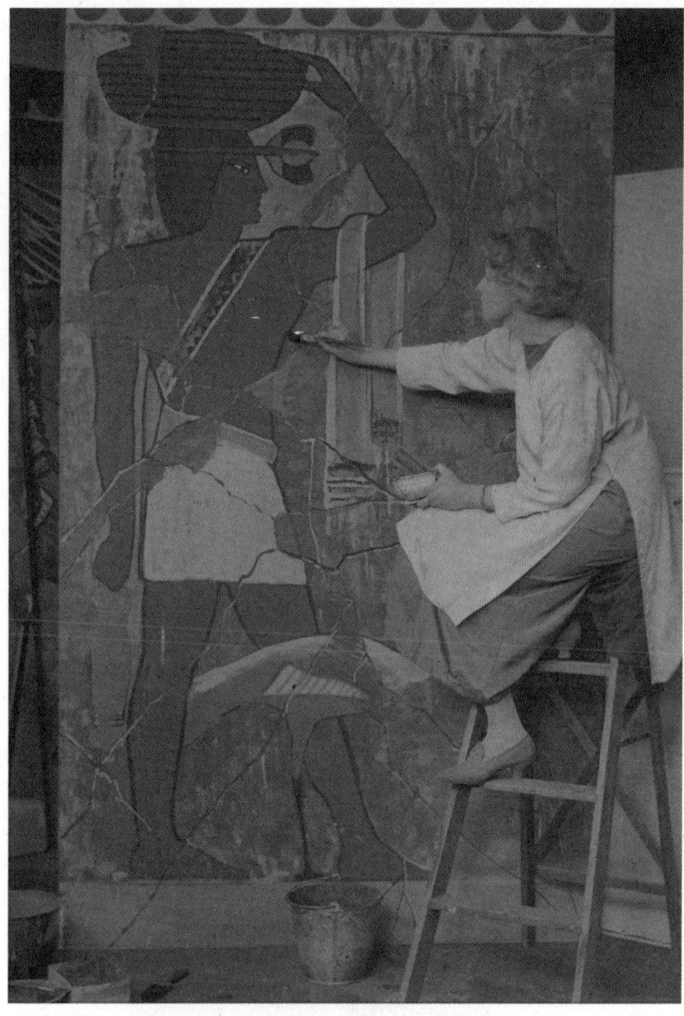

Laura Adams Armer painting scenery at a theater in Berkeley.

In 1909, her photographs achieved their first major national exposure when Alfred Stieglitz published five of them in the January issue of *Camera Work*.

Early the following year Annie separated from her husband and moved in with her mother in Oakland. In February, she traveled to New York, where she stayed for eight months. While there, she visited with Stieglitz and other members of the Photo-Secession and spent much time at their Gallery 291 on Fifth Avenue.

In 1915, along with Francis Bruguiere, she helped to organize the photography exhibit at the Panama-Pacific International Exposition in San Francisco. While many local and Eastern photographers participated, there was much controversy connected with the exhibit. The cause of the disagreement was the decision by the exposition's directors to include the photography exhibit of the Department of Liberal Arts rather than that of the Palace of Fine Arts.

In 1922 and 1923, Annie exhibited in the First and Second Annual International Exhibition of Pictorial Photography in San Francisco. By this time, however, pictorialist photography was declining in popularity with both photographers and the public.

Annie remained in Oakland until her mother's death in 1929 and then moved to Long Beach, California. In Southern California, no longer having the Sierras, Annie turned to the Pacific Ocean shoreline for her inspiration. Throughout the 1930s and 1940s, she continued to produce artistic photographs of subjects ranging from sand erosion to oil derricks. During this period, she also began writing poetry again. In 1941, she completed *Songs of a Pagan*, a collection of thirty-eight poems illustrated by thirty-eight photographs. Her poetry, like her photography, was inspired by the beauty and wildness of the natural world. In addition, it offers a glimpse into her emotional side, revealing something of the passion, sorrow and pain that she felt. Due to the circumstances of World War II, the book was not published until 1949. She died the following year at the age of eighty-one.

Through the medium of photography, Annie Brigman worked to form a mystical union with nature, and the body of work that she left to us fulfilled that goal. Moreover, the fearlessness and independence with which she led her unconventional life has made her an icon as a Bay Area Bohemian artist.

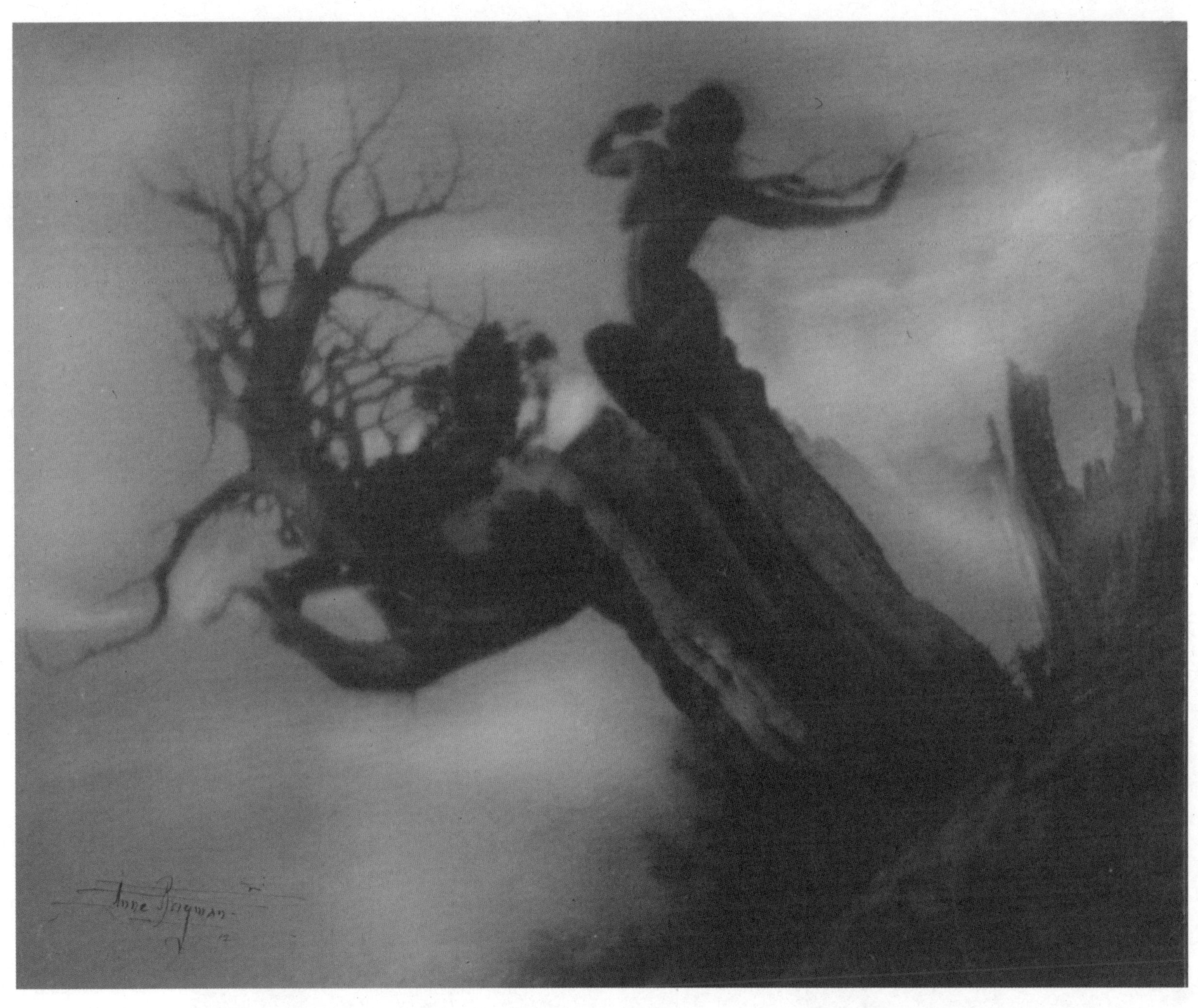

The Storm Tree by
Anne Brigman.

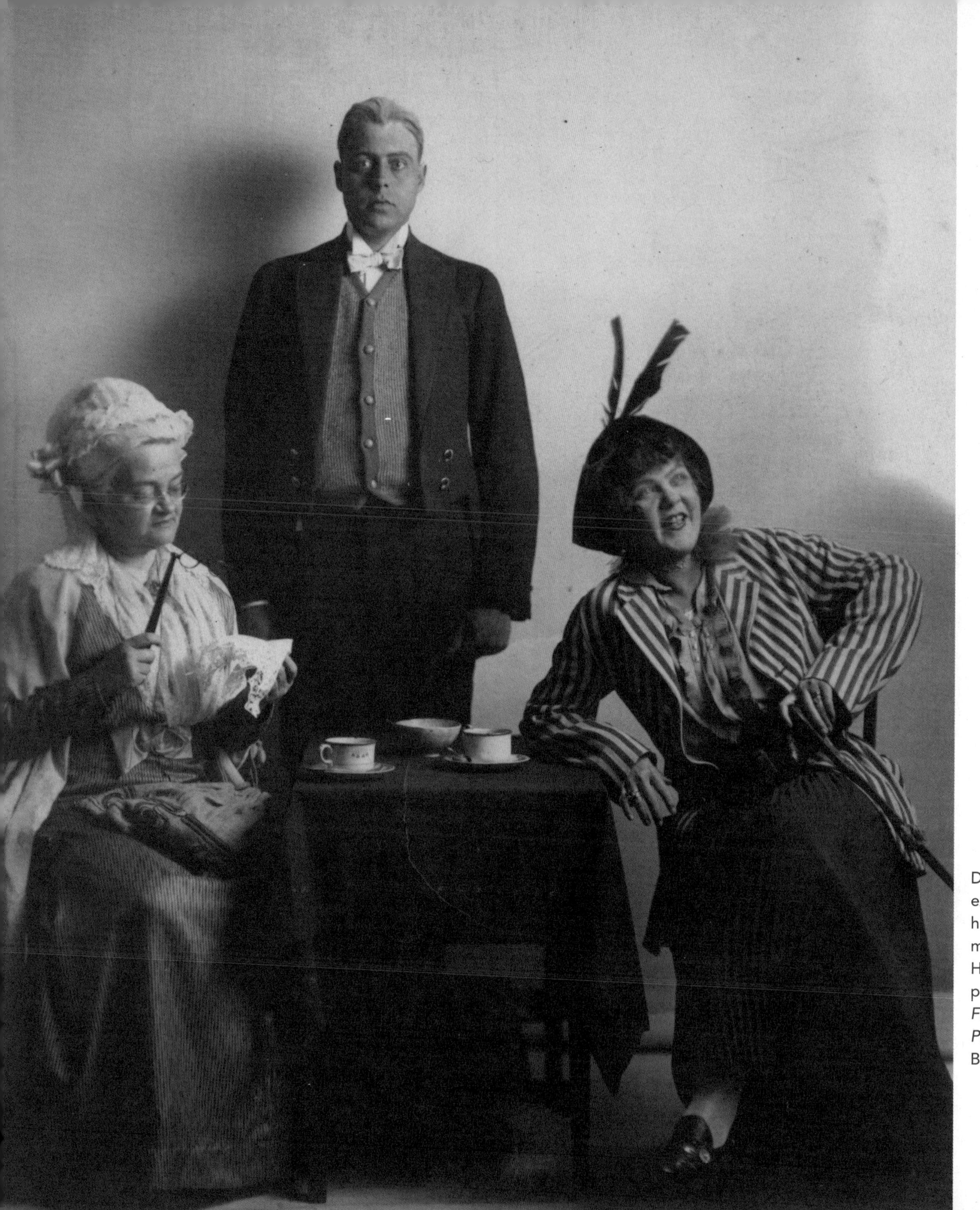

Dorothy Wetmore expounds to her fellow cast members in the Hillside Club's production of *Fanny's First Play* by George Bernard Shaw.

community performances

"All the world's a stage
And all the men and women merely players:
They have their exits and their entrances;
And one man in his time plays many parts,
His acts being seven ages."
—William Shakespeare,
As You Like It

In the early part of the twentieth century, before the days of television, cinema multiplexes and the Internet, Berkeleyans had a more immediate and hands-on connection with the performing arts. Going to the theatre meant going to a live performance, whether it be vaudeville, a famous traveling dance troupe or the opera. Silent films were popular as well; a moving picture parlor, the Varsity, opened on Shattuck Avenue in 1911. There were even earlier movie theatres in South Berkeley, but it wasn't until the advent of talking pictures in the late 1920s that movies began to eclipse live entertainment.

Berkeley residents also participated in performances to a degree unknown today. Throughout the 1910s and 1920s, there was a nationwide mania for outdoor pageants, often based on historical or mythological themes. The little theatre movement, which had its American beginnings in Chicago in 1912, swept the country. Based partly on experimental European theatre, the little theatres were both a protest against the slick commercialization of Broadway and a chance for local citizens to express themselves on the stage.

During the years following the founding of the city of Berkeley in 1878, entertainment in the vicinity of the campus consisted of public lectures, concerts of classical music and student dramatics in rented halls. Various campus groups held musical and literary evenings in private homes, and plays were also performed on university grounds in the Ben Weed Amphitheatre, a natural outdoor arena. For a wider variety, Berkeleyans traveled to Oakland or San Francisco.

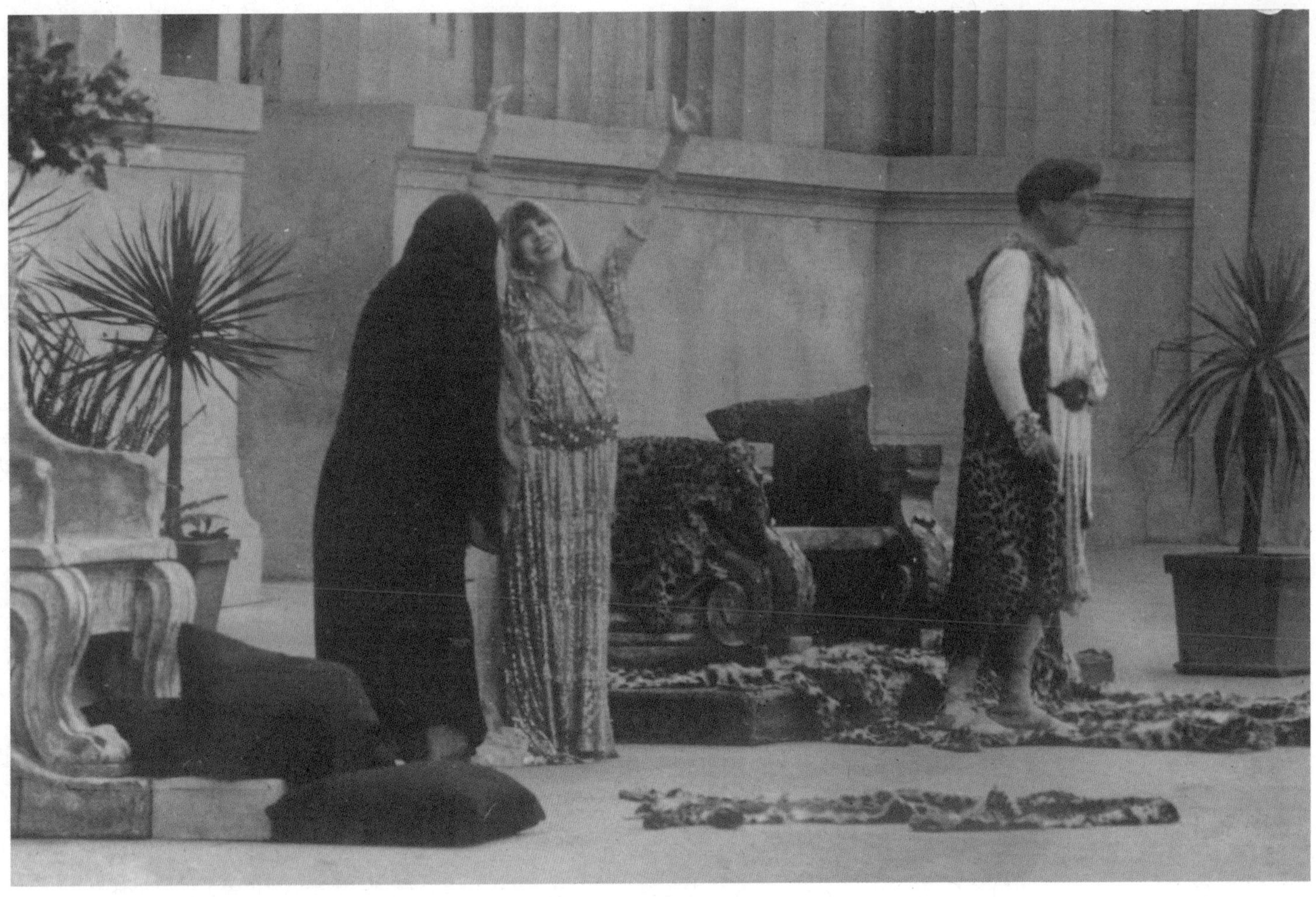

Sarah Bernhardt dazzled the audience in her acclaimed 1906 performance as Phaedra at the Greek Theatre.

THEATRE IN BERKELEY

With the opening of the Greek Theatre on the university campus in 1903, Berkeley at last had a world-class venue for the performing arts. The Greek Theatre was inaugurated with a student production of Aristophanes' *The Birds* on September 24, 1903. One of the first famous performers to appear there was the Divine Sarah Bernhardt. On a nationwide tour in 1906, her scheduled stop in San Francisco was cancelled because the theatre she had intended to perform in had been destroyed by the April 18 earthquake and fire. Instead, Madame Sarah played the title role in Racine's *Phaedra* in Berkeley's Greek Theatre to a rapt audience of earthquake refugees and townspeople.

The Hillside Club, known for its early efforts in preserving the natural beauty of Berkeley, was also an active social club and promoter of the arts. On November 30 and December 1, 1914, the dramatic section of the club, under the direction of Mrs. John

Howell, presented *Fanny's First Play* by George Bernard Shaw. The audience viewed this satire with some astonishment, as it was considered rather modern for conservative Berkeley. Featured among the cast were Robert Wetmore and his daughter, Dorothy Wetmore, then nineteen.

The Wetmore family, Robert, his wife, Amy, and their two daughters, were not typical "bohemians." Mr. Wetmore was in the wholesale fruit business and the family lived in a comfortable home at 2323 Hearst Avenue, then surrounded by scattered houses and open fields, just north of the university campus. However, they had a strong interest in the arts and were among the earliest members of the Hillside Club. Robert Wetmore designed a stained glass window for the clubhouse, both he and his wife took part in theatrical events, and they did not discourage their lively redheaded daughter from her interest in the stage.

Dorothy attended the Hillside School, where among her special friends were Violette Wilson, daughter of J. Stitt Wilson, the socialist mayor, and Merodine Keeler, daughter of Charles and Louise Keeler. In an interview years later, Dorothy remembered that she and a group of costumed classmates sang nursery rhymes at the Greek Theatre as an opener for a program by a noted soprano. Throughout Berkeley High School, where Thornton Wilder was a classmate, and attendance at UC, she continued to perform in plays and entertainments. She was a public health major at the university and graduated in 1917.

The United States had entered World War I by then; during her senior year and the summer after her graduation, Dorothy performed with a group entertaining soldiers and sailors at camps around the Bay Area. In her oral history, recorded in 1977, she remembered:

I was not really sophisticated, but on the other hand, I did know what was what. One of the songs I sang, with another girl—we sort of floated around—was "What One Little Girlie Can Do." The soldiers just adored it![1]

Dorothy parlayed her talent, determination and beauty into a theatrical career, performing with the Marasco Theatre and other stock companies in Los Angeles for almost a year, and then the Maitland Playhouse and the Player's Club in San Francisco for several more. A 1922 review of *The Rainbow* at the Maitland Playhouse praised her: "Miss Wetmore has beauty, a wonderfully rich voice, intelligence and youth. It looks as if she might go very far in the profession of acting."[2]

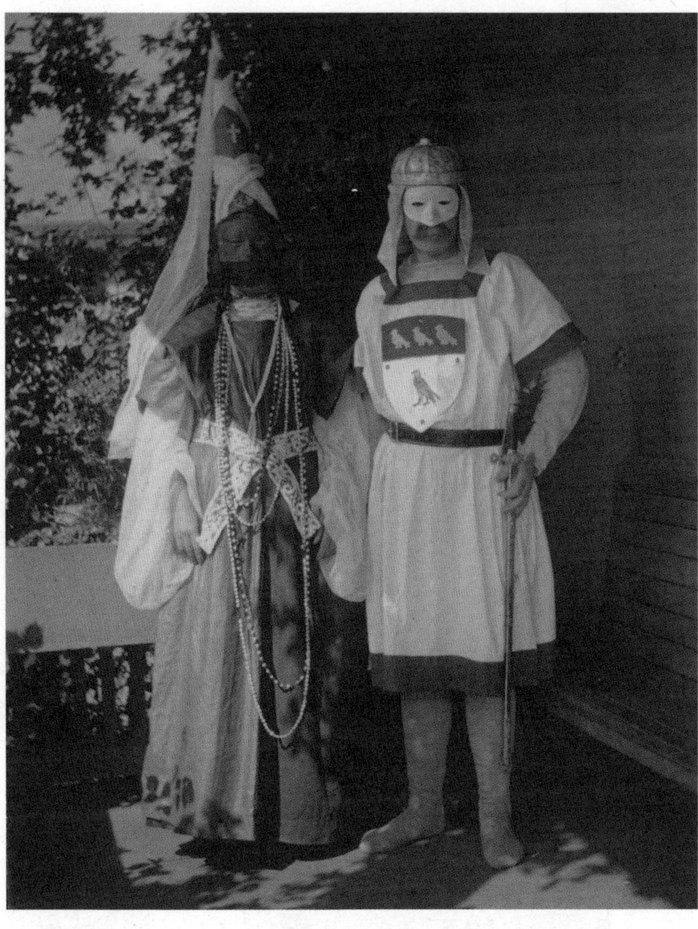

Amy and Robert Wetmore are in fancy dress, possibly for a costume party at the Hillside Club.

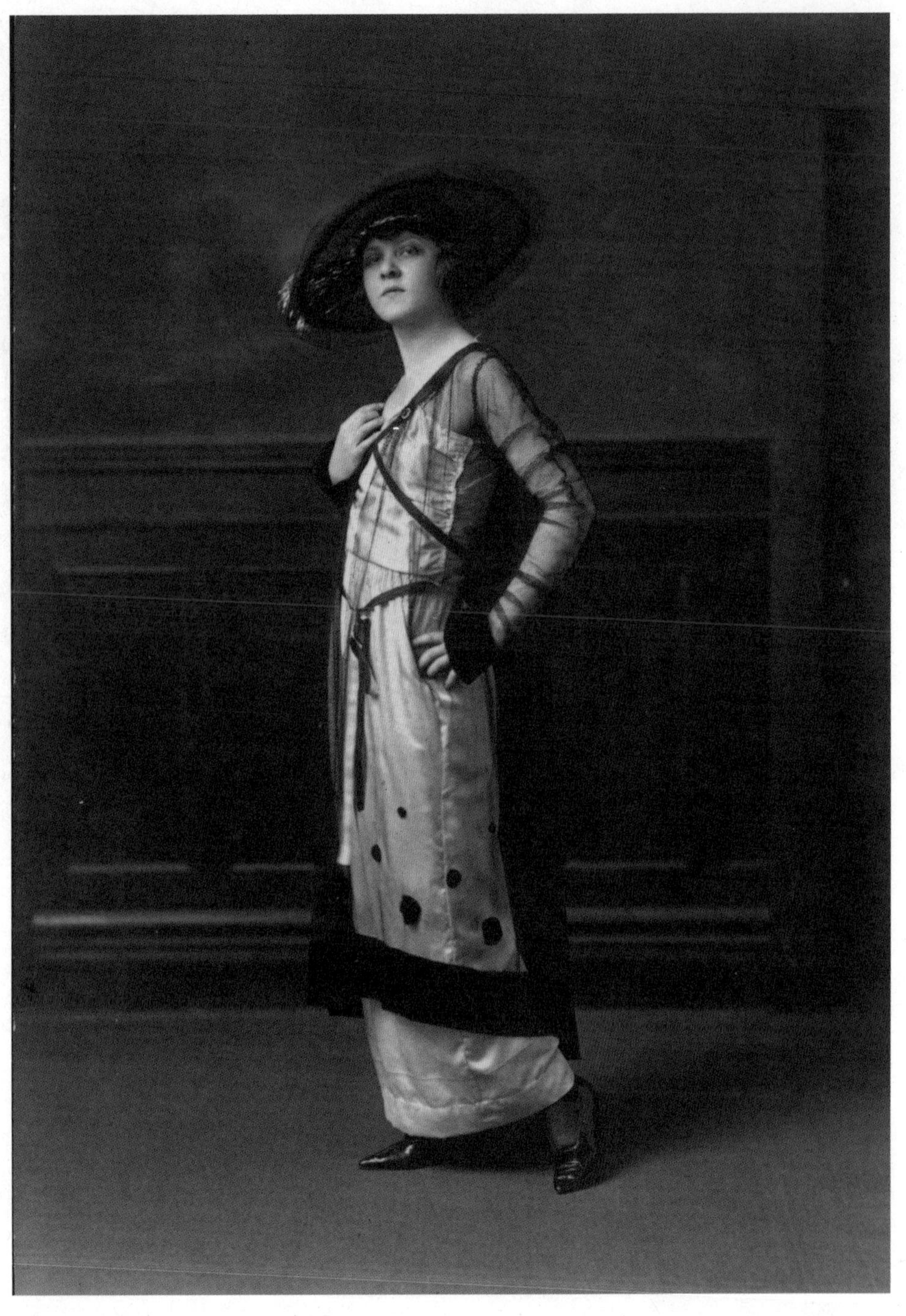

An elegant Miss Dorothy Wetmore appears here as Mabel in *Nothing But the Truth.*

Between afternoon rehearsals and the evening's performance, the young actress had a few hours to kill. She often browsed through the art galleries on Sutter Street, just a few blocks from the theatre district. There she met and became friendly with photographer Dorothea Lange, who had a studio at 540 Sutter Street. Lange had recently married artist Maynard Dixon. Dorothy and an unnamed boyfriend frequently went on picnics to the beach or woods with the other couple. The two women were very close friends at the time, though their paths diverged shortly after.

Not all the little girls who dressed up in costumes aspired to be on the professional stage. In the summer of 1912, a group of north Berkeley children presented *The Rescue of the Princess Winsome* in a Bonita Street backyard. A surviving newspaper clipping pasted in a scrapbook next to two hand-tinted photos of the play describes the scene: "An improvised stage had been erected among the trees in the spacious grounds and more than a hundred friends of the young actresses gathered under the trees and applauded their efforts. The stage and grounds were lit with dozens of Chinese lanterns and made a very pretty effect. The girls had arranged the affair just as a vacation pastime and the result far exceeded the expectations of their friends."[3]

The name of Mrs. John Howell appears many times in the society column of the *Berkeley Daily Gazette* during the 1910s and 1920s. Originally from New Zealand, Rebecca Howell had some training in theatre. Besides her involvement with the Hillside Club, she was artistic director of the Children's Theatre of Berkeley and founded an adult community theatre group. The Howells lived in a house designed by architect Henry Gutterson on Berryman Street. Her son Warren Howell remembers that his mother turned the large living room into an impromptu performance space, where she gave acting lessons and put on plays featuring the local children. The Boynton children, of the Temple of Wings, were among those who took classes there.

From perusing the society columns of the *Gazette*, it appears that Mrs. John Howell's chief rival for the title of "The Queen of Berkeley Community Theatre" was Mrs. Herbert Sanford Howard. This formidable-sounding lady's name pops up everywhere. She was director of the Codornices Club, which presented plays and concerts, performed dramatic readings and tutored young Berkeleyans in the finer points of dramatic recitation.

In 1918, a dynamic personality who was to have a great effect on the performing arts scene reappeared in Berkeley. Samuel J. Hume had been an undergraduate at the university from 1903 to 1908. He had left after his junior year to work and study theatre in Europe. There he met and assisted innovative scenic designer Gordon Craig. The association with Craig, whose mother was British actress Ellen Terry, enabled Hume to meet famous theatrical personalities and to participate in the emerging European art theatre scene.

After spending several years in Europe, Hume returned to the United States in 1912, by now married to Maude Dick of Edinburgh, Scotland. He enrolled in Harvard, finishing his undergraduate degree and completing a master's degree. There followed several years work as director and designer in theatres across the country, including the Detroit Arts and Crafts Theatre. Hume was a proponent of the "New Stagecraft," which sought to use lighting and carefully coordinated design and scenic elements to enhance the performance of the actors and convey the mood of the play. He was also a great believer in the power of drama to educate and enlighten. In this, he hearkened back to the Greek foundations of theatre, whose tragedies and comedies promoted catharsis and community participation.

Hume's appointment in 1918 as a faculty member and the new director of the university's Greek Theatre unleashed a force of nature on the unsuspecting campus and town.

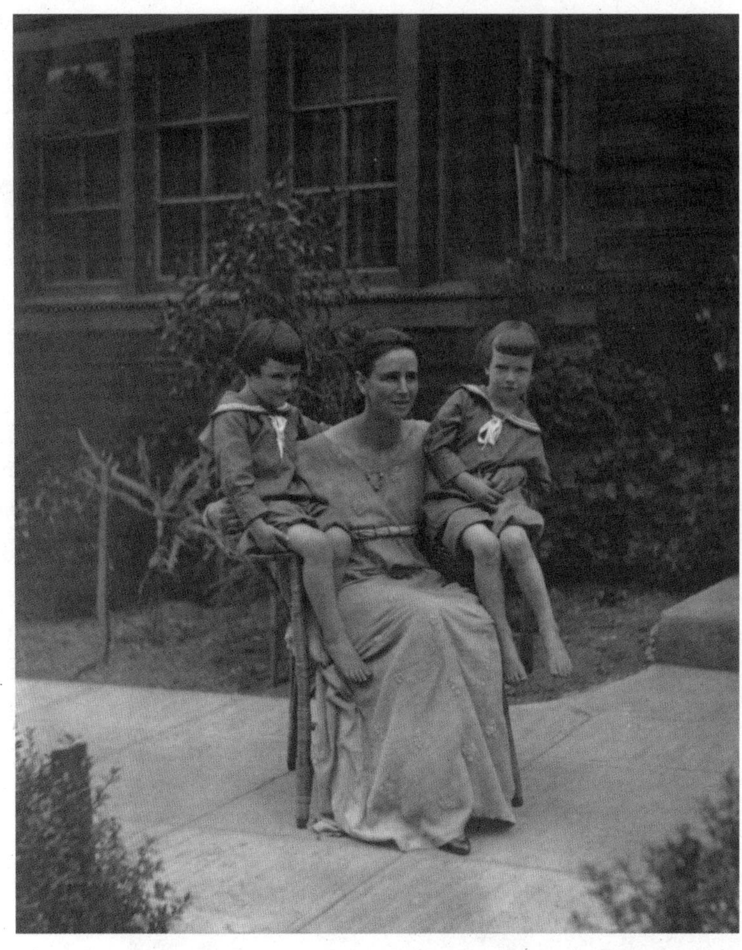

Mrs. John (Rebecca) Howell and twin sons, Warren and Ruskin, are sitting in front of their home at 2033 Berryman Street.

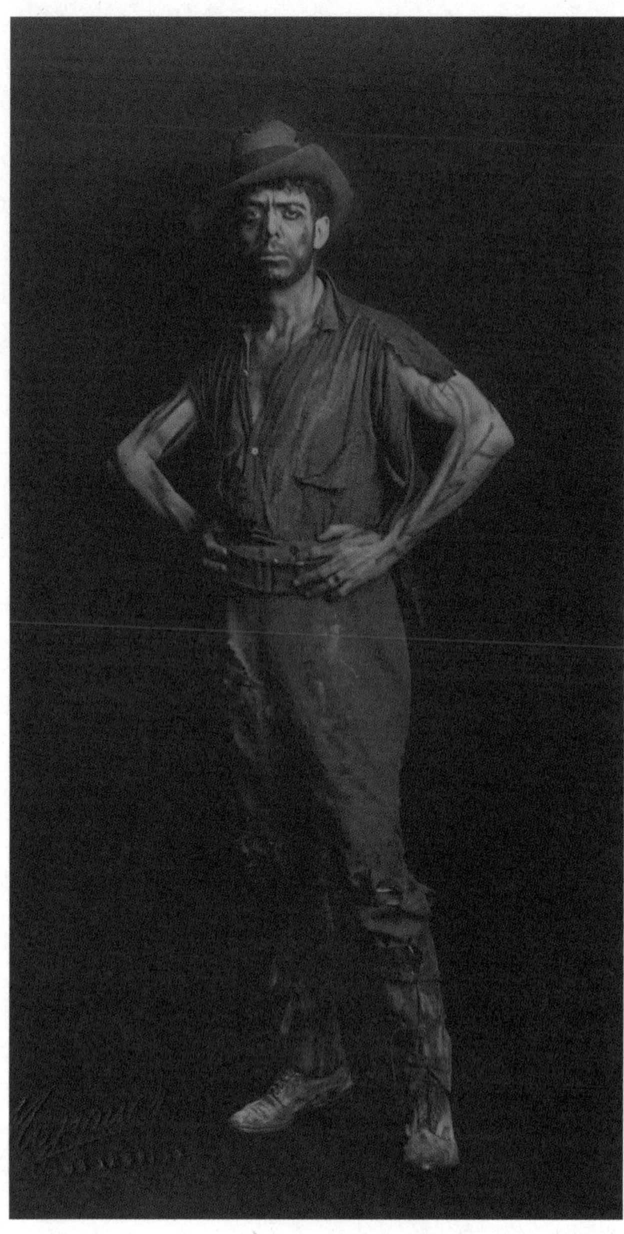

Sam Hume appears in costume for a university play. Note the heavy makeup on his arms.

Under the previous director, William Dallam Armes, performances in the Greek Theatre had primarily consisted of professional touring shows. Hume launched an ambitious program of productions featuring students, townspeople and professional actors. He was also responsible for all concerts, lectures and art exhibitions on the campus.

Correspondence surviving in the archives of the Bancroft Library indicates a man of immense talent, energy and enthusiasm. Hume inspired the same in others. During his six-year tenure at the university, many of the theatre people he had known and worked with in the East followed him out to California.

Frederic McConnell, one of the young men Hume had worked with in Detroit, served with the Army and Navy YMCA in France during World War I. In the spring of 1919, when his tour of duty was almost over, he wrote to Hume to ask if there might be work for him in California. Hume offered McConnell a job in Berkeley as his assistant. McConnell's reply was, "You have the faculty, sir, of filling your subordinates with glee over the prospect of being involved in your endeavors. Your letter reads like a summary injunction to 'go to it'—and I assure you that I will do my damndest."[4]

McConnell managed affairs in Berkeley during the summer of 1920 while Hume worked on directing projects in Pasadena and Santa Barbara. Others who joined Hume included Everett Glass (a friend from Harvard), who wrote from France, "Do you think you'll have any job to offer me if I get back this summer—or next fall? I feel qualified for pastorical, comical, historical, tragic-comical—and as you know, prefer poetry (something we don't get much of in the Army)."[5]

Hume first invited actress Mary Morris out to Santa Barbara to appear in the *Primavera* masque pageant he directed in the summer of 1920. He warned her that he probably couldn't provide her with a salaried position. "Our expenses are fairly heavy and I have to employ certain local people in order not to create any hard feeling."[6]

Actor/director Irving Pichel, married to Dorothy Wetmore's friend Violette Wilson, was another East Coast transplant. Pichel had taken over as director of the Detroit Arts and Crafts Theatre after Hume's departure for Berkeley, and throughout the next couple of years and his service at a Red Cross job in Washington, D.C., Pichel angled for an invitation from Berkeley. "I'd come on wings!"[7]

By the fall of 1920, Pichel was in Berkeley, where he was listed as a co-director of the Wheeler Hall Players. The performance space in Wheeler Hall had not been built as a theatre; rather it was a former lecture hall, with no backstage and a limited playing area. This space required all of Hume's staging ingenuity. There was no proscenium and no curtain, so he utilized techniques such as blackouts and stagehands moving props in plain view of the audience. These are familiar theatrical practices now but were new and exciting for the time. The first year of the Wheeler Hall Players included Oscar Wilde's *The Importance of Being Earnest*, Ibsen's *Pillars of Society*, O'Neill's *Beyond the Horizon* and Shaw's *Pygmalion*, in which Violette Wilson played the part of flower girl Eliza Doolittle. Pichel and Hume frequently acted in these plays as well as serving as general directors. The two men had been good friends and colleagues for a number of years, but their relationship eventually cooled and foundered, ultimately contributing to Hume's severing his ties with the university.

Trouble seems to have begun with the ambitious plan to found a new repertory company in San Francisco, modeled after the New York Theatre Guild. The company included Sam Hume as general director, Everett Glass and Irving Pichel as producing directors, and a group of familiar actors: Mary Morris, Lloyd Corrigan, Dan Totheroth and others. They leased the 1,300-seat Savoy Theatre at 80 McAllister Street. Renaming it the Plaza Theatre, they announced a fall 1922 season of six plays over twelve weeks. Though Hume was still director of the Greek Theatre during this year, his duties were taken over by acting director Max Radin.

The Plaza Theatre was not a success. Plays by Shaw (the West Coast premiere of *Heartbreak House*) and Ibsen (*A Doll's House*) were on the bill. The highbrow fare that played well at Wheeler Hall in Berkeley could not fill a 1,300-seat theatre in San Francisco. Hume left after the first season, leaving the Plaza in Pichel's hands. The new director did not share Hume's distaste for commercialism and the theatre filled out its lease by renting the premises to touring companies.

The experience had left Hume in debt and exhausted. Returning to the Greek Theatre, he resumed his schedule of teaching, directing and corresponding with a wide variety of people. Hume's correspondence indicates that he was responsible for everything from arranging tickets for theatre patrons to answering questions from the general public about the size of the Greek Theatre. There were also a number of play manuscripts submitted by aspiring playwrights for Hume to review and approve.

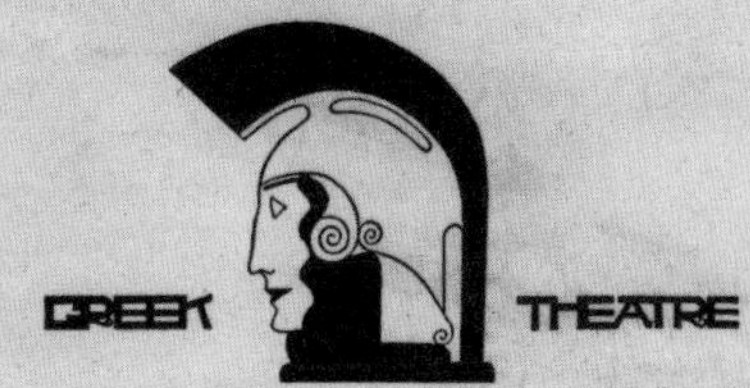

GREEK THEATRE

UNIVERSITY OF CALIFORNIA

WHEELER HALL PRODUCTIONS—FIRST SERIES

THIRD PRODUCTION
November 27, 1920, at 8:15

PILLARS OF SOCIETY
By HENRIK IBSEN

CHARACTERS

Karsten Bernick, a shipbuilder	IRVING PICHEL
Mrs. Bernick, his wife	MINETTA ELLEN
Olaf, their son	DANIEL NORTON
Martha Bernick, Karsten Bernick's sister	OTILIE SEYBOLT
Johan Tonnesen { Mrs. Bernick's younger brother }	DONALD WRIGHT
Lona Hessel, Mrs. Bernick's half-sister	FLORENCE LOCKE
Hilmar Tonnesen, Mrs. Bernick's cousin	J. C. LeCLERCQ
Dina Dorf { a young girl living with the Bernick's }	ELENA•MIRAMOVNA
Rorlund, a schoolmaster	MORRIS ANKRUM
Rummel, a merchant	CLAYTON LANE
Vigeland } tradesmen {	F. S. LeCLERCQ
Sandstad } tradesmen {	ROBERT E. HUTTON
Krap, Bernick's confidential clerk	W. W. B. SEYMOUR
Aune { foreman of Bernick's shipbuilding yard }	GEORGE H. BLACKER
Mrs. Rummel	VERA MORSE
Hilda Rummel, her daughter	EMMA KNOX
Mrs. Holt	ESTHER K. MARTIN
Netta Hola, her daughter	MARY MARTIN
Mrs. Lynge	ELLA M. SHAW

Townsfolk, Visitors, etc.

The four acts of the play take place at the Bernick's house in one of the smaller coast towns in Norway.

———

The autumn season of Wheeler Auditorium Productions will conclude with a repetition of ''Pillars of Society'' next Saturday evening, December 4th, at eight-fifteen. A new series of productions, an announcement of which will be given you during the course of the evening, will be presented after the holidays. Subscription pledges may be handed to the ushers.

These plays presented under the general direction of Samuel J. Hume and Irving Pichel.

The stage decoration by Rudolph Schaeffer and Norman Edwards.

Stage management by James Hull.

A SUBSCRIPTION TICKET TO THE SPRING SERIES OF PLAYS MAKES AN INTERESTING CHRISTMAS PRESENT.

Pillars of Society was one of the many Hume and Pichel productions.

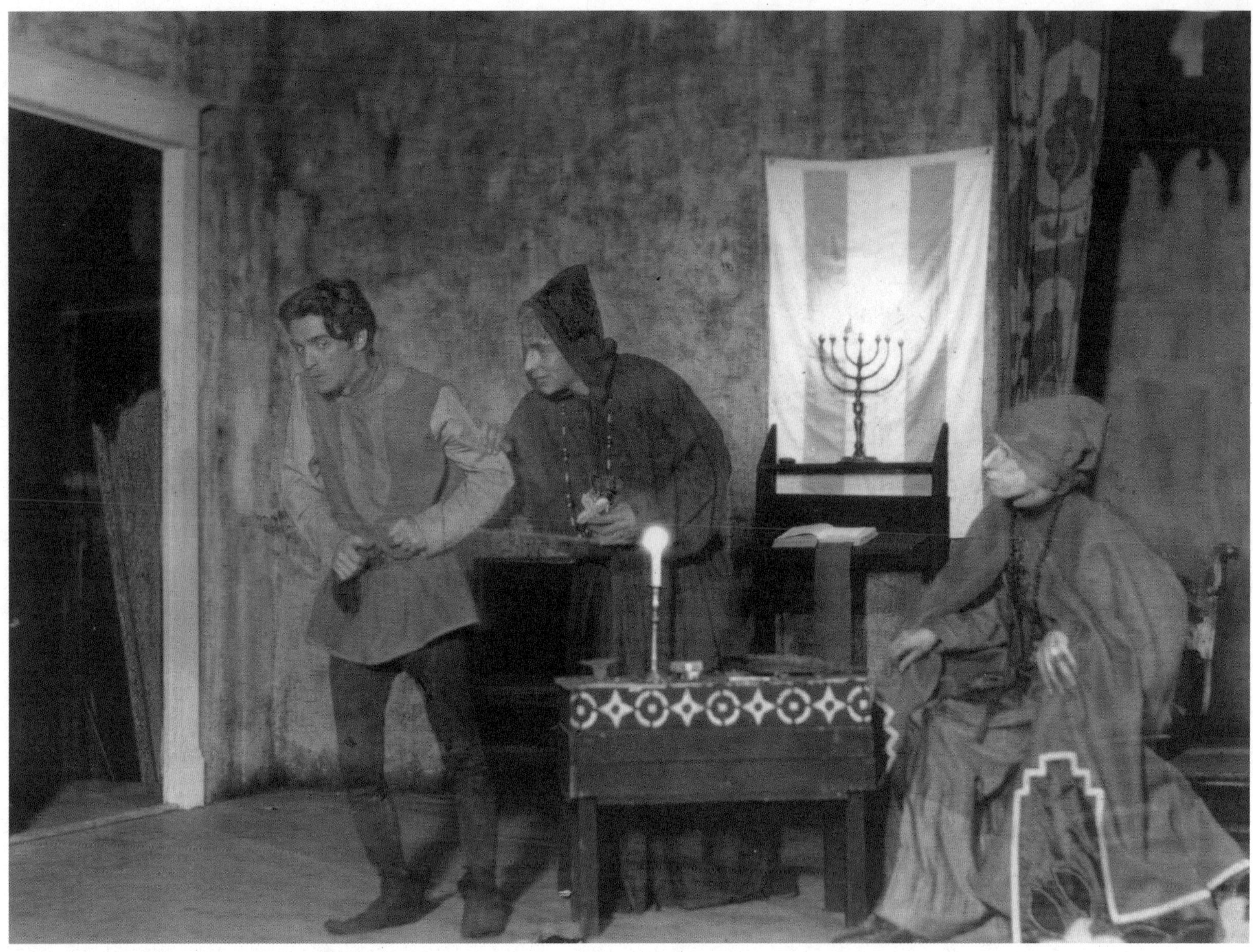

After the failure of the Plaza, Irving Pichel launched yet another new theatre company, the Playhouse Association. Though they eventually took up quarters in the old First Baptist Church on Allston Way, during the summer of 1923, Pichel was hoping that his company could use the Greek Theatre for a production of the *Oresteia* by Aeschylus. He seems to have done an end run around his old friend Sam Hume by first proposing this arrangement to the university administration rather than to Hume. In a series of increasingly formal and distant letters from Hume to Pichel, Hume's pride and the hurt feelings of a relationship gone sour are evident.

These feelings manifested themselves the following winter when Hume wrote a disparaging critique of the production qualities of the Berkeley Playhouse, Pichel's company, expressing concern about the effect on the Greek Theatre Players from having a similar theatre company so close to the campus. This led to a letter of protest from Edward Hogan, the Playhouse business manager. The matter was turned over to a committee studying theatrical activities on campus. The solution the committee came up with was a proposal that the Playhouse, under the direction of Pichel, merge with the Greek Theatre Players, under the direction of Hume. There was no way that Sam Hume could support this suggestion. His refusal to do so led to a letter from the president of the university terminating his contract at the end of the spring 1924 semester.

There may have been additional reasons for Hume's dismissal. He separated and was divorced from his wife Maude while in Berkeley. Maude remained in town for a few years, running an art goods store on Bancroft Way. Sam Hume's second wife, Portia Bell Hume, suggested in an interview that Maude Hume was both vindictive and well connected and that she made efforts to turn the university administration against her ex-husband. Ida Sproul, wife of Hume's good friend Gordon Sproul, refers to Hume's arrogant personality and relates this story: "He antagonized the faculty and then he got divorced from his first wife because he was

seen one morning leaving the home of Mary Morris in his tuxedo, and she was a leading lady in one of the plays and all that kind of thing, and his flaunting it didn't go down well with the Berkeley faculty. It wouldn't have gone down with *all* faculty, I don't think, at that time."[8]

Hume departed for Europe in the summer of 1924, where he authored *Twentieth Century Stage Decoration*, a classic still in use in college theatre design classes today. He also married Portia Bell in Paris in 1927. A graduate of UC and an old friend of Hume's, she had gone to Paris to study sculpture. Returning to Berkeley in 1927, the couple hired architect John Hudson Thomas to build a home modeled after the medieval cloisters of Europe. Hume Cloister, an imposing stone house, still stands on Buena Vista Way.

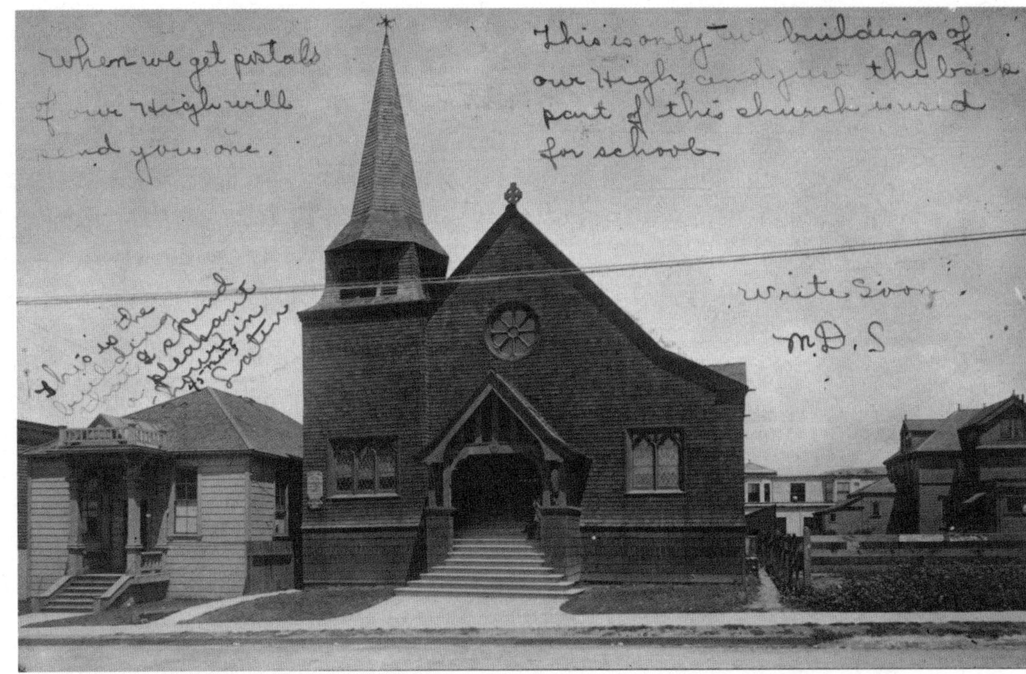

A photo postcard of the First Baptist Church on Allston Way. The rear of the building was used by Berkeley High School before the Playhouse Association occupied the space.

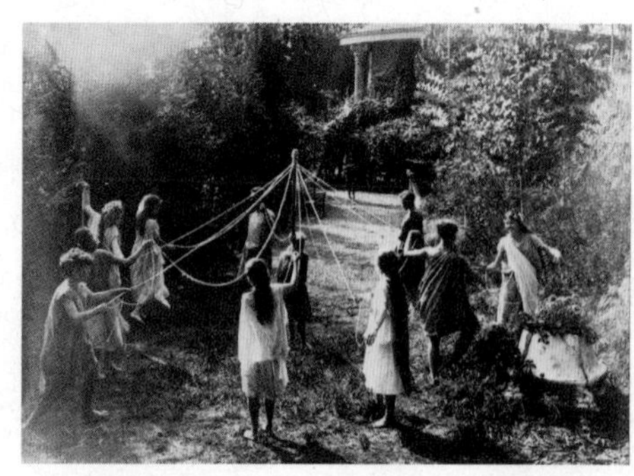

Hume remained an active advocate for educational theatre, teaching and lecturing throughout the state. He ran an art museum on Shattuck Avenue in the 1930s and opened a rare bookshop, the Palindrome, on Allston Way in 1949. Until his death in 1962, Hume was an imposing figure on the Berkeley cultural scene, often walking his two Great Danes through town.

Irving Pichel left for Hollywood in 1926. There he had a moderately successful career as a screenwriter, character actor and director. In 1947, Pichel was one of the witnesses called to testify before the House Committee on Un-American Activities, which was investigating communist activities in Hollywood. He was labeled one of the "Unfriendly 19," though the committee's hearings were brought to a close before he could testify. The Berkeley Playhouse continued under the direction of Everett Glass and, then, Alice Brainerd into the early 1930s. It offered contemporary and sometimes controversial plays, though play selections became much less edgy after Pichel left the scene. By the late 1920s, the Playhouse was offering children's matinees and "delightful social gatherings,"[9] including teas and art exhibits.

DANCE IN BERKELEY

Dance was also an important part of the performing arts throughout the bohemian community. The 1915 Berkeley city directory lists half a dozen dance schools, and there were many more in Oakland. Lessons in social dance were a must for young boys and girls of the middle classes. Dorothy Wetmore Gerrity remembered that "everybody who was anybody at about ten years old in the Berkeley Hills, went to Miss Russell's dancing class (at the Hillside Club). You learned social niceties as well as ballroom dancing."[10]

Equally popular were ballet and "interpretive" dancing. The foremost proponent of the latter was Florence Treadwell Boynton. As a girl growing up in Oakland, Florence had studied dance with her friend Isadora Duncan. At one point, Florence was engaged to Gus Duncan, Isadora's oldest brother. (Family stories say that Florence's father paid him to leave town.) Even after the Duncan family left the Bay Area, Florence remained in touch with Isadora through frequent correspondence.

After her 1899 marriage to the more conventional Charles Calvin Boynton, the growing family lived in Alameda for several years before moving to Berkeley. Raymond Duncan, another brother of Isadora, who shared his family's interest in classical antiquity, visited them there. Duncan had established a school of Greek arts and crafts in Paris, where he and his students made hand-woven fabrics and hand-painted silks. He taught Florence to weave and make sandals, thus giving her the basic skills for creating Greek-style clothing.

A strong and determined character, Florence was a "terrible cook,"[11] according to her daughter Sülgwynn Boynton Quitzow. This may have had something to do with her insistence on a raw vegetarian diet.

Isadora Duncan had studied and taught ballet as a child, and her early professional performances were in Augustin Daly's New

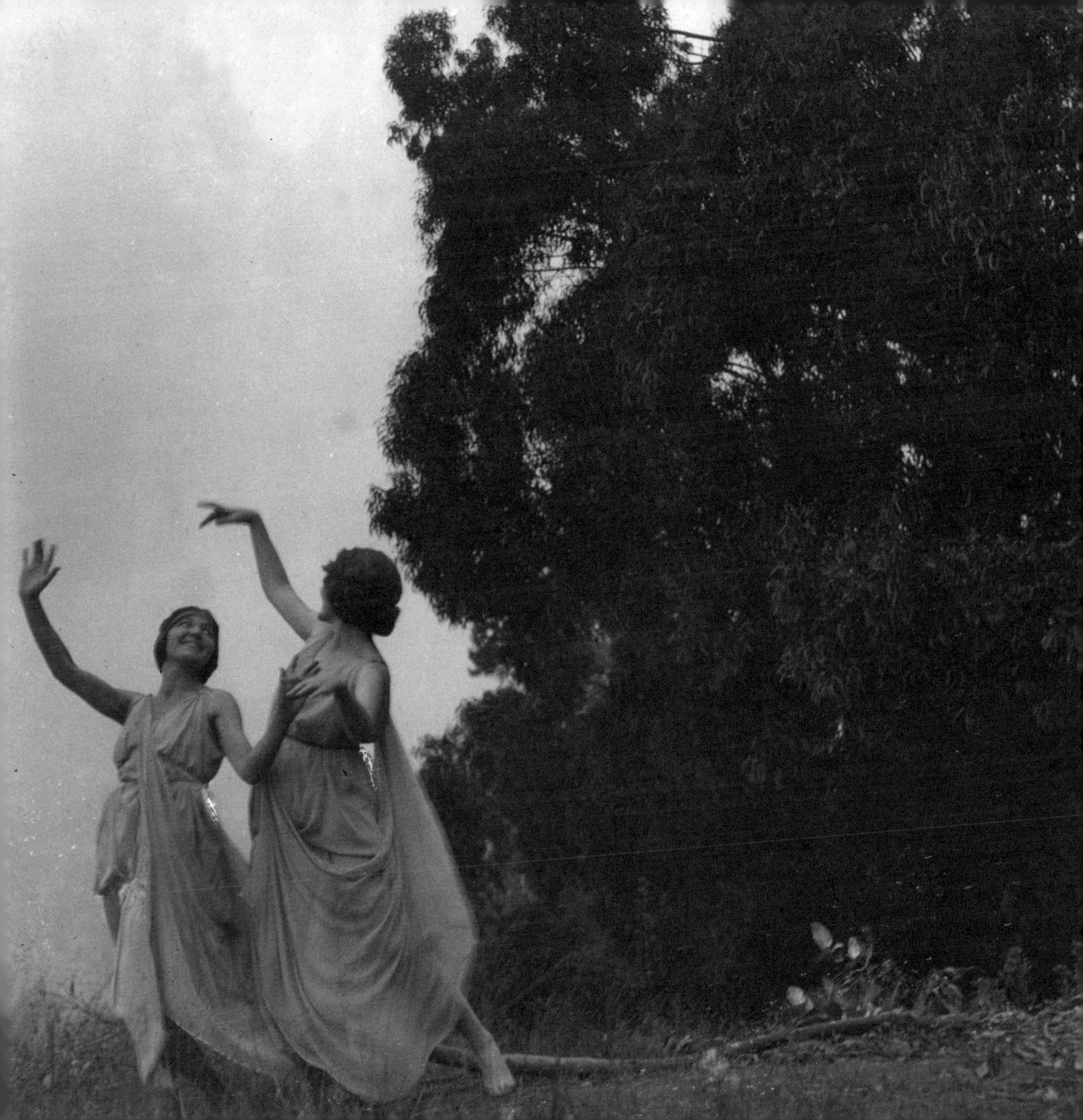

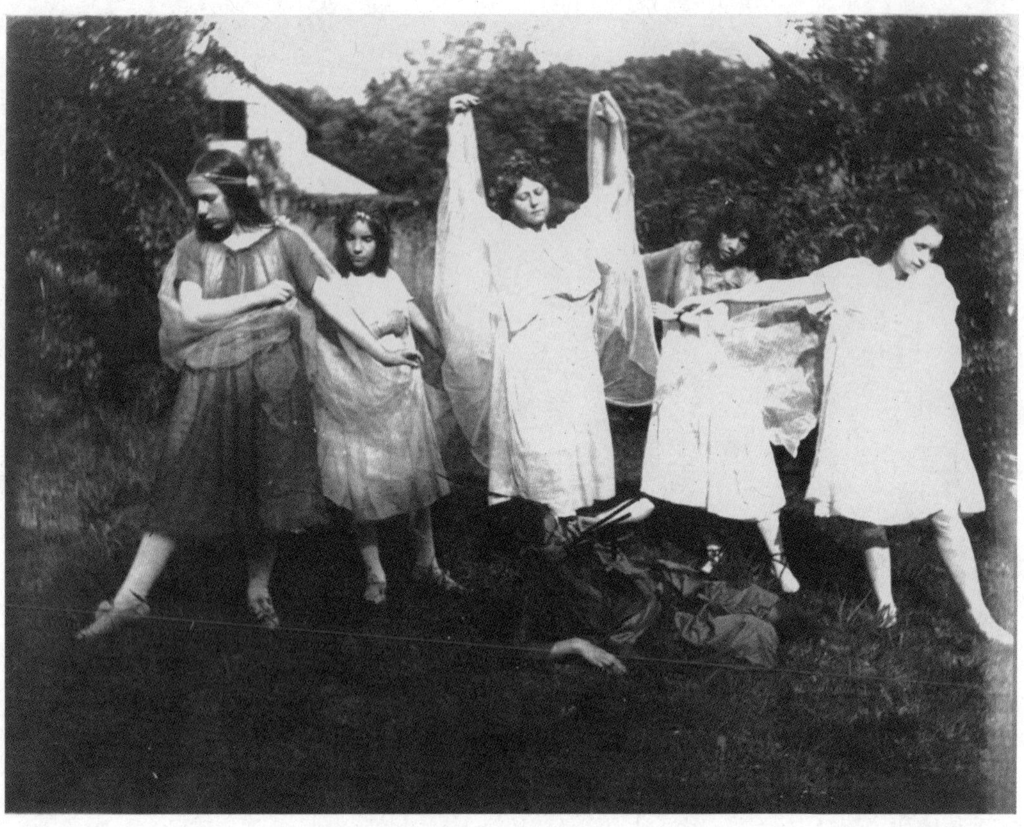

first began performing. Her half-clad limbs and bare feet and her interpretive posing to classical music were considered "arty" and ill-bred. Now, of course, she is recognized as one of the most significant figures in the development of modern dance.

Florence Boynton followed the career of her childhood friend with great enthusiasm and lost no opportunity to promote Duncan. In 1909, she gave an "Isadora Duncan Afternoon" at the Hillside Club. Dressed in a Grecian robe, she read letters from Isadora and performed dances by her childhood friend. Florence also sought to utilize Duncan's philosophy and style at the Temple of Wings. In 1914, she began a series of four seasonal festivals, held in an amphitheatre on the Temple grounds.

When Isadora Duncan returned to San Francisco in November 1917, after an absence of many years, the Boynton family had box seats and attended every performance. They went backstage where the Boynton children finally met the woman who had been held up to them as a role model for all their lives.

There had been hopes that Duncan would stay in the Bay Area for a while and establish a school, but the financial backing for such a venture was not available. The Temple of Wings would remain as the focal point of Duncan-style dancing for many years to come. Several generations of Berkeley children took lessons in free-form dancing at the Temple of Wings, first under the direction of Florence Boynton herself and later from her daughter Sülgwynn. In the archives of the Berkeley Historical Society is a collection of

York company, where she appeared as part of an ensemble of fairies. After traveling to Europe in 1899, she met artists and freethinkers who influenced her in developing a new philosophy of dance. She came to view ballet as a dance form that deformed a woman's body, and she developed her own improvisational style that incorporated natural movements like running and skipping. She taught natural breathing to the rhythm of the ocean waves. She also cast aside heavy costumes and artificial sets, preferring light shifts and simple backdrops, or even dancing outside. Duncan's style of dance was thought scandalous when she clothing from the Boynton family. Some are clearly dance costumes. Lengths of peach and aqua china silk, hand sewn together at shoulder points and side seams, speak eloquently of young girls dancing on the hillside, their tunics swaying in the breeze.

<table><tr><td>MUSIC IN
BERKELEY</td></tr></table>

Music was very much in the air throughout the hills and green streets of Berkeley. Most of the time it was classical music. Ragtime and jazz were not supposed to be played at university functions. The young people interested in such racy music played it at private parties or went to the Garden of Persia Ballroom (later called the Ali Baba Ballroom) in Oakland. Radio KLX also broadcast jazz from the Oakland Tribune Tower. Though a Victrola could be found in half the parlors in the United States by the 1920s, many people played musical instruments for their own amusement and entertainment and for that of their friends. The quantity of sheet music sold rivals the sale of CDs today. Tupper and Reed on Shattuck Avenue sold Victrolas, recordings, sheet music and musical instruments.

For the classically inclined, there were numerous voice and music teachers in Berkeley as well as opportunities to hear classical music performed.

Lyrics and music were intertwined in the Moyle household on Hawthorne Terrace. Gilbert Moyle and his wife, Florida Parrish Moyle (named for the state she was born in), a former concert soprano, moved to Berkeley in 1917. Though Moyle worked in an accounting firm in San Francisco, his true passion was poetry. He was a member of the California Writers Club and published two books of poetry. He collaborated with Charles Wakefield Cadman, furnishing the lyrics for the opera *The Sunset Trail*, as well as for many other songs. In 1921, Moyle served, along with Charles Keeler and Robert Sproul, on the committee that produced the Berkeley Music Festival.

The Moyle's North Berkeley home featured a large living room containing a grand piano. This room covered the entire second floor and served as a music studio and informal recital hall. Here Gilbert Moyle kept his extensive library of music books and Florrie Moyle gave voice lessons. The November 4, 1922, edition of the *Berkeley Gazette* announced, "Mrs. Gilbert Moyle will present four of her pupils in an informal recital Sunday evening at her home on Hawthorne Terrace. Mrs. Estelle Drummond will be featured on the piano and Mrs. Letitia Miller on the violin." During 1922, Mrs. Moyle also offered lessons at a studio at 26 O'Farrell Street in San Francisco.

The house on Hawthorne Terrace burned in the 1923 fire that devastated North Berkeley. It was rebuilt in the same location, but in the meantime, Mrs. Moyle opened a studio for vocal instruction in the Masonic

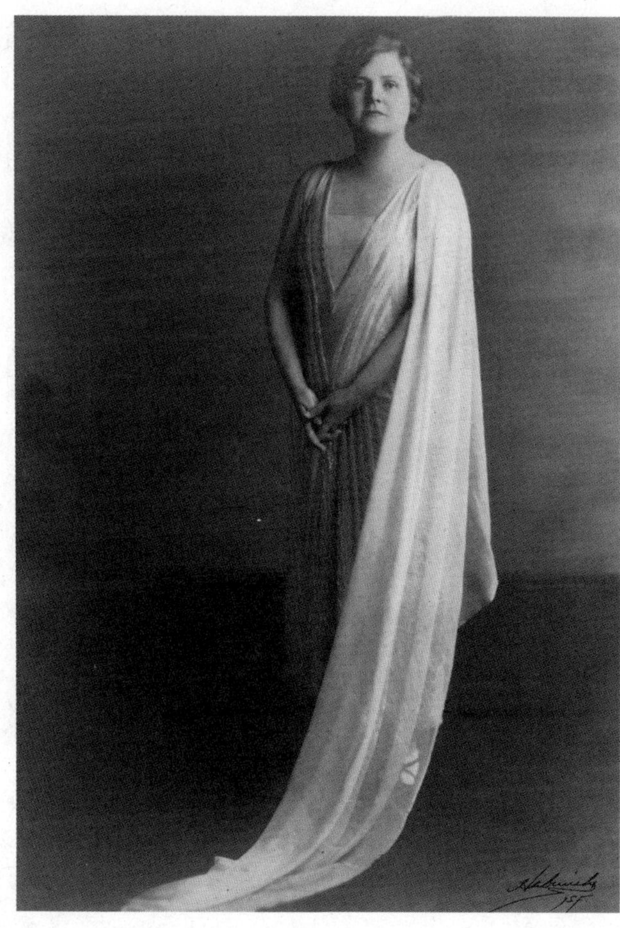

Florida Parrish Moyle used this picture of herself in concert dress as a publicity photo.

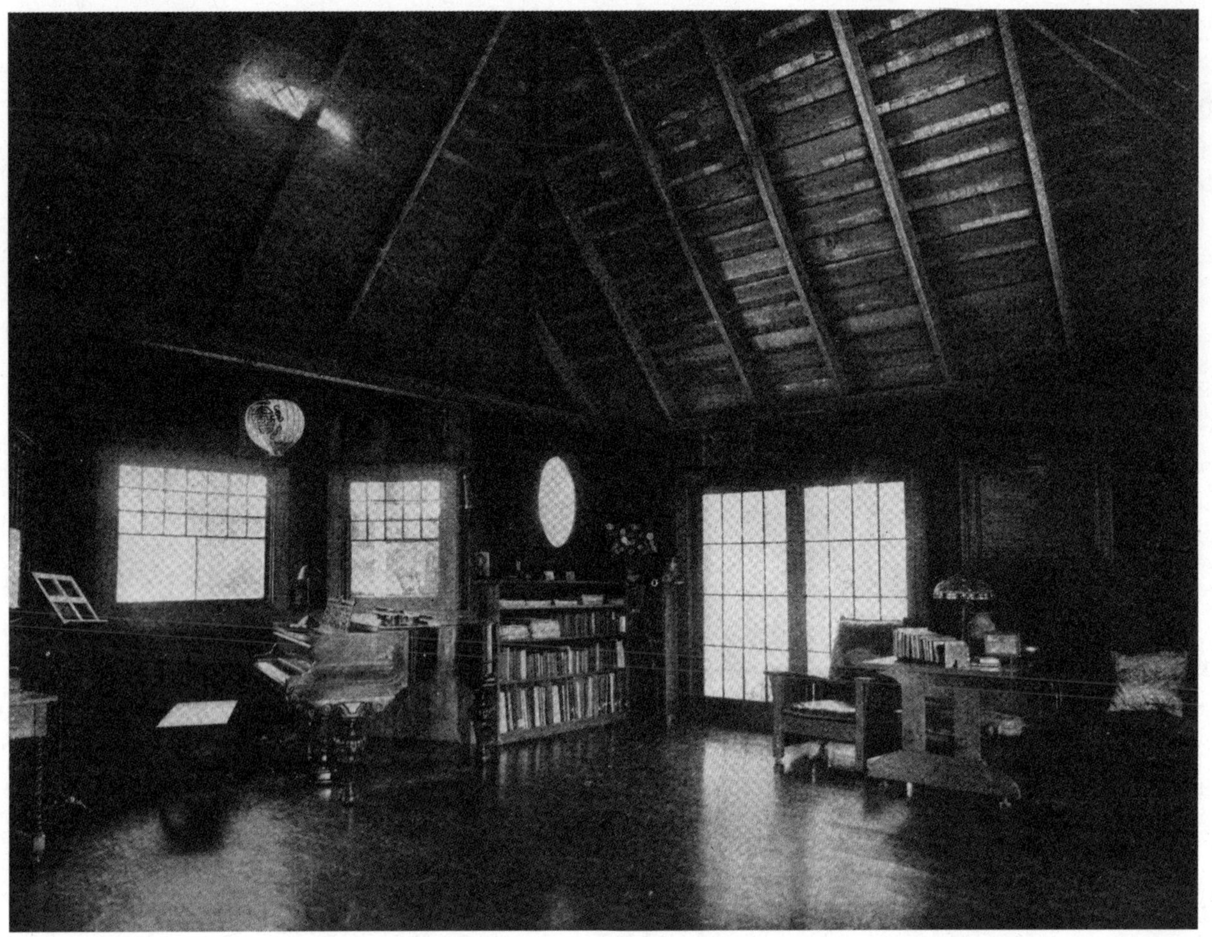

The Cedric Wright Studio at 2515 Etna Street. Not pictured is the swing that hung from the rafters.

Harriet Thompson, a piano teacher living for many years at 2808 College Avenue, offered lessons in her garden studio. Her collection of theatrical and musical programs and invitations, now in the archives of the Berkeley Historical Society, gives a fascinating glimpse into the Berkeley musical scene in the 1920s. Her collection indicates she spent many evenings at Harmon Gymnasium on the campus, where the Berkeley Musical Association presented concerts beginning in 1910. She also enjoyed pleasant afternoons at the Piano Club on Haste Street and student recitals in the studios of her fellow music teachers. She attended per-

Temple building at Shattuck and Bancroft. "The studio is equipped with a large grand piano and has a seating capacity of one hundred."[12] After her husband's early death in 1926, she moved to a home at 2729 Elmwood Avenue, where she again offered lessons, emphasizing, "Young Professional Singers prepared for Radio concert and opera."[13]

The Moyles were not unusual in their home studio. It is an interesting feature of the time that many of the residences in Berkeley artistic circles featured studios or performance spaces.

formances at the Greek Theatre and a few at Wheeler Hall. On many programs, Miss Thompson indicated whom she had gone with and her reactions to the presentation. (She thought Sam Hume's production of *The Jest* at the Greek Theatre in July of 1921 a "horrible" play but "pretty well done.")[14]

Zoning laws apparently were not an issue at the time; many musicians sent postcards and flyers announcing home studio performances. Cedric Wright and his wife, both violinists, presented two evenings of Brahms and Handel in October 1925 in their barn studio at 2515 Etna Street. Admission was seventy-five cents. The "barn" was actually remodeled by Bernard Maybeck. It had a soaring ceiling with room for a rope swing hung from the rafters and space enough for two grand pianos. Jacomena Maybeck remembered evenings at Cedric Wright's studio, when the women wore evening dresses and the men wore tuxedos, and there was much music around the big stone fireplace. Photographer Ansel Adams was a friend of Wright and says in his autobiography, "I became a regular at the frequent, happy and informal evenings at Cedric's Berkeley home, where I met many of the people who were to become so important to me in future years. The route to Berkeley by ferryboat, train, and streetcar was long and circuitous, taking nearly four hours round trip, but the journey was always worth it."[15]

Another unusual performing space was the Berkeley Music Center on Oxford Street. In the 1930s the former Gibson Photography Studio was transformed into a weekly supper club. Dressed in evening wear, patrons ate dinner on trestle tables and then listened to classical music performed by local musicians. Charles Dutton, a music teacher who had lost his elegant home on Tunnel Road after a divorce, cooked the dinners and arranged the evenings. Some local patrons who felt sorry for him set Dutton up in the Music Center. For many years he lived and worked at the center, until in 1946, a notice to vacate came. Dutton walked across the street to the university campus and shot himself, leaving a suicide note saying that at sixty-eight, he was too old to start over.

Nothing now remains of this vigorous performing arts scene except fading memories, a few photographs and piles of yellowing clippings and programs. Did other university towns manifest such a rush of creative performing energy as was found in Berkeley? It is certain that all those who participated in the plays, the dance performances, the concerts and the recitals got a good deal out of it. They were creating culture, not just consuming it; their minds and bodies were actively engaged in problem solving, their spirits were nourished and they were having fun as well, a commodity in short supply today.

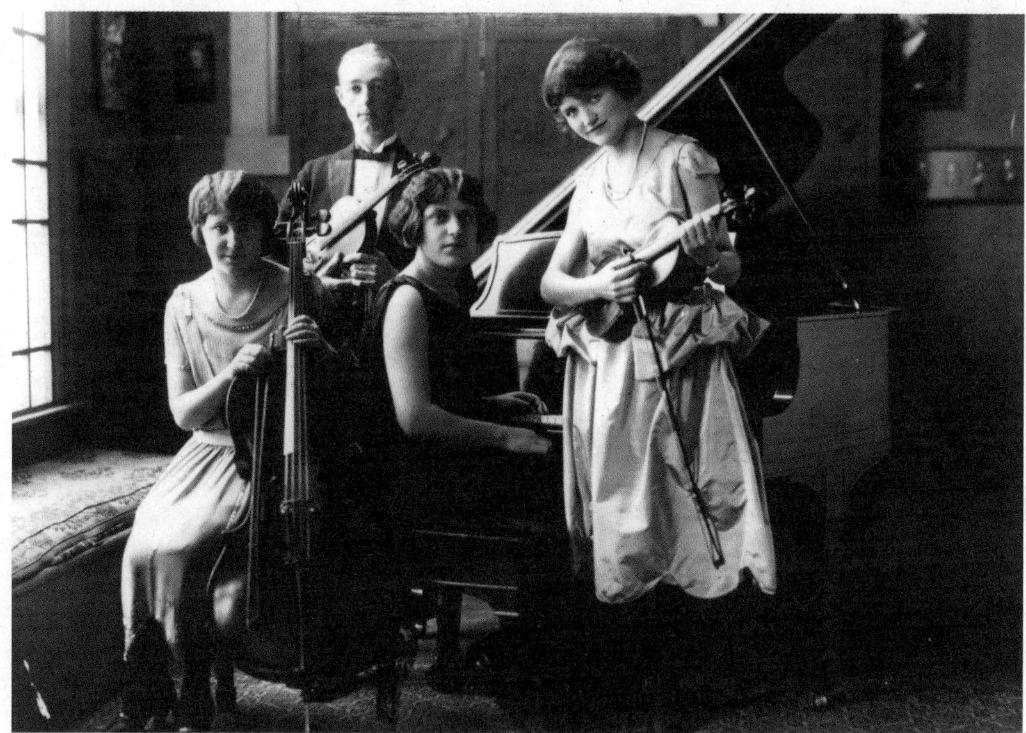

The Muses Quartet, with Antonia Brico at the piano, was photographed in 1921 at the Oxford Music Center.

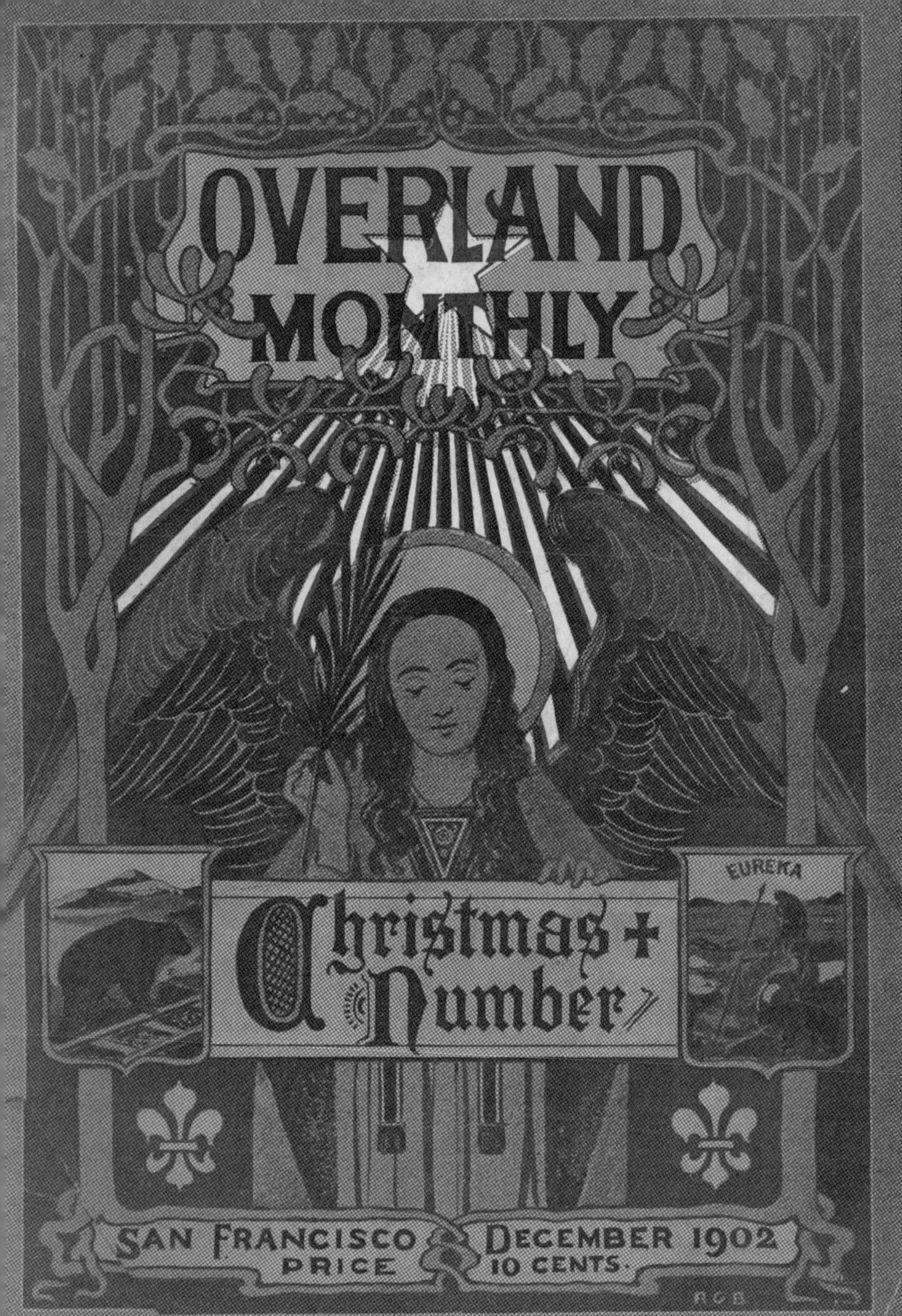

Cover of *Overland Monthly,* December 1902.

literary aspirations

"The craftsmen of the pen, or more properly of the
typewriter, are a nomadic people ever seeking new
characters and new color, and Oakland with its 'Greek
Hights' and cosmopolitan communities that cluster
around the bay have lured such writers."[1]
—*California Writer's Quarterly Bulletin*, June 1913

Young Dorothy Tyrell of Piedmont must have been heartbroken. For nearly a third of her life—since age eleven—she had been kept from school and play by the demands of her sickly and overbearing mother. Her former school friends drifted away during the changes of their teen years, and she had only recently found a few companionable older people through her poetry writing. Now, Mother forbade her to attend the Poet's Dinner because "those bohemians" would corrupt her.[2]

Dorothy had also just lost her advocate and mentor, the poet, womanizer, editor and all-around bohemian George Sterling. He had committed suicide in the San Francisco offices of the Bohemian Club, fulfilling a suicide pact made in Carmel only a few months before. Sterling, apparently with no designs on the teenage girl, had offered to run one of her poems in the *Overland Monthly*, a staid but still important San Francisco-based literary magazine. Dorothy had also published in several newspapers and was "one of the youngest of our poets, the youngest who has appeared in this column," according to a journalist known only by the initials "J.P.A."[3]

Although young and limited by parental restrictions, Dorothy was part of a huge literary movement, the "Berkeley group of authors," as another small newspaper, the *Mill Valley Record*, put it. Berkeley and Oakland were home to a cohesive and chatty group of conference-goers, amateurs and poetry-reading attendees. The East Bay was, in these people's eyes, unique in its ability to produce poets and writers. Because they believed this, they made it come

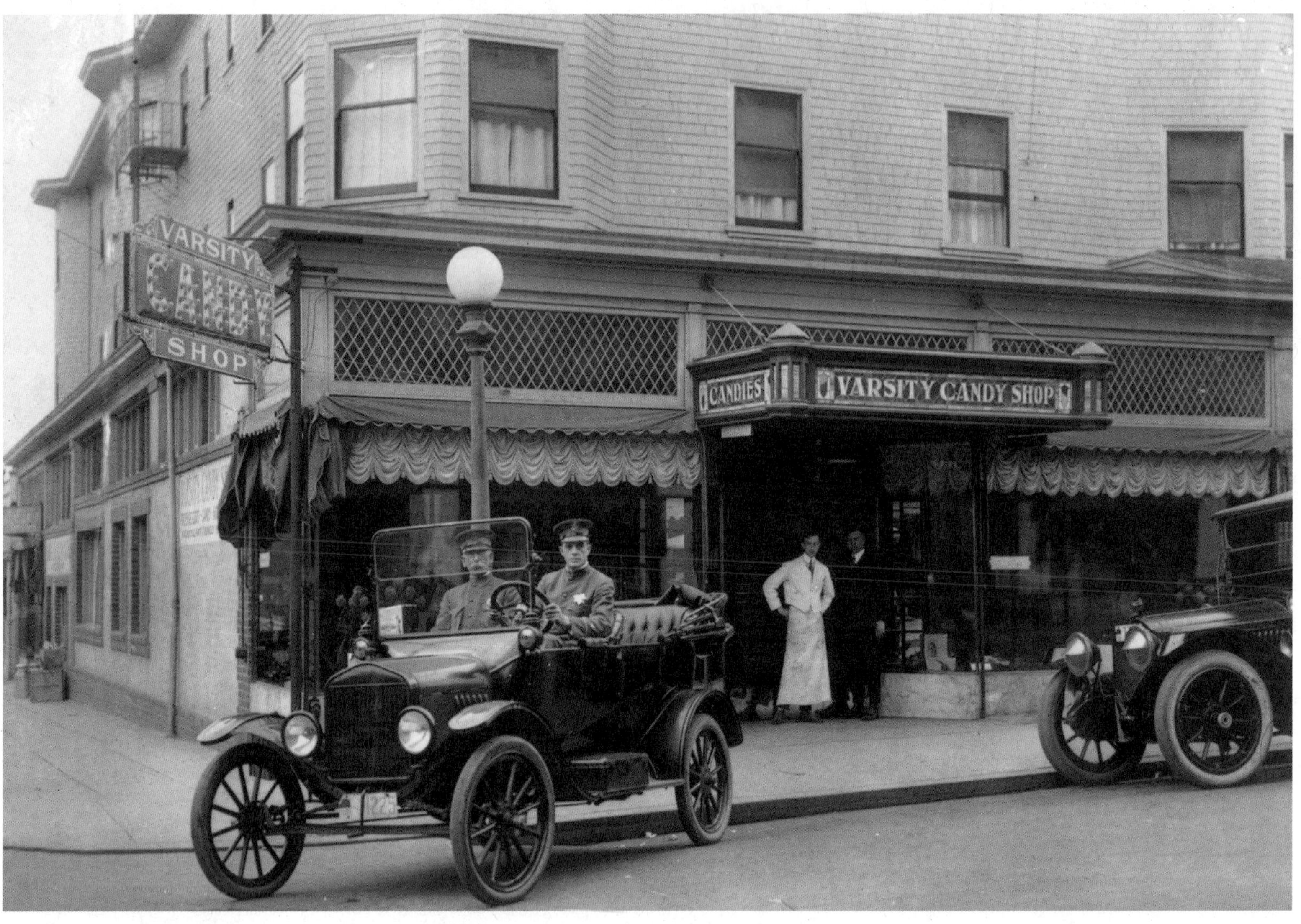

Florence Jury, a student at the university in the 1920s, called the Varsity Candy Shop "a combination candy store and restaurant and a big back room for dancing on Friday and Saturday nights."[31] Due to its central location on Telegraph Avenue, the store's back room was a popular meeting spot for clubs, such as the Poet's Dinner, on weekday nights.

true. When the public library held a "Book Social" in 1894, with each person donating a book in order to attend the literary and musical evening, the library's holdings doubled to 1,400 books in one day. The East Bay offered at least two newspaper gossip columns devoted to poetry, one in the *Albany Herald* and one in the *Oakland Tribune*. Where other gossip columns reported who attended

which party, the poetry columns announced who had published in which magazine.

Addison Schuster, one of these columnists, wrote, "There are more writers of verse in the East Bay than in any section of the United States."[4] His account of poetic greatness was probably inflated. After all, no one actually surveyed the number of poets per capita in Berkeley or anywhere else. But to his readers, his words portrayed a greater truth than any mere fact could. Most writers in Berkeley, and the East Bay in general, were convinced that poets, and other writers, needed a community in order to thrive. With this community came support, jobs, networks and an openness that few other social groups had. The writers shared themes that reflected the uniquely Californian world they lived in, including the natural environment of California, Native Americans, the Pacific Rim and life upon the coast. At the same time, newspapers relished the personal attacks that grew out of debates pitting the supporters of nineteenth-century ideas of poetry against the promoters of new, modernist writing styles.

In March 1927, an announcement went out that the poets were throwing a party. "The Poet's Dinner, first of its kind, will be given at the Varsity Candy Shop, entrance through Hotel Bancroft, Telegraph Avenue and Bancroft Way," said the Alice-in-Wonderland invitation. All poets from the Bay Area were invited. Dorothy Tyrell missed the first year, but she attended the poet's dinner for most of its next fifty years, even once acting as chairwoman. She saw the dinner's popularity grow, so that only five years after the first dinner, the 1933 event had 265 attendees.

The Poet's Dinner was an evening of fun and celebration without structure. In the words of Minnie Knox, one of its organizers, the dinner's strength was its informality. It had "no bylaws, no organization, no officers, no dues, no minutes, no obligations." Anyone who had published in Ad Schuster's column was welcome to submit a poem to the after-dinner contest, which awarded prizes to the best verses.[5] Because the judges did not know the identity of the poets during the judging process, they would occasionally choose beginners over well-established writers, much to the delight of the crowd. Raoul Dorsey, one of the invited, wrote to Schuster's column about his excitement.

I hardly think I'll eat a bite
amid that long-haired crew
But want to be on deck that night
to see the things they do.

A sprinkling of exotic people like Juanita Miller, dressed in an ostrich-feather boa and beauty marks, attended along with the high-school students, retirees and soldiers.

HARRY NOYES PRATT One of the most remarkable of the people at the 1928 Poet's Dinner, the first that Dorothy Tyrell attended, was Harry Noyes Pratt. Pratt was full of contradictions, not the least of which was that he was no longer a Bay Area resident in 1928. Although a native of River Falls, Wisconsin, he devoted most of his life to supporting California arts at a time when most Californians heaped their praises on eastern authors. California, believed Pratt, should be "known world-wide as the Mecca of literature and art." Pratt is now quoted as a "cowboy poet," although there is no historic evidence that he ever left the comfortable urban life of Berkeley

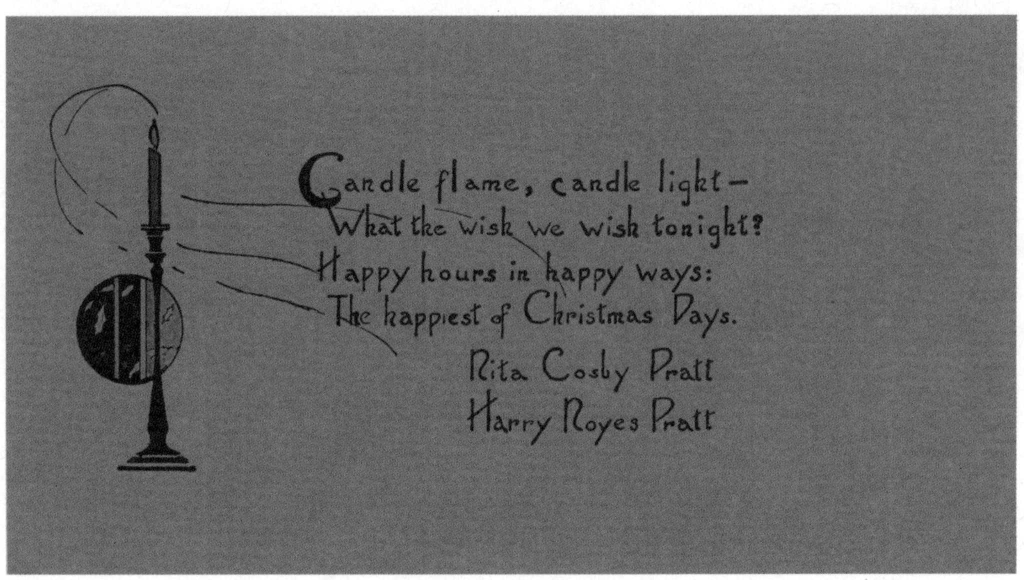

a "little book" of his own writing.[6] Despite his humble words, Pratt hung big hopes on the one hundred copies of his self-published volume. It was his entrance into the local poetry scene. Soon after moving to California, he and his wife called on elderly Ina Coolbrith, one of the state's best-known poets, and he read or recited to her one of the verses from his book. Coolbrith enjoyed the poem, so Pratt presented her with one of his one hundred copies and a sonnet written in her honor. With Ina Coolbrith's approval, he was now one of Berkeley's literary personalities.

Pratt's next step, after reading to his audience of one Poet Laureate, was to read to audiences of dozens of local tastemakers. In part, these readings were a way to make a living through poetry; in part, they were a way to teach Bay Area people about the arts and the importance of supporting them. His goal, as he told voters in a campaign to approve a community building, was to "maintain Berkeley's place as a cultural center."

One way most Bay Area cities created a cultural community was through the local women's clubs. These clubs came to San Francisco in about 1888, according to John P. Young for the *San Francisco Chronicle*, although the newspapers did not start "rating club doings as news" until the 1890s.[7] Berkeley was not a leader in the local women's club movement, despite its role as a cultural center. In 1920, Alameda district of the Federation of California Women's Clubs reported only eight clubs, compared to fifteen clubs in San Francisco and thirty-six

Harry Noyes Pratt used every medium at his disposal—from radio to his Christmas postcards—to promote literary life in the East Bay.

and Sacramento. He desperately wanted to be known as a poet but was ironically much better at promoting art than he was at writing poetry. More than anyone other than the supremely energetic Charles Keeler, he brought a passion for art and culture to a broad middle-class audience.

Harry Noyes Pratt is unknown today, and probably for good reason. His poems are sentimental and stiff, with titles like "The Happy Aspen Tree" and "Hills of Summer." His poetic themes were motherhood and the boys "whom war has rendered men." Like most of his fellow California poets, he was inspired by the natural scene, including the "dew-brushed morn" and "hill trails and open sky." By the time Pratt arrived in Berkeley in 1919, his style of writing was already passé on the East Coast.

He was forty years old, self-educated in the arts and carried a "tiny edition" of clubs in Los Angeles. Of the five Alameda district presidents who attended meetings, none were from Berkeley.[8]

Berkeley women's clubs were often smaller and more limited than other clubs in the region, but Harry Noyes Pratt searched them out and read to most of them. The To Kalon Club, the Adelphian Club, the Berkeley Women's Club, the Americus Talent Club and the San Francisco Branch of the League of American Penwomen all welcomed his lectures. The Ebell Club heard his talk on California novelists, and a program at the Etude Club put his words to music.

Pratt soon took over the presidency of the California Writer's Club from the other most visually prominent poet/lecturer of Berkeley, Charles Keeler. He started a book club on KLX radio Oakland, wrote for the *New York Times* and *San Francisco Chronicle* on "art of the Bay Cities," and started the "Little Gallery at the Claremont Hotel," exclusively to display the work of California artists.[9]

Personality-wise, Pratt was ideally suited to balancing all these different projects. Yes, he was busier than he wanted to be, but he always had confidence in his abilities. He had what he called "the poet's usual egotism" and took joy in announcing his literary successes and publications.[10] Ina Coolbrith soon became a close friend, and Pratt visited and wrote to her often. In his letters to Coolbrith, he is always willing to joke at his own expense, always trying new projects and always flattering his listener, fre-

quently banging his typewriter's exclamation point key—often three or four times in a single page. With such a personality, it is no wonder why he was popular as a speaker.

Pratt was also an irrepressible networker. Through Ina Coolbrith's influence, Harry Noyes Pratt got a job that was perfect for his interests. He was asked to be associate editor of the *Overland Monthly* in 1923—"with salary!"

The sedate *Overland Monthly* was one of California's oldest and most established literary magazines, called "one of the best of the frankly provincial literary periodicals" by the Cambridge History of English and American Literature in 1921.[11] *The Overland Monthly* was founded by Bret Harte in 1868 and had published Ina Coolbrith, Bret Harte, Mark Twain and other geniuses for California's first generation of writers. The original magazine folded in 1875, but a new magazine soon arose to take its name and reputation in 1883, eventually selling 10,000 copies a month. The *Monthly* was one of the first magazines to publish a young writer from

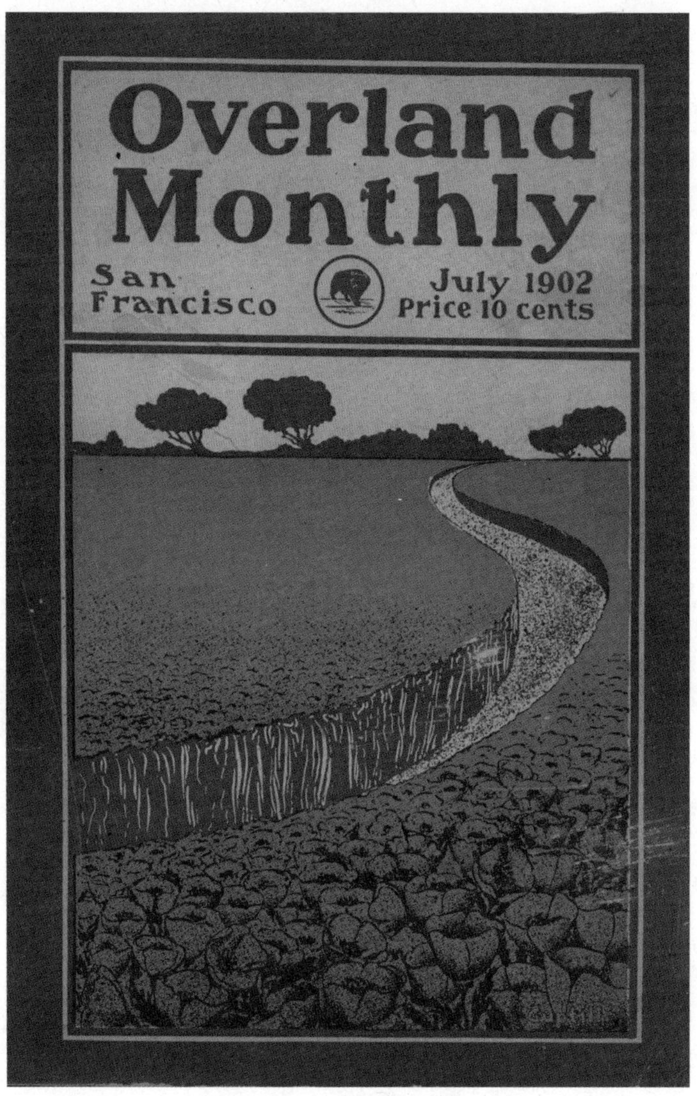

July 1902 cover of *Overland Monthly.*

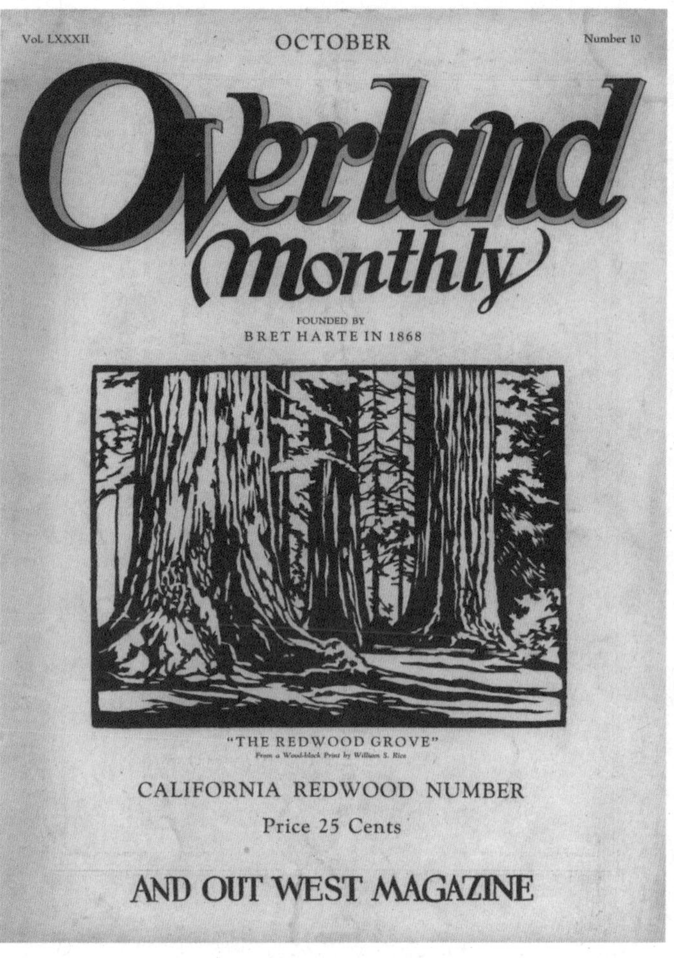

Cover of *Overland Monthly* after it was merged with *Out West* magazine.

Oakland, Jack London. It had even published Harry Noyes Pratt in the months before he became editor.

Pratt had disparaged the magazine only a few months before he got the job, perhaps because he believed that it was delinquent in honoring the great California writers of the past. Pratt had complained to Ina Coolbrith, "I feel it has made no step in advance over the last few years, and I had hoped so much from the new management."[12]

Perhaps because of that complaint, he welcomed a chance to put his ideas into practice. As associate editor, he focused on the great writers of the magazine's past. He interviewed his friend Ina Coolbrith and dragged Bret Harte's daughter through the gold country her father had made famous. When the magazine was bought by New York publisher and merged with *Out West* magazine, he crossed the word "associate" off his letterhead and became simply the "editor." He was briefly one of the most influential people in California literature, able to make careers by publishing new authors.

He also influenced careers through his work with the California Writer's Club. When Pratt became president of the club in March of 1925, it was one of the largest and most prestigious writer's support groups in the state.

THE CALIFORNIA WRITER'S CLUB The California Writer's Club (CWC) was, as one newspaper article put it, a "self-explanatory organization." It was a club for writers who lived in California. Members could be poets, novelists, playwrights, journalists, biographers, political pamphleteers, memoirists, scientists, short-story writers or anyone else who tried to publish. Most of its members were concentrated in the Bay Area.

In 1909, the CWC formed by splitting away from an earlier and more informal group, the Press Club of Alameda. The Alameda club was associated with politically left-wing writers like Jack London, George Sterling and Herman Whitaker. It is hard to say why Austin Lewis (who helped found the Northern California chapter of the ACLU) broke away from the Press Club. Perhaps he wanted to support the local writing culture in a more systematic way than the Press Club did. The club's statement of purpose said that it was formed to "foste[r] talent and giv[e] assistance to struggling authors." The hard-drinking Whitaker, London and Sterling were better known for their long nights of boozing and political discussion than for their organizational skills. Perhaps, too, London and Whitaker's public falling-out over the title of a local socialist party pamphlet made the Press Club unstable. Although most of the local writers sided with London (his fame meant that other writers could ride to publication on his coattails), some of them must have felt that Whitaker was mistreated.

By the time Pratt became president, the club had been around for fifteen years, officially incorporated for twelve. It grew far beyond the membership limits of the Alameda Press Club and was large enough to publish its own quarterly newsletter by 1912. The club began moving its goals more in line with the immediate needs of its increasingly diverse members. These goals included companionship, belief in California's unique literary culture, and mutual support with publication and employment. The California Writer's Club founders believed that the Bay Area, specifically the East Bay, was a unique place for encouraging writers—and, through this perception, made others believe as well.

Companionship was the most important offering of the California Writer's Club and was the only benefit that it could wholeheartedly offer to everyone who was a "craftsmen of the pen, or more properly of the typewriter," as the newsletter stated in June 1913.[13] A writer's life is often solitary and lonely, as the story of young Dorothy Tyrell shows and as many of her contemporaries would agree. The California Writer's Club offered a chance to meet regularly with "people of refined taste" who might engage in "friendly criticism and the thrust and parry of bright wit."[14] They could also commiserate with each other's struggles to get recognition, and celebrate a fellow writer's success at finding a publisher. Diverse settings for these meetings included places so wide-ranging that most members would feel at home in the community.

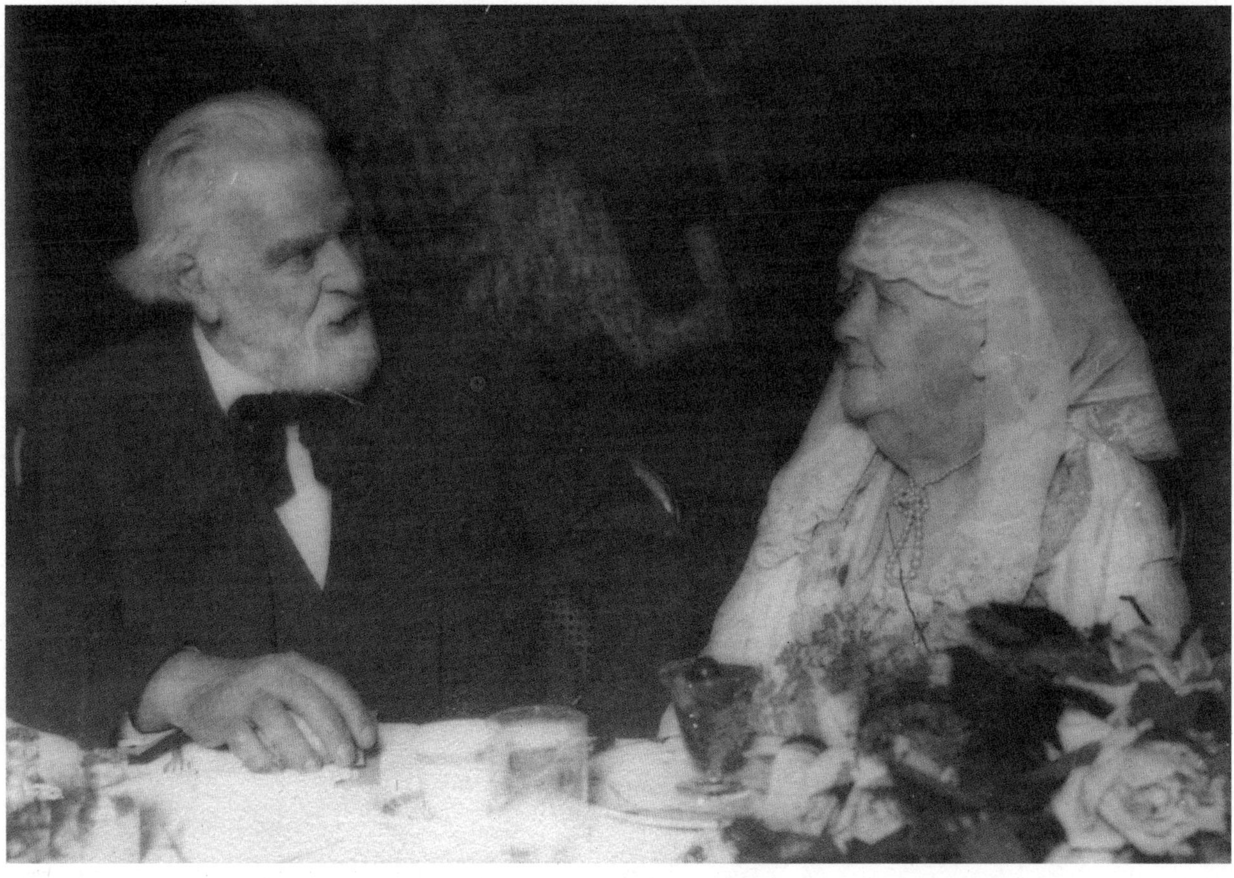

Edwin Markham and
Ina Coolbrith at a
Bay Area literary event.

Perhaps because the club never settled in a clubhouse in one neighborhood, this companionability remained open to people from different occupations, neighborhoods, religions and even races in a way that most Berkeley social organizations did not. Over its early years, the club met in a wide-ranging collection of buildings. In 1924 alone, the club met at the Varsity Club, the Oakland Business and Professional Women's Club and the Live Oak Theater (which was a grand name for what was essentially a ring of seats in Charles Keeler's backyard). Even if the club had outgrown its political roots, Hispanic, Asian and African-American writers were welcomed to the California Writer's Club. The California Writer's Club, like its more playful counterpart, the Poet's Dinner, was one of the few organized interracial social groups in Berkeley.

In 1941, the California Writer's Club presented its first conference. Preserved in the papers of William Nauns Ricks, an African-American writer from West Berkeley, are programs for the event, with his notes on the proceedings—good, very good or bad. Ricks' literary works reflected the Bay Area's literary culture and the California Writer's Club interests, with a focus on topics like the California landscape. His literary works had been published in magazines like *Overland Monthly* since at least 1915. In 1948, Ricks was chairman of the Poet's Dinner and was called "Ever-faithful and much-beloved" by Addison Schuster.[15]

Also, like the Poet's Dinner, the California Writer's Club supported a belief that being Californian gave the writers not only something to write about but also a vigor that spilled into their writing. According to Ina Coolbrith's introduction to the second volume of the California Writer's Club's *West Winds: An Anthology of Verse*, "We are of the West, dear friends," she wrote. "We are ambitious, and still young!"[16]

West Winds shows the strong stamp of Harry Noyes Pratt, the mid-1920s president and friend of Ina Coolbrith. It carried nine poems by Harry Noyes Pratt, compared to only three each by famous poets George Sterling, Ina Coolbrith and Edwin Markham. Pratt's contribution was only equaled by a prolific Oakland poet named Claudius Thayer, an invalid son of Oregon governor William Wallace Thayer.

WITTER BYNNER

Harry Noyes Pratt loved almost everything about the arts in California and was the perfect booster. However, he had at least one rivalry with a poet who had a different vision for California's literary heritage. This poet wrote under the professional name of "Witter Bynner," but was known as Hal Bynner to his friends. Soon after arriving in California, Bynner made the mistake of publicly criticizing California poetry. Pratt, who had invested so much energy in creating a California poetry scene that believed its state was in the vanguard of literature, took it upon himself to chivalrously defend the greats of Miller and Markham from a newcomer he dismissed as a "near-poet" who occasionally wrote in free verse.

It is ironic that Pratt's most public squabble was with a man with remarkable similarities to himself. Bynner was almost exactly the same age as Pratt and arrived in Berkeley less than a year before Pratt did. Like Pratt, he enjoyed the social atmosphere and support of the Berkeley scene and socialized with writers like Jack London, Mary Austin and George Sterling. Like Pratt, he tried to influence the future of literary Berkeley by creating a literary scene focused around his own powerful personality. For Bynner, that scene was centered on his poetry classes at the University of California and on his hotel room, where he held afternoon literary salons for budding student writers.

It is even more ironic that out of their rivalry came Pratt's most famous poem, a bit of doggerel that the local newspapers were thrilled to repeat while eagerly reporting the latest local poetry scandal. The rhyme was a single question that was supposed to put Bynner in his place:

Fame chewed his pencil, scratched
  his head,

Fame—worried-frowned, and
  puzzled said;
I've known 'em all, both saint and
  sinner;
but—who the hell is Witter Bynner?"[17]

Behind the public squabbling of Bynner and Pratt were serious philosophic and literary differences in opinion. Witter Bynner wrote in the new style, distasteful to most of Berkeley's established writers like Harry Noyes Pratt and Charles Keeler. The two men were in the middle of a poetic conflict that shook the entire literary world, in which both sides would routinely mock the successes of the other. Pratt claimed that Bynner "seems more concerned with the technique" of writing than the feeling it should express. And Pratt did not have much respect for the technique. Writing in *Overland Monthly* magazine, Pratt teased that one poet "still clings to some of the outworn traditions. There is, for example, her retention of capital letters. How Victorian! Raus mit 'em!"[18]

Bynner, on the other hand, was equally hard on the more traditional writers. In 1922, he wrote a letter that, according to one of Coolbrith's biographers, "destroy[ed] California's literary past with a few blasé strokes of a pen." Keeler and Pratt didn't even warrant mention in Bynner's letter. The titans of California poetry, like

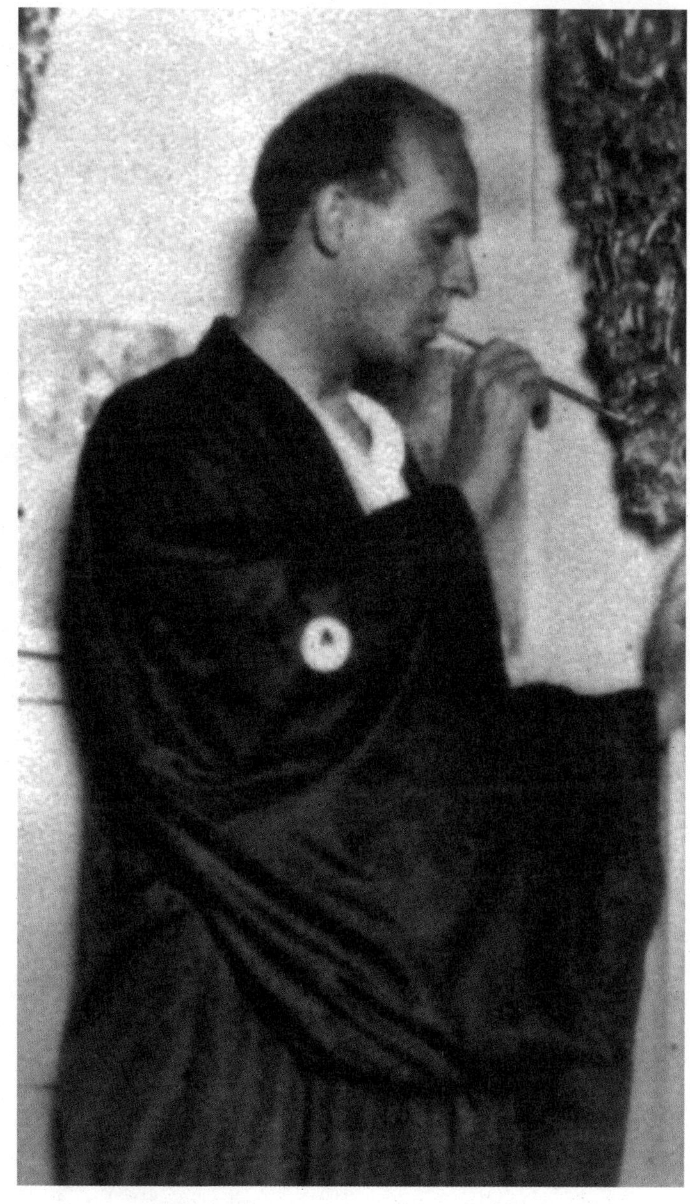

"Some worshipers of beauty find delight
In quaint and ancient things that men have made:
Gold-crusted carvings, bowls and cups of jade,"
wrote Porter Garnett in *WB in California*,
describing Witter Bynner's rooms. Like many
of his neighbors, Bynner enjoyed posing in
unconventional dress.[32]

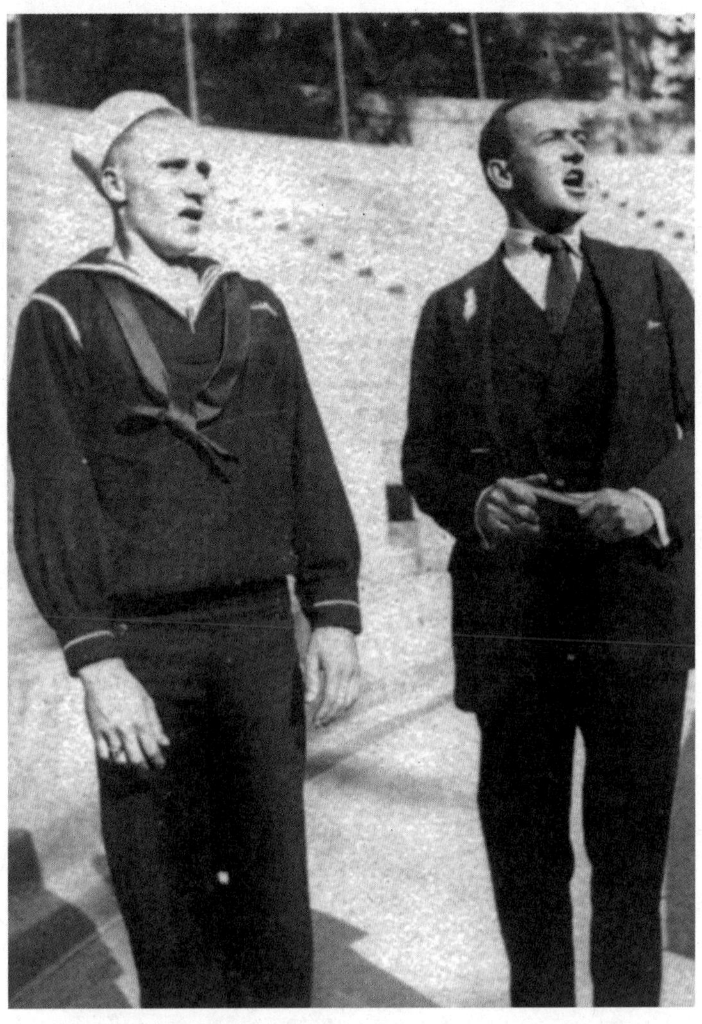

Joaquin Miller, Charles Warren Stoddard and Mary Austin were "boring" and "dead." Of Ina Coolbrith, he said, "I have heard that she is an admirable old lady, What I have seen of her work is commonplace but gentle." Only his own students (who wrote in a style that was strongly imitative of him) and the most modern of the local poets—like Bruce Porter and Yone Noguchi—were worth reading, according to Bynner.

On a more serious level, Pratt and Keeler disagreed with the content of modern poetry, not just the style. Modern artists, according to Keeler, "are in fact psychopathic schizophrenics in whom the normal standards of beauty in nature have been swept away and their grotesque fantasies have supplanted them."[19] Pratt agreed, saying that "the poet, above all men, must have within him love for his fellow man." Both Keeler and Pratt believed in a romantic style that celebrated the best in men and women, not their painful experiences.

In actuality, Bynner was almost chronically upbeat by nature, always looking for the world's beauty, but he had lived through enough trouble to realize that pain was a part of life. Bynner, like most gay people born in the late nineteenth century, struggled to reconcile his sexuality with his upbringing for most of his young manhood and only came to terms with it in middle age. In 1921, he fell in love with a Swiss artist named Paul Thévenaz, a happy man who brought ease and humor to Bynner's life, but who died at thirty-one of a ruptured appendix. One poem, which Bynner published in 1925, explained that "tradition he would set at naught/and never shed a tear."[20] (The poem shows Thévenaz's personality and also shows what Bynner thought about tradition. While it was hard to give up the comforts of knowing that one was following society's expectations, it was also freeing to do so.) By the time Bynner arrived in Berkeley, he was confident in his sexuality and showed it in his dramatic contributions to Berkeley's cultural scene. He hosted an outdoor reading in honor of Walt Whitman's one-hundredth birthday and wrote a performance for male voices to honor the end of World War I, which was recited in the Greek Theater.[21]

Bynner was also wholeheartedly against what Paul Horgan, a friend and literary critic, called the "dainty little basement bohemias" of the literary world, and to him, Pratt's readings to women's clubs were both dainty and insignificant. However, he was friendly with most of the rest of Berkeley's more vigorous bohemians.

When he arrived in Berkeley, Bynner had a job for the war effort, teaching public speaking to the military students of the Auxiliary Training Corps. The war ended almost immediately after he started the position, and the Auxiliary Training Corps was dismantled. Bynner stayed with teaching, leading a class in creative writing and verse the next semester. He often held classes outdoors, with students sprawled around him on the wide lawns of the campus. Twenty eager students and many more hangers-on attended each class, including Hildegarde Flanner, who published her first two books of poetry in the two years after taking Bynner's class, both before turning twenty-two.[22]

Bynner also set up a teatime salon for his students. He invited them to what one student called his "Chinese den," two rooms and a bath on the second floor of the Carleton Hotel that were decorated with ornaments from Bynner's travels in China and Japan. The students enjoyed this entrée into adulthood and literary genius. "Everyone I know has been/made welcome by your genial grin/to pass an hour's pleasant flight," wrote poetry student Eda Lou Walton in a tribute to her popular teacher.[23]

But the students were the only ones who liked Bynner's gatherings. Other professors were shunned for excessive socializing with students, but Bynner lost his job. He was reprimanded by Charles Mills Gayley, the head of the English department, who said that "at no time and under no circumstances should alcoholic beverages be offered to students, whether graduate or undergraduate—especially freshmen."

The next semester, Bynner's contract was not renewed. He stayed in Berkeley for a few months and then decided to go back to China, where he traveled with the sculptor Benjamin Bufano.

The trip to China was the result of Bynner's most important poetic accomplishment during his years in Berkeley. He collaborated with poet Kiang Kang-Hu to translate Kiang's work, resulting in a volume that is still critically praised.

Like Bynner, Kiang was an instructor at the University of California. Wellborn and well educated, he had been a newspaper editor and university professor in his native China and then was made a political refugee after setbacks in the Chinese revolution of 1913. In a 1917 essay, Kiang claimed to have started China's first socialist club in 1911, influenced by the "revolutionary ideas" of novelists and poets from the West. His revolutionary literary thoughts started with the ideas of "Balzac, Victor Hugo, of Byron and Shelley, of Dickens and Mark Twain . . . and, later on, of Kropotkin, Marx, Engels and Bebel."[24] Kiang believed deeply in the political and social power of literature, a belief that he shared with the rest of Berkeley's literary figures. And like Bynner and the leaders of the California Writer's Movement, Kiang helped create a support structure for future writers. Before moving to a better job in Canada, Kiang donated the books that became the core of the university's Asian library.

After returning from China, Bynner traveled around the country on a lecture tour, looking for somewhere to live. In 1922, he settled in Santa Fe, New Mexico, with a former U.C. student with literary aspirations of his own, Walter Willard Johnson, called Spud. Officially, Spud was Witter Bynner's secretary and unofficially his lover.

Santa Fe was one of the emerging hotbeds of American bohemia in the 1920s, home to painters, writers and socialites. One of the socialites was Mabel Gansen Evans Dodge Sterne Luhan (she had four husbands), who introduced Bynner and Spud to English writer D. H. Lawrence, who was visiting the town. Lawrence soon invited them to travel through Mexico with him and his wife, setting the ground for a years-long friendship and for a jealous rivalry with Mabel Luhan, who eventually stole Spud away from Bynner, establishing him as her secretary in Taos.

Bynner loved New Mexico, even running for state legislature one year. After Spud left, Bynner had a string of young male secretaries, some who were lovers and some who were not. In 1931, his friend Robert Hunt arrived in Santa Fe for a visit and stayed until Bynner died in 1968. Their relationship was a marriage in every sense but the legal one, although the handsome Hunt was twenty-five years younger than Bynner. Finally, at age forty-nine, Bynner was able to declare his sexuality to the world. He kept in touch with many of his Berkeley friends, like Samuel Hume, who wrote chatty letters encouraging him to visit Berkeley and act in one of Hume's masques.[25] Another friend, Albert Stern of San Francisco, promised that "whenever you come you can be sure we will do everything we can for you." Stern also kept Bynner in the Bay Area loop by introducing him to Ansel and Virginia Adams, "the two thinnest and hungriest souls alive," who visited Santa Fe that spring. He explained that "I am trying to divide up the heavy responsibility resting on the larder of our dear friend Mary Coolidge" and said, "The better you feed them, the better they will sing and play and take pictures for you."[26]

DANE COOLIDGE

Dane Coolidge was one of Bynner's Berkeley friends referred to above and had known Bynner for nearly thirteen years when Bynner first arrived in Berkeley. Bynner first published Coolidge's story "Bull-Bat" in *McClure's Magazine* in New York, a proceeding that was so successful that Bynner said of it, "I agree with you if I can pass muster that there is 'a blood-brotherhood between us from the land of hidden spirits' and I shall be glad of every token of its existence."[27] In 1908, Bynner had moved on to Small, Maynard and Company publishers, and clearly wanted to maintain the network of writers he had worked with at *McClure's*. He wrote to Coolidge, "I have never forgotten you and the delightful 'Bull-Bat,'" urging him to submit a manuscript, which he did.[28]

Like his more successful neighbor, Jack London, who often published in the same magazines, Coolidge used his youthful experiences and travels to make his stories more authentic. (Unfortunately, unlike London, Coolidge apparently never had the talent to create serious literature. Witter Bynner pointed out that, while Coolidge could create wonderful settings and adventures, his characters were completely two-dimensional.) Coolidge started as "the Boy Naturalist" of Riverside, California, and worked his way through Stanford by writing adventure stories for boys.

After graduating in 1898, Coolidge studied at Harvard and traveled on long expeditions to Mexico, Arizona, Nevada, Italy and France every summer, trapping animals for natural history museums. He eventually settled in San Francisco and, like many San Franciscans, ended up in Berkeley after his home was destroyed in the 1906 earthquake. His obituary said that he joked about the "blessing" of the earthquake, which helped push his writing career. "I came to Berkeley and got a fresh start."[29]

Part of his fresh start was a new relationship. A few months after the earthquake, he married one of his former Stanford professors, Mary Roberts Smith, whose job at a San Francisco settlement house was destroyed by the quake. She was thirteen years older than he and nearly as driven. Like the Londons, the Coolidges had a companionate and physical marriage. She joined him on his horseback trips through the Southwest, bringing her sociological training to his nonfiction books. When Mary Coolidge's friend Clelia Mosher was conducting a survey of women's attitudes towards sex, she wrote that relations with Dane were much better than those with her first husband. She had not particularly

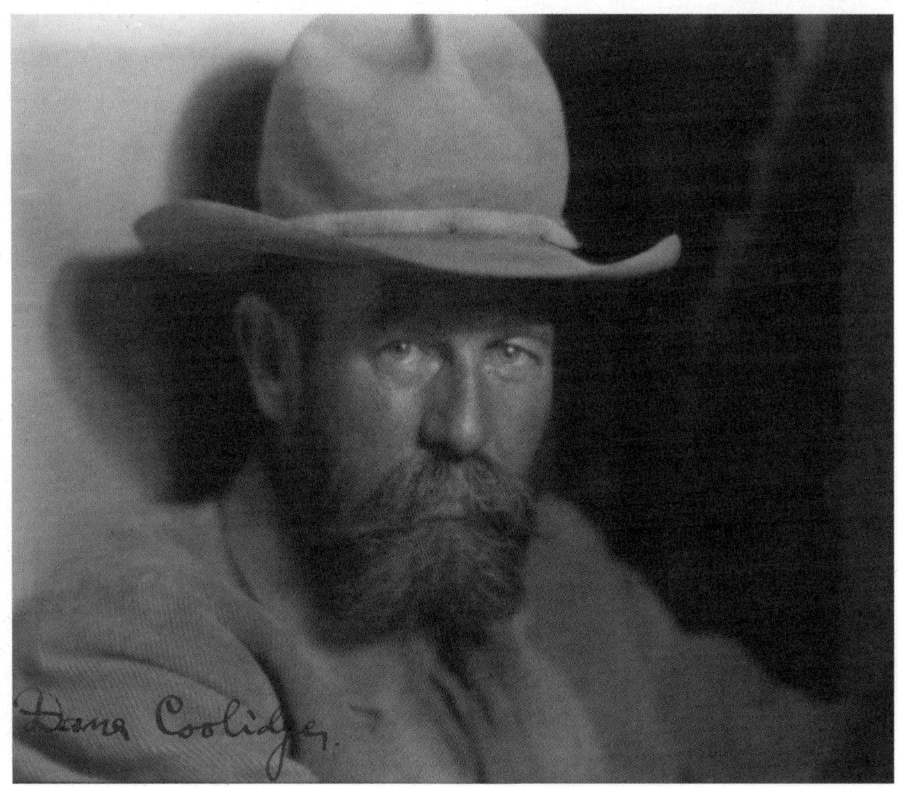

enjoyed sex with her first husband, but she liked the twice-weekly intimacies with Dane, attributing her enjoyment to his (relatively) youthful athleticism.

Even a successful writer like Dane Coolidge needed all the support the Berkeley literary scene could offer. Coolidge left less than $10,000 worth of property when he died in 1940, an amount that was so small as to make the newspaper headlines.[30]

The most famous authors in the Bay Area, George Sterling, Jack London and Mary Austin, found rewards, both spiritual and material, wherever they went. Most of the East Bay's writers, on the other hand, were more like Coolidge, constantly short of

Research trips through the desert made Dane Coolidge as rugged and sunburned as one of the characters from his many novels.

money and dependent on networks like the California Writer's Club. Charles Keeler and Harry Noyes Pratt, both presidents of the club, took odd jobs to support their writing.

Despite this, writers had the community's support of literary expression as an important and respectable path in life. Berkeley's literary community included writers of all kinds, from the academic studies coming out of the university to the newspaper gossip columns that reported on poets. Organizations like the Poet's Dinner and the California Writer's Club were relatively open to members of different backgrounds and encouraged a wide range of people to start writing. They recognized that writers needed both companionship and material aid and supported them through publishing and jobs. Other organizations offered support to writers, too, such as the women's clubs that sponsored readings and lectures that allowed writers to reach larger audiences, or the university, which taught young writers like Hildegard Flanner.

In 1941, the passion of Berkeley's writers for creating and self-publishing found a fitting outlet in *Musings of a Merchant*, the poetry of Lester Hink, the owner of Hink's Department Store on Shattuck Avenue. *Musings of a Merchant* started as a limited edition of five hundred copies but went through at least six printings. Thanks to the work of Harry Noyes Pratt and others, anyone in Berkeley could be a poet, and oftentimes, everyone was.

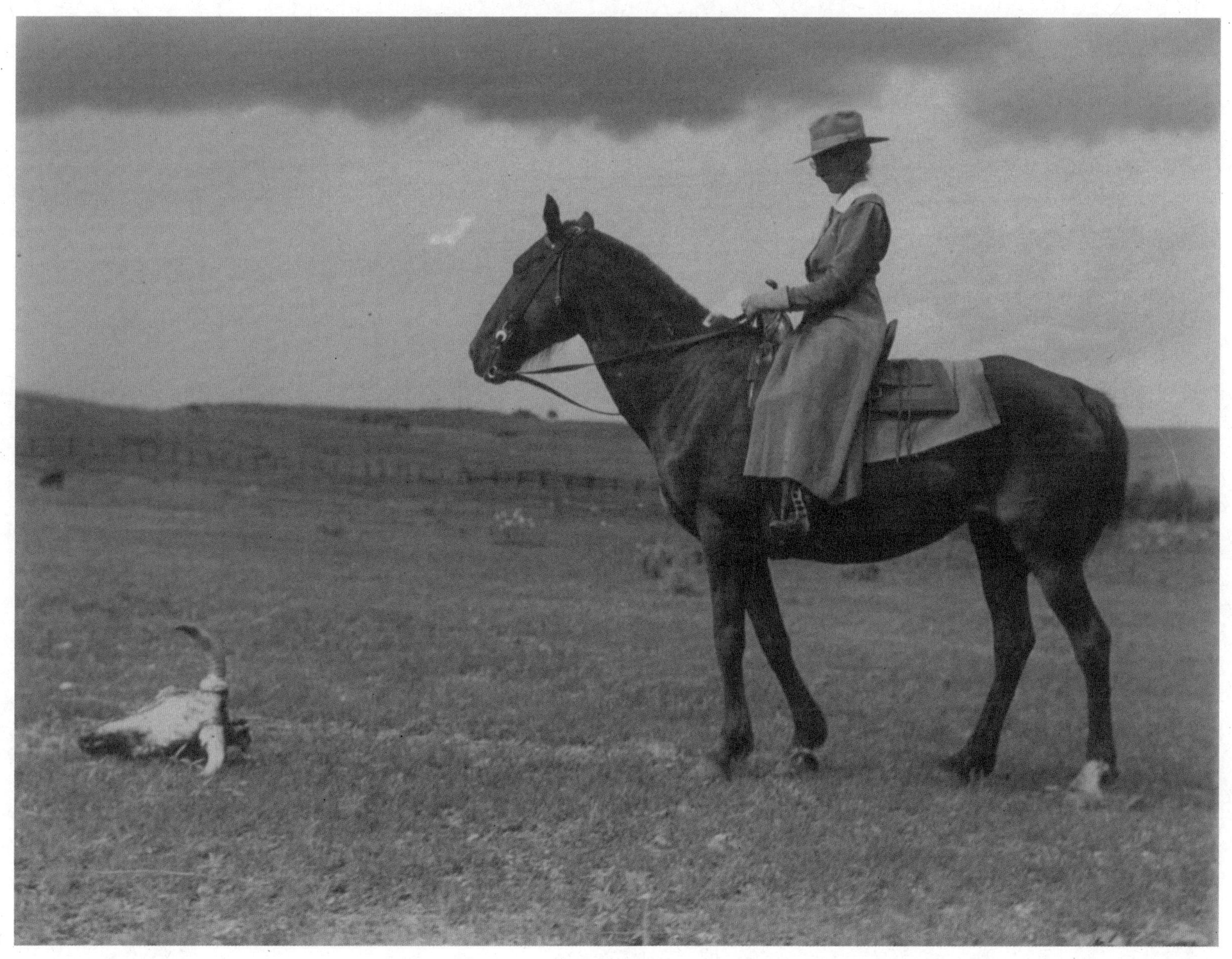

Sociologist Mary Roberts Coolidge joined her husband on his research trips and collaborated with him on his nonfiction works.

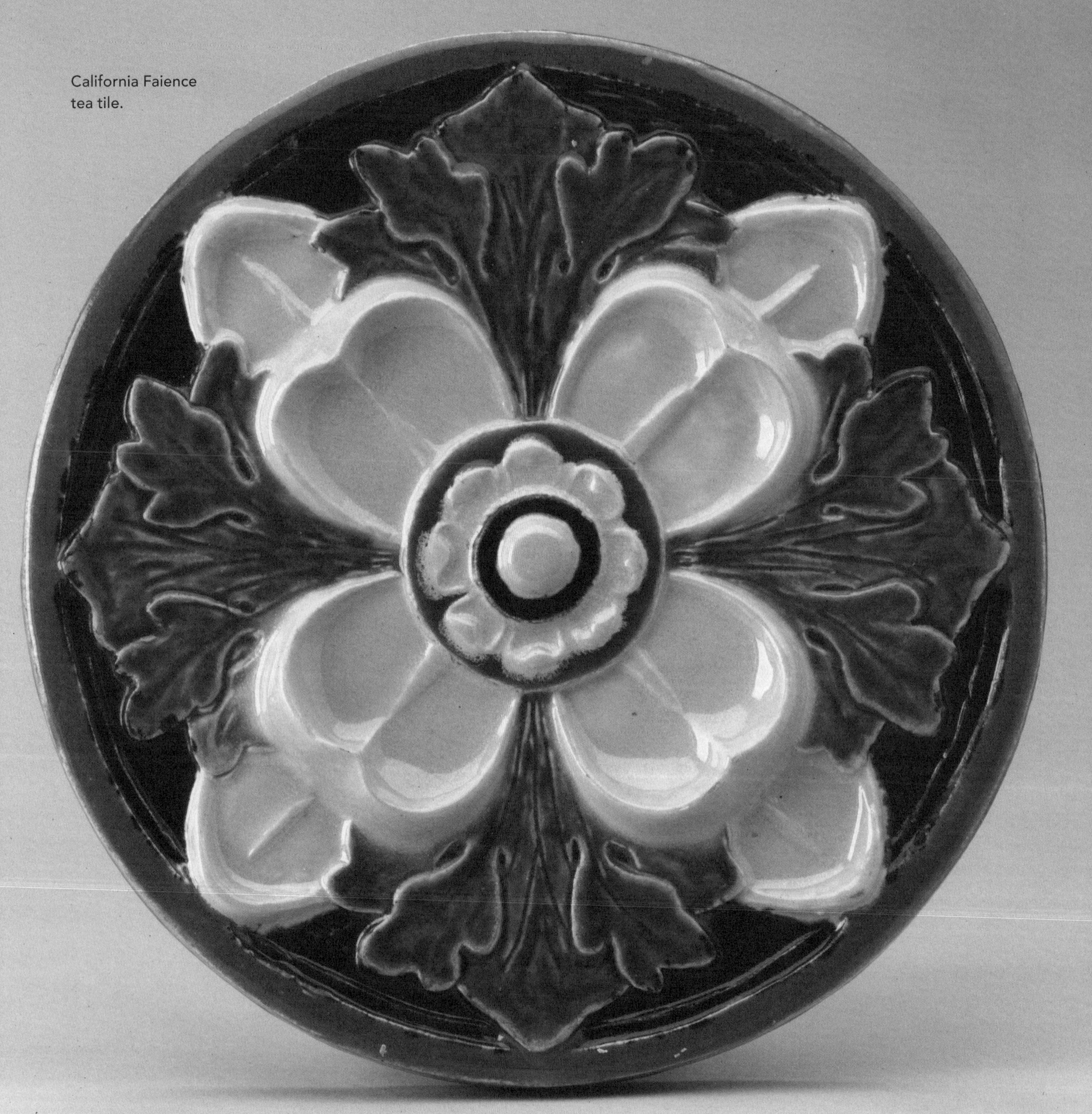

California Faience
tea tile.

crafted by Hand—
The founding of CCAC

The history of the Arts and Crafts movement in the San Francisco Bay Area began with the establishment of the Guild of Arts and Crafts of San Francisco in 1894, the first Arts and Crafts society in the United States. The Arts and Crafts movement had begun a decade earlier in England as a reformist movement in opposition to the worst excesses of the Industrial Revolution and decried the production of cheaply made mass-produced goods. The movement promoted handcrafted items created with authentic and meaningful design and was inspired by the writings of John Ruskin and William Morris.

In Berkeley, Charles Keeler founded the Ruskin Club in 1895, and in 1898, several Berkeley women organized the Hillside Club to protect their neighborhood from the building of "unsuitable and disfiguring houses."

Art education in the Bay Area at this time was centered at the Mark Hopkins Institute of Art in San Francisco. Established in 1893, it was headed, during most of its existence, by painter Arthur F. Mathews and offered courses in painting, drawing, sculpture and related fine arts subjects. Courses and degrees in the fine arts were also offered by the University of California and other local colleges. There were, however, no local institutions that specialized in teaching the crafts and the decorative arts.

In 1906, the San Francisco earthquake and fire completely destroyed the Mark Hopkins Institute of Art. This tragedy created a great void in art education for the entire region.

The Guild of Arts and Crafts of San Francisco had disappeared a few years after its beginning, the victim of internal squabbling among its artist members. In 1903, a new group

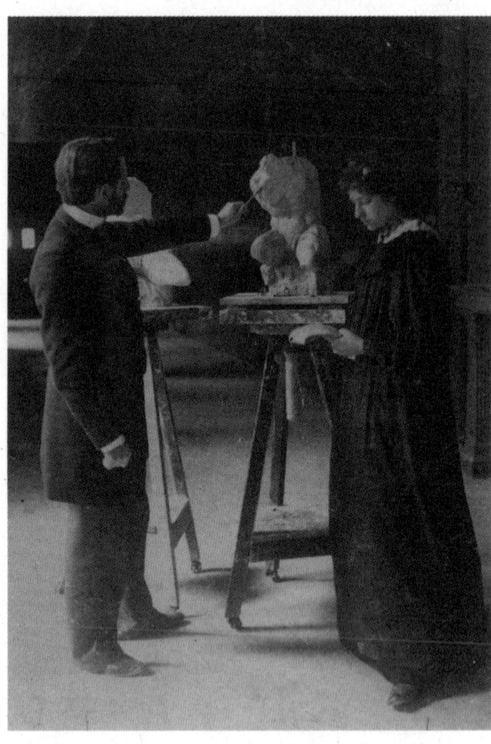

Sculptor Douglas Tilden instructing Laura Adams at the Mark Hopkins Institute of Art in San Francisco.

called the California Guild of Arts and Crafts had been formed.

Shortly after the earthquake and fire, Frederick H. Meyer, an art teacher, furniture designer and member of this new organization, made a statement at a dinner that would prove seminal in the establishment of the California College of Arts and Crafts. This is his description of the event:

After the San Francisco Fire, I attended a dinner at the Arts and Crafts society California Guild of Arts and Crafts of which I was President. We were asked to speak five minutes on what we would like to be doing instead of what we were doing. I spoke about my idea of a practical art school, one whose graduates would earn a comfortable living and instead of teaching only subjects like figure and landscape painting, sculpture, etc., to teach design, mechanical drawing, commercial art, and the crafts, as well as teacher training. Unknown to me, a newspaper feature writer from the *Call* was present and wrote up these ideas in the paper, ending the story, "This is the idea of an Art School, by F. H. Meyer." [1]

There was an immediate public response to the newspaper article. Many of the former students of the Mark Hopkins Institute, now without a school, expressed interest in enrolling in Meyer's new school, if it were created. This strong support for his idea gave Meyer the impetus to seriously formulate a plan to implement it. He initially chose three of his colleagues to help him start his new Arts and Crafts school: Laetitia Meyer, his wife, and artists Perham Nahl and Isabelle Percy West.

FREDERICK H. MEYER Frederick H. Meyer was born in 1872 near Hamelin, Germany (setting for the Pied Piper fairy tale). His father was a forest warden, but one of his uncles was a "maker of fine furniture." Meyer learned the art of cabinetmaking from him and became proficient at it by age fifteen. In 1888, he visited another uncle in Fresno, California, and decided to stay and become a U.S. citizen. He was naturalized in 1893.

Meyer decided to make art his career and enrolled at San Jose Normal School. This school did not offer much art education, so he transferred to the Cincinnati Technical School. Ill health caused him to leave Cincinnati, and he next attended the Pennsylvania Museum and School of Industrial Art. Again Meyer's health caused him to withdraw and this time he went back to Germany and enrolled in the Royal Art School. This new setting produced no health problems; Meyer graduated in 1896 and then returned to the United States.

Meyer once again enrolled in the Pennsylvania Museum and School of Industrial Art and graduated in 1897. He then went back to California, where he worked for an architect in San Jose. He next moved to San Francisco, where he taught at the Lick School and simultaneously worked evenings, illustrating for the *San Francisco Chronicle*. In 1898, he moved to Stockton where he became art supervisor for the Stockton Public Schools. There, he met and married Laetitia Summerville, a fellow schoolteacher, in 1902.

The couple moved to San Francisco in 1903, and Frederick opened a cabinet shop, where he designed and made his own furniture. He was soon teaching again, this time in two different locations: the University of California at Berkeley and the Mark Hopkins Institute. He taught cabinetmaking to other professors at the university, and they built furniture for the Men's Faculty Club that, unfortunately, was disposed of when the club was remodeled in 1958.

During the years immediately preceding the 1906 earthquake, Meyer joined and became president of the California Guild of Arts and Crafts. In the months after the earthquake, when Arthur Mathews opened his furniture shop in San Francisco, he hired Meyer as one of his designers in the cabinet shop. At this time, Meyer resigned his teaching job at the university. In August 1906, his new employer sent him on a business trip to New York, Germany, Norway and Sweden to see firsthand the "modern" furniture being produced. He returned in October 1906, but soon his full energy became focused on planning for the creation of the new art school, and he was forced to give up his position at the furniture shop.

By the following summer, with the help of his three cofounders, Meyer had made his new school a reality and served as its president until his retirement in 1944. He continued to regularly visit his beloved school until his death in 1961. He was and is remembered very fondly by those who studied and worked with him. One of his many extra-curricular activities was the supervision of gardening on the Oakland campus. He had a vast knowledge of exotic plants and was constantly adding new ones to the grounds. His zeal in this area was so well known and respected by the community that he was contacted whenever a local estate was being demolished to inquire whether he wanted any of the rare plants to be saved and transplanted at his college. He did this as a means of providing a more inspirational setting for his art students. This is but one example of his personal commitment to the ongoing task of providing the best possible environment for his school.

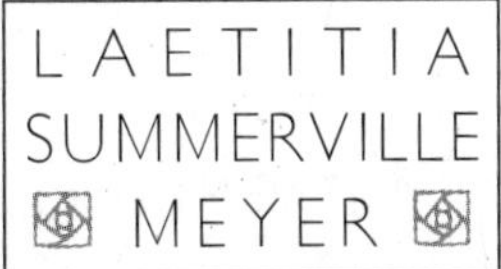

Laetitia Summerville was born in Boston, Massachusetts, in 1860. Her father had been a blacksmith in Northern Ireland and continued his trade when the family moved to Stockton, California. After Laetitia's parents died, she became the head of her family, raising her sisters and brothers as well as two nieces. She helped guide their lives until they finished their education. They all made significant achievements in their education, perhaps foreshadowing Laetitia's abilities as an academic leader. In 1879, Laetitia graduated from high school in Stockton and became a schoolteacher. Like many teachers, she took summer school courses to further her own education. Among these was painting, at which she excelled. She met Frederick Meyer while both were teaching in Stockton, and they were married in 1902.

Once married, Laetitia devoted herself to helping Frederick realize his dream of founding and operating a new style of art school. Her assistance ranged from organizing his work to putting his plans into operation to doing his laundry to making his appointments and seeing that he kept them. She single-handedly organized and ran the art school. This included handling the books, money, admissions and registration for both the day and evening classes.

She was described as a very attractive woman in her youth, but she is remembered most for her dynamic personality. On the surface, she had a stern and rigid bearing, the counterpart to warm and emotional Frederick. One former student described her manner: "She had great dignity and she believed in dignity as a thing in itself, as something to be cultivated and she lived and dressed the part. She had very strong ideas and ideals."[2] However, those who came to know her well found that she was a very warmhearted person. Perhaps the Meyers' daughter summed it up best when she said of her mother, Laetitia, "It was my father's inspiration of course, but the school could never have carried on without her."[3]

PERHAM NAHL

Perham Nahl was born in San Francisco in 1869. He came from a family that had produced artists and sculptors for three centuries. His uncle was Charles Christian Nahl, one of California's greatest Gold Rush–era painters. His father was Arthur Nahl, also a famous artist, who, among his many accomplishments, designed the California State Seal. Growing up in a family where virtually everyone was an artist must have been both a blessing and a curse. It was the custom for the family to provide its children with quite rigid training in art from an early age. While this family background must have been very stimulating, it is likely to have its downside in the form of frequent criticism and comparison from and with other family members. As a young man, Perham studied both painting and lithography in the shop of his father and uncle. He also served an apprenticeship with watercolorist H. W. Hansen and worked at the printing and lithography shop of H. S. Crocker.

He attended the Mark Hopkins Institute of Art from 1899 to 1906. There he acquired the affectionate nickname of "Pops" from his fellow students, alluding to the fact that he was married, a father, and thirty years old upon entering the school. His already-recognized talent enabled him to win scholarships in painting, drawing, design and composition. Somehow, he also managed to find time to work for the *San Francisco Chronicle* while pursuing his studies. It was during this time that he met and befriended Frederick Meyer and Xavier Martinez. These

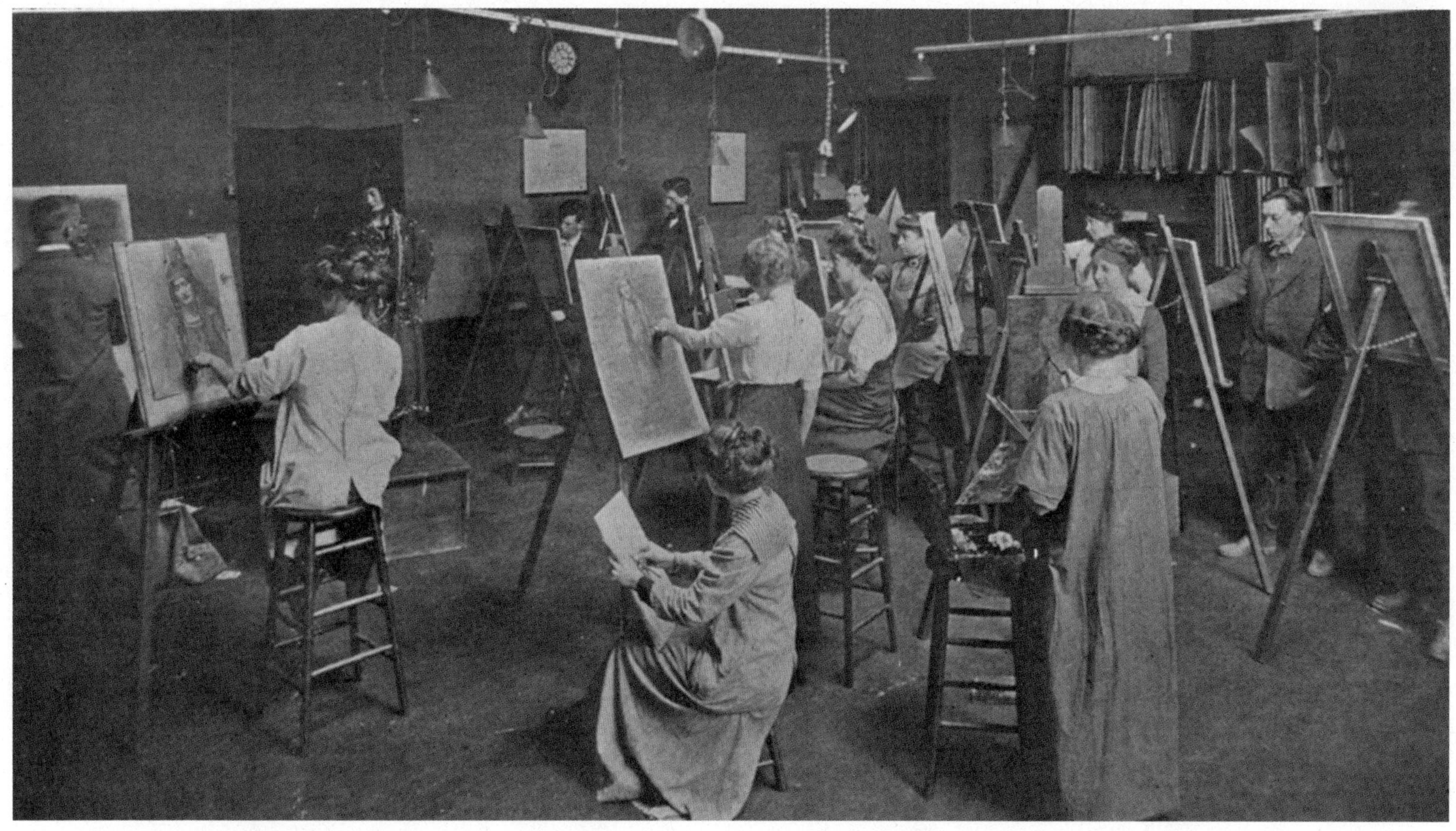

three were frequently seen together at such "bohemian" haunts as Coppa's restaurant.

In January 1906, Benjamin Ide Wheeler, president of the University of California at Berkeley, hired Nahl as a drawing instructor, and he held this post until June, when he resigned in order to pursue his art education in Europe. Nahl arrived in Europe in August, spent several months studying in Munich and Paris, and was back in the San Francisco Bay Area in May 1907. By the end of June, Nahl, along with Frederick and Laetitia Meyer, opened the first summer session of their new art school in Berkeley, where Nahl continued to teach for the next twenty years.

Perham Nahl's greatest talent was drawing, and, not surprisingly, it was also his favorite subject to teach. He taught freehand drawing, antique drawing, life drawing and sketching. His students praised him as an effective teacher.

Harry Dixon, one of Nahl's teaching colleagues, relates that the class most enjoyed by the male students was Nahl's life drawing class. When the model was a woman, the men would be on their best behavior; but when the model was a man, there was

Class sketching from draped figure at the California School of Arts and Crafts.

an unending telling of risqué stories and off-color jokes that was accompanied by raucous laughter. The noise was audible through much of the building on Allston Way, and a succession of people would peek in to see what the commotion was about. These incidents sometimes incurred the disapproval of Frederick Meyer, who did not think that teaching could proceed under such circumstances. However, Harry Dixon insists that the students kept working steadily and never missed a stroke.

In 1913, Nahl was hired as an assistant professor in the art department of the University of California but managed to continue teaching at both schools. One of his more interesting projects during this period was the design for the official poster for the Panama-Pacific International Exposition in San Francisco. His design, entitled "The Thirteenth Labor of Hercules," portrayed the mythic hero forcing apart the continents of North and South America to make room for the Panama Canal. In 1927, he gave up teaching at the School of Arts and Crafts but continued at the university until his death in 1935.

ISABELLE PERCY WEST

Isabelle Percy West was born in Alameda, California, in 1883. Her father was a successful San Francisco architect who designed several of the buildings at Stanford University and the Academy of Sciences Building in Golden Gate Park. Isabelle spent her early childhood in Oakland, attending its public schools. At the age of fourteen, she was sent to finishing school in Maine and, at the age of seventeen, returned to California after her father's death in 1900. Her father had wanted her to be an architect and had instructed her in her childhood in such things as drawing Greek columns.

From 1901 through 1905, she was a student at the Mark Hopkins Institute of Art in San Francisco. During her time there, she met Perham Nahl, a fellow student, and Frederick Meyer, an instructor. In 1901, she rented her father's former architectural office in San Francisco as an art studio. Owing to her studies and other obligations, she was only able to spend Saturdays there. On Saturday nights, she and her student friends would go to local restaurants including Coppa's, San Francisco's premiere bohemian meeting place. There she had the opportunity to meet and speak with fellow artists like "Marty" Martinez and writers such as Gelett Burgess, Bruce Porter and George Sterling. After a time, Isabelle was even allowed the honor of painting a mural on one of Coppa's walls.

In 1905, she traveled to Massachusetts to study at the Ipswich Summer School of Art under Arthur Wesley Dow, whose work became a major influence in her art. Dow, who had published the book *Composition* in 1899, had revolutionized the teaching of art in America through his synthesis of Japanese techniques and the principles of the Arts and Crafts movement. Dow was impressed with Isabelle's talent and persuaded her to enroll in the graduate course at the Teachers College at Columbia

University in the fall, where he was director of the Fine Arts Department. Isabelle's mother then rented out the family home in Oakland and moved her family to New York City. Their temporary home near Columbia became a meeting place for many of the school's interesting people. After the first year, her mother returned to Oakland, and Isabelle shared an apartment with a friend who was in the theatre.

In 1906, after a year at Columbia, Isabelle traveled to Europe where she continued her art studies in England and Belgium. She returned to Columbia in 1907 and completed her Master of Arts degree. She then moved back to California, just in time to help co-found the College of Arts and Crafts in Berkeley. After teaching there for a year and a half, she went back to Columbia for a semester of special classes and then on to Europe to take an art class from Alexander Robinson. During this trip, she also found time to study lithography in Germany. In 1912, one of her paintings was exhibited at the Paris Salon. She returned to the United States in 1913 and exhibited her European work in several American cities. In 1914, she went back to California and soon opened a studio in the Montgomery Block of San Francisco. During this period, she worked with landscape painter Lucy Valentine Pierce, creating painted furniture.

In 1916, she met and married newspaper editor George P. West. The couple moved to an apartment in Greenwich Village in New York City and remained there until 1919. In this East Coast center of

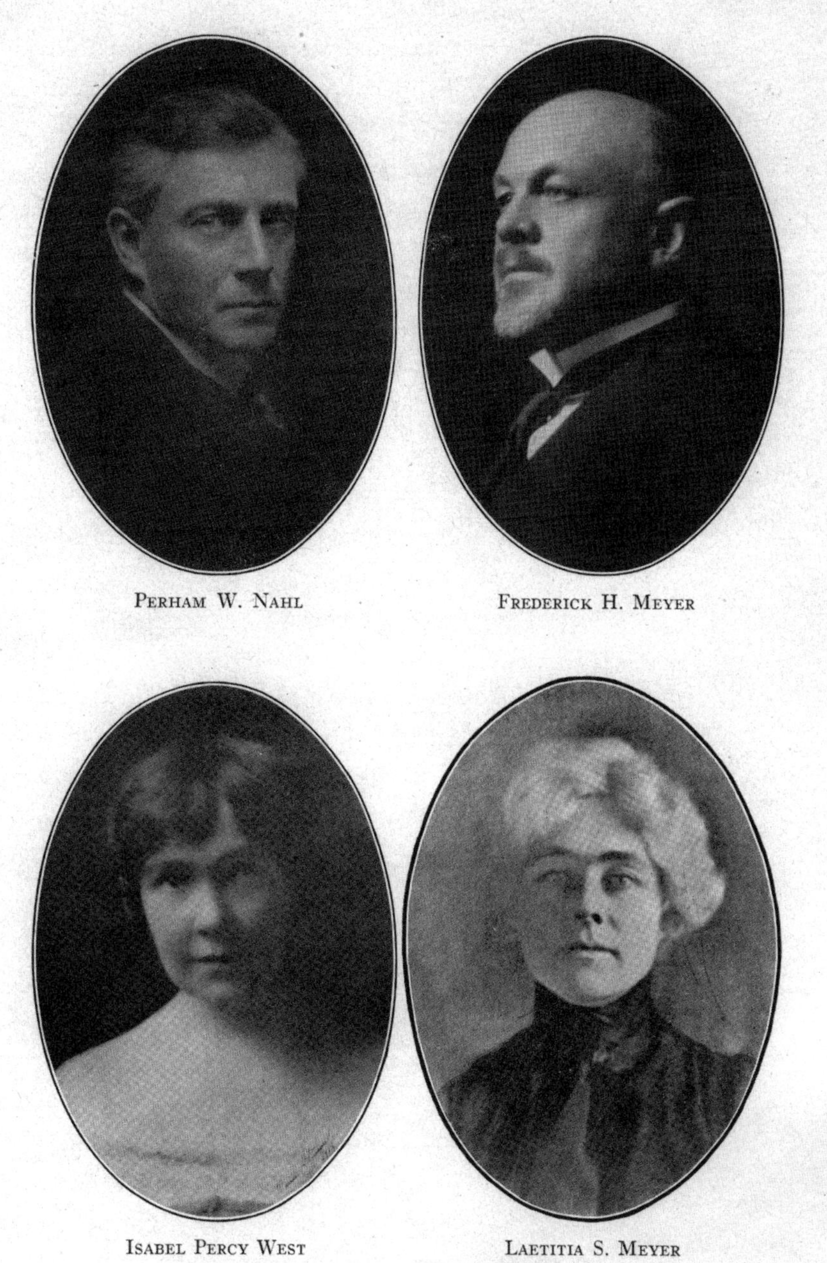

The four founders of the California School of Arts and Crafts: Frederick H. Meyer, Laetitia Summerville Meyer, Perham Nahl and Isabelle Percy West.

bohemianism, the couple counted among their friends John Dos Passos, Jacob Epstein, Ben Hecht, Sinclair Lewis, Walter Lippmann, H. L. Mencken, Carl Sandburg, Upton Sinclair, Gertrude Stein and many others.

In 1920, the couple moved back to California and built a house in Sausalito. Isabelle designed the home and supervised its construction. Her father would have been proud of her efforts. George worked for the *San Francisco Call-Bulletin* and the *San Francisco News*. In 1921, she returned to teaching at the School of Arts and Crafts in Berkeley. Her courses in design were heavily influenced by her studies with Arthur Dow. Students recalled how, for many years, she commuted from her home in Sausalito to the college in Oakland in her electric car with curtains on the window. She continued to teach there until 1941, when she retired. At that time, the school named a gallery in her honor. She continued to paint until her death in 1976.

XAVIER MARTINEZ Xavier Martinez was born in Guadalajara, Mexico, in 1869. His father had a bookstore but spent most of his time creating fine-tooled leather bindings. As Xavier was growing up, he had access to his father's splendid books. At a young age, he began to read and appreciate the poetry of Goethe, Schiller, Heine and some of the French poets whose works were translated into Spanish.

He began painting and drawing at the age of ten. An artist cousin of his father's taught him how to mix his own paints and paint frescoes. He also studied art and graduated from the Liceo de Varonese in Guadalajara in 1890. He attended the university in Guadalajara but did not graduate. While there, he was active in student politics and supplied the illustrations for one of the student political weeklies.

After his mother died during his adolescence, a wealthy and influential woman, Rosalia Sebastida de Coney, helped Martinez. In 1893, he joined the Coneys in San Francisco, California, where Rosalia's husband was consul general of Mexico to San Francisco.

Martinez then became a student at the Mark Hopkins Institute of Art on a trial basis for one year. Due to his lack of proficiency in English, he did not do well, and at the end of the year, Arthur Mathews, director of the school, suggested to Martinez' foster father, *señor* Coney, that he leave the school and not continue in art. Rosalia intervened, and was able to arrange for Martinez to enroll for another year. Fortunately, his understanding of English improved, and he immediately began to excel in all his studies. By the end of the year he had achieved top honors, and Mathews made him his assistant.

Soon Martinez began to be favorably noticed by the local critics. One newspaper article, "San Francisco Illustrators—Curbstone Bohemia," in the *Overland Monthly*, stated, "The most promising rising young illustrator in San Francisco is Mr. X. Martinez, from whose pen I give four sketches. There is more true art and feeling in these sketches than in any others published in this article."[4]

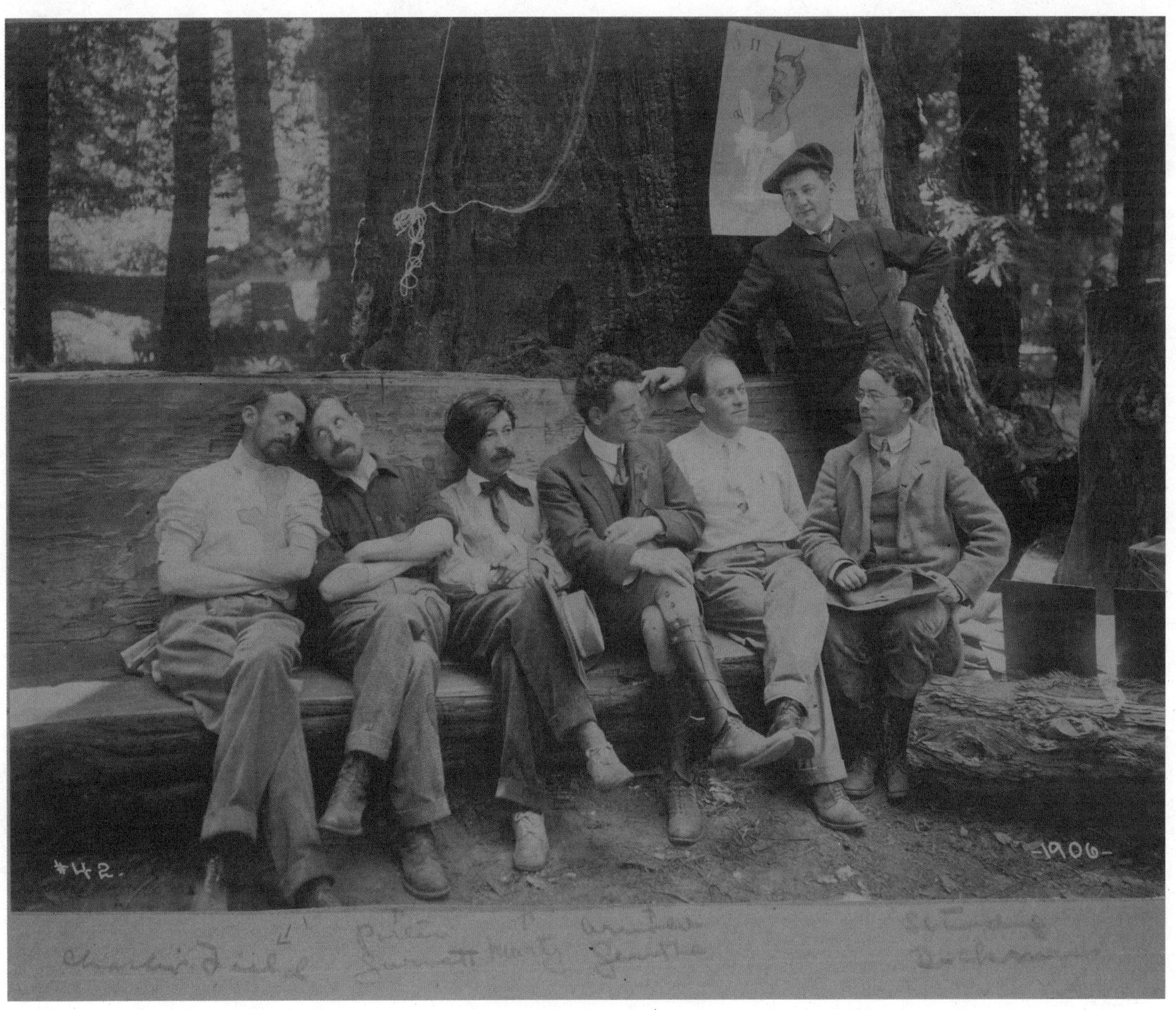

Xavier Martinez (third from the left) and friends at the Bohemian Grove; on his right is Porter Garnett, on his left is Arnold Genthe.

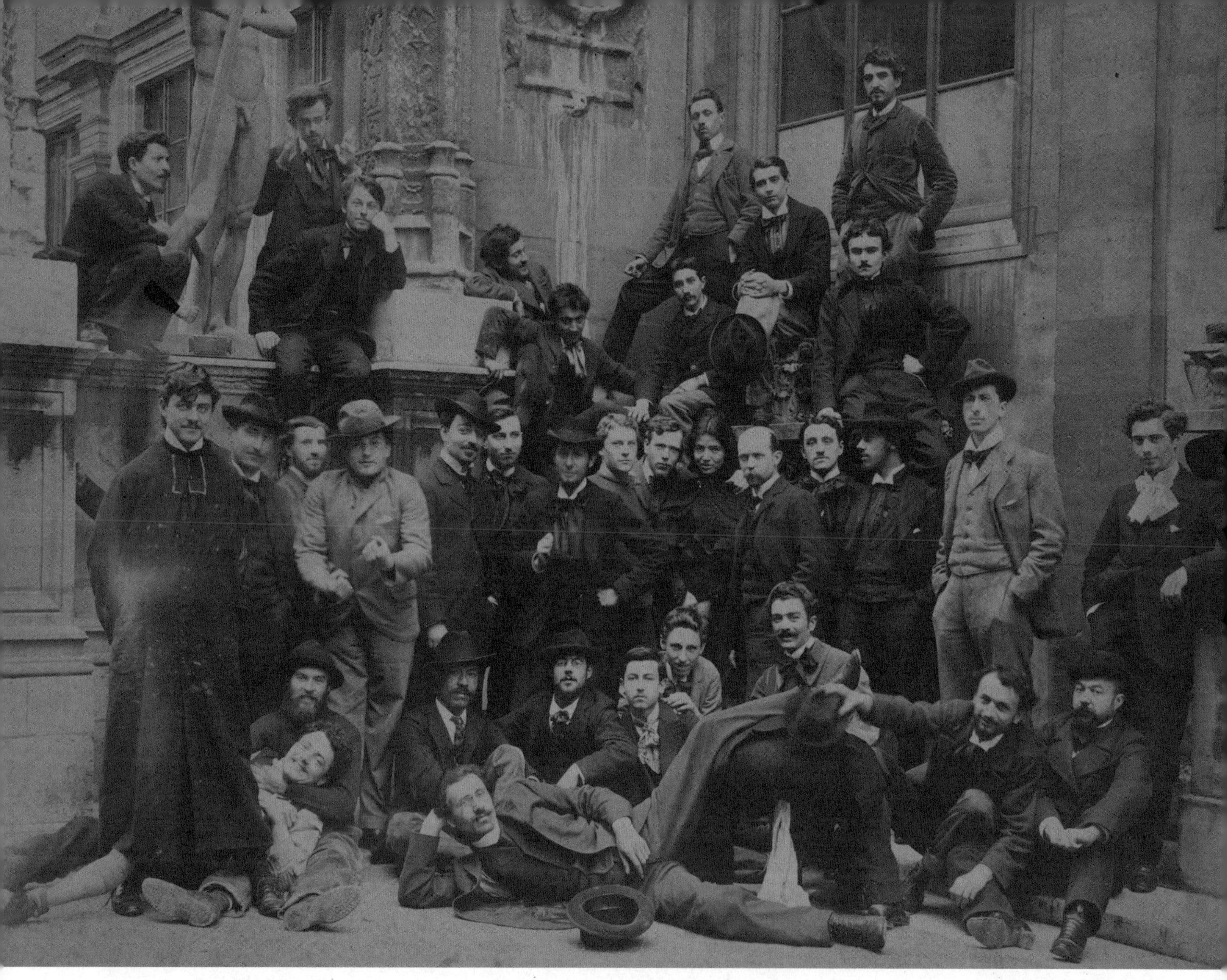

Xavier Martinez and his fellow students of the Ecole des Beaux-Arts in Paris, ca. 1895–1900. Martinez is seated in the front row, second from the left.

In 1895, with the support of his foster mother, Martinez went to Paris. There he studied at the École des Beaux-Arts and the Acadamie Carriere under Gerome and Whistler. In his free time, he was immersed in the bohemian life of Paris of the 1890s. Among his companions were artists Toulouse-Lautrec and Cézanne, and Martinez claimed to have drunk absinthe with Verlaine. Eugene Carriere, noted symbolist painter, is quoted as saying to Martinez, "If you have the courage to remain and starve for six to ten years more I promise you that your name shall be known all over the world."[5] Martinez didn't take the dare. He exhibited three paintings in the Paris Exposition of 1900 and then returned to San Francisco.

Once back in California, Martinez became involved with the local art scene. He was an active member of the Bohemian Club. His personal scrapbooks have many pictures of him posed in groups of his artist friends at their annual Bohemian Grove outings.

He rented a studio in the Montgomery Block, where many of his artistic and literary colleagues would come by and visit. These included Jack London, George Sterling, Gelett Burgess, Porter Garnett, Arnold Genthe, Ambrose Bierce and Joaquin Miller. In the basement of one part of the "Monkey Block" was the original Coppa's Restaurant. Martinez and his bohemian friends were among the regulars here. Martinez painted a frieze of black cats high up on its walls and, underneath, portraits of famous and not-so-famous artists and writers.

On the eve of the 1906 earthquake, Martinez and his friends were out carousing till four-thirty in the morning. When he returned to his studio, he was trying to decide whether to stay up or go to bed when the earthquake struck. He immediately took refuge under a doorjamb and at that moment a brick wall collapsed on his bed. The lesson he took from this experience was that his carousing had saved his life, since if he had been home asleep in his bed, he would have been killed.

The "Monkey Block" survived the fire, but it was heavily damaged. Among the losses were the murals in Coppa's. About a week after the tragedy, some of its denizens decided to hold a kind of wake for the place; they called it the "last supper." An account of this memorable bohemian event is related here:

One night while the great fire was still smoldering, the little crowd of Bohemians, to whom Coppa's restaurant was a second home, gathered there to bid farewell to the old place forever. . . . The food and drink—even the water for the coffee—had to be brought over from Oakland. Permission was secured from Colonel Clem to have candlelight and the soldiers who were bivouacking in the street had orders to allow the party to remain as long as they liked. This proved one of the merriest feasts ever held at Coppa's. An occasional slight earthquake tremor would send the

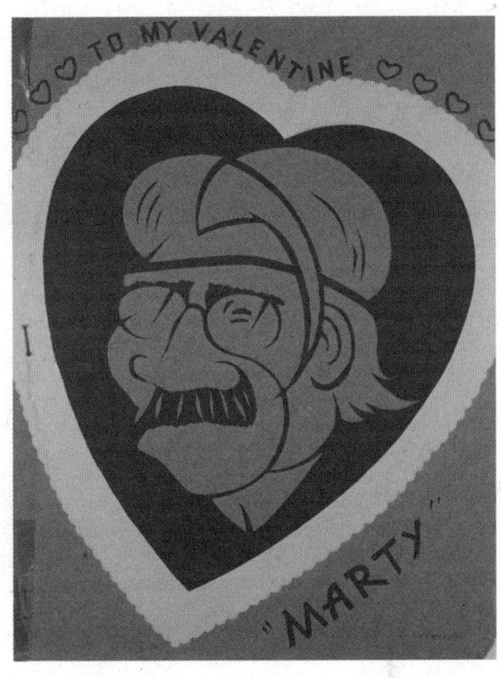

A valentine of Xavier "Marty" Martinez.

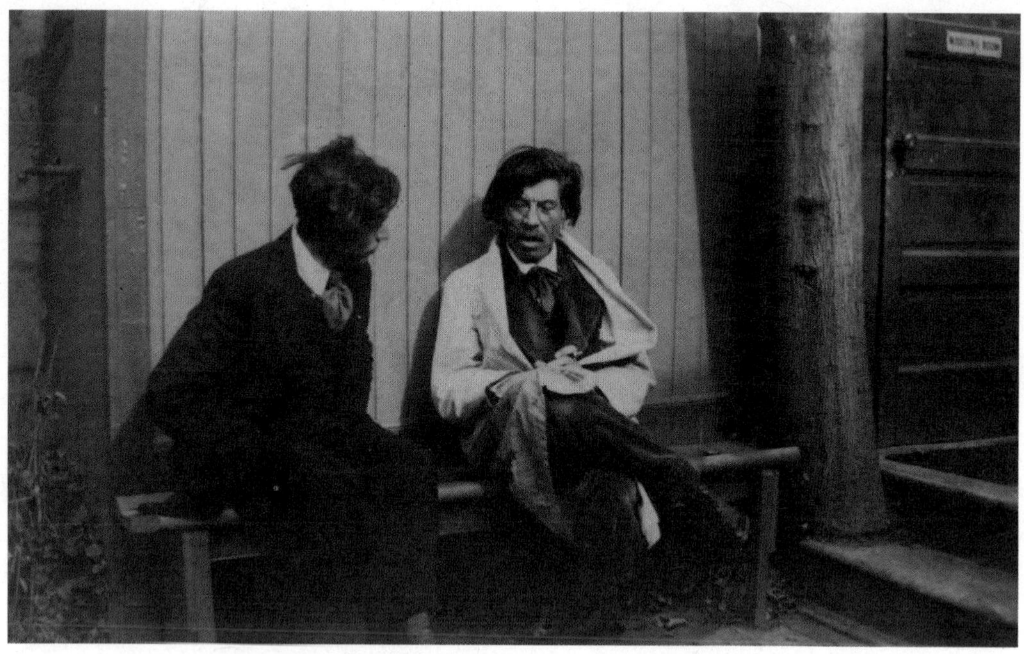

Xavier Martinez and sculptor Beniamino Bufano at the California School of Arts and Crafts, 1922.

girls into the street with their hearts fluttering but they always returned and the wit flowed like precious wine then so scarce in the burned city. After it was all over the company came out into the street, gave the password to the watchful sentinel, and went clambering through the ruins to the ferry.[6]

After the earthquake, Martinez moved to Oakland and then to Piedmont. There, he and several other refugees stayed at the home of writer Herman Whitaker. Whitaker had a daughter named Elsie, and Martinez had met them both at dinner at Coppa's before the quake. He painted a portrait of Elsie, and they soon fell in love. In October 1907, they ran away and were married. Elsie's father was not pleased, as Martinez was then thirty-seven and Elsie was seventeen, and it

proved to be a tumultuous marriage. The couple was very popular socially, and they entertained many visitors at their studio on Scenic Way in Piedmont. In his new East Bay location, perhaps inspired by the beauty of the local scenery, he began to concentrate on painting landscapes in a style known as *tonalism*.

Xavier Martinez was known as "Marty" to his friends. In appearance he was a combination of a Latin Quarter Parisian and an Indian. Although his background was Spanish, Moorish, Scottish and Indian, he was proudest of his Indian heritage. He liked to wear his hair long with a headband binding it. Arnold Genthe described him as "the most colorful figure of the Bohemian artists. With a shock of black hair and eyes like beads of jet, he dressed like the painters in the Latin Quarter—corduroys and always wore a bright crimson flowing tie no matter what the time of day."[7]

Martinez began teaching at the California School of Arts and Crafts in 1909. His arrival made possible the beginning of the fine arts program. In the summertime, he held classes at his home in Piedmont. At these times, students could be seen spread out though the neighboring hills, sketching the scenery, and Martinez stopping at each one to comment on the work.

Elsie and Martinez separated in 1919, but they remained friends. For many years, Elsie lived just across the street and continued to take Martinez to school and back.

Martinez was greatly loved and respected by his students. He taught the advanced classes, and students took pride in being invited to his studio to be part of his "inner circle." His teaching tenure at the College of Arts and Crafts lasted until 1942, when ill health compelled him to retire. He died in 1943, several months after suffering a heart attack. The California State Assembly adjourned in his honor "out of respect to the memory of California's great artist Xavier Martinez,"[8] the only time an artist has been so honored.

FOUNDING OF CCAC, PART TWO

In 1907, the year the art school was founded, Frederick H. Meyer ·was the president of the California Guild of Arts and Crafts. Although there was no financial connection between this organization and the school, there was clearly a connection of spirit, ideas and ideals. Indeed, the original name of the school used from 1907 to 1908 was School of the California Guild of Arts and Crafts. The 1907 school catalogue stated the purpose of the school:

> The demand for instruction in industrial art made by the members of the Guild, as well as by members of the public, led to the formation of a school known as the California Guild of Arts and Crafts. The school specializes in two courses: applied art, for the training of designers, etc., and normal art, for the training of special teachers in drawing and manual training.

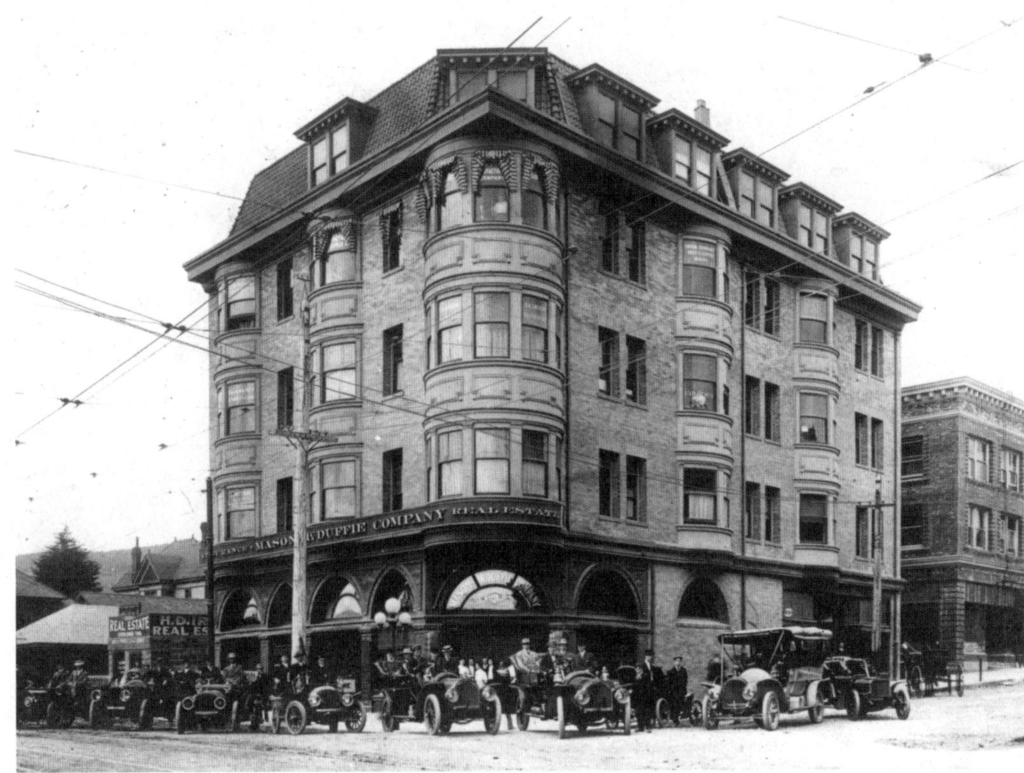

The studio building at the corner of Shattuck Avenue and Addison Street in Berkeley was the home of the California School of Arts and Crafts during its first year, 1907–8.

The school's first location was on the fifth floor of the Studio Building at 2045 Shattuck Avenue in Berkeley. Meyer's choice of Berkeley seems to have been for both moral and practical reasons. His vision was to escape the idea of a romantic bohemian San Francisco art school, as he states, "My experience with students in San Francisco made me think it was better to hold the school in Berkeley where alcoholic beverages were not on sale."[9] So much for the moral issue. As to the practical issue, Meyer writes in the 1907 catalogue:

> Berkeley was chosen as the place for the school on account of its picturesque location, pleasant climate

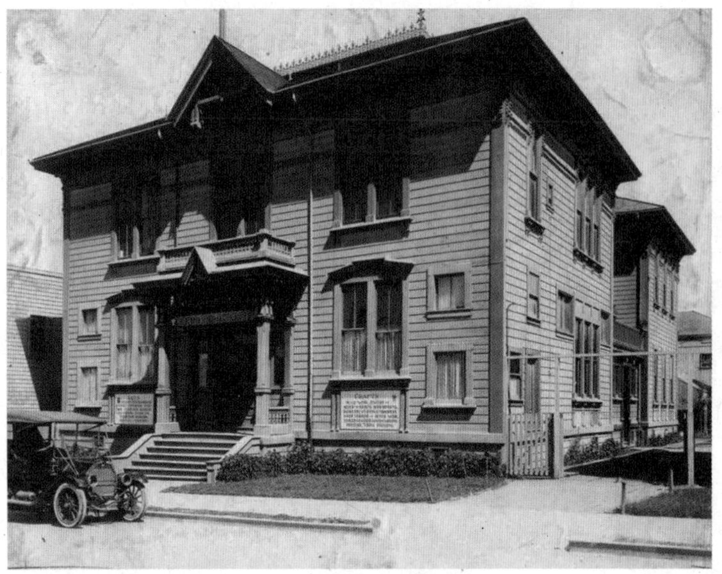

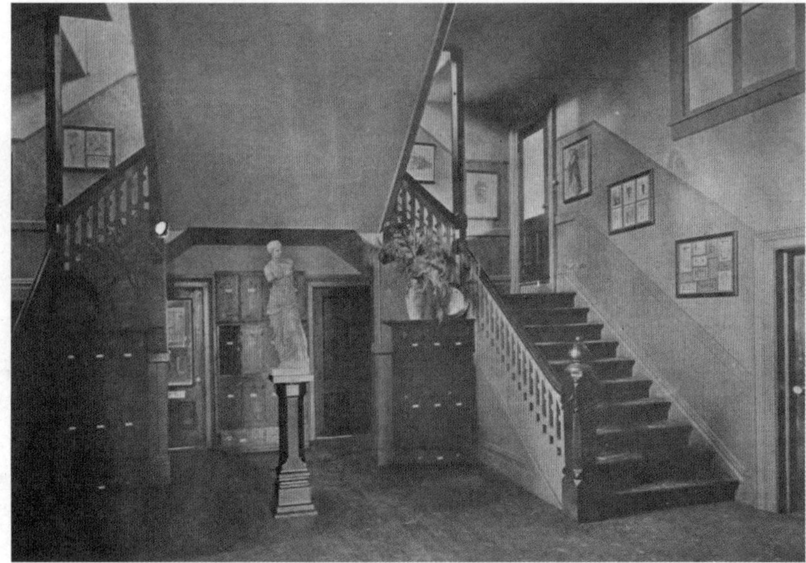

and the fact that it is the recognized educational center of California. The school is located in the well known Studio Building, directly opposite the main stations of the ferry lines, both the Southern Pacific and the Key Route, and the termini of local as well as Oakland street car lines. The school is within one block of the University grounds, which will make it possible for students to take work both at the University and the art school.[10]

The actual opening of the school was the summer session of 1907. The faculty consisted of Frederick Meyer, Perham Nahl and Elizabeth Ferrea. Why Miss Ferrea is not more widely acknowledged as a co-founder is not clear. And of course, Laetitia Meyer was there, providing the entire administrative side of the school, unassisted, for which

immense effort she was accorded the title of secretary.

When the regular school year began in the fall of 1907, Isabelle Percy had joined the faculty. In March 1908, before the end of the first regular school year and to avoid a threatened rent raise, the school moved a short distance to 2130 Center Street, above Al Zeimer's Pool & Billiard Parlor. In May, a graduation was held for five women students. They had been given credit for the years they had previously studied at the Mark Hopkins Institute of Art.

With the beginning of the 1908 summer session, the school ended its implied connection with the California Guild of Arts and Crafts by changing its name to the California School of Arts and Crafts.

In 1909, Xavier Martinez joined the California School of Arts and Crafts faculty, and the school began a fine arts program.

In 1910, needing more space, the building at 2119 Allston Way was leased. Now, at
last, the school occupied an entire building—one that was three stories high. The
building, which was the former Berkeley
High School building, needed remodeling,
and it was not completely ready for use until
1912. When the remodeling was finished,
the school remained on Allston Way until it
had been completely moved to Oakland in
1926. In 1936, it officially changed its name
to the California College of Arts and Crafts.
In 2003, reflecting the increased breadth of
its programs, the college changed its name
to the California College of the Arts.

Throughout its early years, the school
played a central role in the history of the Arts
and Crafts movement in Berkeley. Most of
the local craftsmen had a connection with
the school, either as students or instructors
or both.

As to Frederick Meyer's goal of having an
art school free of bohemianism, the results
were pleasantly mixed. Certainly the nega-
tive side of bohemianism—excessive drinking and carousing—were never associated
with the school. They did have their share of
parties, including their annual Jinx, an event
at which costumed students performed
satirical skits about the faculty, but there is
no record of these or any other school parties ever truly getting out of hand.

On the positive side, the school seems
to have succeeded in imbuing its students
and, to a significant degree, the surrounding community with an appreciation for the
value of an artistic lifestyle. And in this lies

the noble bohemian legacy of this great
institution.

ART POTTERY,
METALWORK
AND JEWELRY—
MAKING IN
BERKELEY

Berkeley's first
art pottery was
the California
Faience Com-
pany, founded
by William Brag-
don and Chauncey Thomas. Both men were
easterners who had studied pottery making
under C. F. Binns at Alfred University in New
York, and both had taught pottery making
at the California School of Arts and Crafts
in Berkeley. In 1915, they started a business
initially called the Tile Shop. Its first location
was at 2336 San Pablo Avenue in Berkeley.
From its early days, its wares included both
tiles and vessels that were marked "California Faience." Their pottery was made from
a low-fired red or buff clay body. The earlier
pieces had subtle matte glazes in keeping
with the style of the Arts and Crafts movement. In their later period, from 1924 through
1933, they primarily used high-gloss glazes
and bright colors. This shift may, in part,
reflect their perception of the evolving architectural styles popular in the San Francisco
Bay Area during these periods. The matte-
glaze ware was in harmony with the brown-
shingle bungalows of the early period and
the high-gloss pieces were more in keeping
with the Mediterranean-style stucco houses
of the 1920s and 1930s.

In 1924, the firm moved to much larger
quarters at 1335 Hearst Avenue and stayed
there for the remainder of its existence. In

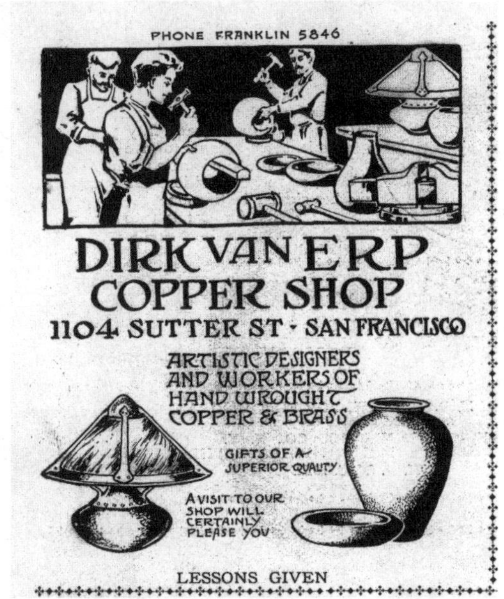

Advertisement in
California School of Arts
and Crafts yearbook.

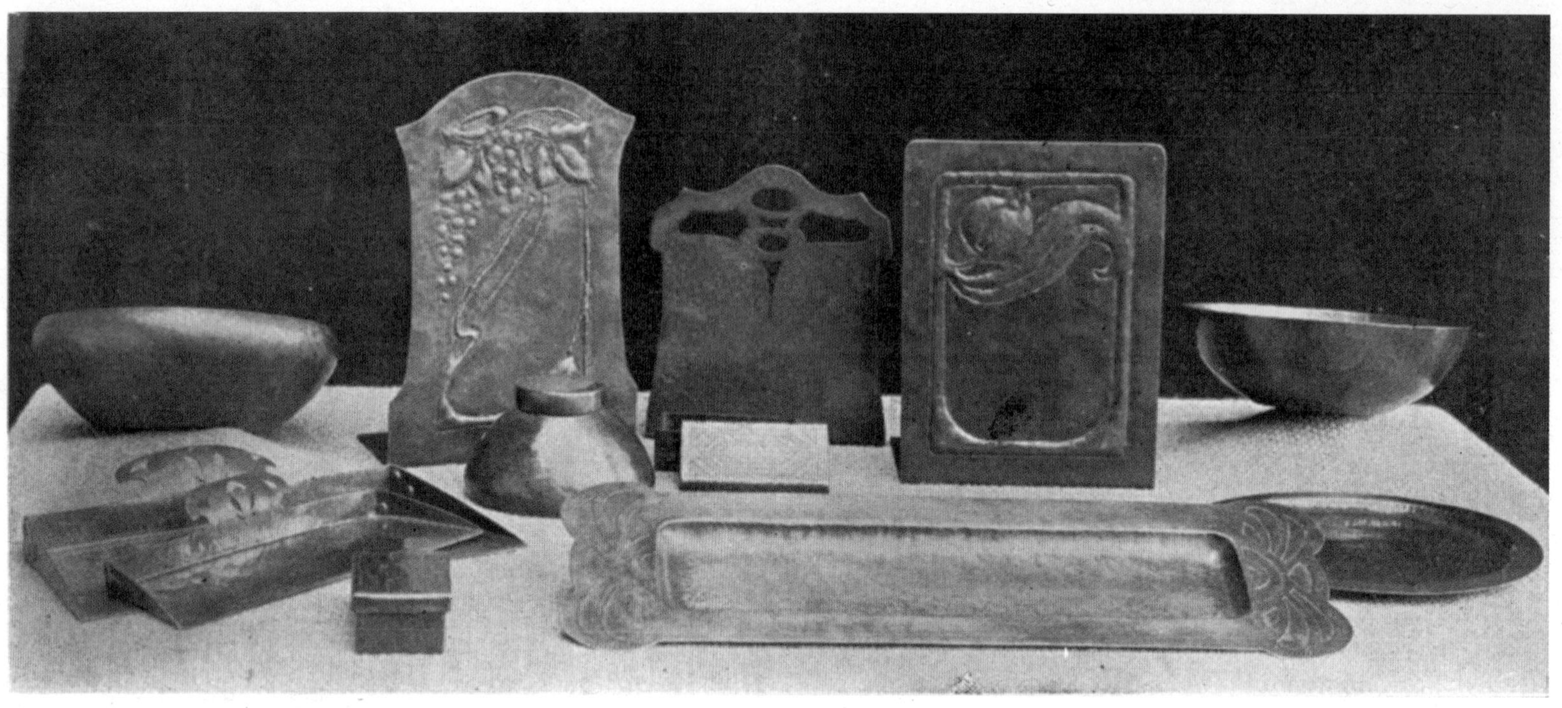

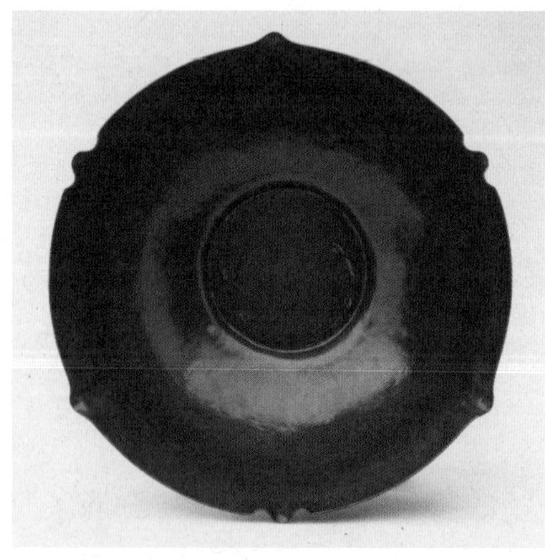

the late 1920s, California Faience received a huge order for tiles for the decoration of Hearst Castle at San Simeon. The company was chosen by the castle's architect, Julia Morgan, who personally designed many of the tiles that were made for this mammoth project. For several years, the tile production for this one project exceeded the total of their other production and helped keep the company in business. In the late 1930s, Thomas sold his interest in the pottery to Bragdon and left Berkeley. Bragdon continued to operate the pottery, primarily as a teaching facility, until his death in 1959.

The other Berkeley pottery operating during this period was Walrich Pottery. James and Gertrude Wall began the business in 1922, and it too was on Hearst Avenue. They also produced both tiles and vessels, and in a wider range of quality than California Faience, but their better items compared favorably. Their wares were mostly single-color, matte-glazed molded items made for gift shops and included figurines, candlesticks, bowls and vases as well as tiles. The firm was quite successful in the 1920s but fell victim to the hard times of the Great Depression and is last listed in business in 1930. Both James and Gertrude Wall remained connected to the ceramics industry after Walrich ceased operations.

Much of the art metalwork produced in Berkeley during this period was connected with the School of Arts and Crafts. In 1908, Mrs. Rufus P. Jennings began teaching metalwork at the school. She was the wife of Charles Keeler's half brother and had been a student of Augustus F. Rose. By 1910, she was also teaching jewelry-making. Harry St. John Dixon started as a student at the school and went on to be an instructor in metalwork by 1911. By 1913, Mrs. Jennings was no longer teaching at the school, but Dixon continued to teach for several more years.

Records show that Mrs. Jennings exhibited her jewelry at the Alaska Yukon Pacific Exposition in Seattle in 1909. Also listed as an exhibitor of handmade jewelry at this event was Katherine Bunnell Gorrill of Berkeley. She was a sister-in-law of Charles Keeler, his wife Louise's sister.

Dirk Van Erp, the most famous of the San Francisco coppersmiths neither attended nor taught at the School of Arts and Crafts. He did, however, live in Berkeley briefly and had his business, the Art Copper Shop, in Oakland from 1909 to 1910. After he moved his business to San Francisco, he placed advertisements in the 1913–14 California School of Arts and Crafts' yearbooks that included the phrase "lessons given."

An advertising postcard for Dirk Van Erp's first shop in Oakland, ca. 1908–9.

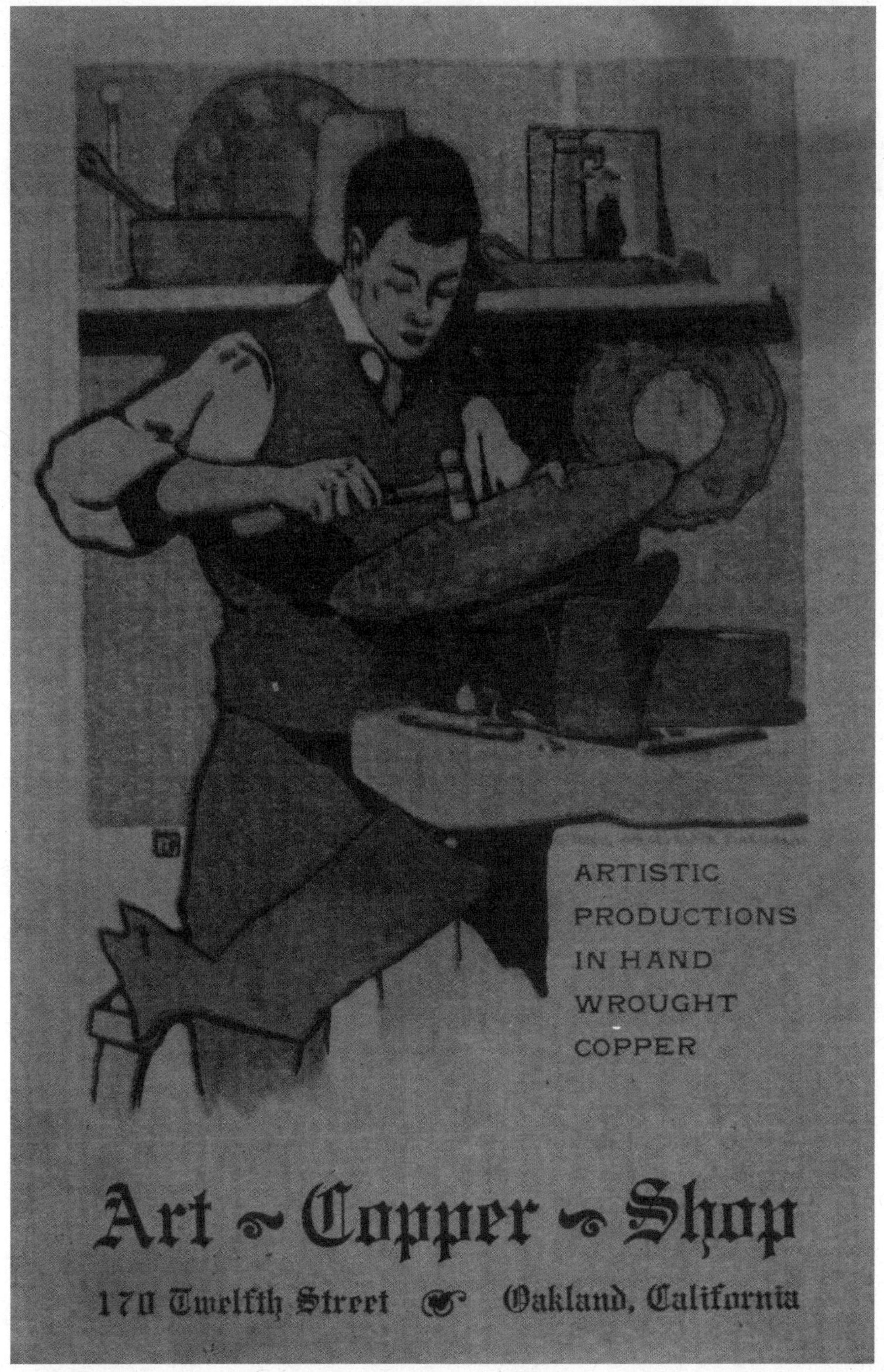

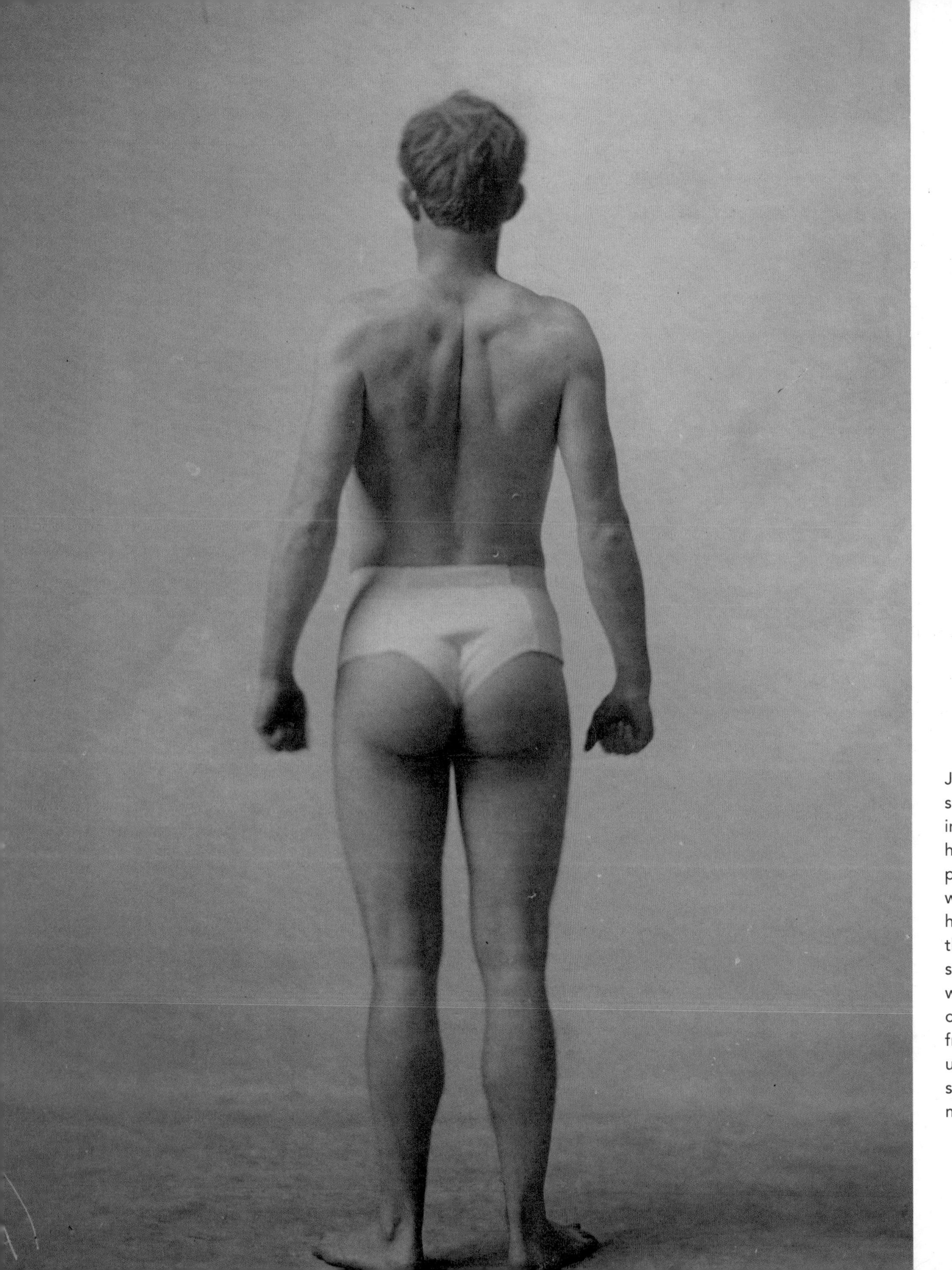

Jack London's physical strength was an important part of both his public image and his personal sense of self, whether he was wrestling his guests or posing for this series of athletic studies. Although these were the most revealing of his portraits, he frequently posed with an unbuttoned shirt collar showing a triangle of his muscular chest.

wild men and revolutionaries

"Intoxication in delusion, dreaming intoxication,
Running, forgetting, absent-minded,
Sadness after pleasure, loss after gain, angry-
Faced by unsuccess—our lives are just like
Childish play."[1]

—Yone Noguchi,
"Childish Play"

Imagine the party at Frank C. Havens's house. More than two thousand lightbulbs supply the glow that glistens off a five-foot-tall gold-lacquered statue of the Buddha. Guests cluster in the Tiffany-designed dining room and wander through an oversized Japanese tea room. Music spills out the windows and drinks flow all night.

Havens, a flamboyant Piedmont real estate magnate who "wore an emerald as big as a pigeon egg,"[2] loved to shock. When he wasn't inspiring the resentment of class-conscious Socialists like Jack London (who hated Havens as "the worst kind of capitalist"), he was disturbing his middle-class neighbors with his avant-guard political ideas and over-the-top spending.

Elsie Martinez, daughter of one of London's old socialist party-mates, remembered one of Havens's parties in particular. At the end of the party, writer George Sterling (Havens's nephew and protégée), Havens and artist Xavier "Marty" Martinez, threw their arms around each other in drunken comradeship "and sang the revolutionary songs—especially the beautiful ones with a Latin rhythm—the famous French revolutionary songs that Marty had taught them. It was delightful. All three holding on to each other and singing at the top of their lungs."[3] There was a radical chic about the bohemians, years before Tom Wolfe popularized the phrase in the 1970s.

Havens's parties, with their infighting artists, heavy drinking and revolutionary leanings, were a window into two of Berkeley's most pressing social issues: prohibition and reform politics. Berkeleyans had fought a battle over alcohol for years, eventually creating what

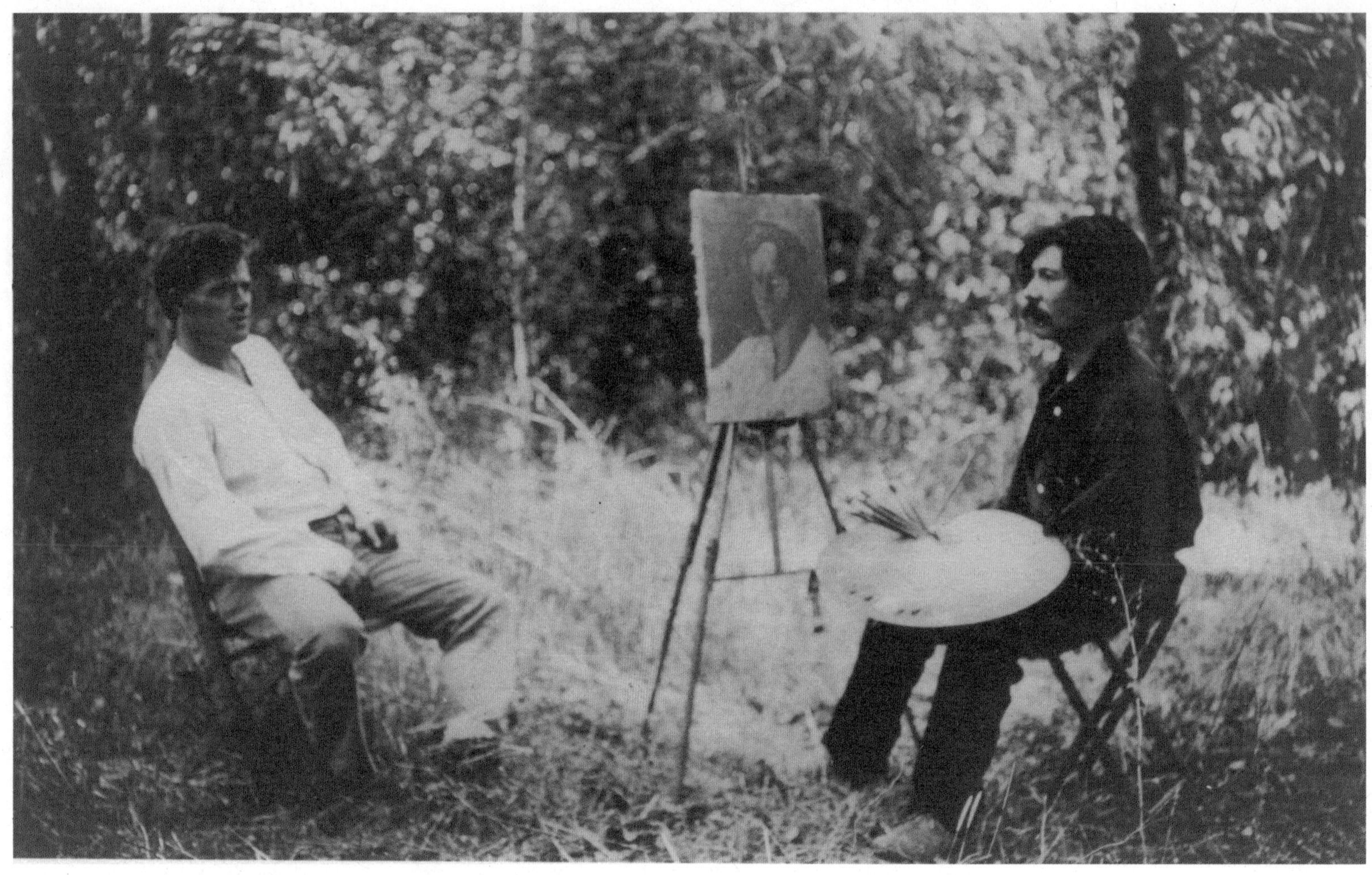

was probably the strictest alcohol ban that the United States would ever see. Politically, the revolutions that wracked the rest of the world played out in small form in the city. Class and ethnicity were crucial in both debates. The bohemians found themselves in the middle of philosophical arguments that seemed so far away from their artistic concerns and yet were formed by their interests in creating a new way of living. The political developments of these years would influence the East Bay for the next fifty to sixty years.

In 1910, Berkeley joined cities like Madison, Wisconsin, in electing a socialist mayor. The new mayor, J. Stitt Wilson, won every precinct west of Shattuck Avenue, which consisted of the working- and middle-class "flats" of Berkeley. He won almost nothing from the east side. Only a few scattered votes came from the eastern hills around the campus, where the left-leaning university intellectuals lived. The differences between the hills and the plains reflected the steep division between the wealthy and the impoverished that was often hidden by Berkeley's middle-class appearance.

Memoirist Jacomena Maybeck estimated that these divisions began in 1877, when "the electric urban trains came up Shattuck Avenue and created a social line—'above and below the tracks.'" The division still exists. As one 2006 writer put it, "Berkeley's wealth, like its houses, is distributed on a steeply inclined plane, with the poor clustered below and the rich perched high in the hills."[4]

Most of the Bohemians were privileged to live above the tracks, far from the worries of the rest of the city. Ansel Adams said of his friend, photographer and musician Cedric Wright, "What was both a curse and blessing for Cedric was that he was always comfortable financially and has absolutely no concept of what the average material condition of most people might be."[5] Most maintained the comfortable, quiet lives of what one historian called an "unnaturally well-to-do middle class." Some, like the popular painter William Keith, became very wealthy but stayed away from the grandeur of the San Francisco rich.[6]

Charles Keeler, figurehead of the Berkeley scene, had typical political beliefs. He joined the mildly reformist Berkeleyans who maintained the class and racial divisions of the town. Keeler was not as financially successful as some of his friends and neighbors; all his life,

he tried to find the perfect lecture series, book or job that would give him enough money to bring up his three children. Selling his brain to the highest bidder, a project that gave the local newspapers a series of funny human-interest stories and that probably helped seal the reputation of "Nut Hill" in the rest of the city's mind, was only the most dramatic of his fundraising projects. Despite his personal money worries, however, he did not believe in the socialist movement that was attracting the attention of so many other worried fathers in town. One of his popular lectures was a warning about the risks of letting Bolshevism move from Russia to California.

Keeler personally disliked racism, especially the anti-Asian feeling that was so powerful in California at the time. When he set up the rules of the Cosmic Religion, he forced its congregations to be racially integrated. Yet he also believed that shared faith should not lead to social integration, especially not friendships that would encourage people of different races to invite each other to their homes. His letters show that he had friendly relationships with many Asian and Asian-American writers, but apparently he did not socialize with them except at poetry readings and artistic salons. In fact, Keeler's most visible work in the city, his job with the Chamber of Commerce, reinforced racial and class segregation. Only businesspeople from the east side of Berkeley could join the group. Forward-thinking business owners from the west eventually formed their own group, the West Side Merchants Association.

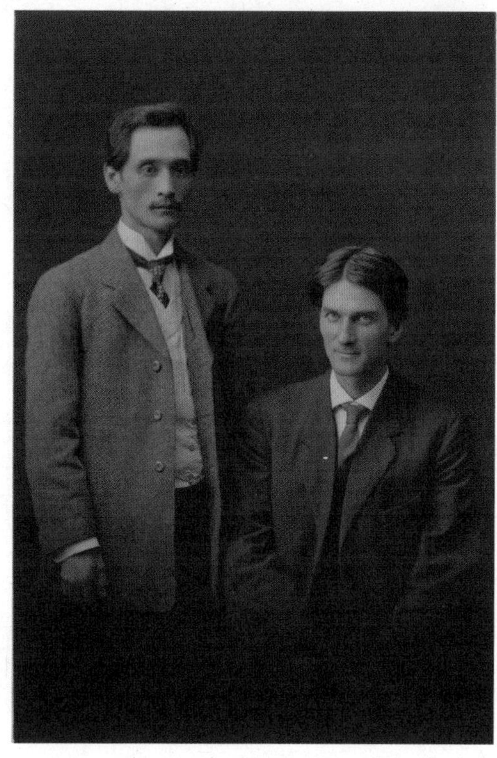

Charles Keeler and Yone Noguchi pose for a studio portrait.

THE 1910 ELECTION The divisions illustrated by these two businessmen's groups played out in the city's 1910 election. Wilson's opponent, Mr. Beverly Lacy Hodghead, was the incumbent mayor. He must have believed himself to be invincible in the polls because he had just put Berkeley on the map as the most progressive, least corrupt city in California. Hodghead's reformist ideas fit perfectly with the utopian urges of most of the bohemians, while his position in Berkeley's social-class divide set him firmly with Keeler and the Chamber of Commerce.

In the early twentieth century, middle-class reformers throughout the United States were horrified by the starvation, disease, drunkenness and cruelty that they saw in all parts of the American capitalist system. They started a movement known as progressivism, a loosely affiliated group of ideas and plans. Progressivism included everything from cooking classes that taught new immigrants to make American white sauce, to clubs that preserved the redwoods. Progressives believed that American politics were corrupt, run by a class of immigrant-dominated machine bosses who only cared about their own wealth, not the needs of the American people. The progressives proposed new ways for Americans to influence their government, like votes for women, the ability to recall elected officials, ballot initiatives and referendums. As historian Ernest S. Griffith put it, they believed that "the cure for the ills of democracy is more democracy."[7]

Hodghead made it his goal to bring almost all of the anticorruption proposals to Berkeley. In 1909, then-candidate Hodghead spoke to the hill dwellers gathered at the Hillside Club, promoting the idea of Berkeley as a "city of homes" despite being a "city of no inconsiderable size" and an "educational center" with "commercial possibilities." Hodghead, with his origins in the city's commercial side, promised to govern the city as a businessman. He was proud to be a political outsider. "I have not been in public life," he explained, "but I imagine that the same rule applies as in private business." In fact, he was running on a ticket so brazenly reformist and anti-politician that he refused to even publish a platform. "There is considerable insincerity in a platform," he explained. A platform is only "a mass of twaddle."[8]

Hodghead, with his antiboss ideas, implemented the Berkeley City Charter of 1909, which was probably the most dramatically progressive city charter in the country at the time. In 1911, a California writer used Berkeley as the example to which all other city charters should be held. The new charter of the city of Berkeley weakened mayoral power and changed the city's government style. In order to break the power of the city's political parties, the charter specified that all city candidates would be nominated by petition, not by primary elections. No candidate's political party appeared on the ballot, making it harder to vote a straight party ticket.[9]

The new city charter also included an antialcohol law that was "one of the strictest [ordinances] ever passed in the state."[10] The new charter proclaimed, "The Council shall have no power to license the sale of any spirituous, malt, vinous, or alcoholic liquors, and every person who within the boundaries of the City of Berkeley sells, barters, gives away, or exposes for sale any such liquors, shall be deemed guilty of a misdemeanor."[11] Under the "give away" provision of the charter, it was illegal to serve alcohol to friends in one's own home. Poet and teacher Witter Bynner was one of the victims of this law. He was forced to leave the university after he was found to be serving cocktails to students in his room.[12]

Berkeley had been struggling with the alcohol issue for more than a generation. In 1873, the California State University Liquor Law restricted all alcohol sales within a two-mile radius of the campus, a law that was changed three years later to a one-mile radius after some of the more distant citizens, in an area that would later become West Berkeley, disagreed with it.

Among them was John E. "Evergreen" Boyd, a writer and public character who "was able to dissolve civic tension with a healthy dose of laughter."[13] Boyd was everything that the teetotalers fought against. He was a convivial joker, who associated alcohol with humor and sociability rather than drunkenness and child abuse. When he was thrown in the Oakland jail for pub-

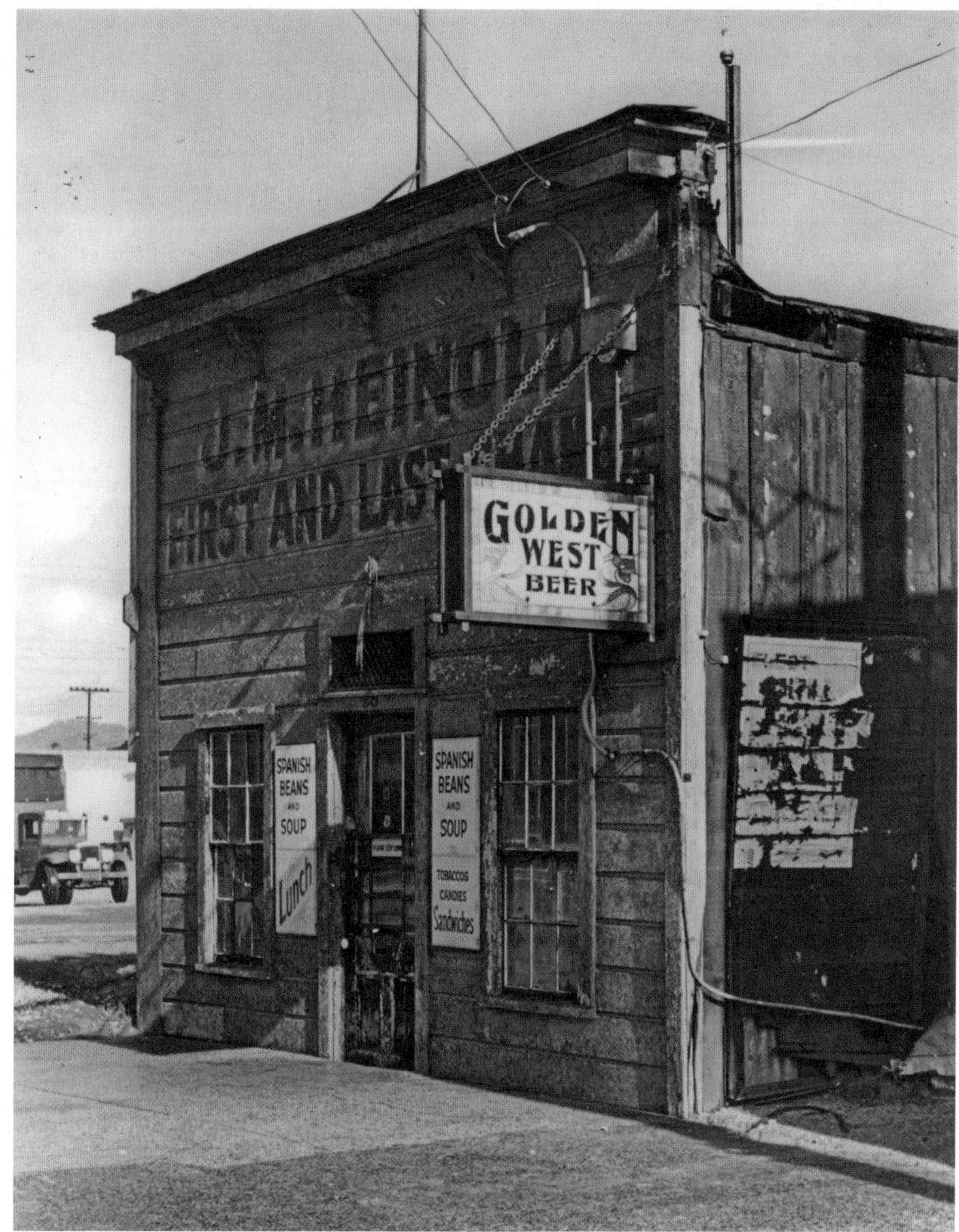

Saloons, including the Last Chance Saloon on the Oakland waterfront, sprang up in a tight ring around Berkeley's alcohol-free zone.

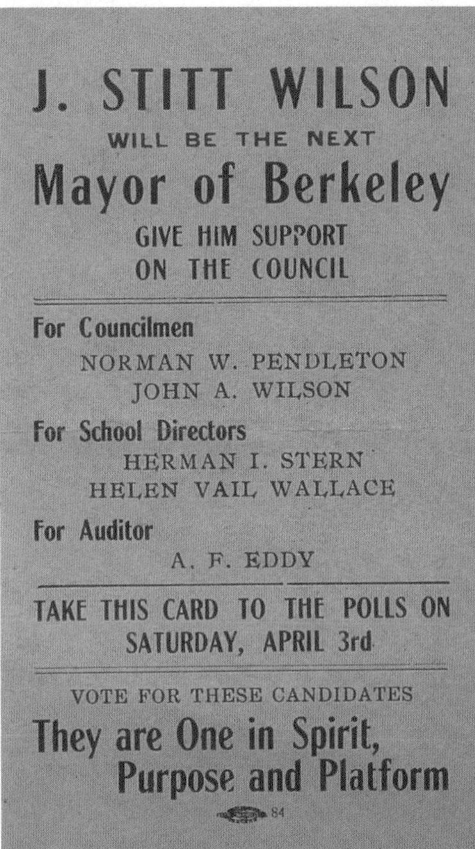

A campaign card from 1910–12 shows that J. Stitt Wilson encouraged other Socialist party member to run for city office.

lic intoxication, he told the newspapers that jail was "the best place to meet the leading citizens of Oakland, and . . . the only place from which they weren't constantly sneaking out to get a drink."[14] He urged the town council to solve the alcohol problems by appointing him Inspector of Beer Saloons and Breweries. He was also not against using the tactics of the teetotalers against themselves, circulating petitions to close a beer parlor that was too closely competitive with one that he supported.

The Berkeley alcohol debate flared up every few years, and the city made continual fine adjustments on the laws. In the meantime, Berkeley had become a showcase for the Anti-Saloon League, a national organization. Naturally, saloons sprang up immediately outside the one-mile ring after the 1876 law was passed. Because of the "sharp contrast" in crime rates between the dry ring and the wet areas surrounding it, the Anti-Saloon League found it easy to argue that vice would disappear if alcohol was banned entirely within the city limits. Once the Berkeley charter was in place, the League hoped to start on other cities, using Berkeley as an example. The antialcohol crusaders conveniently ignored the argument that drinkers would go even farther outside the city to find a bar.[15]

Liquor laws helped determine which artists lived in Berkeley and which didn't. Hard-drinkers like Joaquin Miller, who would often pass around a whiskey bottle with fellow writers Herman Whitaker and George Sterling, tended to stay in Piedmont, even when Berkeley was attracting many of their peers. On the other hand, many of the bohemians living in Berkeley were against drinking. Bernard Maybeck controlled a large chunk of the hill land, thanks to Annie Maybeck's business-oriented mind, and he used his economic power to keep the city dry. The Maybecks insisted that all who bought land from them sign an agreement saying that they would not sell alcoholic beverages on the property. He used the same power to protect his aesthetic standards, forcing the buyers to promise to never paint their houses white. Nancy de Angulo, who disliked Maybeck and his restrictions, made a point of having drunken parties in her house on Maybeck land. Her wandering anthropologist-poet husband, Jaime, would occasionally get so smashed that he would roll down the hill into the Maybeck's yard.[16]

MAYOR J. STITT WILSON

Stitt Wilson, who stepped in to lead this socially divided city, took the reform even further. With the support of the conservative local paper, the *Berkeley Gazette*, he was elected for a two-year term against the incumbent mayor, Beverly L. Hodghead.

Despite his popularity with the national progressive movement, was less careful about maintaining his popularity at home. He had made enemies at the *Gazette* while pushing through the dramatic changes of the 1909 charter. In his anticorruption campaigns, he attacked the local Republicans who ran the paper. The newspaper kept the grudge going by supporting Hodghead's opponent in the next election, even though Wilson was even more critical of the paper's ideas than Hodghead was. (Wilson was savvy enough to refrain from attacking the paper's supporters directly.) When Wilson won 2,749 votes to Hodghead's 2,468, the paper proclaimed it "truly [a] victory for the people, the plain people, the common folk."[17]

Wilson's political success led to "the greatest political gathering ever witnessed in this city" up until that time, according to the *Gazette*. More than 2,100 people gathered outside Berkeley High School for a preelection rally in support of Wilson. After the polls closed and the votes were counted in Wilson's favor, his supporters broke into a spontaneous parade. They carried the new mayor down Shattuck Avenue, the heart of downtown and a stronghold of Hodghead-supporting businesses.[18]

Like many of his supporters, Wilson was an immigrant. His life story is dim, though, and different sources disagree as to whether he came from Canada or England. In either case, he moved to the United States in his youth and grew up in a strictly religious family. Following the faith of his childhood, he was trained as a Methodist minister at Northwestern University in Evanston, Illinois. Evanston was a short train ride from booming Chicago, where Wilson started as a minister.

Yone Noguchi, coming from San Francisco, with its beauties and dandies, first saw Chicago about the same year that J. Stitt Wilson was working as a young minister: "'Smoke' means Chicago as 'flower' means Japan."[19] The world Wilson saw was even worse than what Noguchi described. Men, women and children lived and worked in inhumanly dangerous conditions. Working in the slums of Chicago radicalized Wilson. He used his training as a minister as a powerful rhetorical tool. God was on the side of the reformers, not on the side of the rich.

Wilson resigned his Chicago clergy position and moved to Berkeley in 1901. Once in Berkeley, he dedicated himself to promoting socialism, writing pamphlets that were distributed throughout the United States and England. These pamphlets, which he turned into a self-published book, *How I Became a Socialist*, were filled with religious imagery. He spoke of "industrial wolves and the beasts of prey which devour even the lambs of the flock," and the "Goliath of Capitalism."[20] In contrast to the industrial wolves, he offered "the Kingdom of God on the earth—the Kingdom or condition of Social Justice, brotherly love, and spiritual inspiration and fellowship among men . . . and the abolition of the present capitalist system and the establishment of the Socialist Co-Operative Commonwealth."[21] Some of Wilson's speeches were intended to bring more people into socialism, but others were intended to get him elected. The year before he ran for mayor, he ran for California governor on the socialist platform and won fifty thousand votes. He gave stump speeches from the "Red Special," an automobile that attracted attention wherever it went on the mostly car-free roads.

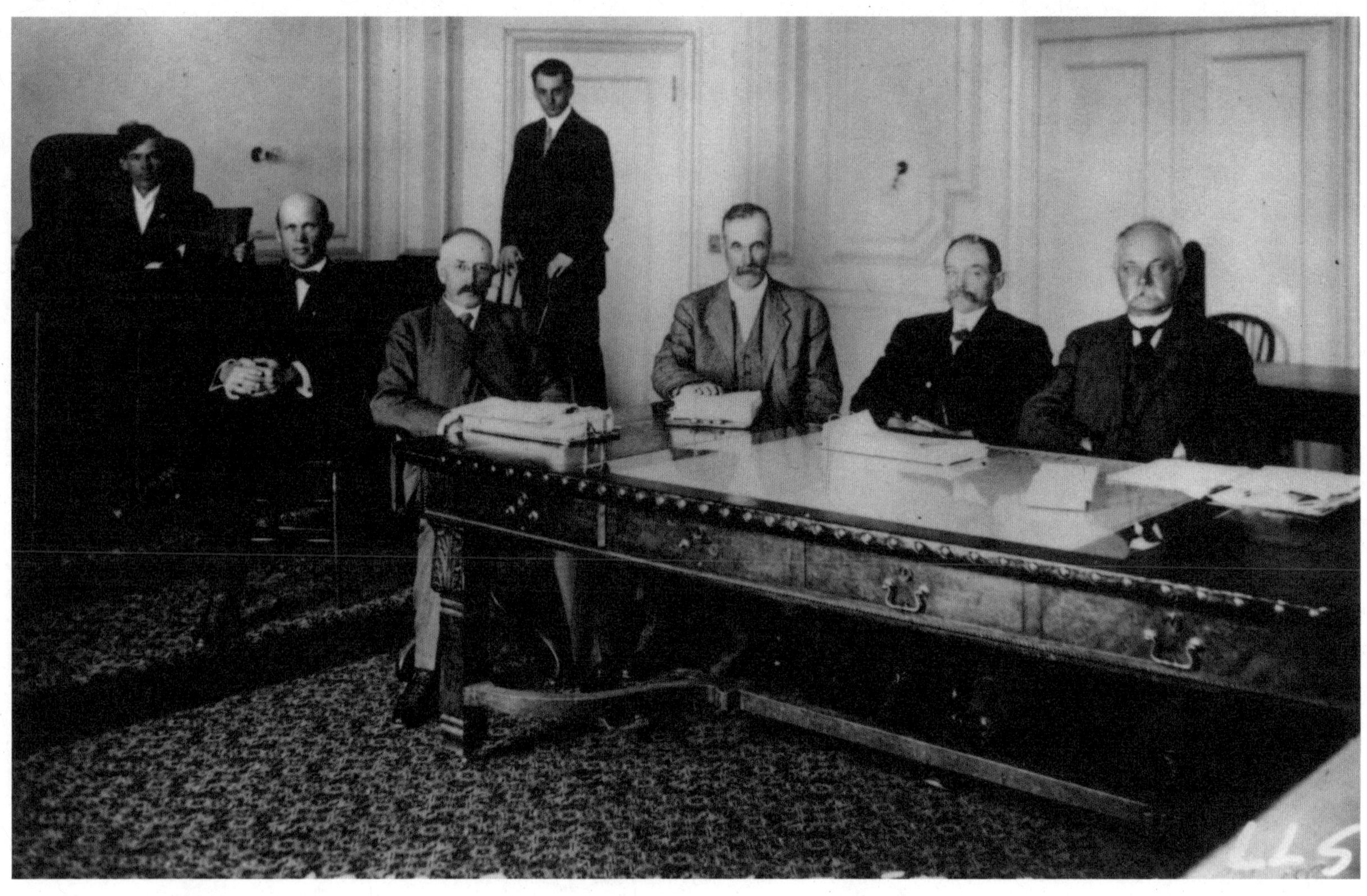

Mayor J. Stitt Wilson and the Berkeley City Council in 1912.

Most of Wilson's mayoral platform was centered on quality of life issues. All of his proposals advocated improving the lives of the citizens through government regulation and control, mostly through expanded city programs. He advocated street improvements, new sewer bonds, better firefighting and better police technology with "the perfection of the police flashlight system." (This last plank was perfect for a city that was already a leader in police work, thanks to pioneering police chief August Vollmer.)

On a more socialist bent, Wilson called for municipal ownership of utilities and regulation of rates, and he also advocated taxation of empty lots (presumably to stop land speculation and to encourage landowners to turn the lots into productive uses.) He supported free textbooks and kindergartens for the young. He wanted a municipal employment bureau for the jobless. Even these more radical planks were not unusual in the Bay Area of Wilson's time. In 1912, Oakland established a public wood yard, which provided jobs to all able-bodied men in the city.

Nor did Wilson ignore what Berkeleyans of the time considered one of the most important quality-of-life issues of the day—alcohol and vice. Most of Wilson's support came from the "wetter" areas of town, in the west and south of the city where the saloons flourished. However, it is doubtful that any Berkeley mayor could have won without a commitment to temperance.

Unlike the other reformers in Berkeley, however, Wilson found the blame for vice not in the degeneracy of the individual but in capitalism. "Economic injustice . . . lies at the root of our problem of prostitution," he stated in one lecture, which he found so important that he published it.[22] He blamed San Francisco leadership for their boost-erish clean-up campaign of the Barbary Coast, calling it a "pseudo-excitement of ten days." The prostitutes would work wherever they ended up, he said, especially because they would find it hard to find work in any other job. "Less than 2 percent ever had even high school advantages—and over 80 percent never went through the pri-mary grades," he pointed out. Prostitution is "a Man's business" for profit; "the women are merely tools."[23]

At the end of his two-year term, Wilson decided to resign from electoral politics and turned down his party's nomination for the next election. He pointed out as he left office, "The finances of the city of Berkeley were never in better condition and everybody knows it." But Wilson was still disappointed. He did not succeed in his larger goal, to "make some progress" in the fight against capitalism, and complained that he was "handicapped by a reactionary council."[24]

However, Wilson did have some success in bringing other socialists into city office on his coattails, and in his resignation letter to the Berkeley Socialist party, he encouraged his compatriots with the reminder that "on the day I went out of office Comrade Elvina S. Beals took her seat on the school board, thus placing three socialists in one voting body for the first time."[25] After he resigned from the mayorship, Wilson had a regular speaking arrangement at the grand Scottish Rite Auditorium in San Francisco. He spoke every Sunday morning, almost as if he had returned to the pulpit.

THE OAKLAND SOCIALIST PARTY

Wilson's run was an anomaly in Berkeley, promoting socialism for only a few years. The rest of the East Bay, however, had a thriving radical left movement for most of the twentieth century, mainly centered on the docks and immigrant neighborhoods of Oakland. William McDevitt, one-time edi-tor of Oakland's party organ, the *Socialist World*, could brag that "the socialist groups of the Bay counties [were] . . . the best orga-nized similar group anywhere in the U.S.A." with the nation's "most active free-speech

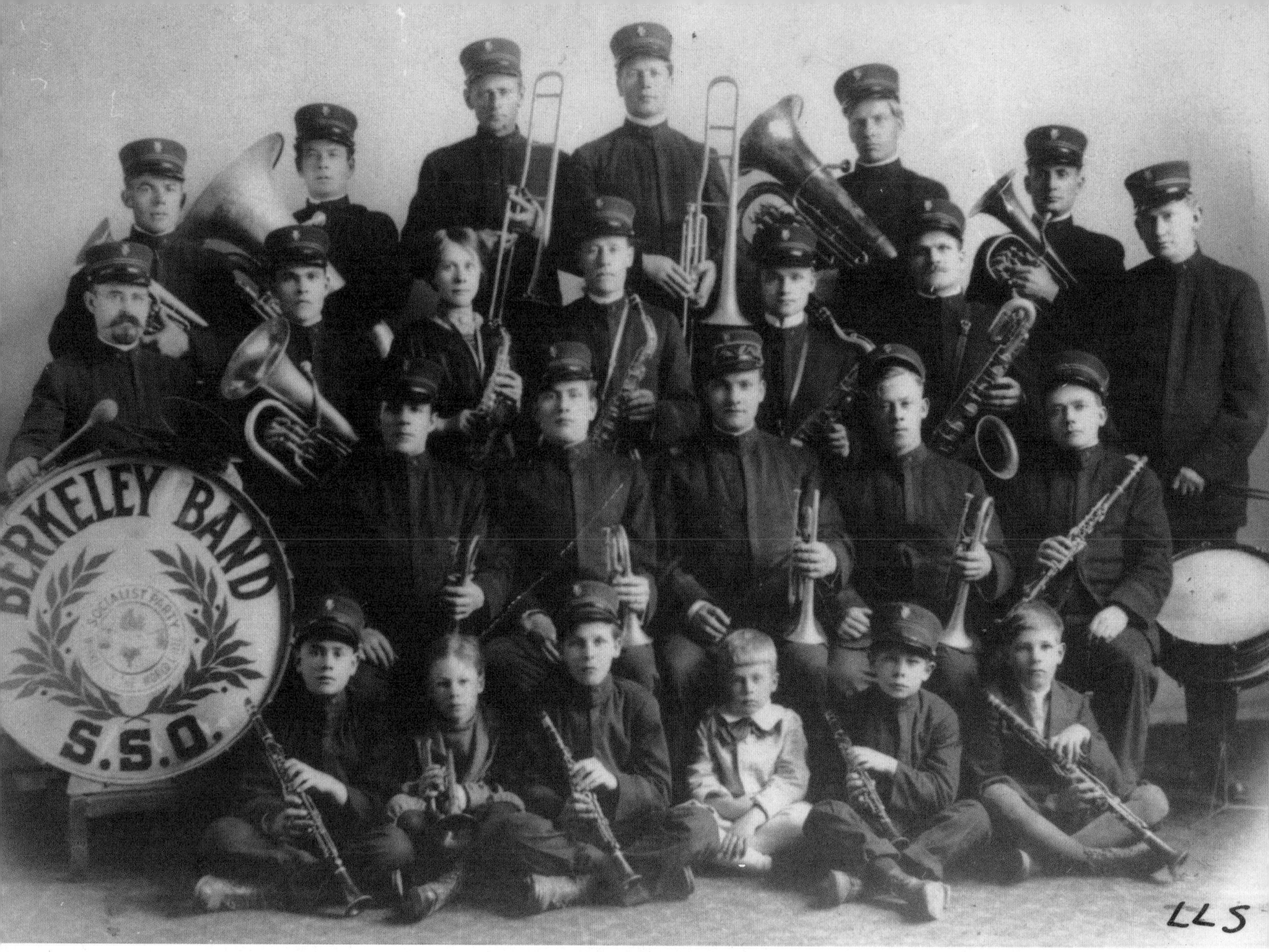

Socialists in Berkeley and Oakland recognized that songs could be as powerful as speeches in recruiting new members.

open air forum." There, the most dramatic figure in the early part of the century was the "boy Socialist," Jack London. According to Elsie Whitaker, who knew London, he was the heart of a multiethnic crew who tried to bring broader thoughts to the local socialist party, "three Englishmen, four Germans, several Scandinavians, and three Americans." Elsie claimed, "His enthusiasm was what propelled the young socialist party. It wasn't the logical Germans, Swedes and English that kept the party going, it was Jack London."[26]

Any practicing socialists in Berkeley probably attended meetings and lectures with the Oakland group. Like the Oakland Socialists, they might have spoken on a soapbox on the "fighting corner" of Tenth and Broadway in front of Oakland City Hall or risked being hauled away to the Oakland city jail. At the end of the evening, they probably ended up chatting with Oaklanders like Herman Whitaker, who usually were found drinking from the "big coffee cups that held almost a pint" at Coffee Dan's cafe.[27] Originally founded in San Francisco in 1879, Coffee Dan's offered all comers good food and a friendly, chatty atmosphere. *Twenty Minutes at Coffee Dan's*, a 1916 Variety Stage Play from San Francisco, has among its characters an old man, a college boy, a shop girl, a soldier and a drunk.[28]

Elsie Whitaker gives a vivid picture of what one of those meetings was like. Although only a little girl, she joined her father at meetings wearing a "little blue cap with a red feather in it." Her jaunty feather brightened up the Labor Temple on Twelfth Street in Oakland, "a hideous old place with old wooden benches and sort of a dank, musty smell about it." Despite the grim surroundings, the lecture-goers often got caught in the excitement of the event. One debate between her father and Stanford's strict president, David Starr Jordan, left the building "filled to the doors."[29]

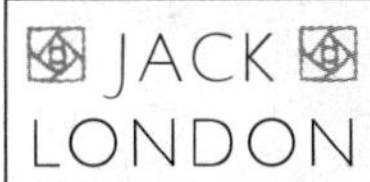

Even though Whitaker could fill a room, Jack London outshone him. The party ran London for mayor, knowing that he could draw votes like no other candidate. In 1905, the *Oakland Tribune* reported that he was the first political candidate who could ever draw a paying crowd to his campaign rallies. London's appeal was tied up in his youth, his speaking ability, his athleticism and his Bobby Kennedy–like good looks. Even the elementary school girls who played with his younger daughter were impressed by his dress sense.[30] His followers were less likely to admit that his appeal also came from his reputation for adventure and sexual intrigue. London was too smart to not realize that he cultivated a "romantic" image. When he was a teenager, he said, "I was branded a 'red-shirt,' a 'dynamiter' and an 'anarchist'; and really decent fellows, who liked me very well, drew the line at my appearing in public with their sisters."[31] By his twenties, people followed him in part because he was being seen in public with a wide range of other men's sisters.

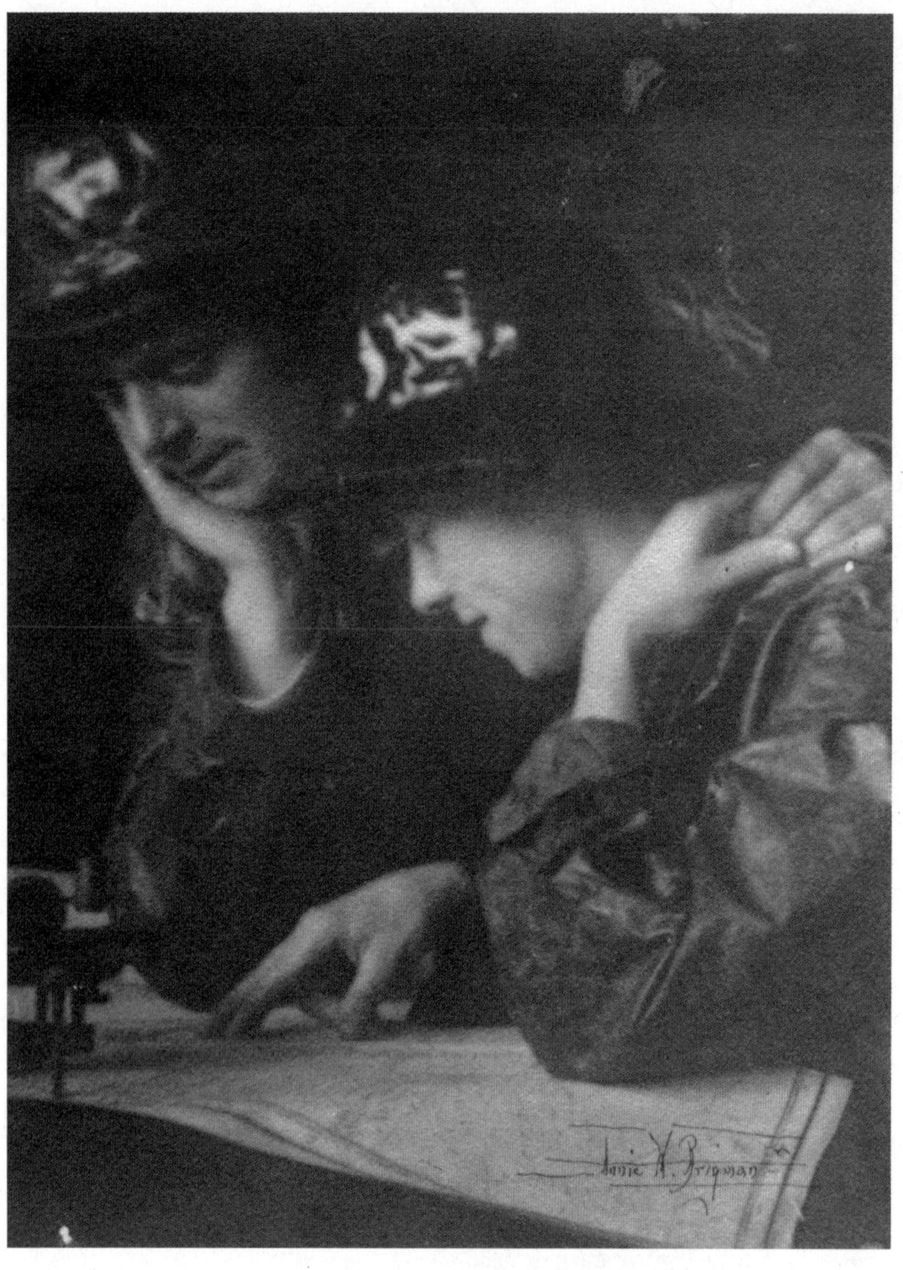

Charmian Kittredge and Jack London on board their yacht, *The Snark*, in a photo by pictorial photographer Annie Brigman. Brigman's signature soft-focus technique adds a tender mood to the portrait of her friends.

London's life during his twenties had so many sensational highlights that it is hard to summarize without making it sound like one of the melodramatic movies of the time. He had frequent affairs, sometimes with his fellow Socialist party members. When one of them dared to turn him down, he became stunningly angry. He once broke a date with typist Charmian Kittredge to marry someone else, a schoolteacher named Bess Madden. Under the influence of an essay that claimed romantic love was unimportant, he decided that Bess was his best chance to create solid Anglo-Saxon children without diluting his bloodline.

London's unhappy marriage to Bess showed one of his biggest contradictions. He combined radical socialism with a belief in Anglo-Saxon superiority. (This belief must not have been very popular in the mostly immigrant socialist party of his time.) Austin Lewis, an Englishman who had translated Marx and who frequently joined the socialists in Oakland, said, "Jack stood with one foot planted in the soil of social democracy, but the other foot was already being dragged in the morasses of the philosophical teachings from which have sprung fascism."[32] Although they may seem contradictory, both beliefs came from the same source: Jack London's impoverished childhood. On the one hand, he did not want anyone else to live through what he had. On the other hand, he needed to feel more important than the people who surrounded him, and believing in the superiority of his ethnicity was a way to do so.

As biographer Clarice Stasz points out, his beliefs were common in the Bay Area at the time.[33]

When London left Bess, she blamed famous socialist Anna Strunsky for the divorce. Strunsky had actually refused to sleep with London several years before, although she did spoon with London as he took her to the theater in San Francisco. She broke off the affair when she learned that he was still sleeping with Bess, contrary to his claims.[34] The real reason for the divorce was his affair with the woman who would become his second wife, Charmian Kittredge. (The second marriage almost did not happen because he had a short affair with theater critic Blanche Partington while waiting for his divorce.)

Charmian Kittredge was raised in Oakland in the most bohemian of circumstances by her aunt Ninetta Eames Payne, later a follower of Charles Keeler's Cosmic Religion. Charmian was a wild horsewoman and bicyclist, who matched Jack London in her physical abilities. She also shared his socialist beliefs. Although Jack insisted that she resign from the party when he did in 1916, she reinstated her membership after his death, when she was "one of only two registered socialists in the town of Glen Ellen," the Londons' Sonoma Valley retreat from the Oakland social scene. Charmian and Jack were married while he was on a socialist lecture tour, and she was proud to share him with the party on what was essentially their honeymoon.[35] At about the same time as their marriage, London helped found the Intercollegiate Socialist Society of America. More than fifty years later, the ISS was still influencing Berkeley politics. After many name changes and mergers, the ISS became the Students for a Democratic Society, or SDS.

HERMAN WHITAKER Devoting much of his life to a careful cultivation of his masculine identity, London enjoyed boxing, wrestling and fencing with his guests, both men and women. One of his competitors and fencing teachers was Herman Whitaker, a well-born Englishman who settled in Canada because of family problems. Whitaker became a socialist because of his "experience of pioneering, with its hardships and harshness," according to his daughter Elsie.[36] He arrived in Oakland in 1895, with a wife and six children, in the middle of an economic depression. "Looking like a gentleman he tramped the streets and byways getting any job he could—washing windows, cleaning floors, gardening, and once digging ditches."[37]

The Whitakers ended up traveling from one immigrant neighborhood to another. Because he was an Englishman, he moved out of the Irish neighborhoods particularly fast. In these neighborhoods, he learned about how the socialist movement proposed to solve the economic inequalities of life in Oakland and the world, and to bring America out of the depression of the 1890s.

While the socialists of Oakland were mostly laborers, they supported the bohemian intellectuals among them. Whitaker

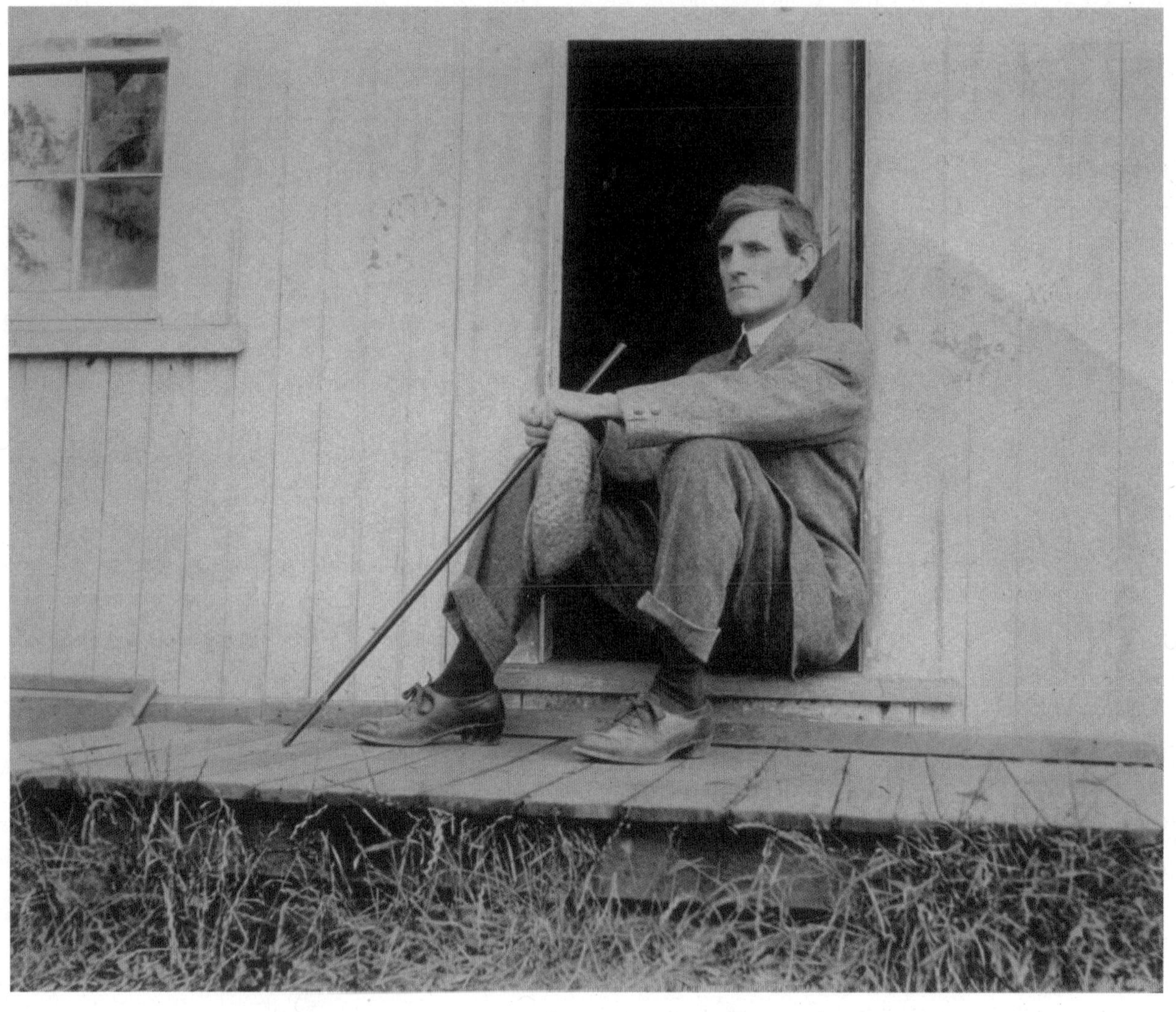

Herman Whitaker, probably after his disagreement with Jack London drove him out of the Oakland Socialist party and away from politics.

Martinez (who married Whitaker's daughter Elsie when she was seventeen and he was thirty-seven.)

Despite everything the party had done for him, Whitaker felt that the Oakland contingent did not value his contributions of speeches and pamphlets. Whitaker resigned the party in anger when he fought with Jack London about strategy. The long-brewing disagreement came to a head over the title of a pamphlet. London wanted it to read, "Let the Capitalists Tremble," while Whitaker thought that the title was too inflammatory. Since the intellectual property of all Oakland Socialist party pamphlets were owned by the group rather than by an individual, London insisted that they put the title to a vote. Naturally, the party members followed their famous figurehead, and Whitaker resigned in frustration. He lost most of his bohemian friends at the same time. Only a few people, like Ross Reed Cheney, stayed friendly with both sides. The more ambitious artists all sided with the more successful writer, hurting Whitaker deeply.

found a job in a socialist cooperative grocery store run by a German, Halvor Hauch, who later encouraged Whitaker to write short stories. While Whitaker holed up in his study, writing sixteen hours every day, Hauch supplied the family with oatmeal, canned milk and an occasional slab of bacon.[38] Whitaker eventually moved to Piedmont and joined the whiskey-loving men of Bohemia, visiting with George Sterling, Joaquin Miller and Xavier "Marty"

<table><tr><td>CARLETON
◈ PARKER</td></tr></table>

While the Socialist party in Berkeley was led by ex-clergyman Stitt Wilson and the Oakland party was dominated by the immigrants and hard-scrabble workers, the region had a third style of socialist who centered on the university. Wilson's style was radically progressive electoral reform, and the Oaklanders favored speeches, rallies and pamphleteering. The university radicals, on the other hand, preferred to work through intellectual problems and make recommendations for change from within.

A wildly adventurous, red-haired man named Carleton Parker attended the university in the years immediately before and after the turn of the twentieth century and later returned to teach there. Parker always had a complicated relationship with the university, but then he had a complicated relationship with almost everyone but his wife, Cornelia, who adored him without reservation. Cornelia felt that no one—not the university, not the town, not the artists he met in the homes of his fellow professors, not even the International Workers of the World—respected him the way such a great man should be respected. Nothing was good enough for her Carl unless he was idolized as a "genius" and a true friend to everyone.

Carl Parker was the kind of college student who made his own bear jerky (shooting the bear himself in Idaho) and served it to girls when he took them out for picnics. He was at Berkeley from 1896 to 1904, taking a few years off to labor in the mines of California and Canada. While working there, he joined the Western Federation of Miners, a group that would incorporate itself in 1905 into the "One Big Union," the Industrial Workers of the World (IWW), also known as Wobblies.

Returning to Berkeley after an education at Harvard and the University of Heidelberg, Parker was one of the first academics to study the problems of migrant labor camps in California's central valley, including his hometown of Vacaville. He was sympathetic to the needs of workers, yet also believed that the IWW and other groups that mobilized the migrant workers were overly violent in their protests. He theorized that psychological analysis was the way to understand the problems of worker/employer relationships. Poor working conditions and worker dissatisfaction were sicknesses, and strikes were only a symptom of these problems.

Parker served as executive secretary in the state Immigration and Housing Commission and "put the migratory on the map" of socialist concerns.[39] One of the most dramatic incidents he covered was the Wheatland Hop-Picker's riot. On a Sunday in August 1913, the men, women and children who harvested hops for California's beer went on strike because they had no water. The closest well was more than a mile away. The rancher, "true to his position and perhaps his type," according to Parker's psychological approach, called the sheriff's posse to arrest the strike leader. The posse drove up in a caravan of cars as the crowd was singing an IWW song, and "after a short

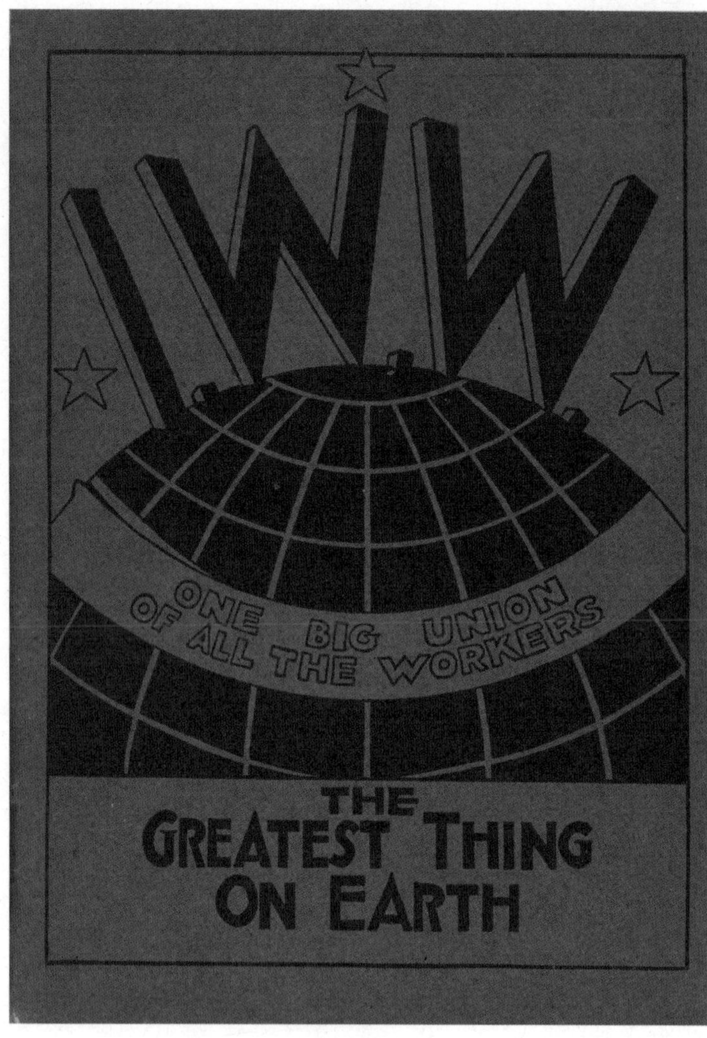

The enthusiastic title of "One Big Union of All the Workers: The Greatest Thing on Earth," was typical of the IWW's promotional materials.

and typical period of skirmishing," a member of the posse fired a gun in the air and started a true riot that left two hop-pickers and two of the sheriff's men dead.

The Wobblies were blamed for the riot. About one hundred of the two thousand eight hundred workers were IWW "card men," including the leader, Richard "Blackie" Ford, and had been involved in speeches and protests from San Diego to Spokane. Another four hundred or so knew the words to the union's memorable songs and could help organize their fellows into the sing-along. Parker advised changes in the laws, making the camps more sanitary and more humane so that IWW radicals could not get a hold in the camps.

When they moved to Berkeley, Carleton and Cornelia Parker bought a house as high in the Berkeley Hills as possible, "where we would realize as much privacy as possible, and where our friends could reach us—if they could stand the climb."[40] Like most of the hill-dwellers, their home was full of the simple luxuries that hill living offered, like Sunday tea parties and a picture window overlooking the Golden Gate. On Tuesday nights, students would brave the hill to talk about life and labor psychology with their thirty-something teacher, grabbing a midnight snack of "ham sandwiches, or sausages, or some edible dear to the male heart" from Cornelia's stash in the kitchen.[41]

"Berkeley socially had become too much of a strain," Cornelia complained, because her husband had made enemies of his fellow teachers by being too free and social with his students, and yet made enemies of the students by grading too hard.[42] (Probably Cornelia's complaints that $1,700 dollars a year and an associate professor's position was not good enough for her brilliant husband also had something to do with their lack of popularity.)

Even more discouraging for their neighbors, the Parkers had almost no interest in the artist feeling that many other Berkeley residents loved. They enjoyed movies, and Carleton could recite "Casey at the Bat," but that was about it for their artistic lives. Bruce Porter, the Russian Hill (San Francisco) artist who helped start the *Lark* and who lived for art, chided Carleton: "You need beauty—you need verse and color and music—you need all the escapes." Parker responded that "the world will improve only through thoughtful social effort. . . . Lives are happy only in that effort. And with it all there will be time for beauty and verse and color and music" after social reform was finished.[43]

After a few years at Berkeley, Parker took a sabbatical to research and write a book, and then accepted a position at the University of Washington as Head of the Department of Economics and Dean of the College of Commerce. Finally, Cornelia was happy with the family finances—she could afford to hire a cook, go to the movies and put frosting on the Sunday cake. She was thrilled that Carleton was getting recognition for his work, acting as the doctor to a strike-ridden patient. But this period lasted only seven months. By March 1918, Carleton Parker was struck down with pneumonia, with a temperature of 105 degrees, and was dead within three days, just short of his fortieth birthday.

Parker left a legacy in Berkeley in the faculty members he radicalized. He had support from the famous anthropologist A. L. Kroeber, who put forward the unpopular proposal that no student be allowed to graduate until he had "supported himself with the labor of his hands for one year."[44]

JAIME DE ANGULO

Parker also had the support of one of Kroeber's fellow anthropologists, Jaime de Angulo, who frequently breezed through town on his way to and from the artist colony in Carmel. Although he stopped by to visit with Kroeber, the city's main attraction for de Angulo was Lucy "Nancy" Freeland, who also taught in the university's anthropology department. The divorced de Angulo was shunned by the respectable people of Berkeley—including the Maybecks and the Keelers—for his affair with Freeland. Kroeber also disapproved

of the relationship and felt that de Angulo lacked the discipline to handle a teaching schedule at the university.

But even if respectable Berkeley disapproved, Jaime was popular with Carmel artists like George Sterling and with the graduate students who were on the fringe of Berkeley's social scene. At least some of the students who followed him must have shared his belief that political justice was more important than academic success. As de Angulo put it, "I must get out of my ivory tower and into the seething street, before it is too late!"[45]

For de Angulo, socialism was the natural reaction to the stifling of his Spanish Catholic upbringing. His rebellion started when he was eight or nine and fascinated by the plumbing in the Place de Concorde fountain in Paris. No one would explain plumbing to him, and instead everyone insisted on telling him "about sin . . . about the state of grace, all sorts of things which bore me." By twelve, he said, "I could no longer believe my parents, my teachers. I was on my own; if there is a truth then I must find it myself."[46]

While running away from his heritage, he dabbled in life as a cowboy, a collector of Native Californian songs, a translator, a transvestite and a poet. Although most of the community rejected de Angulo, he often showed up at local parties, thumbing his nose at the more sedate members of the local bohemian scene. Nancy, who eventually married him, encouraged his behavior as a way to get back at her neighbor, Bernard Maybeck.

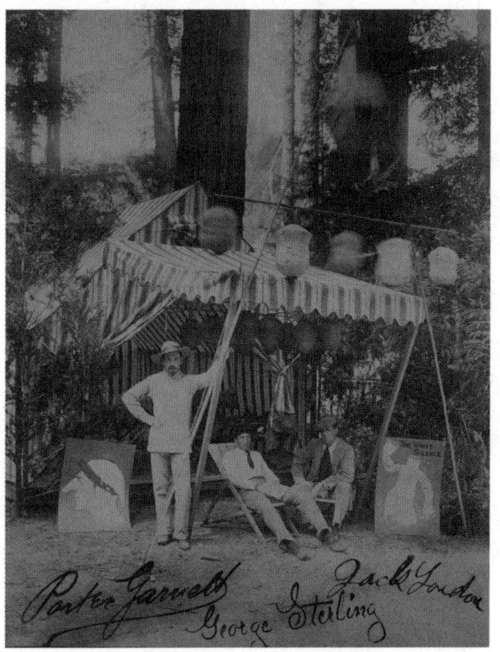

Porter Garnett, George Sterling and Jack London relax at the Bohemian Grove, ca. 1915. Despite their interest in left-wing politics, all three men enjoyed socializing with San Francisco's elites in the Bohemian Club. Sterling would later shoot himself in his room at the club.

Jaime de Angulo would have felt at home with music professor Charles Seeger. In about 1914, Seeger and his friend Herbert A. Cory, an English instructor and poet, were talking to "a group of our young faculty and graduate students," Seeger relayed in a 1966 interview, "and we thought we did a beautiful job" explaining immorality. A quiet man in the back interrupted them, saying that "we just didn't live in a real world. We were sitting up in an ivory tower talking nonsense, and we could talk our heads off and it wouldn't make *any* difference to *anything* at *all*, and we were just children and damn fools. Well, we rather liked that."[47] The quiet fellow was Carleton Parker, and Seeger was almost instantly inspired.

After meeting Parker, Seeger and Cory traveled with Parker through California's Central Valley, watching migrant workers and learning about how the Industrial Workers of the World (IWW) were trying to organize. "On this ranch we saw the handcarts and the wagons (I don't remember any automobiles) that the workers came to the ranch in. . . . There were a lot of children around, some animals, and there was a latrine, nothing but a board over a ditch."[48] Everyone over six was working in the fields.

Seeger, a graduate of Harvard, was a young hotshot in the music world. When U. C. President Benjamin Ide Weever personally asked Seeger to become a music professor at Berkeley, the already cocky young man was made even more self-confident. He was a full professor at twenty-six, a remarkably young age. "There were people over twice my age who were still associate professors," he remembered. Seeger's wealthy family background was much like Whitaker's. His disdain for others came from his father, who believed that "about 70 percent of the people in the world were just stupid and couldn't do anything for themselves, and about all you could do was just keep them from rioting and making trouble." Seeger, in his youth, seemed to keep himself deliberately ignorant of social reality. Although he loved debates, he believed that reading newspapers was "a foolish occupation for a composer."[49] He knew little other than how to write and play music.

Seeger settled in a house on La Loma Avenue and started teaching, soon realizing he didn't actually have much to say to his students. He needed to teach himself something—anything—that he could then relay to his pupils. What he found was the history of music, a subject that would make him a pioneer and would justify his earlier self-confidence. After demanding that the library buy some books on the history of music ("by this time I had begun to be aware that there were sources," he said), he set up an Introduction to Musicology class, "apparently the first course in musicology given in the United States." Because the class was so radical, Seeger could choose what he wanted to teach. For the class on Native American music, he played the round wax-cylinder field recordings that Jaime de Angulo had made of the songs of the Northern Californian Indians.[50]

Parker's comments and exposure to the world combined with Seeger's growing studies of history to inspire a political awakening in Seeger. This new-found radicalism was nurtured by his friendship with German emigrant Emil Kern, "an old Kautskian socialist who lived more or less by his wits in San Francisco and had a shack over on the Pacific." Within a few months, Seeger's philosophy moved to the other side of the economic spectrum, from "nineteenth-century laissez-faire" capitalism to extreme radicalism.[51]

Like Whitaker, Seeger balanced parties at the homes of San Francisco's most wealthy people with lectures to the immigrant left. He had a Maybeck-designed home pushed up against the Berkeley Hills, but he spoke at the Radical Club, "which met in small restaurants on the border of what they used to call the Barbary Coast."[52] He summered in the artist's colony of Carmel and then led lectures to the IWW in a loft on San Francisco's Market Street.[52]

Seeger's biggest adventure was a camping vacation during the fall and winter of 1920, when he and his wife, Constance, decided to travel from the northeast to their waiting house in California, stopping along the way to earn money by performing at churches and schools. Seeger spent a year creating a trailer out of oak and iron and then retrofitting his Ford so it could carry the weight of the "well-over-a-ton" trailer. The family packed clothes, dishes, toys, food, a violin and a collapsible harmonium in their homemade trailer and started on the road.

"The outside of it was wood, the top was canvas like a prairie wagon, and it could collapse for getting under low bridges," said Seeger. His description of the family sounds almost as if the Seegers belonged in the 1960s. "You should have seen us driving down Fifth Avenue," he said. "The Ford full of children looking out from under the collapsible top, and the rather pretty woman sitting in front, and the man with the beard driving."[54] The Seegers ended up spending the winter in rural North Carolina. As always, they divided their time between the humble and the glamorous. One afternoon, Seeger repaired a roof with his dirt-farmer friends and then returned to the same house a few hours later for a black-tie dinner.

These dinners, like Frank C. Havens's parties and the late nights at Coffee Dan's, epitomized the Easy Bay radicals' political experiences. There was always an element of surprise and playfulness in their politics. Many cities in the early part of the twentieth century had radical mayors, progressive legislation and antialcohol laws. Every college town had new thinkers and political extremists. But what city in the United States, apart from Berkeley, forbade people from serving alcohol to their friends? Who else had the good clothes sense of Jack and Charmian London, the bear jerky of Carleton Parker and the revival-hall language of J. Stitt Wilson's campaign speeches? The East Bay, divided as it was between dry and wet, reformist and revolutionary, had something for everyone.

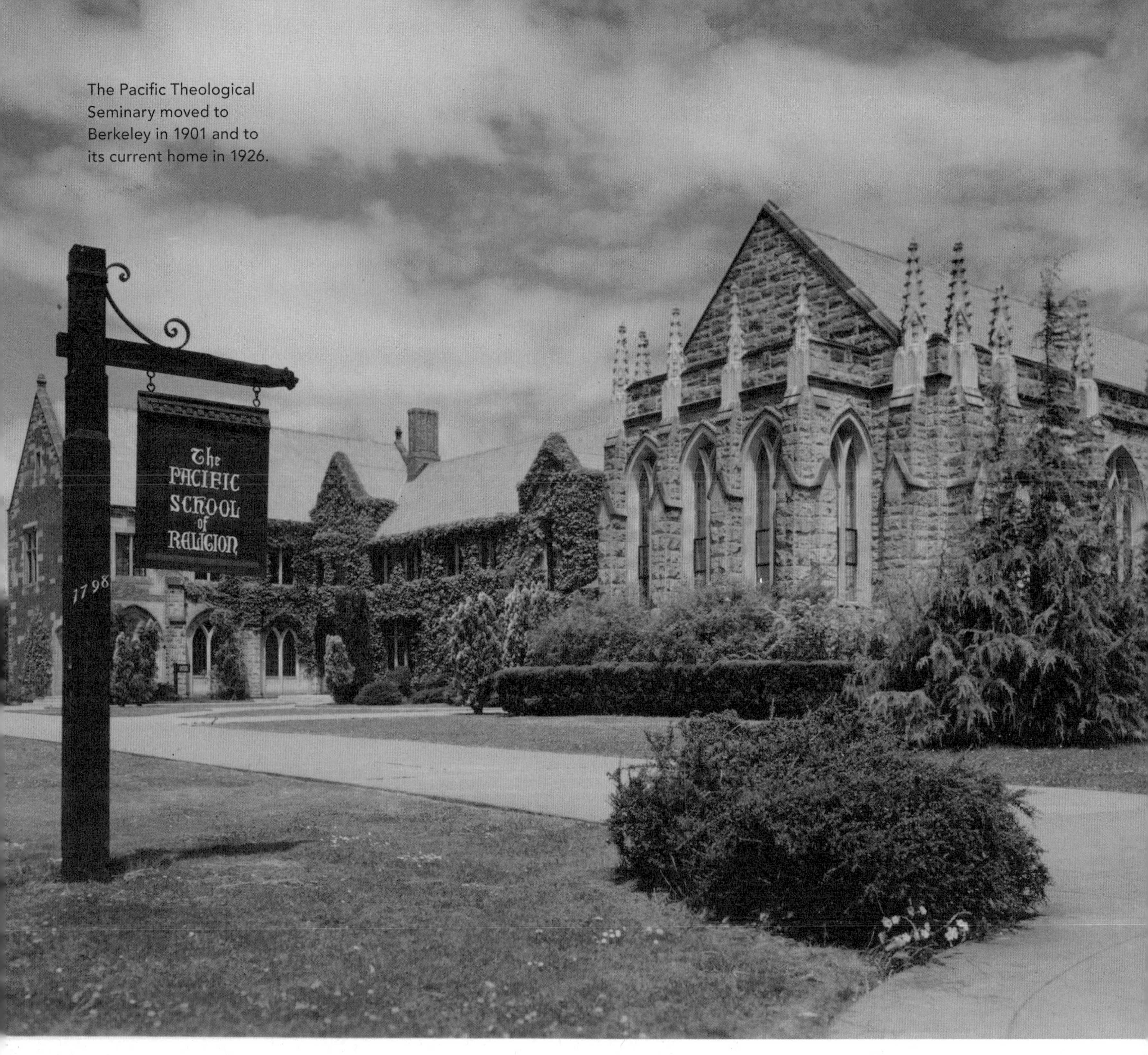

The Pacific Theological
Seminary moved to
Berkeley in 1901 and to
its current home in 1926.

cosmic thoughts

"The mighty Buddha uprose
And spake in the startled gloom:
When the winds of time have blown
Thy dust to the east and west
Thou wilt know that Christ is my brother
And God is the end of our quest."[1]
—Charles Keeler,
"Buddha to the Knight," *1894*

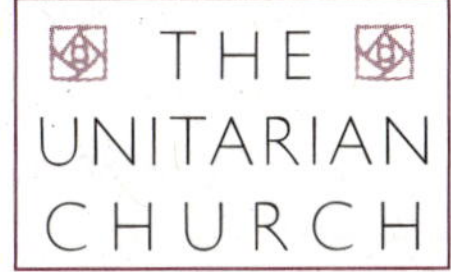

"In those days we were all Unitarians," wrote dancer Florence Boynton, describing Berkeley when she moved there in 1911.[2] Bernard Maybeck, who built Boynton's home, was a Unitarian and architect of the First Unitarian Church. Her neighbors, poet Charles Keeler and artist William Keith, were both Unitarians. Editor and author Ninetta Eames Payne was married to a Unitarian minister, and composer Henry Bickford Passmore spent his Sundays as the Unitarian church organist.

Unitarianism was perfectly suited to the bohemian life. Its emphasis on ecumenism, pacifism, scientific thought and, most importantly, artistic beauty left a lasting impression on Berkeley's cultural scene. As the years went on, however, many Berkeley residents explored emerging religious outlets. World War I brought new problems, especially for the pacifist bohemians. Their traditional faith did not explain how to rescue a civilization "now on trial" from poison gas and fear of war, as Charles Keeler put it. In his mind, "religion must unite the world" that had been pulled apart by war, and Unitarianism did not go far enough in encouraging that unity.

Throughout the 1910s and 1920s, Berkeley and the Bay Area were rich with religious ideas that were available in few other places in the country. Without an established religious culture, people of diverse religions (even new or obscure ones) were able to rise to positions of influence. Joining a new religion or even starting one's own might have brought a few odd glances, but it was not likely to lead to social isolation. This freedom meant that Berkeley's bohemians could look around themselves for new ways to express their spiritual sides.

Florence Boynton's perspective was typical of the bohemians, as she gave up Unitarianism and socialism for Christian Science soon after moving to Berkeley. Meteorologist Lazar Blochman practiced spiritualism in addition to Judaism. Missionary Yehan Numata started a magazine to bring Buddhist thought to America.

The high point of this religious freedom and creativity was an entirely new religion, the International Cosmic Society. Inspired by Unitarianism, spiritualism and Buddhism, the Cosmic Society (also known as the Cosmic Religion) offered a spiritual community for those who questioned the dogma of more traditional beliefs. Its founder, Charles Keeler, also ensured that the Cosmic Society offered personal attention and support.

From the very beginning, the Bay Area had a unique religious history. One of the first buildings in San Francisco was a church, Mission Dolores, built just as the United States was fighting for its independence from England. Missionaries from Mexico and Spain built the structure to convert the local Native Americans to Catholicism and to force them into ranching. In the 1840s, San Francisco's second religion appeared—the Church of Jesus Christ of Latter-day Saints, whose followers were called Mormons. The religion was less than twenty years old at the time, and Mormons were persecuted throughout the United States. The tiny

Mexican-owned city of San Francisco was a safe haven to set up Mormon life, complete with schools and newspapers. Almost immediately after the Mormons arrived, the California gold rush changed the city forever, but the Bay Area stayed open to new and unconventional religions.

In the next fifty years, all of the world's religions came to the Bay Area. In 1906, the U.S. Religious Census found that San Francisco had one of the most diverse religious populations in the country. Only 36 percent of San Franciscans were traditionally religious, and only 7 percent of San Franciscans belonged to the Protestant denominations that made up most of the rest of the country.[3]

Religiously, Berkeley was considered a bastion of traditional native-born Protestantism. However, within the mainstream Protestant denominations, the city's educational culture helped spread new ideas through its densely packed theological schools. "When Berkeley has become an Oxford, Oakland a Brooklyn, and San Francisco a New York, it will then be a very great advantage to have a school of liberal progressive theology of long standing," said an early religious leader.[4] Soon Berkeley was the home of a large Protestant theological training center focused around the Pacific Theological Seminary. Unitarians, Baptists, Congregationalists, Episcopalians and others trained their clergymen in Berkeley, disseminating a liberal and ecumenical Protestant culture. In 1916, the institute changed its name to the Pacific School of

Religion to emphasize the influence of other religious traditions.

The most liberal Protestants in Berkeley were the Unitarians, who included most of the people in this book. Unitarians of the time believed that "the church is profitable for edification, but not for doctrine."[5] It was a fitting religion for people who strove to develop new artistic developments and philosophies. In the Unitarian tradition, God can be understood through human reason and exploration. The religion's name comes from the Unitarian belief in the unity of God, as opposed to the trinity. Earlier American bohemians, like the 1830s transcendentalists Ralph Waldo Emerson and Henry David Thoreau, influenced the denomination and encouraged Unitarians to recognize the value of a wide variety of religious traditions. In 1890, Berkeley's Unitarians were still debating how far they should go to support the "latitudinarian tolerance" of non-Christian traditions.

Berkeley's Unitarians, like those elsewhere, believed in supporting science and new knowledge, just the belief that a university town needed in order to thrive. Stanford University President David Starr Jordan, the man who had brought Unitarianism to California, pointed out to the Berkeley Unitarian Club that belief in the new, strange scientific world that was so booming in the nineteenth century came from the same source as beliefs in religion. In both, a person needed to step outside his or her own experiences and understand something more complicated than him- or

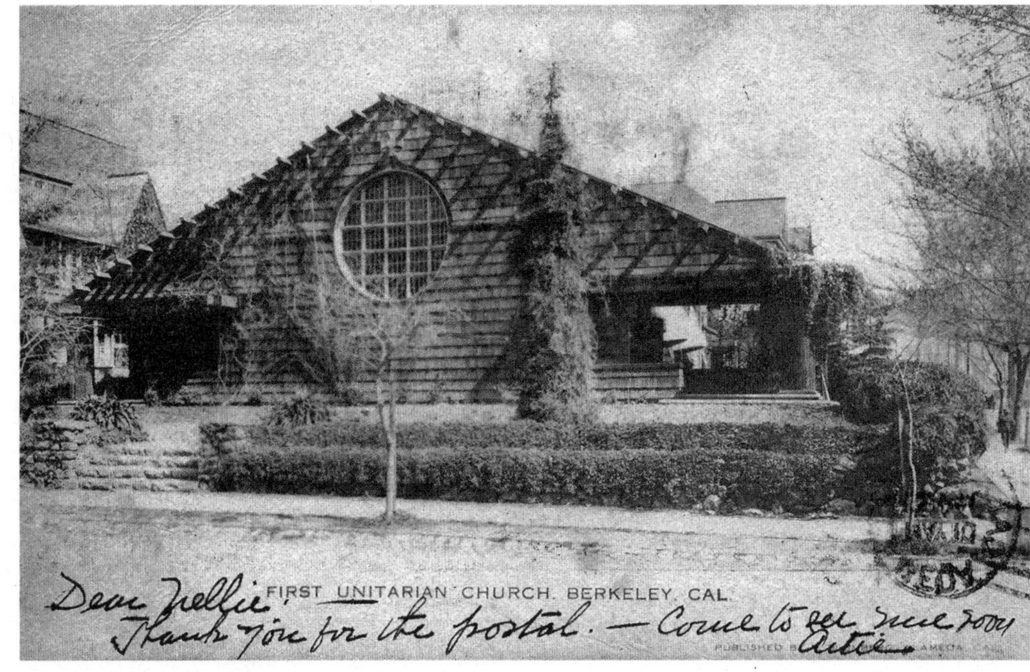

herself. Jordan even felt that "much of what we call religion today is simply the debris of our grandfather's science."[6]

In 1891, the Berkeley Unitarians hit a turning point just as the city's bohemian movement was starting. That year, thirty-two families "signed the book" to say that they were officially members of the First Unitarian Church of Berkeley. By the end of the year, more Unitarians had come forward to support the local church, so that one hundred families were members by January 1892. Seven years after its founding, the church's board raised enough money for member Bernard Maybeck to design a new building, propped up with large redwood pillars. The new structure was dedicated that November, with four Unitarian ministers

The First Unitarian Church of Berkeley, built by architect A. C. Schweinfurth of the office of A. Page Brown & Co., San Francisco. The company also employed the soon-to-be famous Bernard Maybeck, who was a member of Berkeley's Unitarian congregation.[7]

and a rabbi participating in the opening ceremony. By 1908, the church had 534 families as members.

This was the local Unitarian church's period of greatest strength. After the changes of World War I, membership dropped. In 1922, only 340 members remained.[8]

Around the time when membership in the Berkeley church was declining, artist Bruce Porter of San Francisco wrote to a friend in Berkeley about his experience with the Unitarian idea of God. "The word 'God,' spoken in the comfortable (almost smug) atmosphere of the old Unitarian congregation, took my breath and tanked me into a vision of a great flood of light, and *only* light." God, Porter said, should not be frightening, not a "monster" of olden times, but a new and fresh idea of truth, goodness and beauty.

As the Unitarian church faded away, Berkeley's citizens were leaving behind older forms of worship and exploring the new ideas that were springing up around the globe in the nineteenth and early twentieth centuries. One of the first to appear in Berkeley was spiritualism, which was first established in New York in 1848 and was practiced in the Bay Area since at least the 1880s.

SPIRITUALISM Although we do not known much about spiritualist Lazar Blochman besides his niece's recollections, his story shows how an adventurous person with liberal beliefs could turn to unconventional believer despite a traditional religious upbringing. Blochman probably passed the bohemians in the streets, libraries, theaters and hiking paths of Berkeley. He might have met them at civic and charitable functions. But his interests lay outside of those shared by most of the people in this book. Blochman was a pacifist, an avid bicyclist and nature lover who turned to meteorology as an outlet for his passions. He also was a vegetarian and, according to his great-niece Mary Hoexter, would haul around his dinner, "one pound of yellow cheese," whenever he went over to someone else's house for a get-together.

Lazar Blochman had adventure in his genes. His father was a Jewish emigrant from France and his mother was from Germany, but the family had been in California since at least the late 1850s.[9] Lazar's Uncle Abraham Blochman was a gold-rush era businessman who lost his fortune in the 1870s but built it right back up again in the 1880s (he, too, was an avid bicyclist). By 1886, Uncle Abraham was able to fund the first Jewish congregation and religious school in San Diego. Another Blochman brother died in the Sierras and was "packed down to Sacramento on mule back so he could be buried in a Jewish cemetery."[10]

As a young man, he married Ida Mae Twitchell, a schoolteacher who loved botany, and settled in Santa Maria. After a life of hard work, the couple discovered oil on their property and decided to retire from professional life and take up study. To them, the perfect place to do this was in Berkeley, home of the university. In 1909, the family

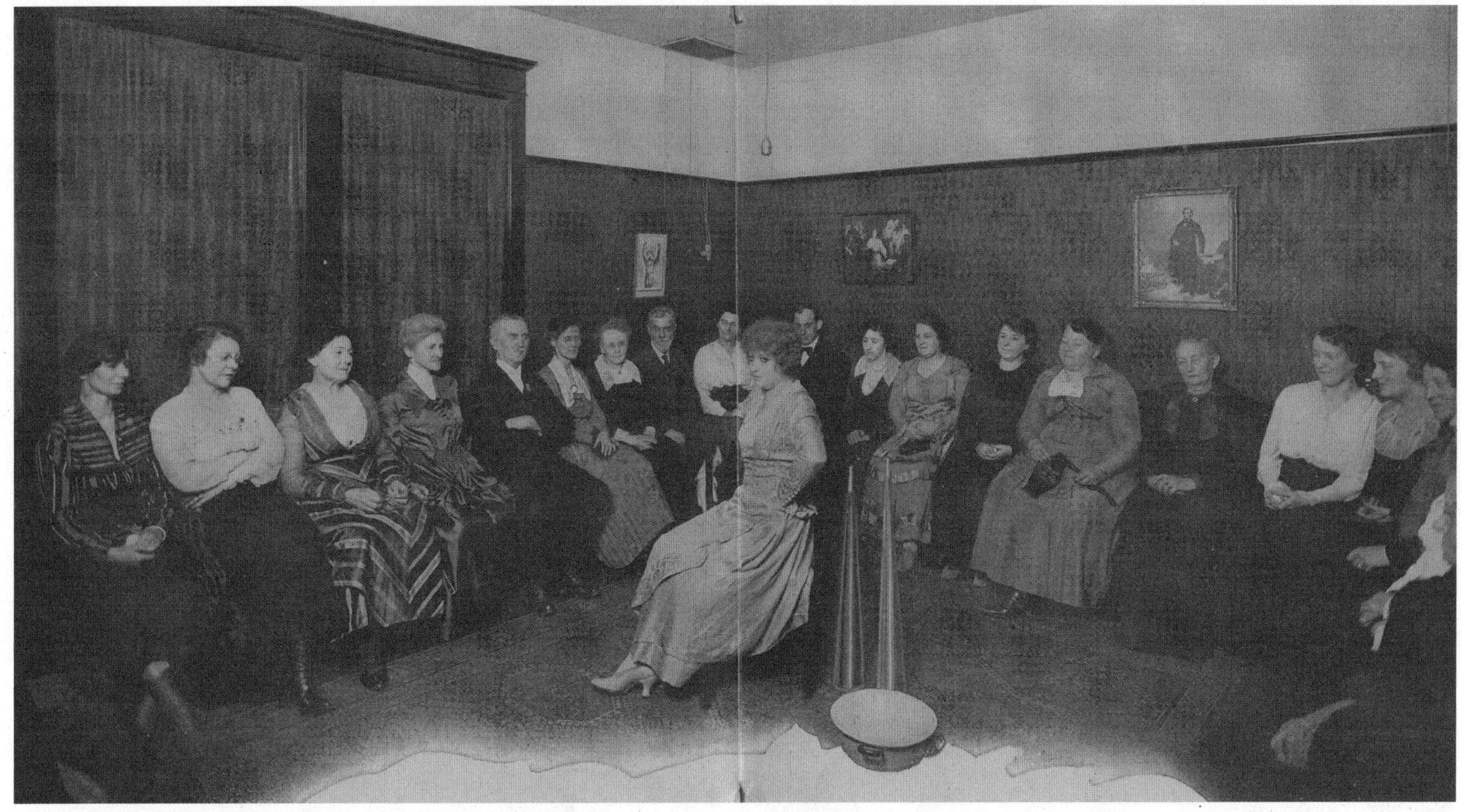

Spiritualists sit in a circle around a medium in an early 1920s séance in Illinois.

moved to Berkeley, where Ida served eight years on the Berkeley Board of Education and nineteen years as the president of the Berkeley Charity Commission. Lazar was even busier. At fifty-nine years old, he decided to attend college. Within six years, he had studied geography, meteorology, Spanish, history and philosophy, and then he earned a teaching certificate and a Master of Science degree. In his spare time, he hiked Mt. Tamalpais in Marin County until he was injured at age eighty.

Lazar was always an unconventional and creative person, but only this combined with tragedy made him a spiritualist. After Ida's death in 1939, he started attending séances in order to talk with her and his deceased younger sister Hannah.

Spiritualism, the belief that Lazar Blochman followed, was a way to "communicate with the dead."[11] For its believers, it offered proof that humans never die. Once people leave earth they go to "spheres" that surround the earth, each time being born into a higher sphere, keeping their personality. They also keep their habits after death; for example, clothes are worn in the spirit world.[12] Like Lazar Blochman, those who

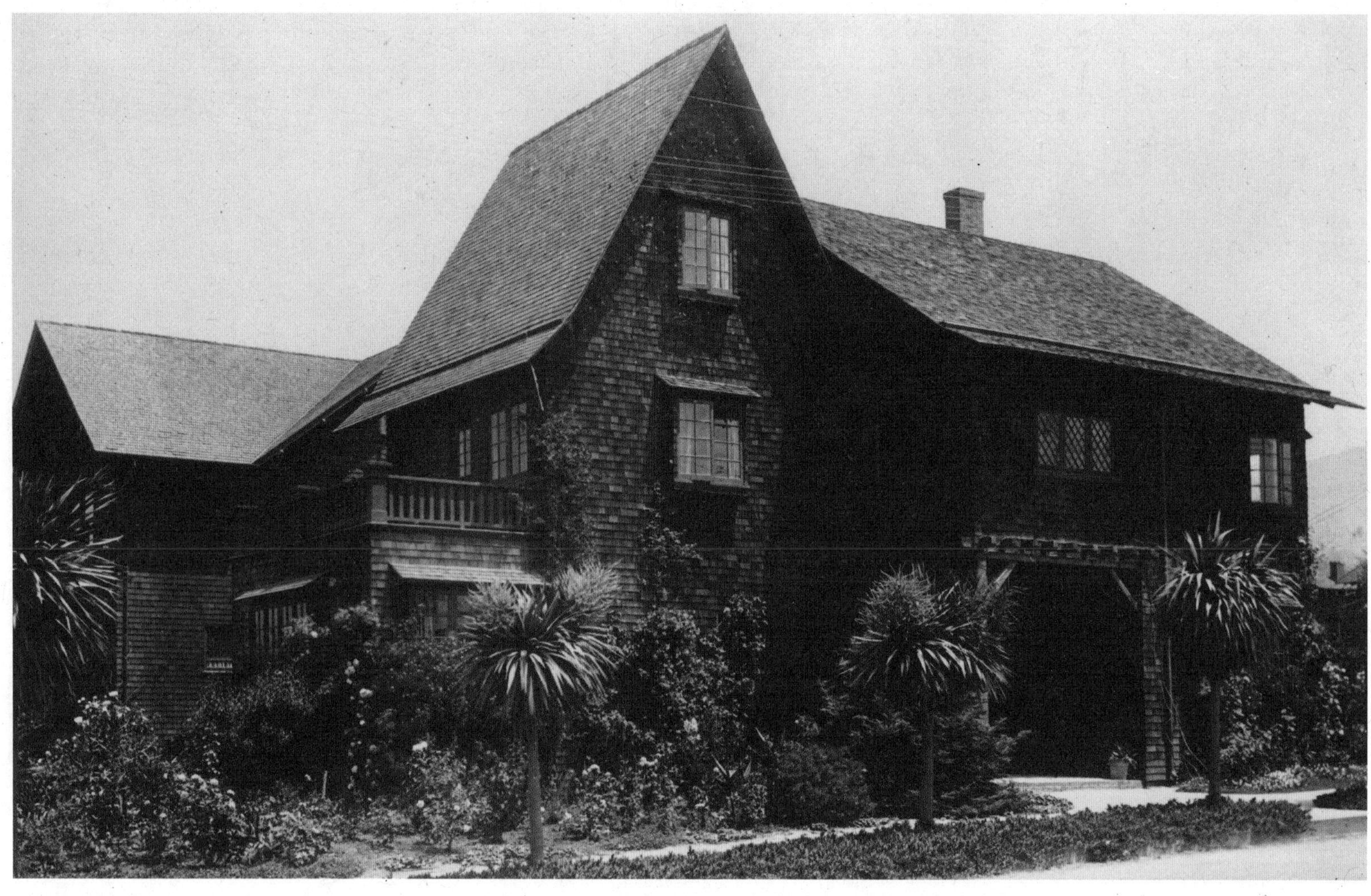

found it too hard to wait until they could be rejoined with those who had passed to the other side could communicate with the spirits through mediums.

Mediums were "sensitive to vibrations in the spirit world," according to the *Spiritualist Manual*.[13] Spiritualists maintained that the gift of sensitivity could appear in anyone, regardless of belief or goodness. Although spiritualist beliefs are counter to those of the Judaism that Blochman grew up with, at least one 1922 spiritualist advertised in Hebrew.

Mediums around the country offered rapping sounds, spirit writing materialization (in which the person appears as a filmy form in front of the medium) and other methods of contacting those who had passed on. Sometimes the medium would channel many different people in one session. S. H. West, a spiritualist believer, wrote that he received spirit writings on slates from five different people, each of whom had a different style of message and each of whom wrote in a different handwriting. His doctor asked about his health, a friend debated politics, and his parents discussed family matters. In a later San Francisco séance, he spoke with fifteen different people, including an ancient Greek girl named Pansy.[14]

CHRISTIAN SCIENCE Like Lazar Blochman, Florence Boynton adopted new beliefs in response to troubles. First drawn to the local Christian Science church because of its Maybeck design, she soon came to enjoy the beliefs of the religion. (Perhaps her claims that she converted on her second visit to the church were exaggerated, but her point is clear. She adopted Christian Science very quickly.) Maybeck's brilliant plan for the church was completed in 1910, and Florence Boynton probably converted soon after. The Christian Science religion appealed to her in part because of her aesthetic sensibilities. The church was built of natural wood and fit with Boynton's own beliefs about structures that combined the natural with the human.

For Florence Boynton, one of the most important passages of *Science and Health*, an important Christian Scientist document, was, "The Structure of Trust and Love; whatever rests upon and proceeds from divine Principle."[15] As she said, she turned from socialism (striving for worldly equality) to Christian Science (striving for spiritual perfection). Her con-

version was probably influenced by the political changes in the 1910s as the world rushed into war and America was torn apart by labor problems. In the Christian Scientist worldview, sin, evil and death are simply illusions. Even though mortals see them as real, they are nothing but urges that lead one away from God. For someone struggling with reports of a violent world, the thought that such things were not real must have been a huge relief.

In 1866, the religion was discovered and founded by forty-something Mary Baker Eddy, who suffered from spinal disease. In 1875, Eddy published *Science and Health* for the first time and founded the Church of Christ (Scientist) in Boston in 1879. By the 1890s the religion was nationwide, though in the years after 1920, it was increasingly centered on the West Coast.

Boynton was part of a trend in Christian Science conversions. Between 1916 and 1926, the religion was steadily growing, and California had the biggest jump in members of any state. Mostly an urban religion, it drew people from similar backgrounds as Florence Boynton.

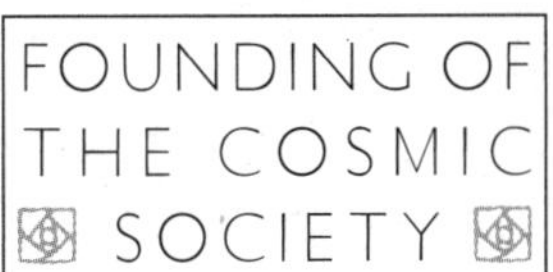
FOUNDING OF THE COSMIC SOCIETY Out of this religious stew of Berkeley beliefs came Charles Keeler's Cosmic religion. Keeler was influenced by the beliefs that swirled around his social circle in Berkeley. In 1925, he wrote *The Epitome of the Cosmic Religion*, a slim stapled pam-

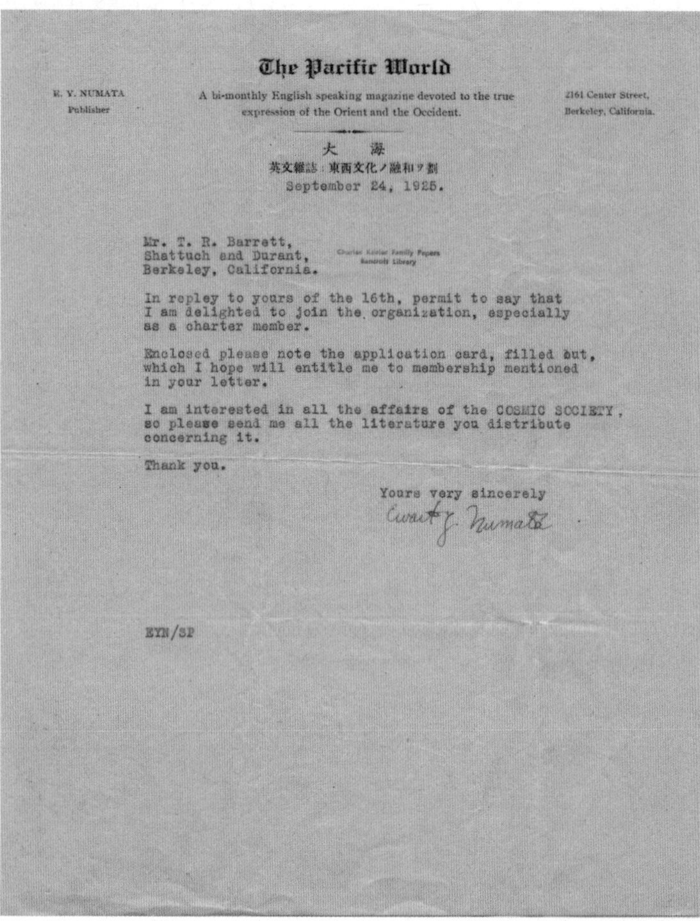

The Pacific World

E. Y. NUMATA
Publisher

A bi-monthly English speaking magazine devoted to the true
expression of the Orient and the Occident.

2161 Center Street,
Berkeley, California.

大　海
英文雜誌：東西文化ノ融和ヲ割
September 24, 1925.

Mr. T. R. Barrett,
Shattuch and Durant,
Berkeley, California.

In repley to yours of the 16th, permit to say that
I am delighted to join the organization, especially
as a charter member.

Enclosed please note the application card, filled out,
which I hope will entitle me to membership mentioned
in your letter.

I am interested in all the affairs of the COSMIC SOCIETY,
so please send me all the literature you distribute
concerning it.

Thank you.

Yours very sincerely

EYN/SP

Yehan Numata responds to an invitation to join the Cosmic Society on the letterhead of the *Pacific World* magazine.

phlet that introduced what he hoped would be a worldwide belief system headquartered in Berkeley. It would offer a chance for "those who have outgrown traditional faiths" to "become reconsecrated to the ideal" through the guiding hand of the Cosmic faith. Soon afterwards, his friends started urging him to set up meetings for followers of the goals, beliefs and organization outlined in the *Epitome*.

Keeler made it very clear that he thought his religion was nothing like the mystical beliefs of theosophy, spiritualism or Christian Science. He did not want his new faith lumped with what he saw as the "cranks" who dismissed rational experiments for "half-baked, undigested or visionary theories." In one letter to Dr. L. Esterbrook, he wrote, "I am frankly afraid of Theosophical doctrines. . . . Of all the queer, intangible and sometimes mad conceptions of life and the universe that I have heard, they certainly had a monopoly." Keeler also dismissed Christian Science, especially for its tenets about healing. If someone announced that he found "a cure for cancer, before believing it I would like to know what the research men of the Rockefeller Institute . . . thought of it," Keeler said.[16]

Even though he would have denied doing so, Keeler still drew ideas—perhaps unconsciously—from his neighbors. Like the Unitarian church of which he was once a member, Charles Keeler believed in the sanctity of all religious traditions, "Christ and Buddha, Mahomet and Confucious, Lao Tze and Zoraster," a trinity composed of three abstract ideals and acceptance of rational truths derived from research.[17] As outlined in the *Epitome*, the "trinity" of the cosmic religion was not the Father, the Son and the Holy Spirit but rather Love, Truth and Beauty. Love, as defined by the Cosmic religion, was "unselfish," a "desire to promote the well-being of others," while truth was the facts as laid out by accredited experts, like "college professors" and "government investigators."[18] As befitting Keeler's love of both poetry and wildlife, he said that beauty could be found in both art and nature.

Keeler encouraged chapters of the Cosmic Society to accept members of different races. He even suggested "international quotas" of different races and ethnicities in each chapter "whenever it is expedient and practical to do so." This would "encourage friendly association of individuals of diverse races and nations."[19] His own chapter had members of "half a dozen nationalities" among its seventy founding members, according to a 1926 newspaper article. But Keeler was hesitant about, or maybe even afraid of, social integration. Like most people of his time, he was not entirely comfortable with complete racial mixing. "Such association as fellow members of a religious organization, however, need not imply any further association in home or social life," he reassured his flock.[20]

YEHAN NUMATA

Because of Keeler's belief in racial equality, he invited members of many Berkeley communities to join his faith. In September 1925, a devout young Buddhist named Yehan Numata wrote to Keeler to accept the invitation, saying that he was "delighted to join the organization, especially as a charter member."[21]

Numata was a thirty-year-old student in statistics at the University of California and a leader in the Japanese-American student community. He had graduated from elementary school twice, once as a child in his small hometown in Japan and once as a nineteen-year-old in Hawaii. His father, a priest, taught him the Jodo Shin sect of Buddhism. As Numata's biographer explained, this branch taught that everyone could be saved, not just those who could afford to donate money to the temple. Numata was sent abroad to follow his father's religious example, acting as a missionary to Jodo Shin followers in Hawaii and later in California.

Once he arrived in California, racism and isolation hurt his spirit, while tuberculosis hurt his body and a natural disaster took his home. During his junior year, the 1923 wildfire burnt down the Japanese student's dormitory, along with houses in the Berkeley Hills. Neighborhood homeowners refused to let the Asian students rebuild on the highly desirable hill land, which was officially restricted to white people. Numata, as befitting his role as a missionary, stepped up as a leader of the students. He presented their case to the mayor of Berkeley and won permission to rebuild.

In July 1925, Numata started yet another project. He no longer wanted to be a priest like his father and, instead, decided to promote Buddhism as a layperson. He and some other young men who were "striving to bring the Old and the New Worlds into closer relationships" started a magazine called the *Pacific World*. A magazine for "all the Children of Mother Earth," the *Pacific World* tried to reduce the animosity towards Asian-Americans by educating white America about Asian culture. The magazine had a goal that must have attracted and influenced Charles Keeler as he started to develop the Cosmic religion. It focused on the "one great underlying force that is present in all men, that is Love."[22]

The first issue of the *Pacific World* reached most of the places where Mother Earth's children lived. Numata and his fellows sent copies to India, England, Germany, Ceylon, Japan, the Philippines and all parts of the United States, from the Philadelphia Public Library to the University of Chicago to Boston, New York and Iowa City. Every department in the U.S. cabinet received a copy, as did the U.S. postmaster general and the vice president.

While they were happy to get free copies of the magazine, not enough of the *Pacific*

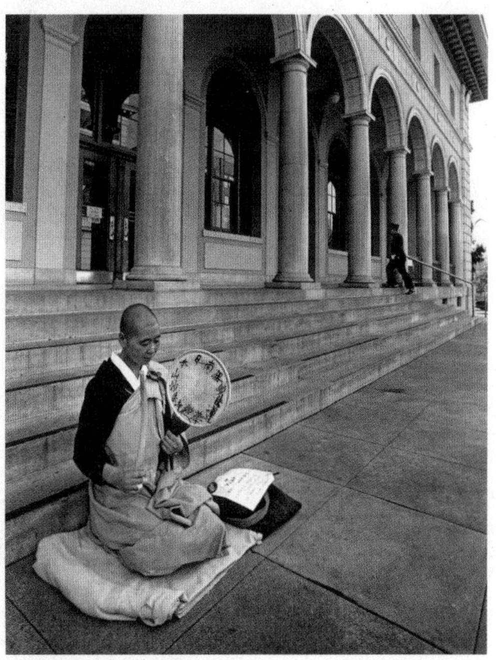

A Buddhist monk continues Yehan Numata's activist tradition.

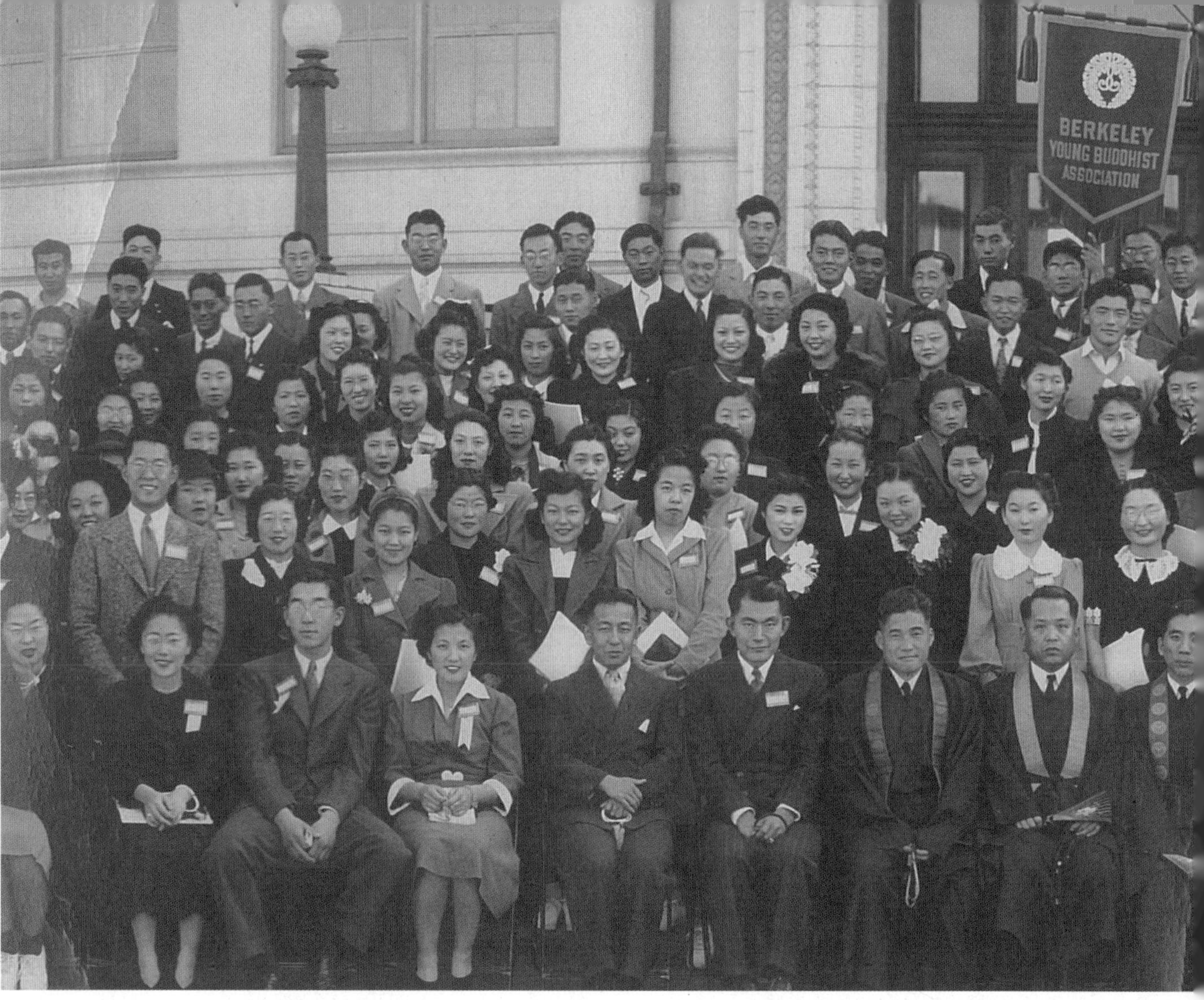

The 11th Annual Bay District Buddhist Conference, held in Berkeley, California, on October 27, 1940. This group portrait shows the growing strength of Berkeley's Buddhist community on the eve of World War II, a community that had its roots in the student groups and immigrant families served by missionaries like Yehan Numata.

World's supporters were willing to spend money on it. The *Pacific World,* ambitious as it was, ended up short of money. Numata's magazine lasted only a few years until the students ran out of money and were forced to stop publication. Numata returned to Japan after finishing his education and vowed that he would become so rich that none of his Buddhist projects would ever have to close from lack of support. He succeeded in both projects, founding a successful laboratory tool company and donating most of his money to religious causes, including reviving the *Pacific World* in 1982. The magazine is now distributed free of charge to anyone who is interested.

NINETTA EAMES PAYNE Other followers of the Cosmic religion brought their own talents and own concerns. One was Ninetta Wiley Eames Payne, a difficult and

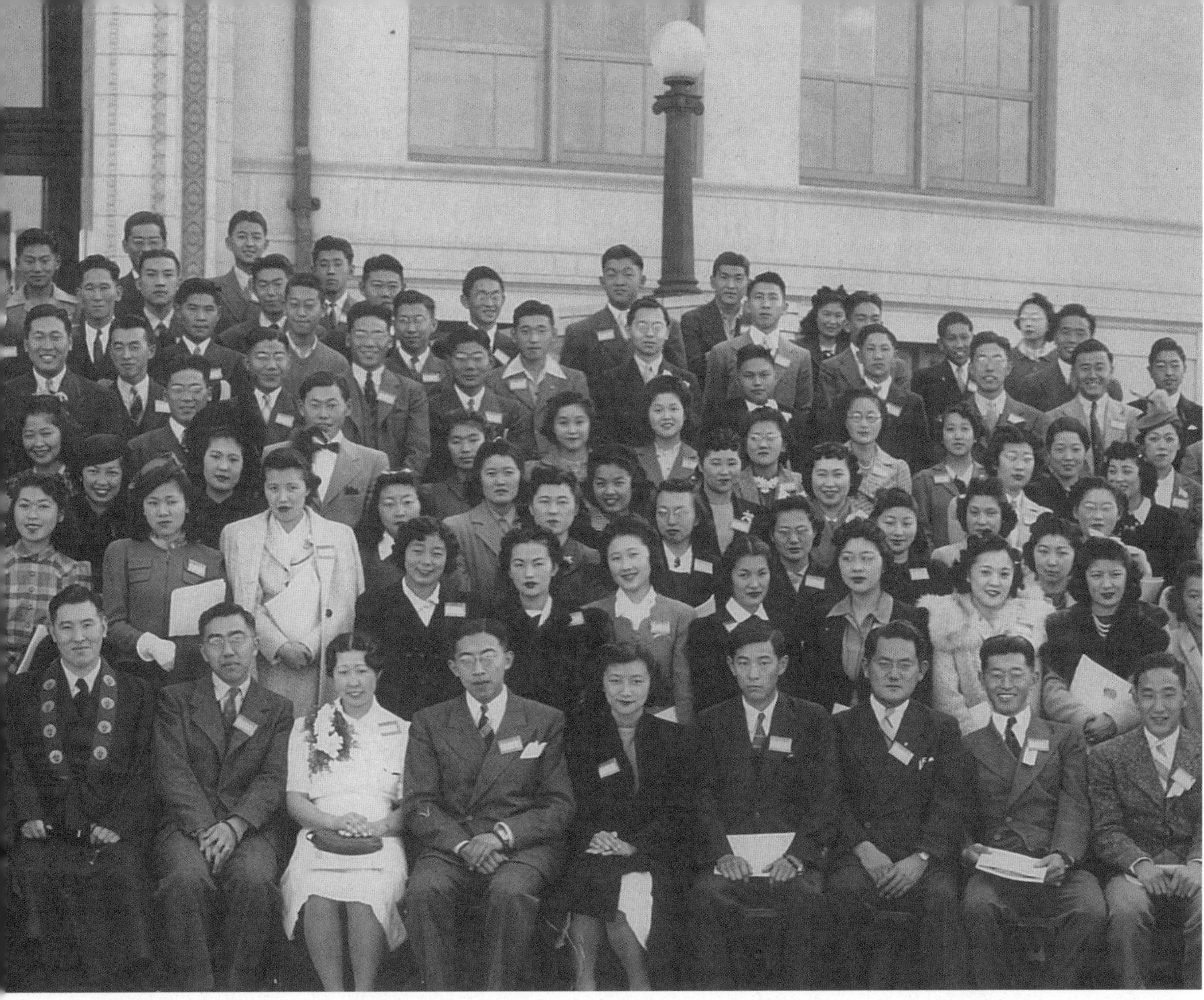

self-centered woman known as Netta. By the time she joined the Cosmic religion, she was an elderly woman, living off her niece Charmian's money and her nephew-in-law Jack London's fame. In 1926, only her fascination with whole-wheat bread made her happy until she found a friend in Keeler and a new project in the Cosmic religion.

Netta was never a conventional woman. "I know I am fanatical. But I cannot help it,"[23] she once explained. She was part of California's first wave of bohemians and deeply connected with the *Overland Monthly*, one of the first literary journals in California, which she and her first husband, Roscoe Eames, treated like the family business. Roscoe, a former shorthand teacher, was the magazine's business manager. Netta threw in her services for free, taking on "editorial duties" and writing articles.

Netta and Roscoe Eames also shared a belief in free love, following the ideas espoused by radical feminist Victoria Woodhull, who believed that "I have an inalienable, constitutional and natural right to love whom I may, to love as long or as short a period as I can; [and] to change that love every day if I please."[24] Roscoe would occasionally disappear with another woman, while Netta brought home "protégés" picked from the artistic young men of Oakland. She set up a *ménage a trois* with Roscoe and her second husband, Edward Biron Payne, who worked on the *Overland Monthly* with Netta and Roscoe. When Roscoe decided to permanently stay with one of his lovers, she divorced him and married Edward in 1910.

Edward Payne had been kicking around Berkeley's bohemian scene since the 1870s. He started out as a Berkeley Congregational minister who converted to Unitarianism and Christian socialism and then moved on to spiritualism. He helped found the Altruria Community, one of a trio of utopian communes that set up in Sonoma County in the 1890s. The eighteen men, women and children of the community managed to build seven houses in nine months and were starting to sell their produce at the Altrurian Store in San Francisco before they got the idea that a hotel would be a more profitable business. The community's ambition kept growing, however, until the unfinished hotel's many additions ate up their capital. Unable to stay on the land, the Altrurians moved back to the Bay Area's cities.

Ninetta Eames was likely one of the Altrurians' investors. Even though money was tight, she would probably have thrilled at the chance to help create a new and more equitable society. Three decades later, she was definitely supporting the Cosmic religion. In March, she promised a "monthly stipend" to support the society financially. Each time she wrote to Keeler, she reminded him that she was doing her part. In April, she pointed out that she had "contributed [her] mite" and in May that she was sending "another small check to help a little in your able work."[25] Ninetta Eames was making sure that Keeler knew how grateful he should be.

In return, Ninetta gained a devoted correspondent who offered her his "gracious kindness and consideration" and made her feel a part of his "nobel [*sic*] work for mankind." With the attention from the founder of a religion, Ninetta felt that she could finally die contented, or in her words, "race happily towards an ever-radiant summit, both hands scattering feather-weight cares like butterfly wings afloat."[26]

Although Ninetta Wiley Eames Payne was convinced she was going to die soon, she continued to have a vibrant and dramatic life into her ninth decade. She married her third husband, Fred Springer, in 1937 at the age of eighty-five.

LIFE IN THE COSMIC SOCIETY

The Cosmic religion needed Netta's help, and the help of every other member, just in order to survive. "The Berkeley Chapter of the Cosmic Society has not been a success if by success one means a large and grow-

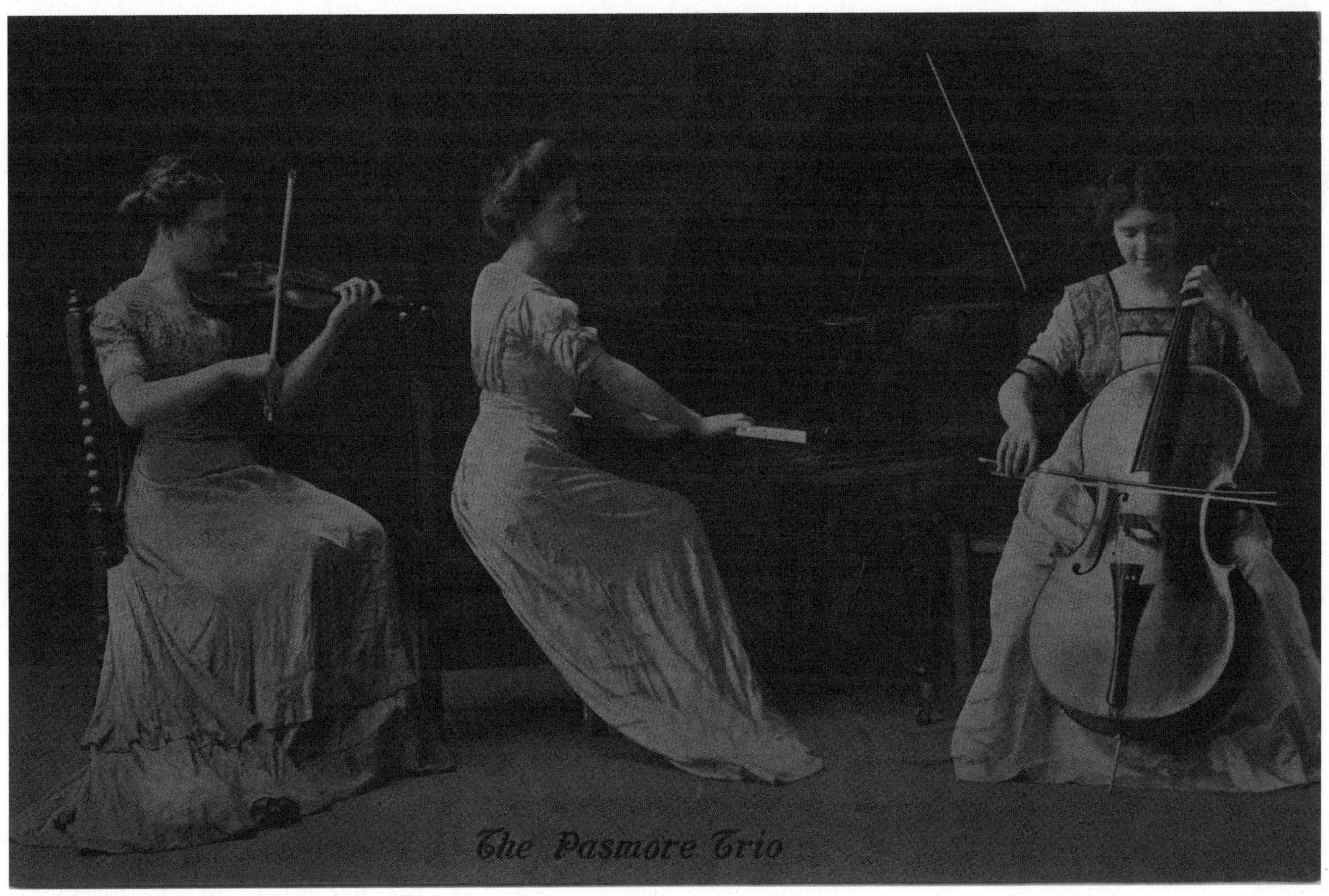

ing following and ample financial support," reported Charles Keeler in a May 1926 letter. Keeler sounded disappointed but still hopeful. After all, he was still frequently receiving letters from supporters such as the spiritualist believer in reincarnation, Laura Gearns Nelles, who wrote that Keeler's faith had found "the heart of life" and "the naked truth" that was "almost smothered by [contemporary life's] trappings of superstition, custom and materialism."[27] Members who could not give money gave their time and talents. One woman translated the *Epitome of the Cosmic Society* into braille, receiving free membership for herself and a friend in return. Composer H. Bickford Passmore, who had written hymns for the local Unitarian church before persuading Keeler to start a chapter of the Cosmic religion, played music at the Cosmic ceremonies.

Dorothy, Mary and Suzanne Passmore—"just three young girls from the Pacific Coast"— who performed internationally as the Passmore Trio.[28] They were the daughters of Henry Bickford Passmore, who composed the hymns for the Cosmic religion.

Keeler felt that a religion needed to express beauty in order to attract members, and he liked to incorporate pageantry and pomp into the meetings of his new faith. Unfortunately, the Cosmic religion could not afford to pay artists or architects, so Keeler and Passmore's talents dominated the Cosmic religion's ceremonies. Keeler did not leave any record of the Cosmic religion's rituals, but he did lay out some guidelines for meetings. The group usually met in a member's backyard, lit by candles, and heard music from a soloist. Cosmic religion followers recited autosuggestion chants, rhyming couplets with a strong rhythmic beat. Sometimes these little poems seem to have a jazzlike syncopation. Each chant was intended to bring something good to the chanter, like peace, health or prosperity. Rather than appealing to a higher force, the chants imply that the singer can bring good things on himself or herself simply by believing in them. The "Auto Suggestion for Prosperity" includes the rhyme "O I am a magnet of wealth and power/Good things come in a ceaseless shower."[29]

At some point during the evening, the followers listened to one of Keeler's sermonlike speeches on their faith's primary beliefs about nature, beauty, world affairs and various cultural ideas of God. Occasionally, Keeler would talk about one of his other interests, like Mother's Day, patriotism, or even fairies. Often, the sermon would build on the previous week's theme.

The Cosmic religion never drew more than a small huddle of believers, gathered in the chilly garden every Sunday evening. Perhaps they held their candles, or perhaps the candles burned in lamps around them. Perhaps they sang or chanted as a group, or perhaps they sat and listened to a performer. Most likely, the scant ritual appealed to those who already knew the Keelers and appreciated their style of hospitality.

Many of the tiny band of followers moved on to other beliefs after their experiment with the new religion. As Yehan Numata's experience shows, membership in the Cosmic religion in no way stopped some people from practicing other faiths. In the end, the Cosmic religion lost members quickly and was moribund by the 1930s. Charles Keeler was the second person to have the Cosmic religion burial rites read over him—words he had written himself many years before. His daughter was one of a few to be married by the Cosmic religion rituals.

Even though the city's experiment with the Cosmic religion lasted only a few years, most Berkeleyans respected and understood the urge that led Keeler on the ambitious path of creating a new religion. The Cosmic religion was the ultimate example of how the city's combination of creative people, religious diversity and willingness to experiment helped drive people to new beliefs in the trying years during and after World War I, as belief in traditional religions like Unitarianism declined. Not only did Berkeley's religious experimenters try to understand a world that was more complicated and violent, but they also tried to make the world more beautiful through their faiths.

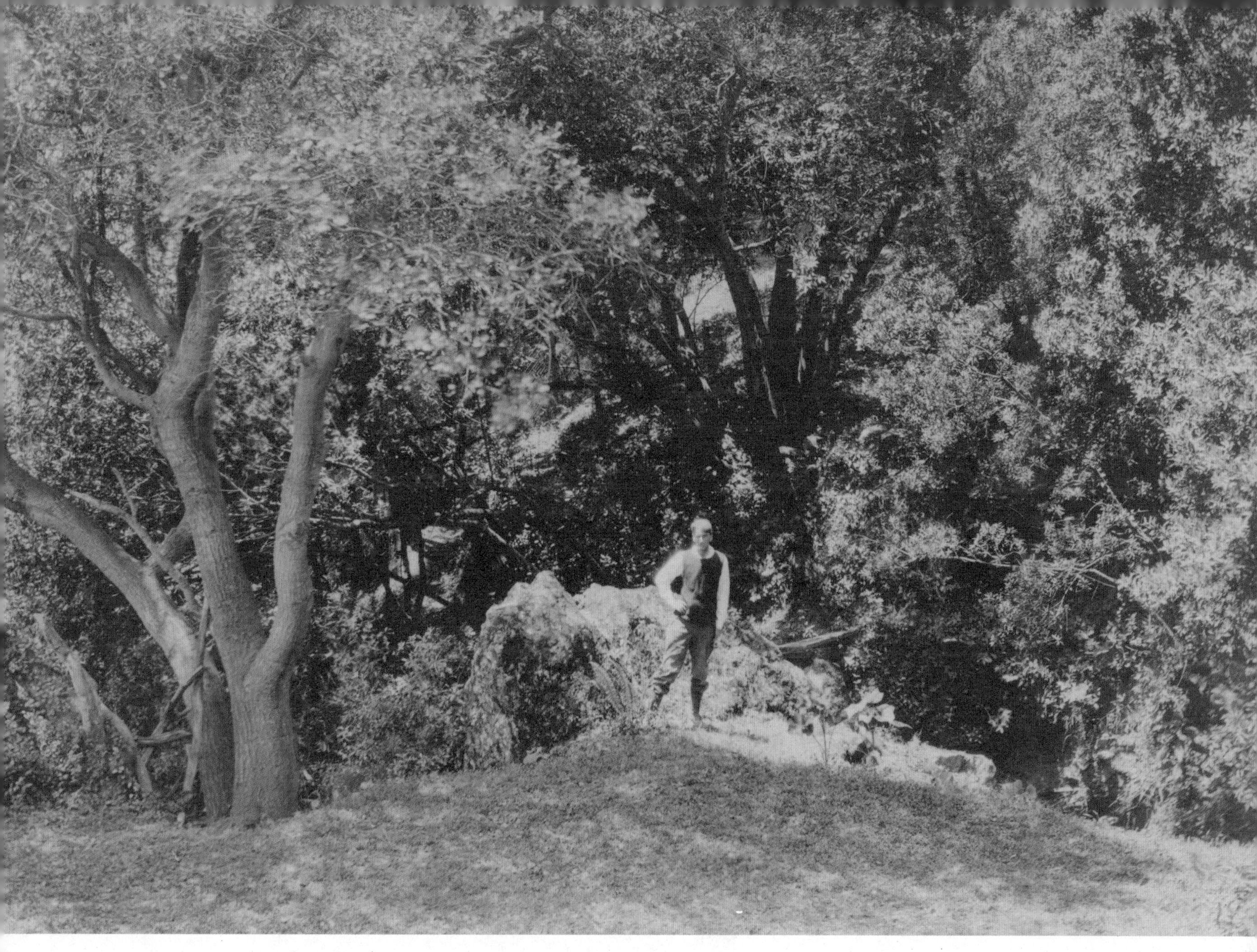

Charles Keeler on stage
at his amphitheatre.

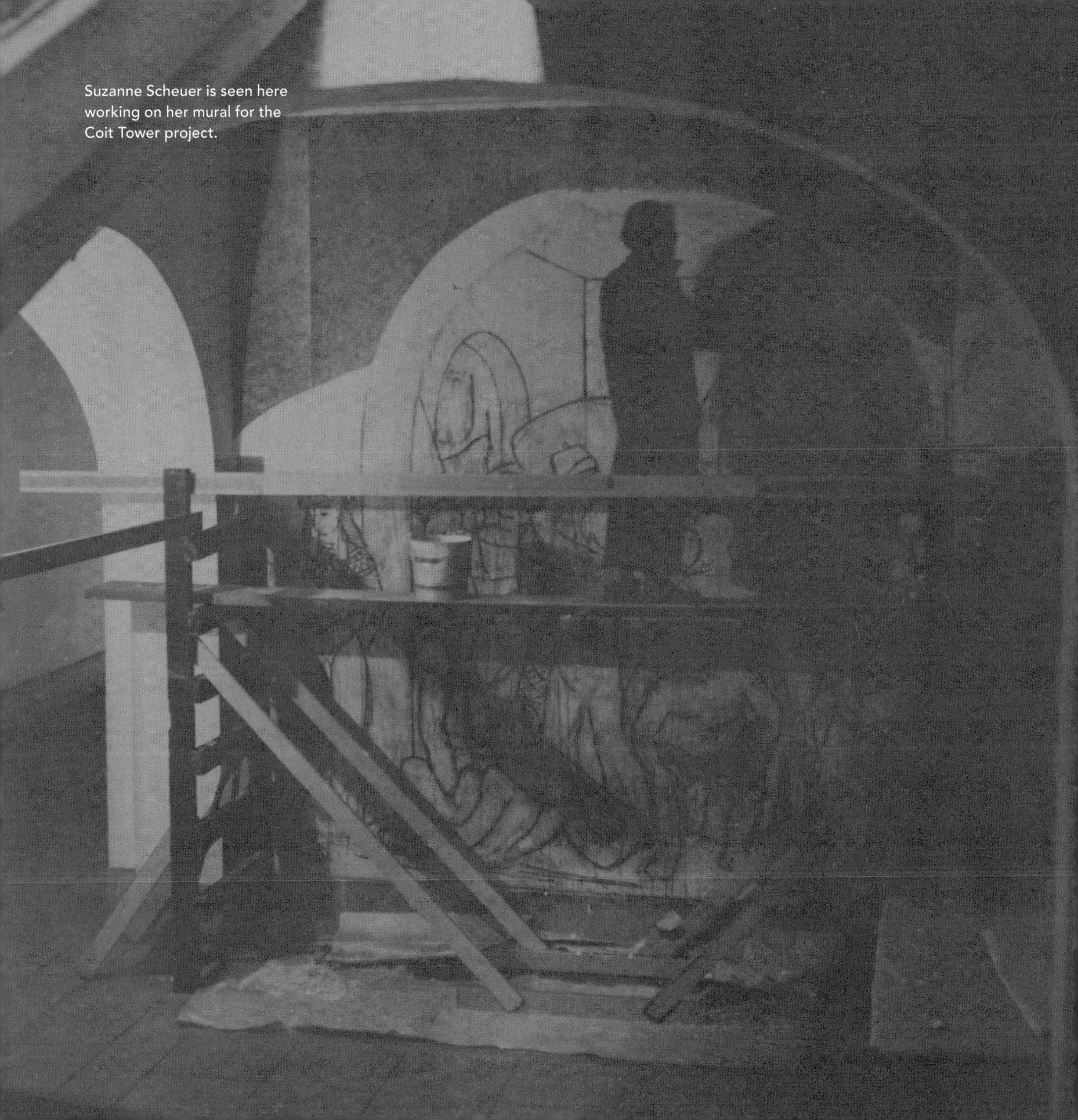

Suzanne Scheuer is seen here working on her mural for the Coit Tower project.

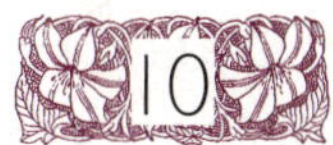

HOW the WPA kept art alive

"Now, who's gonna vote on election day?
Who's finally gonna have his say
Who's gonna cause a change—hey, hey!
It's the poor forgotten man!"[1]
—Bob Miller,
"The Poor Forgotten Man," 1932

With the stock market crash of 1929, America entered hard times. The post–World War I exuberance and optimism of the 1920s was over. Almost overnight, fortunes were lost and the extravagant lifestyle of the decade's newly rich was curtailed. Those who had been on top of the world now found themselves in reduced circumstances, and those who had been living a more modest lifestyle now found themselves in poverty.

Though Berkeley was somewhat insulated from the effects of the Great Depression by the presence of the university and the jobs it provided, many factories and businesses in the city and in the surrounding area either closed or laid off workers. Throughout the country, 25 percent of the workforce was unemployed.

If life in the early 1930s was difficult for farmers, salesclerks and factory workers, it was even more difficult for Berkeley's artists, writers and performers. Wealthy art patrons were now feeling the pinch and were not buying art or supporting the performing arts. Many local artists had supplemented their incomes by teaching an occasional class or giving private lessons in art, dance or music. The money for such lessons dried up, and the young people who had been taking them often had to go to work themselves to help their families survive.

By 1934, actress Dorothy Wetmore was the wife of artist and scenic designer John Emmett Gerrity and the mother of five young children. They lived on Sterling Avenue, high in the North Berkeley hills. It was not far from the neighborhood where Dorothy Wetmore had grown up, but the comfortable middle class existence she had known had vanished.

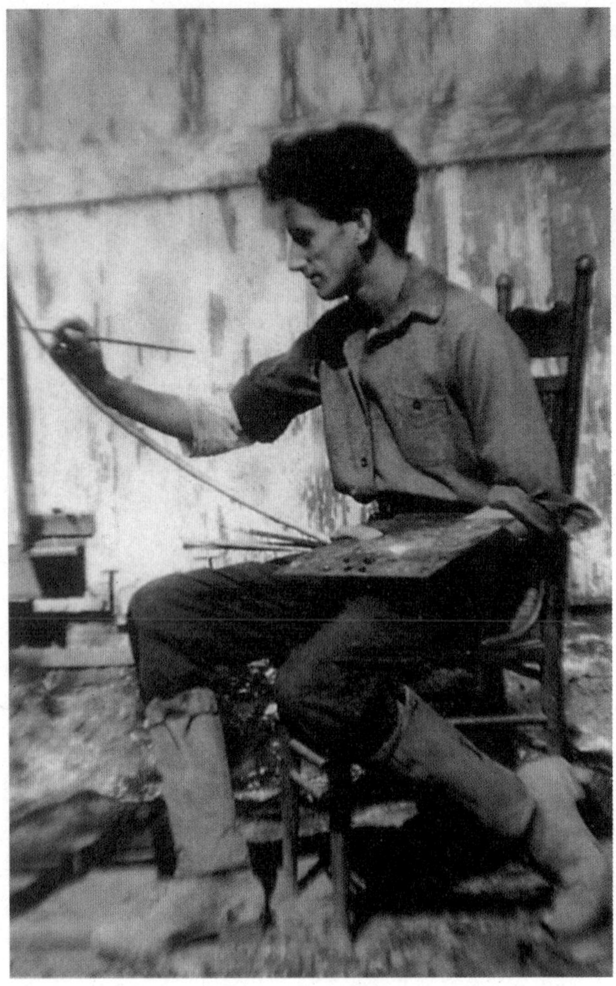

John Emmett Gerrity,
ca. 1917.

"We were Catholic and we were poor," their daughter Mary Bucher remembers. "We weren't really part of the Hillside Club crowd."[2]

Her father, John Emmett Gerrity, said in his 1965 oral history, "I used to have a school here, classes. About twenty, twenty-five people used to paint up here at my studio. And they all quit; as the Depression came they all left."[3]

After several long and desperate years, during which the U.S. economy stubbornly refused to rebound, Franklin Delano Roosevelt was elected president. When Roosevelt took office on March 4, 1933, he promised a "New Deal" for Americans. Plans were quickly put into effect to put America back to work, including the artists. Thus, the Federal Art Projects were born.

THE PWAP

The Coit Tower murals, one of the first public art projects in California, were done under the auspices of the Public Works of Art Project (PWAP). This project had a mandate to employ skilled artists to decorate already-existing public buildings. There was no requirement that the chosen artists be eligible for the welfare rolls, as there would be later. Twenty-six artists and nineteen assistants were hired to decorate the first two floors of the tower (a monument to San Francisco firefighters) with murals done in fresco. Many of the artists had studied or taught at the California School of Fine Arts in San Francisco, thus coming under the influence of Diego Rivera, who was commissioned to paint a mural there in 1931.

Dorothy Cravath did not work on the Coit Tower murals, but she knew most of the artists who did. "We all knew each other in the thirties. There weren't so many artists or dancers or musicians. Almost all of us knew all the others or most of the others."[4] Years later, Cravath was hired by the City Parks department to restore the murals. She stated in her 1964 oral history, "I learned about mural technique from Diego Rivera, which is why all these WPA murals look rather Rivera-ish. I think we all learned about fresco from watching Diego Rivera do the mural in art school."[5]

Among the artists hired on the Coit Tower project were two sons of Berkeley architect John Galen Howard, who was the supervising architect of the university campus for twenty-three years, designing many of its most famous buildings. Robert Howard, the elder of the two, attended the California College of Arts and Crafts while it was still in Berkeley and then went to the Art Students League in New York. After a brief stint in the army during World War I, he was discharged in France and spent several months traveling around Europe on a bicycle, carrying only his overcoat and watercolor supplies. He was impressed by the sculpture he saw in Europe, and upon his return to California in 1922, he began taking jobs that would give him training in sculpting and mural techniques. Howard worked with Ralph Stackpole on the reliefs for the San Francisco Stock Exchange and made connections with working architects that kept him employed when others were struggling. "I was very busy during the first part of the Depression. I had some very good jobs. While everyone else was having a hard time, I was the only one that had any kind of work that I knew of, except for the people of the PWA."[6]

Robert Howard's contribution to Coit Tower, a cement phoenix over the front entryway, was not part of the PWAP project but was commissioned by the architect, Arthur Brown. He also visited the project often and made a film of the artists painting. "I remember going up quite often because my sister-in-law, Jane Berlandina, was painting her piece and I think my wife, Adeline Kent, was helping her and I'd go up and have lunch with her and I'd go on the rounds and get hold of my friends, most of whom would be working very hard because it was all done in fresco and they had to paint while the mortar was fresh."[7]

Robert's younger brother, John Langley Howard, had a more pivotal role in the controversy that surrounded the murals. John Howard had a degree in engineering from the University of California. He also attended CCAC and the Art Students League in New York, and had his first solo exhibition of paintings in San Francisco in 1926 at the age of twenty-four. The younger

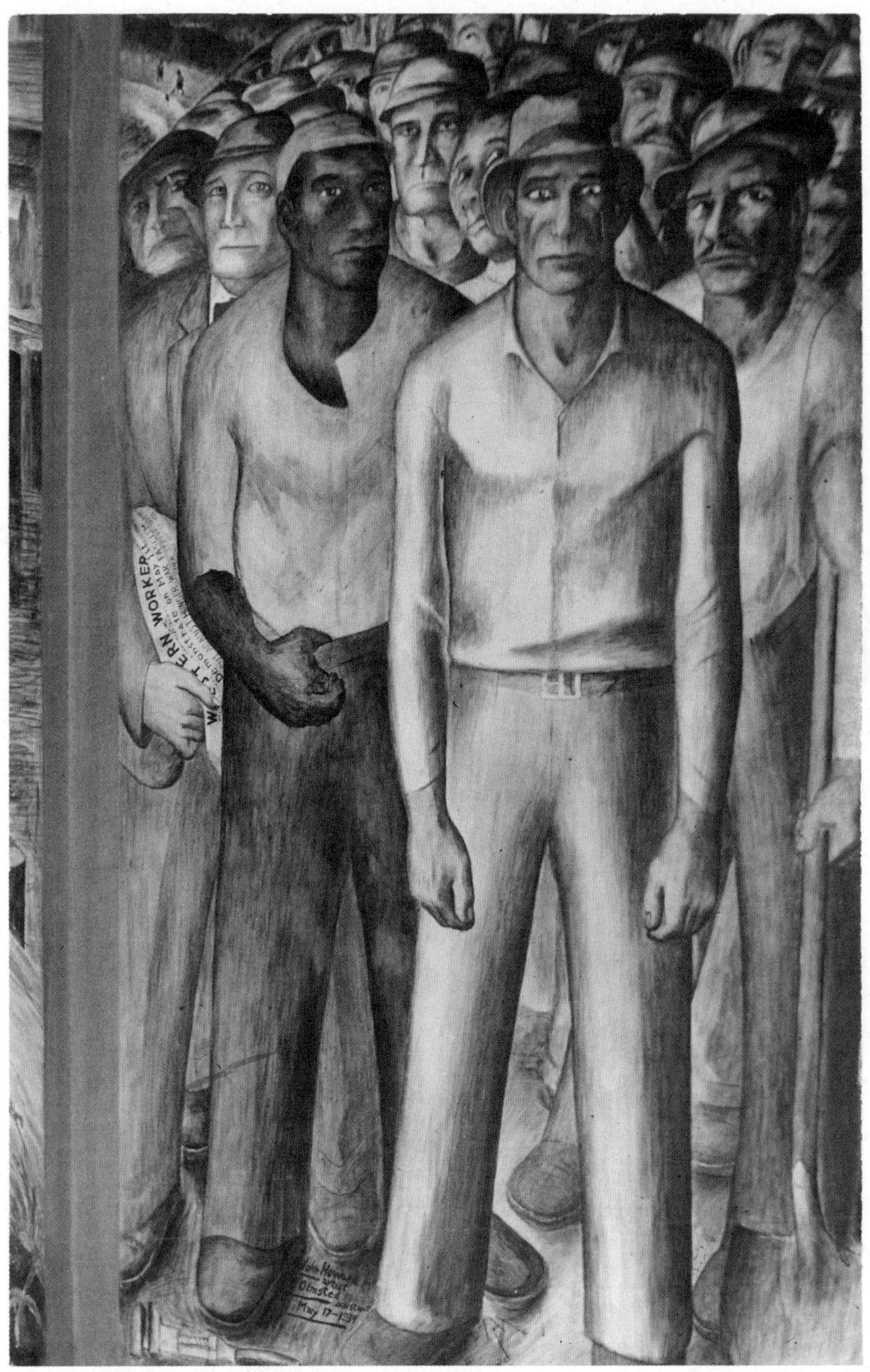

California Industrial Scenes, the controversial Coit Tower mural by John Langley Howard.

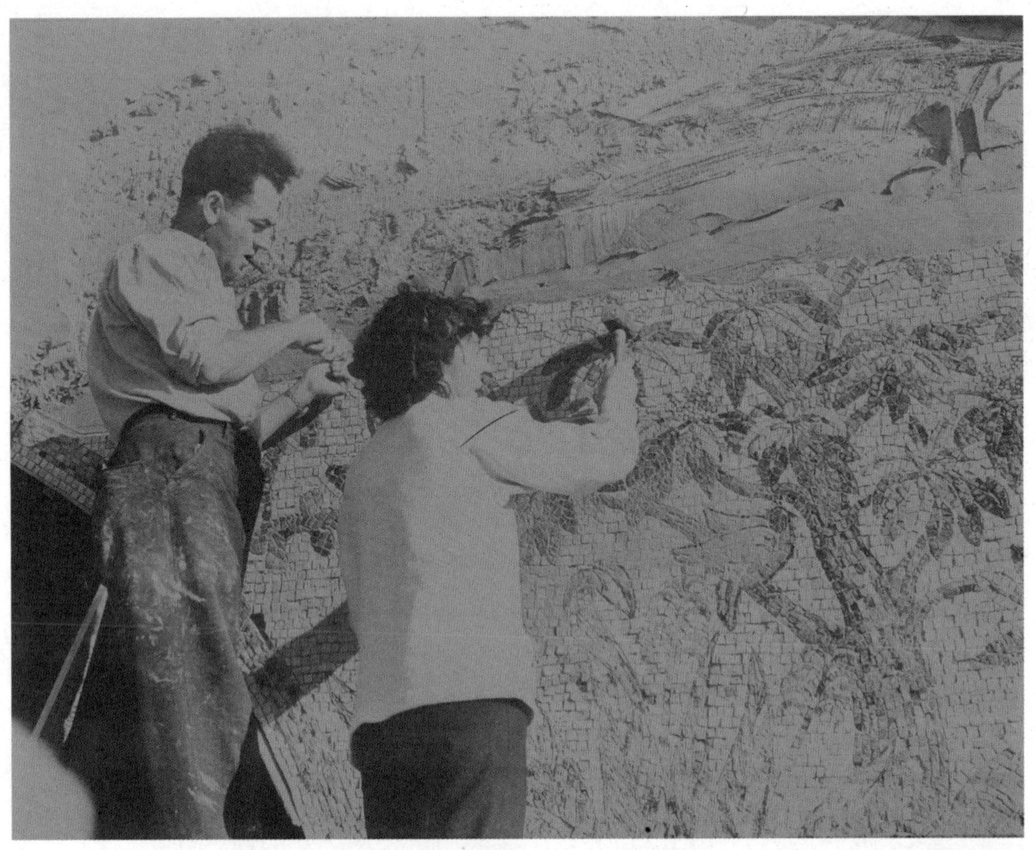

Mosaic technician Primo Caredio and artist Maxine Albrio were photographed setting marble mosaic for the San Francisco State Teacher's College mural.

author Andrew Hemingway wonders why, given this fact, the Regional Committee of the PWAP chose to put the project in their hands. Most of the murals were innocuous, depicting grape growing and wine making, fields and orchards, sports, colorful street scenes, office workers and prosperous-looking factories.

Though the initial sketches had been reviewed by the PWAP Regional Committee, some unsettling details crept in. Bernard Zakheim's public library mural included intense readers clutching newspapers with alarming headlines, as well as a portrait of John Langley Howard reaching for a copy of Karl Marx's *Das Kapital*. Howard's own painting, titled *California Industrial Scenes*, features a crowd of gaunt and menacing-looking workers, one of them holding a newspaper with the headline "Western Workers Demonstrate on May 1st Against Hunger, War and Fascism." Worst of all, Clifford Wight, an English artist, had added some unauthorized panels above his portraits of California workers. These included a hammer and sickle and the slogan "Workers of the World." All this was taking place while the threat of a longshoreman's strike was building on the San Francisco docks. The city was tense and violence was in the air. The *San Francisco Examiner* fanned the flames of the ensuing uproar by printing a composite photograph showing the hammer and sickle superimposed on the library scene. In May 1934, near the completion of the project, it was shut down and the artists barred from the site. It was not until Wight's

Howard was more political than his brother and was interested in socialist ideals. When the artists began work at Coit Tower, they each chose a wall space and began quickly sketching out their ideas in charcoal on large sheets of paper tacked to the walls. They only had funding for four and a half months, so time was of the essence. The overall theme of the murals was California industry and agriculture. The project was under the direction of Bernard Zakheim, who was responsible for the overall conception, and Victor Arnautoff, who supervised the execution. These two men had substantial radical connections. In *Art on the Left*, offending panels were removed and the longshoreman's strike was settled that the artists were able to finish and the Coit Tower murals were at last opened to the public.

THE WPA The PWAP was short-lived. Later the arts projects were organized under the umbrella of the Works Progress Administration (WPA) and included the Federal Theatre Project, the Federal Writer's Project and the Federal Music Project, as well as the Federal Art Project. A means test was established and 90 percent of the people employed on a particular project had to come from the relief rolls. Maxine Albrio, who worked on the Coit Tower murals as well as later projects with her husband, Parker Hall, explained the difference.

"They called it the WPA then because it was a workers relief project, and it was only for people who needed it to live on. Any of us who had a little bit, we were interviewed to find out exactly what we did live on and if they found that we had a home and enough to eat, why those were put off. Then later they took us back on again."[8]

In spite of the indignity of submitting to a means test, most artists were grateful for the work, even if it was sometimes temporary, as funding levels rose and fell. One of those eager to sign up for WPA work was Elizabeth Ginno. A third-generation Berkeleyan, Elizabeth was a slender young woman with enormous eyes and a rambunctious spirit that belied her delicate appearance. The daughter of two dentists (her mother, Dr. Lenore Ginno, was the

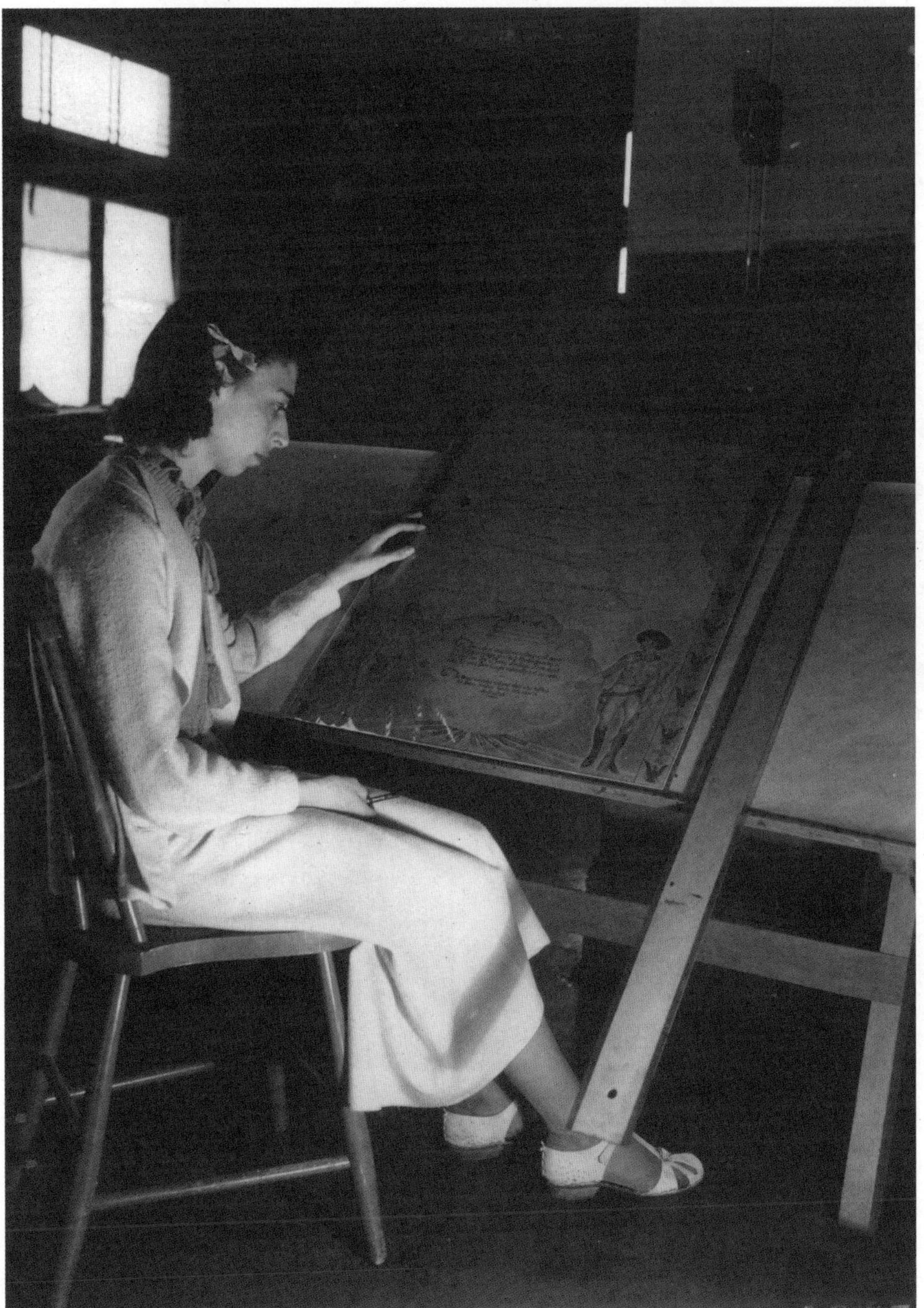

Elizabeth Ginno at her drawing board in the National Park Service project office.

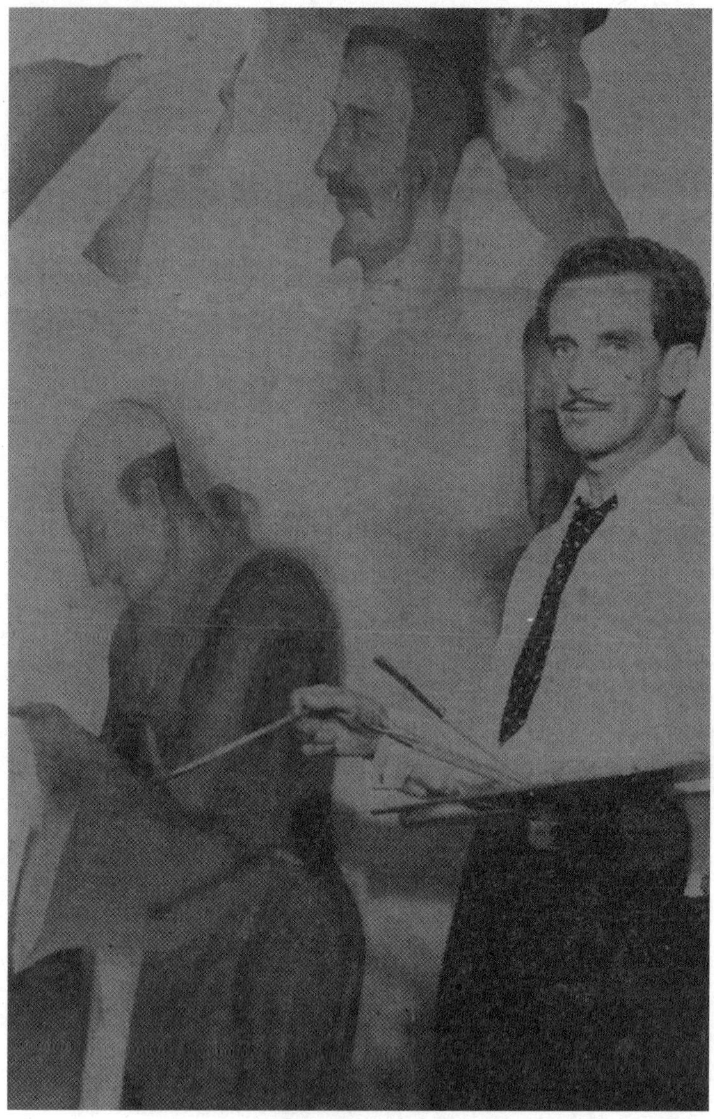

first female dentist in Berkeley), she enjoyed a comfortable childhood in her parent's large house at 1151 Oxford Street, attending local schools and Mills College as a drama major. Active in community and little theatre productions, including some at the Berkeley Playhouse, she married scenic designer Carol Aronovici in 1930. The marriage only lasted a few years, but the couple started Stagecraft Studios, a theatrical lighting and costume business, in a family garage. They were divorced in 1934, leaving Elizabeth a single mother with two small children. By this time, her mother had lost the family home on Oxford Street to the bank, lacking the payment of $600, and Elizabeth was forced to temporarily foster out her children and stay with a friend.

Under the WPA, she worked in art education in the Oakland schools; then in 1937, she got a job in the Museum Project operated by the National Parks Service. This project, headquartered at the Western Regional Laboratory at 2223 Fulton Street on the university campus, employed over one hundred artists who created murals, dioramas and paintings for display in Western National Parks. As a senior artist, she was paid $1.81 an hour though her initial assignment was only for seventy-eight hours of work. This was actually an excellent rate of pay. The Coit Tower muralists were paid an average of $33 a week and supervisors on other projects made $120 a month. It was possible to live on this amount during the Depression, with enough for rent, food, carfare and a little extra.

Florence Jury, a good friend of Jacomena Maybeck, had attended the university in the 1920s. She returned to Berkeley in 1932, the worst year of the Depression, to work on the *Berkeley Gazette*, where she had been employed part-time during her college years. In a series of articles published in the Berkeley Historical Society's *Exactly Opposite the Golden Gate*, she gives details about everyday life during the Depression: "I stayed at the Carlton Hotel while I looked for an apartment which I found within a few days, at the top of Virginia Street for $25 a month. It was spacious and furnished: a large living room, a dining room with a red brick corner fireplace, a large kitchen opening onto the lawn and clothes line. A dressing room and bath, and a large sleeping porch with a view of the Bay! After a few months I wrote to the landlady, whom I never saw, that I thought it would be helpful if she reduced the rate to $22.50 a month. She did, without resistance."[9]

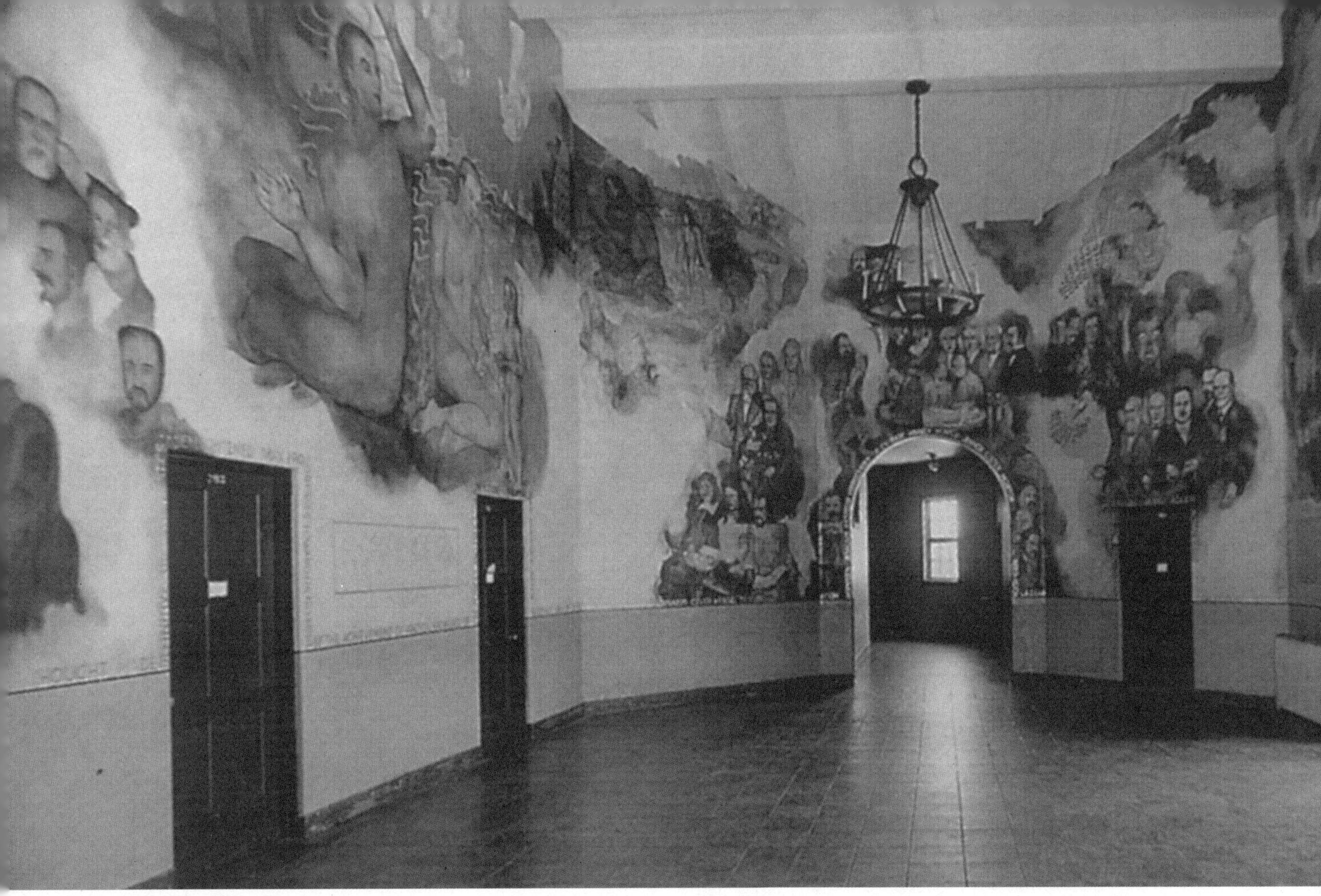

Rent and food were cheap in proportion to wages as long as one had a job. Clothing was another matter. Good wool coats and suits cost at least $18 to $25. Jury remembers that the female employees of the *Gazette* were pleased when the publisher, Charles Dunscomb, known for his elegant attire, announced that he was going through his closet and getting rid of some of his suits. "Suddenly, by way of some ingenious tailoring, many old suits were transformed and made new again, with the jackets looking feminine and the trousers turned into skirts."[10]

John Emmett Gerrity, today considered a major force in California Modernism, also found work with the Federal Art Project. His first assignment was to do watercolors and

The completed Gerrity mural *Inventions of Man* at the State Teacher's College.

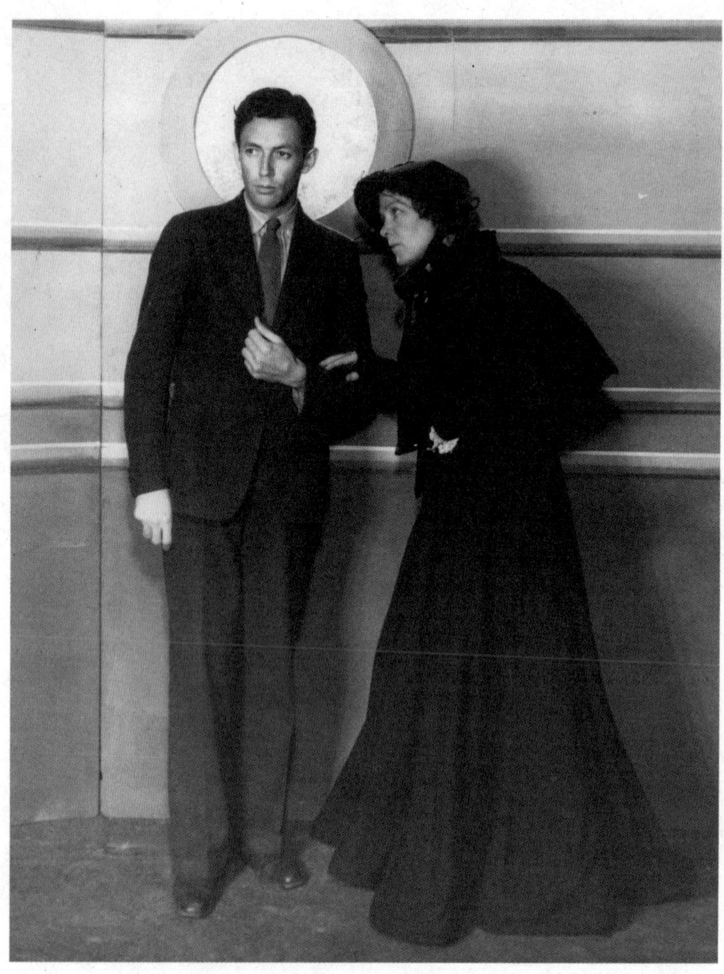

Leon Forbes and Dorothy Gerrity in the Federal Theatre production of *Outward Bound*.

paintings in his home studio and simply turn the finished product into the office supervising the Painting Project. This arrangement was not unusual; when there was no site-specific public art project available, the artists on the relief rolls were still kept working. Their work, mostly smaller pieces, became the property of the government. One of the stated purposes of the WPA Federal Art Project was "to open up new vistas of enjoyment to the public by providing schools, libraries and other public buildings with fine examples of contemporary murals, easel paintings, prints and sculpture."[11]

To this end, the Berkeley Public Library received twenty-five lithographs from the Federal Art Project in November 1936, having agreed to hang them in suitable locations throughout the building and to not remove them from the premises without written authorization.

Gerrity's next commission was a mural project at the State Teachers' College at Haight and Laguna Streets in San Francisco. These were not done in fresco, but in oil on canvas, stretched and attached to the walls. The paintings decorated the entrance to the Life Sciences Building and were, unlike most of the other WPA murals, done in very bright colors. Maxine Albrio was assigned to a mosaic project in the same building, but since it was so large, the various artists working there rarely saw each other.

In the interview done by the Smithsonian Archives of American Art in 1965, Gerrity crustily insisted that he was a self-taught artist and that other artists did not influence his technique. "And then Diego Rivera was here and everybody began to paint like him with sort of stovepipe legs. There was a lot of work like that, strongly influenced by various painters. So, being an independent character, I set out to do the thing I felt was closest to myself. And so I worked that way."[12]

Gerrity remembered that the project took almost four years, as he and his assistants were sometimes reduced to three days a week when funds got low.

John Gerrity's wife, Dorothy, found work with the Federal Theatre Project. A photograph in her scrapbook shows her in a scene from the play *Outward Bound* and may be from the FTP Oakland production of that play. "I played a couple of good parts in that [FTP]; when that closed I went into radio."[13] The FTP Radio Division broadcast from the KPO station on Van Ness Avenue in San Francisco. Mary Bucher remembers listening to her mother's radio programs from their home in Berkeley. Her two older sisters were sometimes allowed to accompany their mother to the radio station, but Mary was too young and had to stay at home.

The aim of the Federal Theatre Project was not only to provide employment for unemployed actors, directors, stagehands and technicians, but also to introduce live theatrical performances to rural areas and remote communities through touring companies. Some plays were chosen at the national level; lists of approved plays, along with guidance on staging, costuming and staffing levels, were distributed to the various production units around the country. Individual production units were also encouraged to come up with their own ideas.

The FTP included many sub projects, such as Children's Theatre, Vaudeville and Circus, Marionette Theatre, Dance, Radio and Negro Theatre. The Bay Area FTP employed more than five hundred people at its height, and in its first two years presented some twenty-two different productions. Everett Glass, who had come to Berkeley to work with Sam Hume many years earlier, was first the general supervisor of the Alameda County Federal Theatre Project, which presented productions of over a dozen different plays in Oakland. He later became one of two drama supervisors for the San Francisco Project, headquartered at the Alcazar Theatre. He also directed four one-act plays for a production called *Americana* in 1936. Project supervisors did not have to pass a means test and could be hired for their ability and expertise in a given field. Glass presumably fell into this category. He later went

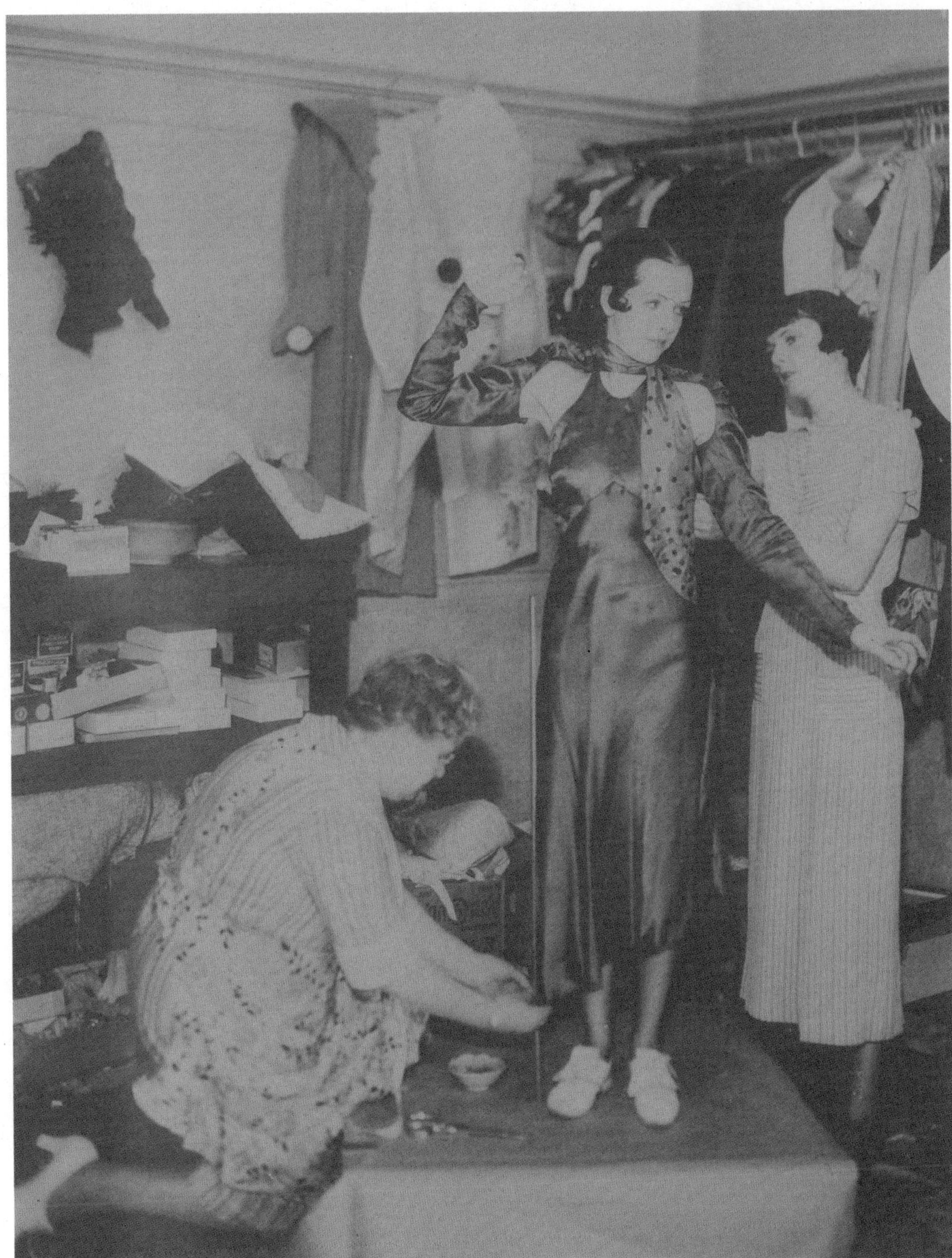

Backstage in the costume shop of a Federal Theatre production in Oakland.

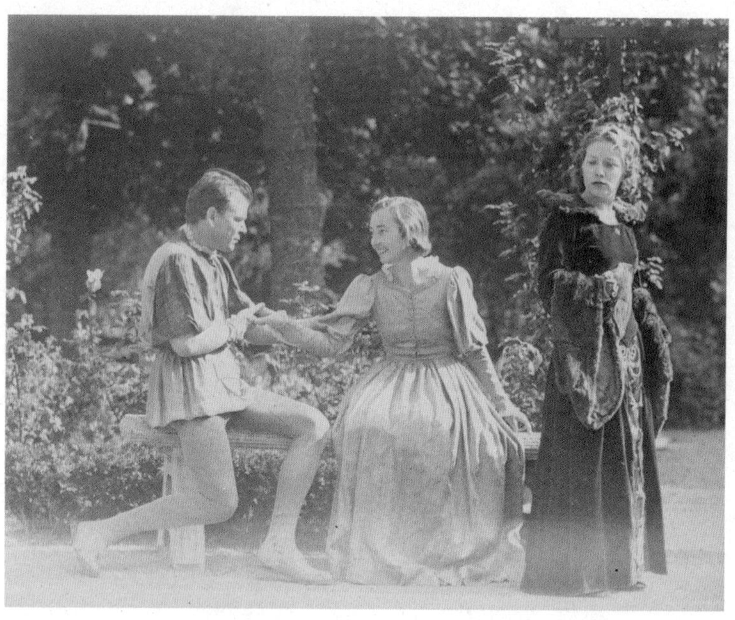

The WPA Division of Recreation sponsored this California Community Players production in Berkeley's Live Oak Park.

to Hollywood and became a well-known character actor in films of the 1940s and 1950s.

Another Berkeley resident who worked for the FTP was Lois Foster. She had been assistant director for the Children's Theatre associated with the Players Guild in San Francisco. In the early 1930s she was Samuel Hume's secretary and collaborated with him on a book called *Theatre and Schools*, aimed at facilitating the organization of school drama programs. Foster began work in December 1935 as supervisor of the Research Division of the San Francisco FTP. The task was to write a history of San Francisco theatre, including Chinese theatre, as well as to keep track of the productions and accomplishments of the FTP in San Francisco. She had a staff drawn from the welfare roles, "whose backgrounds varied from journalism to character work on the stage and poets and propagandists."[14] In a report titled "Toward a Living Theatre: A History of the San Francisco Federal Theatre Projects, November 1, 1935, to August 1, 1936," Foster delineates both the accomplishments of the first few months and the problems the Theatre Project faced. The latter included attacks from the press, uncertain and fluctuating funding, plays that

had to be shelved after weeks of rehearsal because they were deemed "unsuitable," professional actors who complained about the assignment of parts, and bickering and drunkenness at the theatre. Nevertheless, Foster concludes that the project was well worth it: "Theatre craftsmen and actors are given the opportunity to practice and improve in professions in which they have been specifically trained and experienced; hundreds of personal problems have been solved, temporarily or permanently; the spirit of individual cooperation engendered has made for a fine loyalty and for creative contribution from many employees who had arrived at a stage of mental and even physical degeneration through continued disappointment and failure in the past."[15]

Lois Foster received a notice of termination of employment in June 1937. "In one of those arbitrary decisions which were practically a way of life for WPA, the research project division was dissolved. Actually, a special division of the writer's project took up the study of San Francisco theater history and produced a series . . . of mimeographed studies."[16]

Other arts projects included the Oakland Music Project, which consisted of the Oakland Concert Orchestra, the Northern California Colored Chorus, the Oakland Mixed Chorus and the Oakland Dance Band. Ruth Acty, who later became Berkeley's first African-American public school teacher, sang with one of the choruses and appeared in several FTP productions, including *Swing Mikado*, first presented at the Alcazar Theatre in San Francisco and then in a theatre at the Golden Gate International Exposition on Treasure Island.

From 1938 to 1940, Berkeley was also home to the WPA California Folk Music Project, under the direction of Sidney Robertson. Later the wife of composer Henry Cowell, Robertson had worked as an assistant to Charles Seeger in Washington, D.C., traveling through Appalachia to collect examples of American folk music with a portable recording device utilizing acetate discs. She conceived the project as one that would collect examples of folk music from all types being performed in Northern California. The project was cosponsored by the Music Department at the University of California, which provided office space, and the Library of Congress. The WPA provided twenty workers from the relief rolls. In addition to recording songs, they collected photographs of musicians in performance and sketches of the musical instruments used.

The Berkeley division of the Federal Writers Project was based at the Bancroft Library on the university campus. Thomas C. Fleming, a young African American with two years of college and some previous writing experience on the *Oakland Tribune*, was assigned to this project at a pay of $94 a month. He was the only black person in the group of thirty people, some of them PhDs and former newspaper writers. They researched the history of California, utilizing the immense collection of the Bancroft Library and filling notebooks with their handwriting. "These guys were rebels. One of the first things they did was to form a union. They were always demanding certain changes of the government, and threatening to strike if we did not receive a higher wage. The Federal Writers Project was the most rebellious unit in the WPA, and got in disfavor all over the country."[17] This particular project lasted only six months because funding, as usual, ran out. A later Writer's Project produced a book, *Berkeley: The First Seventy-Five Years*.

In addition to providing employment for many residents, WPA projects contributed to the beautification of the city. On

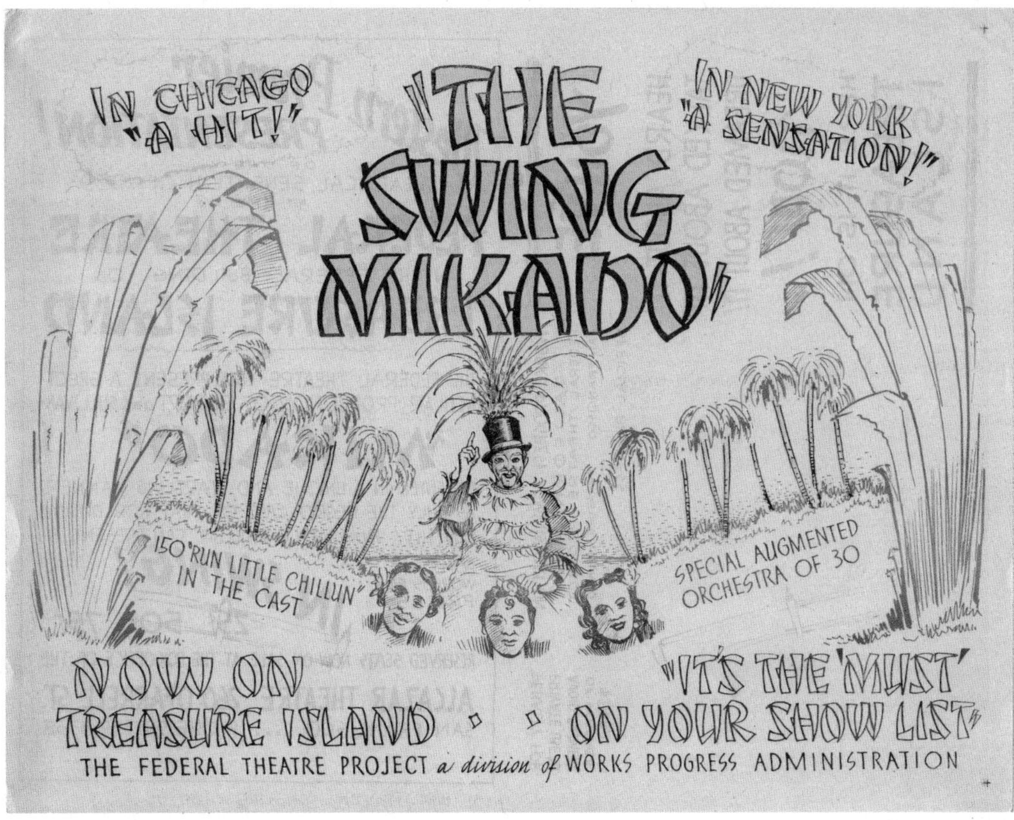

A flyer for *Swing Mikado*, a production done by many Federal Theatre groups around the country.

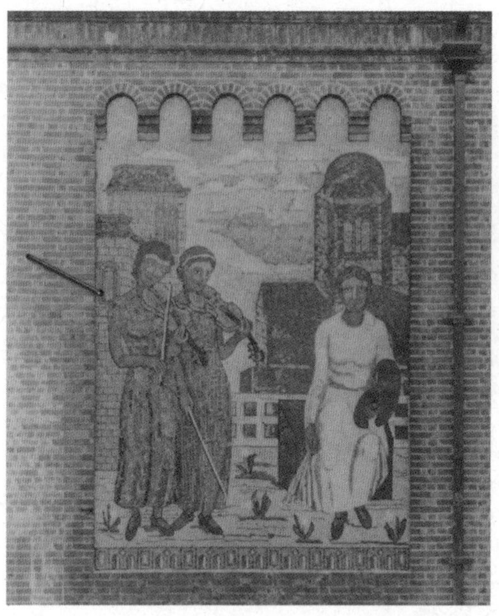

The Bruton and Swift mosaics at the UC Powerhouse depict music and painting on the left (shown above) and sculpture and dance on the right (shown below).

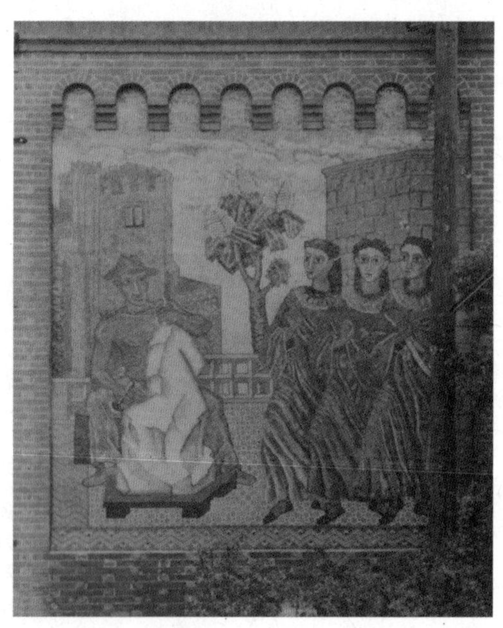

January 5, 1934, the *Gazette* announced, "Mural Will Adorn Council Chambers." The mural, done in fresco, was to be a large map of Berkeley and the surrounding area. Its creation was under the direction of Berkeley artists Marian Simpson and Ray Boynton. The same article announced a plan for the "decorative redesigning of the waiting room at the Health Center."[18]

Suzanne Scheuer, one of the Coit Tower artists, decorated the main post office with an interior mural. David Slivka, a young sculptor, received the commission for a relief of four postal workers on the front porch. The old powerhouse, a small brick building on the university campus designed by John Galen Howard, had been converted into an art gallery in 1934, using private funds. In 1936, Helen Bruton and Florence Swift installed WPA-sponsored mosaic panels. These, still in existence today, as is the post office artwork, have art and artists as their theme, depicting music, painting, sculpture and dance.

More massive WPA projects created the Berkeley Rose Garden on a terraced hillside and John Hinkle Park, complete with a small stone amphitheatre used for many theatrical performances in the years since.

Many of the most searing and emotionally powerful images of the Depression years were captured on film by photographer Dorothea Lange. After a decade as a successful studio photographer, Lange took her camera out onto the street in 1932 and began making pictures of the people she saw there: old men in bread lines, workers on strike and the many unemployed with their faces of despair. She eventually exhibited these photographs, which were unlike anything she had done before, at a small gallery in Oakland. Located at 683 Brockhurst, the space had formerly been the studio of Pictorialist photographer Annie Brigman. Now, Willard Van Dyke, Ansel Adams, Edward Weston and other young photographers who were interested in simple and direct presentations of their subjects formed a loosely knit association called Group f/64. Though Lange was older than most of the people in the group and never joined it, Van Dyke put on an exhibit of her photographs in 1934. This led to a meeting with Berkeley economics professor Paul Taylor, who had long been interested in the uses of photography in documenting social conditions. Taylor's chief focus was the study of migratory labor. He had pursued this on his own while in graduate school and subsequent years of teaching. In 1935, he was hired by the State Emergency Relief Administration (SERA) to do research on the thousands of migrant workers who were pouring into California from the Dust Bowl. Taylor asked for the services of a photographer who could document the human face of the mass migration as he conducted interviews for his report.

Though there were no provisions for a photographer and Lange had to be hired under the job description of clerk-stenographer, she began accompanying Taylor and his team as they traveled up and down the state, visiting picking fields and migrant camps. She soon became an invaluable member of the crew, speaking easily and naturally with the people they were observing and questioning, and only photographing them after putting them at ease, as she had done with the wealthy patrons in her portrait studio. The dramatic depiction of the plight of the migrant workers contained in the Taylor-Lange report led to the creation of the first government sponsored camps for the workers. These offered sanitation, places for the children to play, dry tents or cabins to sleep in and a small measure of dignity to the thousands who had been living out of their cars since they left the Midwest.

Dorothea Lange's marriage to artist Maynard Dixon had been precarious for years. They had two sons, and Dixon had a daughter from a previous marriage. Lange had a troubled relationship with all three children, and the Dixons had often left the children with various friends and relatives while they traveled or worked on projects. Though there was still much of the societal pressure on a woman artist to take care of her family before taking care of herself, which Ina Coolbrith had bowed to sixty years before, Lange was of a different temperament than Coolbrith had been. If the children got to be too much for her, she farmed them out to friends and relatives and went about her business, though not without a great deal of guilt.

After several months of traveling and working together, Taylor and Lange realized they were in love and asked their respective spouses for a divorce. They were married on December 6, 1935, and moved into a

rented house on Virginia Street in Berkeley. They now had a combined family of five children, which Lange ruled with a firm grip. Fortunately, Paul Taylor's warm and thoughtful personality balanced Lange's mercurial one and though the children had to do as they were told by "Dictator Dot," the home was a loving one with many good times.

Lange was hired on her own by the Resettlement Administration and given assignments to document conditions in

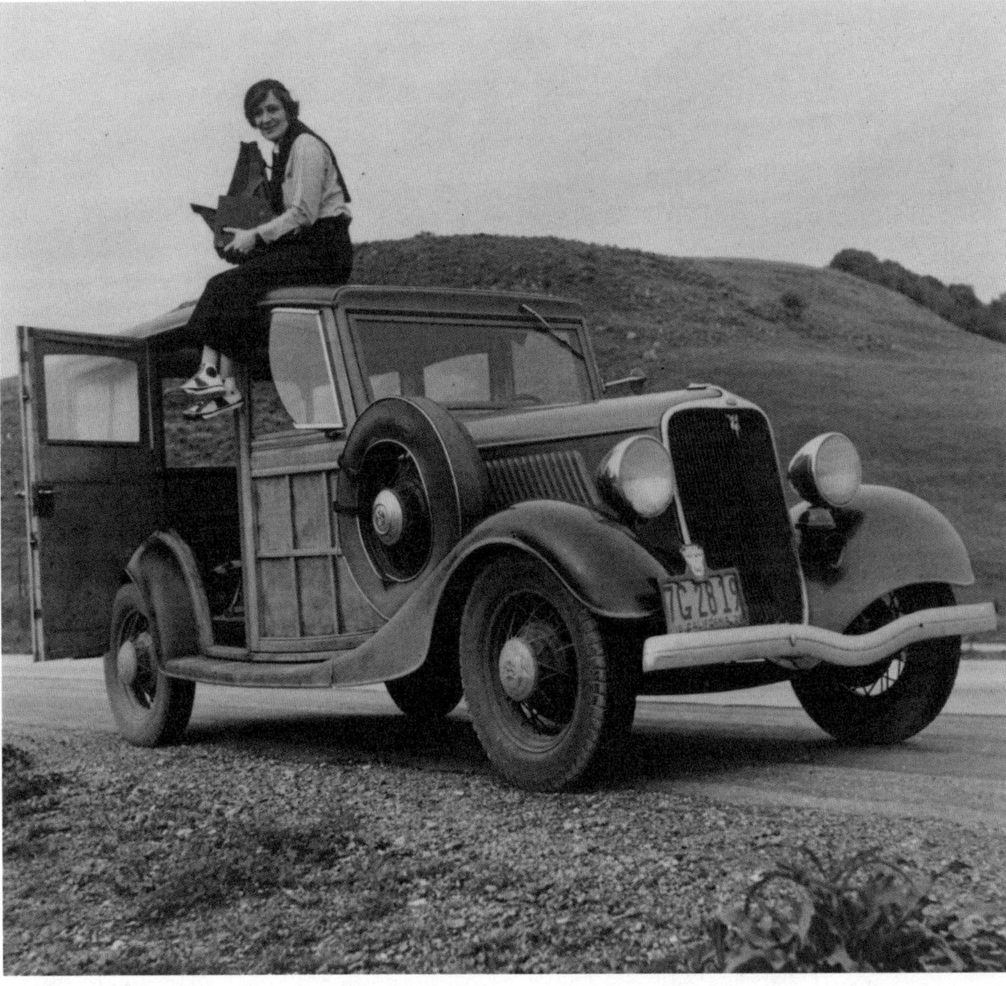

Dorothea Lange during one of many road trips through California.

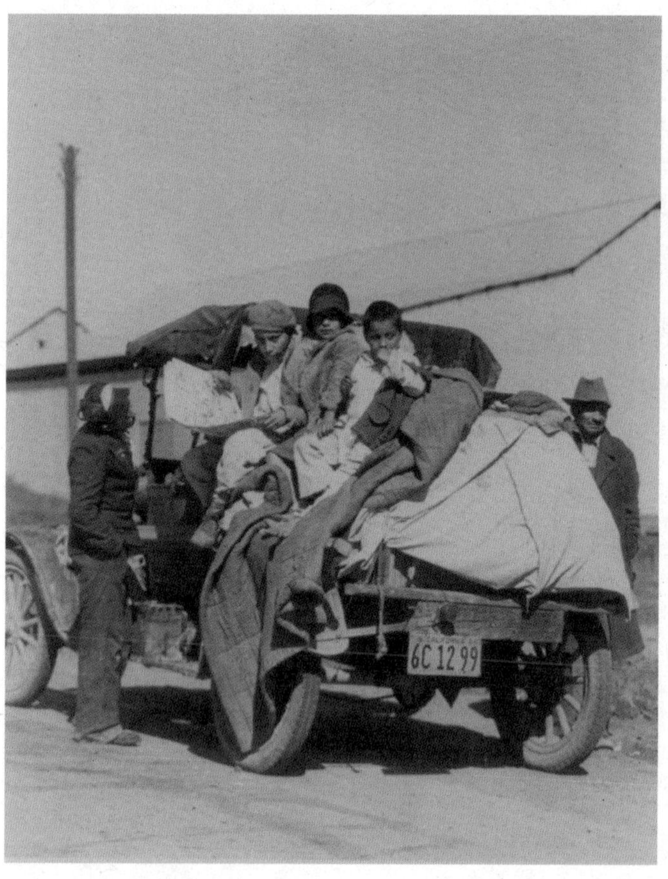

Travelers on the road to nowhere, hoping to find a new life. Photographed by Dorothea Lange.

specific areas. She sometimes traveled alone and sometimes with an assistant, often Ron Partridge, the son of her old friend, Imogen Cunningham. It was in March 1936, towards the end of a month on the road by herself, that Lange made one of the most famous photographs of her career. She was on her way north in the rain, anxious to get home to Berkeley, when she passed a small roadside sign that said "Pea-Pickers Camp," in Nipomo, California. She drove past and kept going for another twenty miles before something made her turn around and go back to the camp.

I saw and approached the hungry and desperate mother, as if drawn to her by a magnet. I do not remember how I explained my presence or my camera to her, but I do remember she asked me no questions. I made five exposures, working closer and closer from the same direction. I did not ask her name or her history. She told me her age, that she was thirty-two. She said that they had been living on frozen vegetables from the surrounding fields and birds that the children killed. She had just sold the tires from her car to buy food. There she sat in that lean-to tent with her children huddled around her, and seemed to know that my pictures might help her, and so she helped me. There was a sort of equality about it.[19]

The woman was Florence Owens Thompson and the picture became known as *Migrant Mother*, the face of the Depression. Lange continued her documentary photography work for several more years, eventually traveling not only through all of California, but through the southwest and southeast, taking pictures of former slaves and sharecroppers, Dust Bowl tenant farmers who no longer had farms, and people on the road, traveling to what they hoped was a better life.

After the December 7, 1941, attack on Pearl Harbor and the entry of the United States into World War II, all persons of Japanese ancestry on the Pacific coast, even if they had been born in America and were citizens, were forced out of their homes into internment camps. The War Relocation Authority (WRA) hired Dorothea Lange to document the resettlement process. More than one hundred and ten thousand Japanese-Americans, including one thousand three hundred Berkeley residents, sold or rented their homes and businesses, stored their belongings, and boarded buses for assembly centers. From these, they were dispersed to hastily built camps in remote areas throughout the West. Lange was on hand with her camera and photographed her subjects in a way that captured their humanity and dignity.

Thirty years later, the Smithsonian Archives of American Art conducted a series of oral history interviews with surviving WPA artists. All were asked their opinion about the quality of work done under the WPA and whether they were in favor of government support of the arts. While there was a certain amount of grumbling about the busywork involved and the fact that jobs were sometimes assigned by need rather than merit, all agreed that the WPA Arts Projects had been worthwhile. Ruth Cravath commented, "I think that probably it enabled some of them to keep on being artists, really, at the time. . . . Many of them would have done something else to earn a living which is a little bit hazardous for an artist, sometimes, because it is hard to get back to it or keep on doing it."[20]

Her sister-in-law Dorothy Cravath said, "I think it was terrifically important because it gave a great many artists the subsidy they needed to make a real start. And it was also important because it educated the public. People began to think that possibly walls of buildings needed murals or could stand murals, and it hadn't occurred to them before. I think most of the American public felt that all real painting had been done in the Renaissance and stopped there."[21]

Robert Howard's comment was the most succinct: "Well, it kept them from starving to death."[22]

The WPA Arts Projects and all the other projects of the New Deal did not end the Depression; it was only when the nation began gearing up for World War II that well-paying jobs became plentiful. But the WPA gave people the means to exist through a very dark decade and kept art and hope alive.

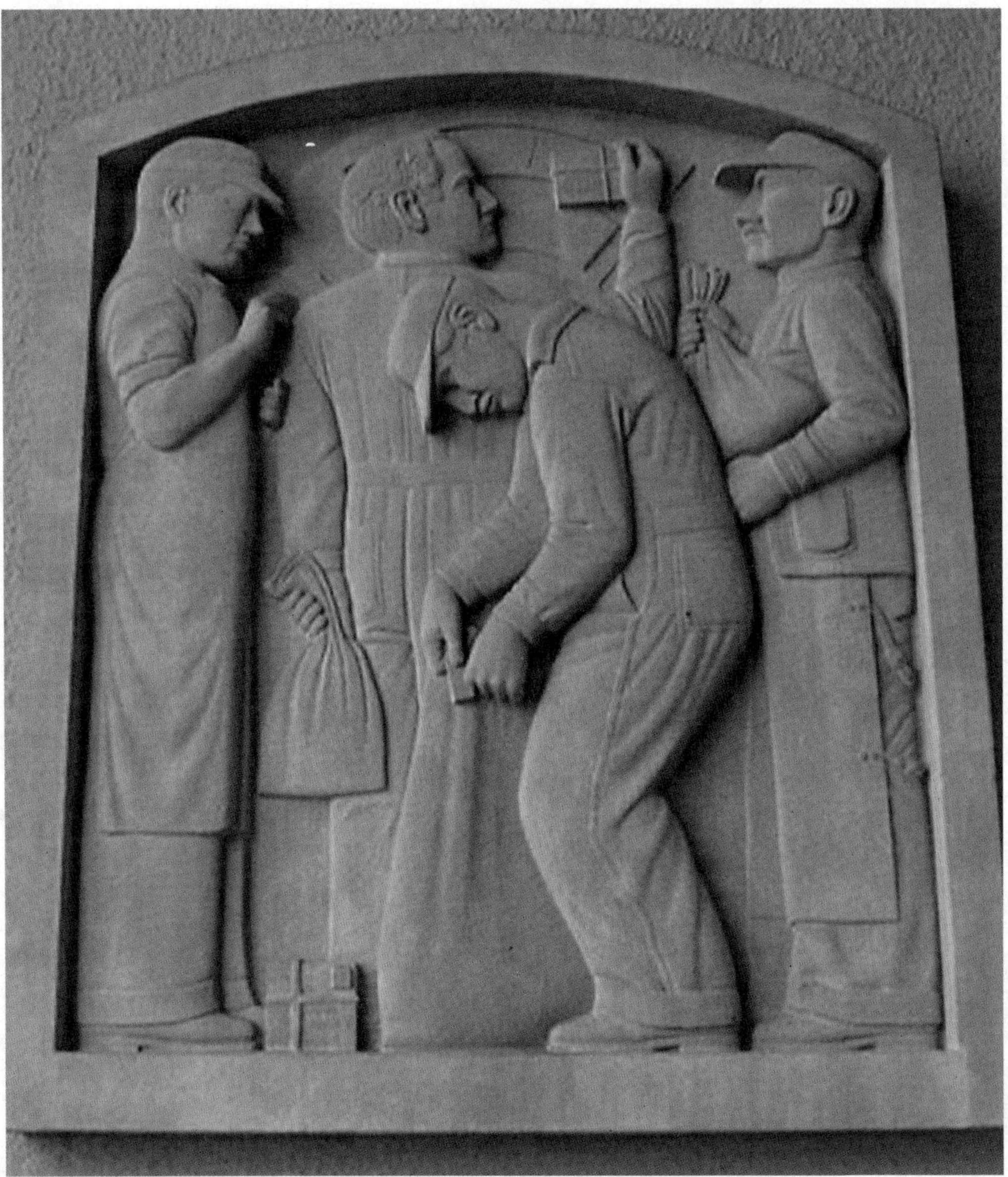

The relief in the porch of the main Berkeley post office was done by young artist David Slivka in 1937. He later went on to become a well-known sculptor in New York.

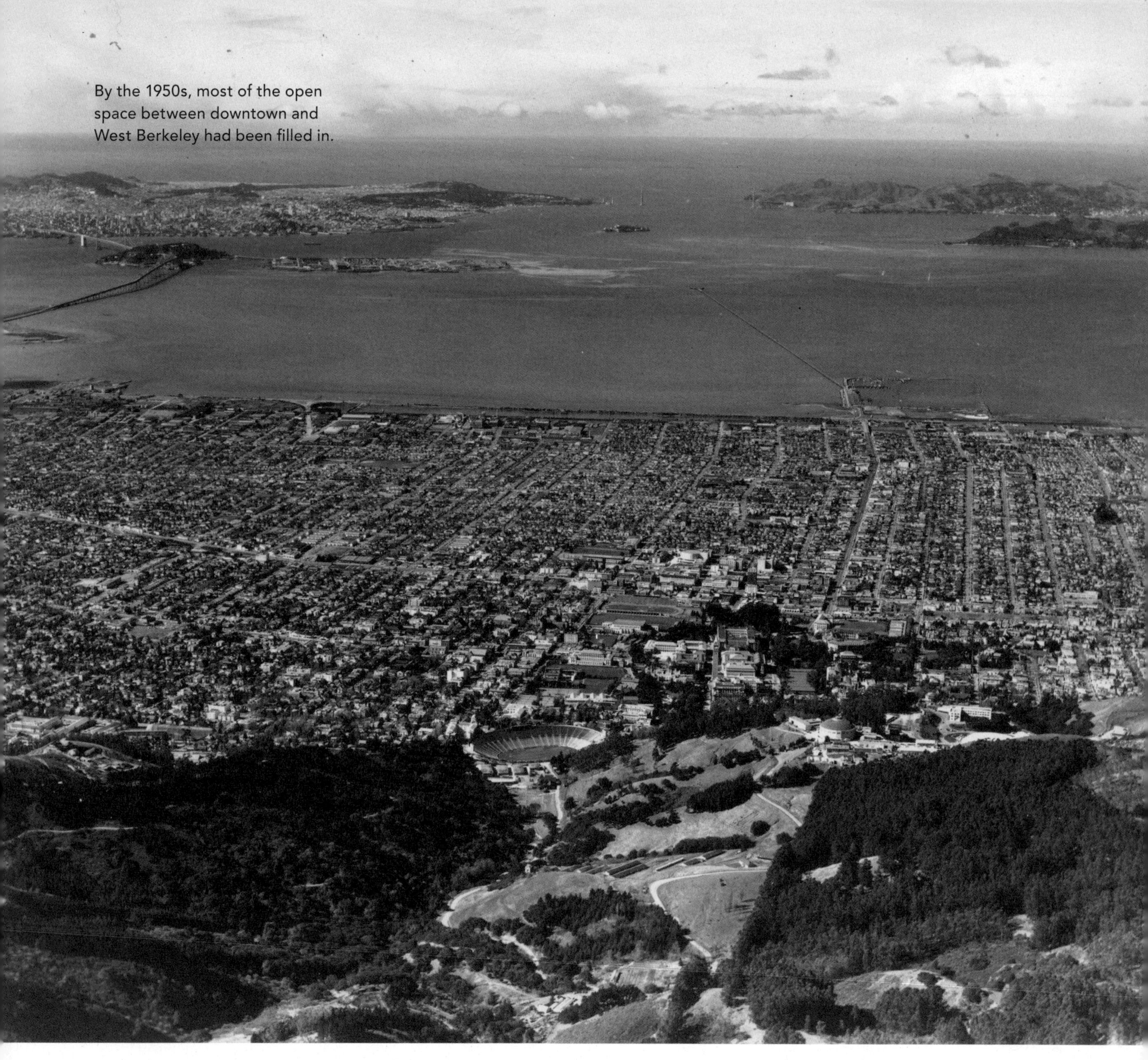

By the 1950s, most of the open
space between downtown and
West Berkeley had been filled in.

Legacy

"We are the music makers,
  And we are the dreamers of dreams,
  Wandering by lone sea-breakers,
  And sitting by desolate streams;
  World-losers and world-forsakers,
  On who the pale moon gleams:
  Yet we are the movers and shakers
  Of the world forever, it seems."[1]
  —Arthur O'Shaughnessy, "Ode"

After World War II, Berkeley was a changed place. The community had been upended by the war years, with so many of the young people leaving to serve in the armed forces, an influx of African-American workers from other parts of the country arriving to work in the Richmond shipyards, and the removal of its Japanese population to internment camps.

When the war ended, Berkeley, like the rest of the country, wanted things to return to "normal." But those days were gone. Even as students and professors streamed back, the G.I. Bill affording many new students the opportunity of an education; even as families were reunited and lives picked up again, change bubbled and fermented beneath the seemingly placid surface of the city.

In the late 1940s, the university community was shaken by the controversy over the newly instituted loyalty oath required by all academics. In the 1950s, Allen Ginsberg wrote "Howl" in a cottage on Milvia Street. In the 1960s came the Free Speech Movement and a resurgence of student radicalism. In the 1960s and 1970s, it was as if the social and cultural experiments of the early part of the twentieth century had merely been a dress rehearsal.

Instead of small pockets of bohemians dotting the hillside and quiet streets, large sections of the youthful population of Berkeley adopted at least the surface appearance of the new bohemianism. Eccentric clothing, vegetarianism, anarchy, communal living,

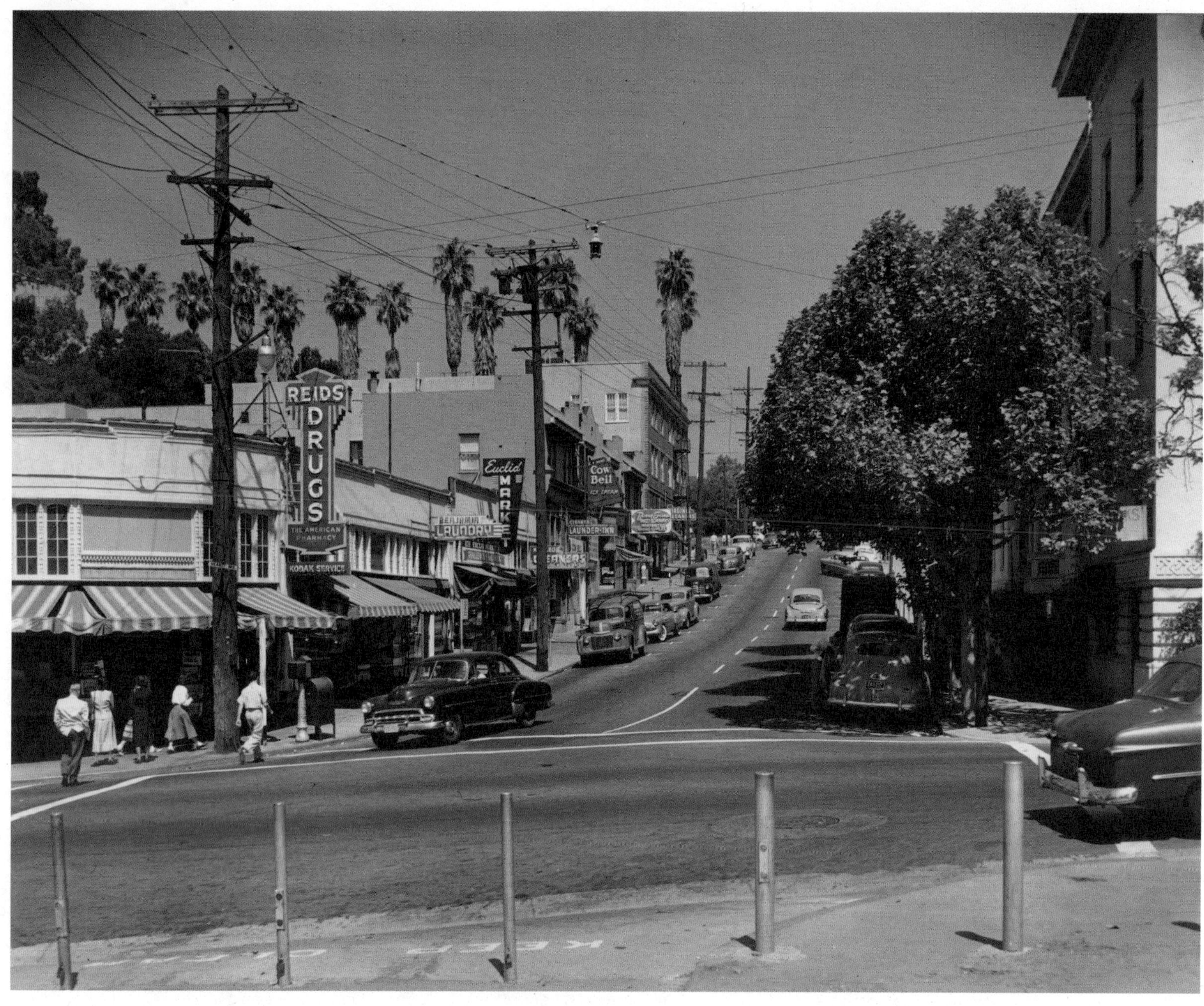

A post–World War II view of Euclid Street, just north of the university campus.

experiments with prohibited substances, new religions and wild parties—little did they know that it had all been done before.

Berkeley has always been home to writers. Post–World War II Berkeley was no exception. Author and walking-tour leader Don Herron points out in *A Guidebook to the Literary World of San Francisco and Its Environs*, "Berkeley has been a major site in the development of modern science fiction and fantasy."[2]

Ursula K. Le Guin, author of the Nebula and Hugo award-winning *The Left Hand of Darkness* and *The Dispossessed*, was the child of renowned anthropologist A. L. Kroeber and his wife, Theodora, and grew up in a home on Arch Street. Perhaps it was her parents' anthropological studies as well as the unique community she lived in that helped Le Guin imagine and eloquently depict alternate forms of society.

Anthony Boucher set his first mystery novel, *The Case of the Seven of Calvary*, published in 1937, in the neighborhood of the University of California campus, where he had been a graduate student. After the war, Boucher became the founding editor of the *Magazine of Fantasy and Science Fiction*. As such, he was responsible for introducing authors like Ray Bradbury to the American public.

George R. Stewart taught in the English department on the UC campus for thirty-eight years. His haunting novel *Earth Abides*, a tale of the world after a great plague, is set in Berkeley and environs, with descriptions of the city, its neighborhoods and public buildings as they slowly crumble into ruin, populated only by a small band of survivors.

Philip K. Dick, perhaps most famous for his short story *Do Androids Dream of Electric Sheep?* (made into the 1983 film *Bladerunner*), lived in Berkeley, as did Marion Zimmer Bradley, author of *Mists of Avalon* and most of the Darkover novels. Ernest Callenbach, whose 1980s novels *Ecotopia* and *Ecotopia Emerging* foreshadow the ecological woes in today's news headlines, was a Berkeley author. Dorothy Bryant, author of *The Kin of Ata Are Waiting for You*, still lives in Berkeley. She was the subject of an oral history interview conducted by the Berkeley Historical Society and published in 2007 and is a frequent author of letters to the editor about a variety of community ills.

If some of the early bohemians presented in these pages were to return today, would they feel at home in twenty-first century Berkeley? Charles Keeler would be pleased to see downtown designated as the "arts and commerce" district. He would enjoy the poetry, including some of his own verses imbedded in the sidewalk on Addison Street. Joaquin Miller, who surrounded himself with visitors, would delight that his old home at the Hights has been turned into

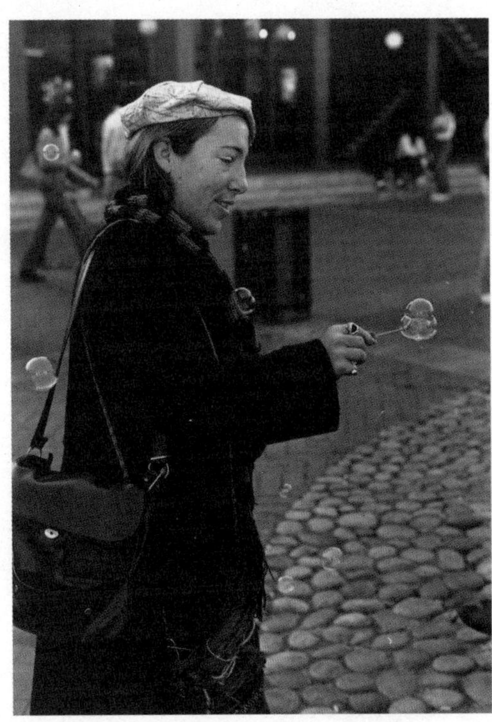

ABOVE: Local poet Julia Vinograd, here shown ca. 1969, is known as the Bubble Lady.

BELOW: Harvey Grosser, Dan O'Leary and Michael Chastain, burning draft registration forms at an antiwar rally.

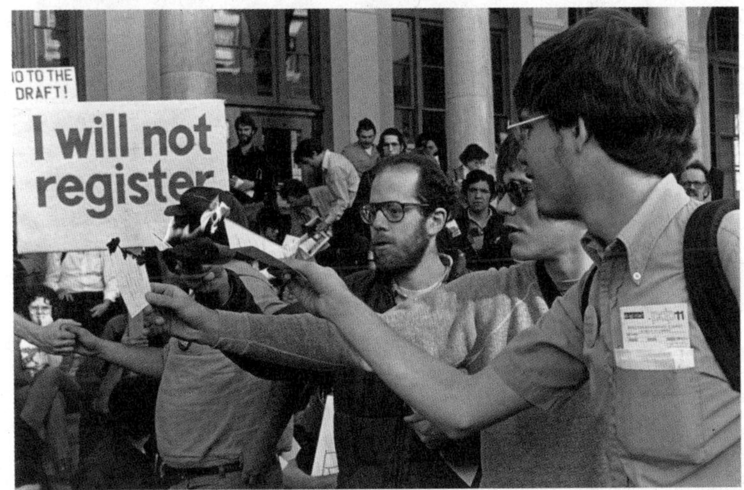

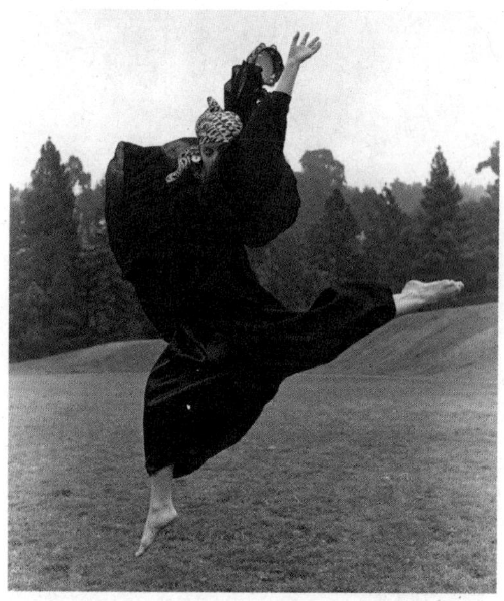

ABOVE: **The spirit of Isadora Duncan lives on in this barefoot dancer from the Creative Dance Theatre of Berkeley.**

BELOW: **In a good example of creative reuse of a historic building, the 1902 Golden Sheaf Bakery has been transformed into an education center for Berkeley Repertory Theatre.**

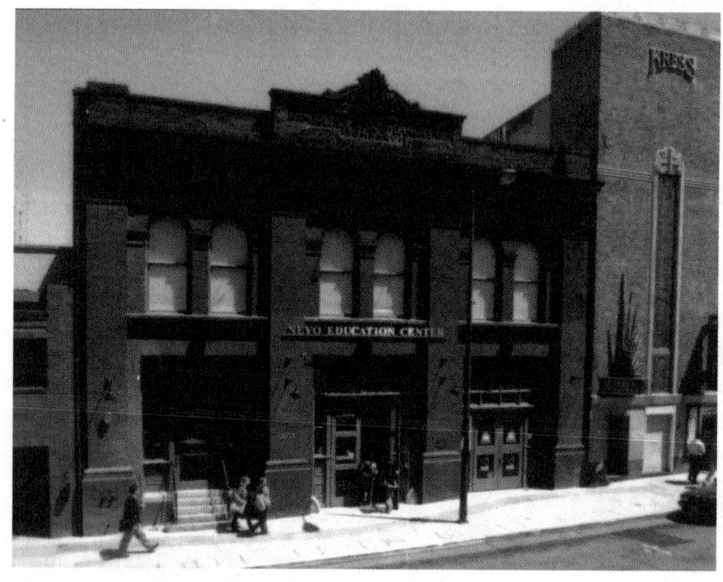

a park for the people of Oakland to enjoy. John Muir would walk in Tilden Park, its public hiking trails winding along the tops of the hills. Florence Boynton might smile to see dancers in flowing robes still leaping and turning in the open air. The Poet's Dinner is still held annually, and Dorothy Tyrell, who missed the first one, might be pleased to find that the grand prize is given in her honor. The Ina Coolbrith Memorial Circle awards an annual prize in her name. Sam Hume would be glad to see Berkeley's many theatres and excellent acting, innovative stagecraft and new scripts presented.

The California College of Arts and Crafts, which gave a start to so many artistic careers, is now the California College of the Arts, with campuses in Oakland and San Francisco.

Berkeley has always been a home of visionaries, and this continues to translate into a kaleidoscope of different visions of what the city is and should become.

Today Berkeley is experiencing many of the problems typical of urban areas around the United States. Though neighborhood shopping districts are lively and well traveled, it has a city center with many vacant storefronts. Efforts by the city to promote downtown have met with some success, though Shattuck Avenue lacks destination stores and businesses. There is a continual fight about lack of parking versus the importance of using public transit.

With no opportunities to expand its borders, there is impetus to build up, which meets with cries of outrage from traditionalists who have no wish to see their beloved town turned into a forest of high-rises. In the 1960s and 1970s, many older buildings in the areas north and south of the university were torn down to make way for apartment buildings and student residence halls. A strong preservationist movement arose, leading to the founding of BAHA, the Berkeley Architectural Heritage Association. Many significant examples of older architecture have been saved through the efforts of concerned citizens, though others accuse them of "nimbyism" and intolerance of progress.

The University of California and other churches, institutes and nonprofit entities own approximately one fourth of the land within the city, permanently removing it from the property tax rolls, while bringing thousands of people into the city who utilize its services. The tension and conflicts that ensue from this situation fill the City Council meetings and the letters to the editor columns in Berkeley newspapers.

For all its problems, Berkeley is still an attractive place to live. It is still a city of trees and gardens, and the local nurseries are busy on weekends. Skyrocketing housing costs, like most of California, have made Bernard Maybeck's "simple homes" worth millions, while even simpler bungalows in the flatlands are out of the reach of many working families. Strict rent-control laws, passed in the 1980s, have allowed some ex-students and artistic types to remain in the city. Their presence helps maintain vestiges of early bohemianism. Strange garden sculptures, eccentric dress, a love of nature and a tolerance for nonconformity are all present in twenty-first-century Berkeley, just as they were one hundred years ago. If the early-twentieth-century bohemians we have been discussing in these pages were to return to the present day, they would find much that is changed but also much that feels familiar. Street musicians play on downtown corners, and the many local bookstores offer literature and news from around the world. Poetry readings, musical offerings, community festivals and art shows are available every day of the year. More importantly, it is a city of involved and concerned citizens who believe that they are not just citizens of a city but of the world.

To the early bohemians, art and creativity were as important as breath. They were believers in community and in the healing power of the natural world.

If they did not individually accomplish all that they hoped or wished for, they nevertheless collectively kept alive for future generations a fierce determination to speak truth, create beauty and question the status quo. This is their legacy.

"We remember the details of our story, we do not invent them."[3]
—Graham Greene

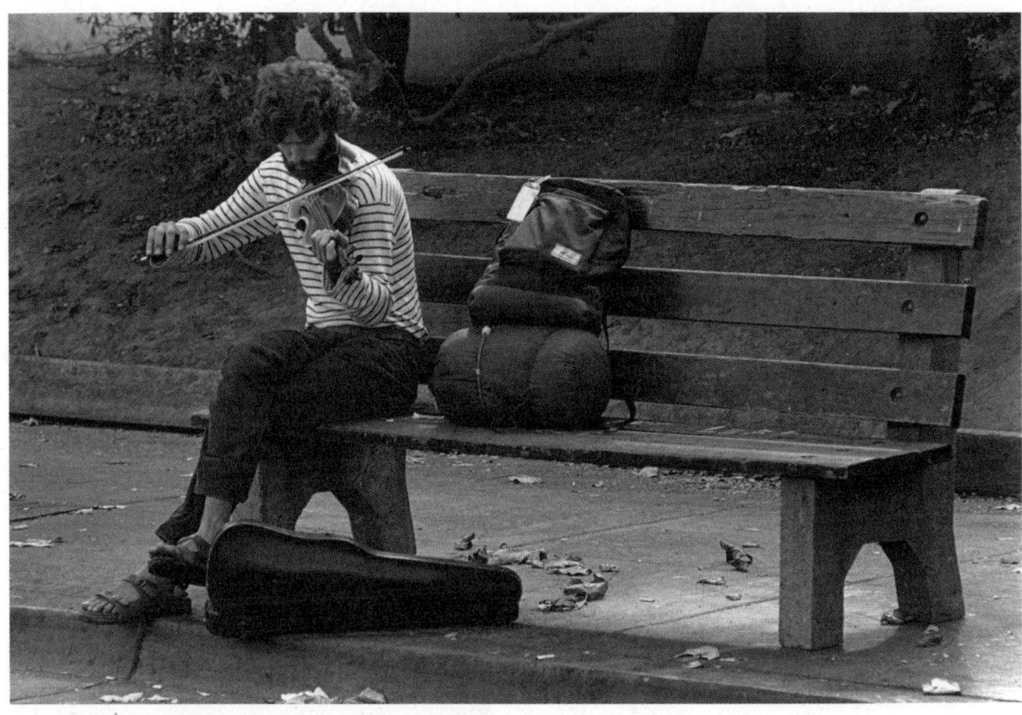

ABOVE: A lone musician, Dan Burke, plays his violin while waiting for the bus at the corner of Sixth Street and University Avenue.

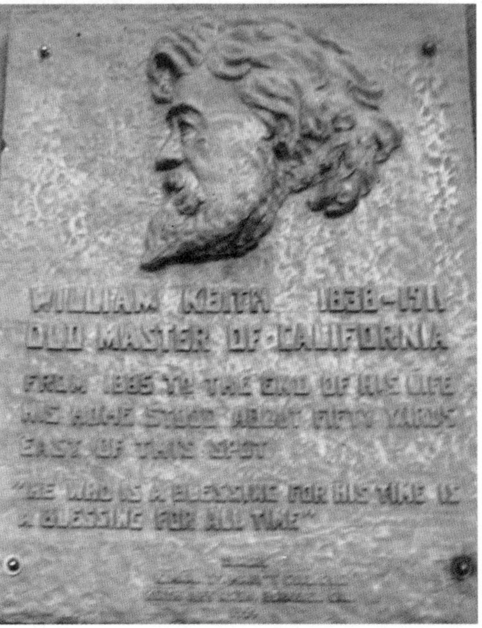

LEFT: A memorial plaque to artist William Keith was placed on the wall of Edwards Stadium, the university track arena built on the location where Keith's home once stood.

Notes

INTRODUCTION

1. Dell, *Love In Greenwich Village*.

CHAPTER 1

1. Contract dated July 14, 1856, in Keith-McHenry-Pond Family Papers.

2. B. P. Avery, "Art Beginnings in the Pacific," *Overland Monthly* 1, no. 2 (August 1868). Keith-McHenry-Pond Family Papers.

3. Pauly, "William Keith," 4.

4. John Muir, letter to William Keith, May 19, 1902. Keith-McHenry-Pond Family Papers. The note in Muir's handwriting is dated 1902, but President Roosevelt's visit to Yosemite took place in 1903.

5. Keith-McHenry-Pond Family Papers.

6. J. W. Gally, *Overland Monthly* 15, (December 1875). Keith-McHenry-Pond Family Papers.

7. Newspaper clipping, 1885. Keith-McHenry-Pond Family Papers.

8. Wagner, *Joaquin Miller*, 227.

9. Ibid., 228.

10. Ibid., 86.

11. Noguchi, *The Story of Yone Noguchi*, 57.

12. Wagner, *Joaquin Miller*, 137.

13. Martinez oral history.

14. Sinclair, introduction to *Martin Eden* by Jack London.

15. Norris, "The Santa Cruz Carnival," 1.

16. Everett, "Frank Norris in His Chapter," 560.

17. Burgess, *The Lark*, no. 15, July 1896.

18. Ibid., no. 1, May 1895.

19. Porter, *The Epi-Lark*, no. 25, May 1897.

20. Ina Coolbrith, letter to William Keith, July 18, 1907. Keith-McHenry-Pond Family Papers.

21. Rhodehamel, *Ina Coolbrith*, 358.

CHAPTER 2

1. Keeler, *A Season's Sowing*, 5.

2. Keeler, *The Simple Home*, 3 and 52.

3. "Open-Air Drama," *San Francisco Examiner* (San Francisco, CA), October 23, 1904.

4. Keeler, *Friends Bearing Torches*, 50.

5. "To Present Play of Famous Poet," unattributed newspaper clipping in Keeler family scrapbook.

6. "Poet's Daughter an Artist—Paints Nature on the Bay," *San Francisco Examiner-Oakland Edition* (San Francisco, CA), November 30, 1919.

7. "Children to Play Queer Instruments at This Concert," *San Francisco Chronicle* (San Francisco, CA), 1921.

8. "Art Center Development C. of C. Plan," *San Francisco Chronicle* (San Francisco, CA), December 4, 1921.

9. "Keeler Outlines Commerce Body's Tentative Program," *Berkeley Daily Gazette* (Berkeley, CA), December 1921.

10. "Poet Keeler's Brain Listed for $75,000 in Contract," *Oakland Tribune* (Oakland, CA), February 6, 1920.

11. "Charles Keeler Delights Crowd at First Soiree," *Berkeley Daily Gazette*, (Berkeley, CA), September 22, 1920.

12. "Poet's Brains Capitalized for $75,000," *San Francisco Chronicle* (San Francisco, CA), January 23, 1921.

13. Keeler, *An Epitome*, 3.

14. Ibid., 31–32.

15. Keeler, *Friends Bearing Torches*, 4.

16. Ibid., 6.

CHAPTER 3

1. Seeger, *Reminiscences of an American*, 88.

2. Clayes, "Evening in Berkeley," 23.

3. Ibid.

4. Tinniswood, *The Arts and Crafts Home*, 12–18.

5. Peixotto, *Romantic California*, 5.

6. Stern, letter to Witter Bynner, April 5, 1929.

7. Whitaker, *Berkeley the Beautiful*, 138.

8. Baker, "Past and Present of Alameda County."

9. Robinson, "The Hillside Problem."

10. Keeler, *The Simple Home*, 1–4.

11. Ibid., 3.

12. Ibid., 28.

13. Keeler, *Suggestions for Hillside Homes*, 5.

14. Whitney, *Childhood Memories*, 6.

15. Maybeck, *Maybeck: The Family View*, 17.

16. Ibid., 18.

17. Millie Robbins, "Millie's Column, A Wacky House on a Grizzly Peak," unpaginated clipping. *San Francisco Chronicle*.

18. Ibid.

19. Shipounoff, *Intro to the Simple Home*, xxiv.

20. Boynton, "The Way," 2.

21. Jury and Maybeck, *The Four-Year Stretch*, 31.

22. Hoexter and Hoexter, "The Blochmans of San Francisco," unpaginated essay.

23. Maybeck, "Maybeck: The Family View," 27.

24. Whitney, *Childhood Memories*, 6.

25. Maybeck, *Maybeck*, 36.

26. Seeger, *Reminiscences of an American*, 102–3.

27. Jury and Maybeck, *The Four-Year Stretch*, 31.

28. Palache, "Six Weeks."

29. Gibson, *A Record*, 10.

30. Young, *Journalism in California*, 166.

31. Cummings and Dunne, *California for the Sportsman*, 33.

32. Colby, letter to *Collier's* magazine.

33. Gibson, *A Record*, 10.

34. Colby, letter to *Collier's* magazine.

35. Cohen, *The History of the Sierra Club*, 30.

36. Bamford, "God Immanent," 6.

37. *California History*, "A Century of Environmental Activism," 241.

38. Adams, *Ansel Adams*, 30.

39. Stern, letter to Witter Bynner, April 5, 1929.

CHAPTER 4

1. "The Berkeley Girl Whose 'Omar' Photos Startle Literary Critics," *Oakland Tribune* (Oakland, CA), March 19, 1906.

2. Brigman, "Starr King Fraternity Exhibition," 229.

3. "Arts and Crafts Exhibit Ready," *San Francisco Chronicle* (San Francisco, CA), October 19, 1908, 5.

4. Maurer, unpublished autobiographical typescript, 5.

5. Maurer, "A Plea for Recognition," 60.

6. Hicks, "A Few Words," 121.

7. Brigman, "The Prints at Idora," 465.

8. Robert H. Fletcher, quote from notes accompanying a 1915 interview of Laura Adams Armer, Artists Index, California State Library.

9. Hicks, "A Few Words of Criticism," 122.

10. Brigman, "Starr King Fraternity Exhibition," 229.

11. "Fear Retards Woman, Avers Mrs. Brigman," *San Francisco Call* (San Francisco, CA), June 8, 1913.

12. Brigman, "The Prints at Idora," 466.

CHAPTER 5

1. Dorothy Wetmore Gerrity oral history, Berkeley Architectural Heritage Association, 1977.

2. Dorothy Wetmore Gerrity scrapbook.

3. Pat Pothier scrapbook.

4. Frederic McConnell, letter to Samuel Hume, June 11, 1919. Department of Dramatic Art Papers, Bancroft Library.

5. Everett Glass, letter to Samuel Hume, February 25, 1919. Department of Dramatic Art Papers, Bancroft Library.

6. Samuel Hume, letter to Mary Morris, March 5, 1920. Department of Dramatic Art Papers, Bancroft Library.

7. Irving Pichel, letter to Samuel Hume, December 25, 1918. Department of Dramatic Art Papers, Bancroft Library.

8. Sproul oral history, 144.

9. Program for *The Beaux Stratagem* at The Playhouse.

10. Dorothy Wetmore Gerrity oral history.

11. Boynton-Quitzow Family oral history. Berkeley: UC Regional Oral History Office, 1973.

12. Newspaper clipping supplied by Lee Palsak.

13. Ibid.

14. Handwritten note on program of *The Jest*.

15. Adams, *Ansel Adams*, 29.

CHAPTER 6

1. *California Writer's Quarterly Bulletin*, June 1913, 2.

2. Atkinson, *The Singing East Bay, 1927–1976*, 18.

3. Ibid.

4. Atkinson, *The Singing East Bay*, 19.

5. Ibid., 15.

6. Harry Noyes Pratt, letters to Ina Coolbrith, July 28, 1919. Harry Noyes Pratt Papers, Bancroft Library.

7. Young, *Journalism in California*, 168.

8. Gibson, *A Record*, 20–21.

9. "Pratt, Harry Noyes," biographical file in archives of the San Francisco Public Library.

10. Harry Noyes Pratt, letters to Ina Coolbrith. May 25, 1923. Harry Noyes Pratt Papers, Bancroft Library.

11. "The Cambridge History of English and American Literature in 18 Volumes" (1907–21), *The Overland Monthly* 17, Later National Literature, Part II. Reprinted online at http://www.bartleby.com/227/1214.html.

12. Harry Noyes Pratt, letters to Ina Coolbrith, May 25, 1923. Harry Noyes Pratt Papers, Bancroft Library.

13. *California Writer's Quarterly Bulletin*, June 1913. Clipping in "Pratt, Harry Noyes." Biographical file in archives of the San Francisco Public Library.

14. Ibid.

15. Atkinson, *The Singing East Bay*, 47–51.

16. Coolbrith, Introduction to *West Winds*.

17. The Clubman, "Alameda Singer Raps Bynner for Criticism," *The Post-Enquirer* (Oakland, CA). November 18, 1922. Clipping in the Harry Noyes Pratt papers, San Francisco Public Library.

18. "Poets and things," *Overland Monthly and the Out West Magazine*, 468.

19. Charles Keeler, letter to Dr. Esterbrook, 1929. Charles Keeler Papers, Bancroft Library.

20. Kraft, *Who Is Witter Bynner?*, 48.

21. Gay Bears! Collection of the University Archives. "The Hidden History of the UC Campus." http://sunsite.berkeley.edu/gaybears/.

22. Gioia, *California Poetry*, 61.

23. Walton, poem from *WB in California*, online.

24. Chiang Kang-hu, "Socialism in China," *The Masses*, October 1917. Reprinted online at www.marxists.org.

25. Samuel Hume, letters to Witter Bynner, 1920–1922. Department of Dramatic Art Papers, Bancroft Library.

26. Stern, letters to Witter Bynner.

27. Bynner, letters to Dane Coolidge.

28. Ibid., March 17, 1908.

29. Ibid.

30. According to EH.net, a Web site created by economic historians, $10,000 in 1940 would translate to $139,000 in 2006 dollars using comparisons to the Consumer Price Index. Using the calculation of nominal GDP per capital, Coolidge's estate would be $547,590 in 2006 dollars. This amount included his home and all of its contents.

31. Jury and Maybeck, *The Four-Year Stretch*, 31.

32. Garnett, poem from *WB in California*.

CHAPTER 7

1. Meyer, "Why an Art School?"

2. Wessels, interview by Margaret Penrose Dhaemers, 64.

3. Meyer, interview by Margaret Pearce Dhaemers, 62.

4. "San Francisco Illustrators—Curbstone Bohemia," *Overland Monthly*, July 1895, 74–76.

5. *The Recorder* (San Francisco, CA), January 9, 1943. In Martinez scrapbook no. 4, collection of the Oakland Museum of California.

6. Griswold, *Western World*.

7. Hailey, ed., *California Art Research*, 54.

8. *House Resolution*, California State Assembly, no. 35 (January 19, 1943).

9. Meyer, "Why an Art School?"

10. *Catalogue*, School of the California Guild of Arts and Crafts.

CHAPTER 8

1. Noguchi, "Childish Play" from *Seen and Unseen*.

2. Statz, *American Dreamers*, 96.

3. Martinez, oral history interview, 155.

4. Bilger, "The Lunchroom Rebellion," 77.

5. Adams, *Ansel Adams*, 29.

6. Walker, *Classy City*.

7. Griffith, *A History*, 67.

8. Hodghead, Campaign Speech to the Hillside Club.

9. Griffith, *A History*, 68 and 136.

10. Ostrander, *The Prohibition Movement*, 92.

11. Ferrier, *Berkeley, California*, 305.

12. Ostrander, *The Prohibition Movement*, 92.

13. Pettit, *A Berkeley Antebellum*, 55.

14. Ibid.

15. Ostrander, *The Prohibition Movement*, 92.

16. De Angulo, *The Old Coyote*, 141.

17. Lance Gilmore, "The Day Berkeley Went All-Out Socialist," *Berkeley Gazette*, April 15, 1975, 1.

18. Ibid.

19. Noguchi, *The Story of Yone Noguchi*, 93.

20. Wilson, *How I Became a Socialist*, unpaginated.

21. Ibid.

22. Wilson, *The Harlots and the Pharisees*, 1 and intro.

23. Ibid., 11.

24. Ibid., 28 and 30.

25. Ibid., 31.

26. Martinez, oral history interview.

27. Ibid., 155.

28. Grauman, "Twenty Minutes at Coffee Dan's," 4.

29. Martinez, oral history interview, 124–25.

30. Lozier, *My Recollections*, unpaginated.

31. London, *War of the Classes*, 1.

32. Statz, *American Dreamers*, 74.

33. Ibid., 130.

34. Ibid., 105.

35. Ibid., 133.

36. Martinez, oral history interview, 5.

37. Ibid.

38. Ibid., 19.

39. Parker, *An American Idyll,* 70.

40. Ibid., 90.

41. Ibid., 91.

42. Ibid., 89.

43. Ibid., 131.

44. Seeger, *Reminiscences of an American,* 120.

45. Leeds-Hurwitz, letter from Jaime de Angulo to John Collier, 10.

46. De Angulo, "Marceline, vous êtes."

47. Seeger, *Reminiscences of an American,* 114.

48. Ibid., 115.

49. Ibid., 115–16.

50. Ibid., 106–8.

51. Ibid., 118–19.

52. Ibid., 121.

53. Ibid., 129–31.

54. Ibid., 43–47.

CHAPTER 9

1. Keeler, *Songs of the Cosmos,* 40.

2. Boynton, "The Way," 4.

3. Anderson, "A True Revival," 28.

4. Ferrier, *Berkeley, California,* 293–302.

5. Howison, "Cooperation of Religion," 39.

6. Jordan, "On the Conflict of Science," 26. Addresses at the thirtieth meeting of the Unitarian Club of California, held at San Francisco, California, April 26, 1987.

7. http://www.berkeleyheritage.com/ berkeley_landmarks/1unitarian.html.

8. Hasselmann, *The First Unitarian Church of Berkeley: A History,* 1–14.

9. Black, "Abstract of the 1870 Federal Census."

10. Caspar, "The Blockman Saga," online.

11. Braden, *These Also Believe,* 323.

12. Ibid., 336.

13. Ibid., 330.

14. West, *Life and Times.*

15. Boynton, "The Way," 6.

16. Keeler, letter to Dr. L. Esterbrook.

17. *Oakland Tribune,* "Keeler Starts New Creed in Berkeley," March 2, 1926.

18. Keeler, letter to Dr. L. Esterbrook.

19. Keeler, *An Epitome of the Cosmic Religion,* 23.

20. Ibid.

21. Numata, letter to Charles Keeler.

22. Editorial, *Pacific World,* June 1925. Reprinted in "Letters to the Pacific World," 5.

23. Statz, *American Dreamers,* 14.

24. Victoria Woodhull quoted in Frisken's "Sex in Politics," 90.

25. Payne, letters to Charles Keeler, March–May 1926.

26. Payne, letter to Charles Keeler, March 7, 1926.

27. Nelles, letter to Charles Keeler.

28. "The Pasmore Trio and Charles Edward Clarke," 1910.

29. Keeler, *Auto-Suggestion for Prosperity,* unpaginated manuscript.

CHAPTER 10

1. Music and lyrics by Bob Miller, ca. 1932.

2. Mary Bucher, conversation with Shelley Rideout, April 20, 2006.

3. John Emmett Gerrity, oral history interview by Mary McChesney, 7.

4. Dorothy Cravath, oral history interview by Mary McChesney, 6.

5. Ibid.

6. Howard, oral history interview by Mary McChesney, 3.

7. Ibid.

8. Albro and Hall, oral history interview by Mary McChesney, 16.

9. Jury, "How the City Weathered," 306.

10. Ibid., 307.

11. "Purpose of the Federal Art Project," Works Progress Administration. Swingle Collection, Berkeley Public Library History Room.

12. John Emmett Gerrity, oral history interview by Mary McChesney, 4.

13. Dorothy Wetmore Gerrity, oral history interview, 1977.

14. Foster, letter to David Kahn.

15. Foster, "Towards a Living Theatre," unpaginated typescript.

16. Foster, letter to David Kahn.

17. Fleming, "Working for the WPA."

18. "Mural Will Adorn Council Chambers," *The Berkeley Gazette,* January 4, 1934.

19. *Popular Photography,* February 1960. Cited on the Library of Congress Web site http://www.loc.gov/print/list/128_ migm.html.

20. Ruth Cravath, oral history by Mary McChesney, 12.

21. Dorothy Cravath, oral history interview by Minette Martin, 7.

22. Robert Howard, oral history interview by Mary McChesney, 7.

CHAPTER 11

1. O'Shaughnessy, "Ode."

2. Herron, *A Guidebook,* 190.

3. Greene, *The End of the Affair,* 25.

photo credits

ARONOVICI, JOHN GINNO

pages 96, 175

BANCROFT LIBRARY, UNIVERSITY OF CALIFORNIA, BERKELEY

pages 18 William Keith (POR-20-10046148B),
28 Porter Garnett (POR-17),
62 (0012384_31a 1960.010 ser. 1:0198—PIC),
90 Samuel Hume (01:54 1971.031.1914.09:38-ALB),
104 (00006310), (BANC MSS C-H 23),
115 Mary Coolidge (POR-3),
148 Herman Whitaker (POR-2),
162 (00006308), (BANC MSS C-H 105),
167 (00006307), (BANC MSS C-H 105)

BERKELEY ARCHITECTURAL HERITAGE ASSOCIATION

pages 20 (BAHA.D44),
38 (BAHA.D46),
54 (BAHA.D19),
55 (BAHA.D85),
56 (BAHA.34),
57 (BAHA.D13),
58 (BAHA.443),
61 (BAHA.D80),
68 (BAHA.D74),
71 (BAHA.D75),
72 (BAHA.D67),
75 (BAHA.D72),
80 (BAHA.D32),
89 (BAHA.289),
93 (BAHA.290),
94 (BAHA.D82),
98 (BAHA.39),
160 (BAHA.33)

BERKELEY HISTORICAL SOCIETY

pages 8,
10 (114.189.0628),
12,
13 (123.190.0686),
14 (233.189.1939),
33, 34, 35, 36, 37, 39, 40, 41, 42, 44, 45, 46, 48, 49 (Keeler Collection),
50 (494.190.1577),
53 (490.190.3262),
65 (480.190.2132),
67 (Keeler Collection),
91,
92,
99 (473.192.6692),
102 (214.191.3233),
129 (213.190.1305),
137 (Keeler Collection),
142,
144 (450.191.7034),
154 (264.195.2179),
163 Mike Musielski, photographer (543.980.1323),
169 (Keeler Collection),
186 R. L. Copeland, photographer
188 Cliff Bond, photographer (114.195.0626),
189 (upper), A. Moon, photographer (492.196.2007),
189 (lower), (543.198.0297),
190 (upper), Margaret Moore, photographer (478.199.6863),
191 (upper), Russell, photographer (471.198.6749)

BUCHER, MARY, MARGARET LOVERDE & KATE SATER

pages 84, 87, 88, 172, 176, 177, 178, and front cover

CALIFORNIA COLLEGE OF THE ARTS

pages 123, 128, 130 (left)

Bibliography

Adams, Ansel. *Ansel Adams: An Autobiography.* Boston: Little, Brown and Company, 1996.

Albro, Maxine and Parker Hall. Oral history interview conducted by Mary McChesney. Smithsonian Archives of American Art, 1964. http://www.aaa.si.edu/collections/oralhistories/transcripts/albro64.htm.

Anderson, Douglas Firth. "A True Revival of Religion: Protestants and the San Francisco Graft Prosecutions, 1906–1909." *Religion and American Culture* 4, no. 1 (1994).

Atkinson, Ruth. *The Singing East Bay and Beyond: Fifty Years of the Poet's Diner, 1927–1976.* Oakland: Wuerth Letter Shop, 1976.

Baker, Joseph E. *Past and Present of Alameda County, California.* Chicago: S. J. Clarke Pub. Co., 1914. Reprinted at http://www.calarchives4u.com/history/alameda/1914-ch16.htm.

Bamford, Fredrick I. "God Immanent." From *West Winds.* Ina Coolbrith, editor. San Francisco: California Writer's Club, 1925.

Berson, Misha. *The San Francisco Stage: From Golden Spike to Great Earthquake 1869–1906.* San Francisco: San Francisco Performing Arts Library and Museum, 1992.

Bilger, Burkhard. "The Lunchroom Rebellion." *The New Yorker,* 82, September 4, 2006.

Black, Edward. "Abstract of the 1870 Federal Census, San Francisco County, California—ED 48: File 7 of 20." http://www.rootsweb.com/~cenfiles/ca/sanfrancisco/1870/ed48/sanfrancisco/ward08/precint02/sanfrancisco-j07.txt.

Bolin, John Seelye. *Samuel Hume: Artist and Exponent of American Art Theatre.* PhD dissertation, University of Michigan, 1970.

Boynton, Florence. "The Way (The Consciousness in Which We Live) No Age (Atmosphere of Unfoldment)." From the Florence Boynton Papers, Berkeley Historical Society, ca. 1925.

Braden, Charles Samuel. *These Also Believe: A study of modern American cults and minority religious movements.* New York: Macmillan, 1953.

Brechin, Gray. "Built by FDR: How the WPA Changed the Lay of the Land," *SF,* January 1990. Reprinted online at http://www.graybrechin.com/GbrechinArticle5.html.

———. "The Temple of Wings" *San Francisco Magazine,* April 1991.

Brevda, William. *Harry Kemp—The Last Bohemian.* Lewisburg: Bucknell University Press, 1986.

Brigman, Anne. "Starr King Fraternity Exhibition." *Camera Craft,* April 1905, 229.

———. "The Prints at Idora." *Camera Craft,* December 1908, 465–66.

Burgess, C. A. *Pictorial Spiritualism.* Chicago: Illinois State Spiritualist Association, 1922.

Burgess, Gelett. *The Lark.* no. 1, May 1895.

———. *The Lark.* no. 15, July 1896.

Bynner, Witter. Letters to Dane Coolidge, October 3, 1905. Dane Coolidge Papers, Bancroft Library.

"A Century of Environmental Action: The Sierra Club, 1892–1992." *California History* 71 (summer 1992).

California Writer's Quarterly Bulletin, June 1913. Clipping in "Pratt, Harry Noyes" biographical file in archives of the San Francisco Public Library.

Cardwell, Kenneth. *Bernard Maybeck: Artisan, Architect, Artist.* Santa Monica: Hennessey and Ingalls, 1996.

Carlin, Eva V., ed. and decorated by Louise M. Keeler. *A Berkeley Year.* n.p. The Women's Auxiliary of the First Unitarian Church of Berkeley, California, 1898.

Caspar, Trudie. "The Blochman Saga in San Diego." *Journal of San Diego History* 23, no. 1 (1977). Reprinted at http://www.sandiegohistory.org/journal/77winter/blochman.htm.

Catalogue. Berkeley: School of the Guild of Arts and Crafts, 1907–08.

Cerney, Susan Dinklespiel. *Berkeley Landmarks: An Illustrated Guide to Berkeley, California's Architectural Heritage*. Berkeley: Berkeley Architectural Heritage Association, 2001.

Clark, Jean Hannah and Shirley Sargent, eds. *Dear Papa: Letters Between John Muir and His Daughter Wanda*. Fresno: Panorama West Books, 1985.

Clayes, Mary Bird. "Evening in Berkeley." *Twigs from the Berkeley Branch*. Evelyn E. Underwood, editor. Berkeley: Press of Lederer, Street & Zeus Company, ca. 1927.

Cohen, Michael P. *The History of the Sierra Club, 1892–1970*. San Francisco: Sierra Club Books, 1988.

Colby, William. Letter to *Collier's* magazine. San Francisco, May 12, 1908. Reprinted online at http://balrog.sdsu.edu/~putman/445/colbyhetchletter.htm.

Coolbrith, Ina. *Wings of Sunset*. Boston and New York: Houghton Mifflin Company, 1929.

———. Introduction to *West Winds: an Anthology of Verse*. San Francisco: Harr Wagner, 1925.

Cornelius, Brother. *Keith, Old Master of California*. New York: Putnam, 1942–57.

Cosmic Society. "The Seventh Anniversary of the Founding of the Berkeley Cosmic Society." Handbill, October 9, 1932. Charles Keeler Collection, Berkeley Historical Society.

Cravath, Dorothy. Oral history interview by Minette Martin. Smithsonian Archives of American Art, 1964. http://www.aaa.si.edu/collections/oral histories/transcripts/cravat64.htm.

Cravath, Ruth. Oral history interview by Mary McChesney. Smithsonian Archives of American Art, 1965.

http://www.aaa.si.edu/collections/oral histories/transcripts/cravat65.htm.

CU-36 Records of the Department of Dramatic Art 1911–1977. Berkeley: The Bancroft Library, University of California.

Cummings, A. M. and Allan Dunne. *California for the sportsman; being a collection of hints as to the haunts of the wild things of hoof, claw, scale and feather of California's land and water; the way to reach them, and some suggestions as to approved methods of capture*. San Francisco: Southern Pacific Railroad, 1911.

"Dane Coolidge." *Handbook of Texas Online* http://www.tsha.utexas.edu/handbook/online/articles/CC/fco56.html.

De Angulo, Gui. *The Old Coyote of Big Sur: The Life of Jaime de Angulo*. Berkeley: Stonegarden Press, 1995.

De Angulo, Jaime. "Marceline, vous êtes une cochonne." Undated essay. Jaime de Angulo Papers, University of California Los Angeles, Collection 160 Box 2.

Dell, Floyd. *Love in Greenwich Village*. New York: George H. Doran Company, 1926. http://home.swbell.net/worchel/dell/proem.htm.

Dempster, Fred H. *A Brief History of the Hillside Club; its First Quarter Century, 1889–1924*. Berkeley: Hillside Club, 1973.

Dicker, Laverne. "Laura Adams Armer: California Photographer." *California Historical Society Quarterly*, summer 1977.

Ehrens, Susan. *A Poetic Vision: The Photographs of Anne Brigman*. Santa Barbara: Santa Barbara Museum of Art, 1995.

Everett, Wallace W. "Frank Norris in His Chapter," *The Phi Gamma Delta* 52, no. 6 (April 1930). http://phigam.org/history/Magazine/NorrisatUC.htm.

Ferrier, William W. *Berkeley, California: the story of the evolution of a hamlet into a city of culture and commerce*. Berkeley: self-published, 1933.

Fleming, Thomas, "Working for the WPA," *The Columbus Free Press-Reflections on Black History*. February 17, 1999. http://www.freepress.org/fleming/fleming70.html.

Fonar, Philip S. *Jack London, American Rebel*. New York: Citadel Press, 1947.

Foster, Lois. "Towards a Living Theatre: A History of the San Francisco Federal Theatre Project, November 1, 1935 to August 1, 1936." Typescript in the collection of the San Francisco Performing Arts Library and Museum.

———. Letter to David Kahn, May 15, 1977. San Francisco Performing Arts Library and Museum.

Frankiel, Sandra Sizer. *California's Spiritual Frontiers: Religious Alternatives in Anglo-Protestantism, 1850–1910*. Berkeley: University of California Press, 1988.

Frisken, Amanda. "Sex in Politics: Victoria Woodhull as an American Public Woman, 1870–1876." *Journal of Women's History* 12, no. 1 (spring 2000), 89–111.

Frost, O. W. *Joaquin Miller*. New York: Twayne Publishers, Inc., 1967.

Gagey, Edmond M. *The San Francisco Stage: A History*. New York: Columbia University Press, 1950.

Garnett, Porter. From *WB in California*. Reproduced on Gay Bears! Collection of the University Archives. "The Hidden History of the UC Campus." http://sunsite.berkeley.edu/gaybears/.

Gay Bears! Collection of the University Archives. "The Hidden History of the UC Campus." http://sunsite.berkeley.edu/gaybears.

Gerrity, Dorothy Wetmore. Tapes of oral history interview. Berkeley Architectural Heritage Association, 1977.

Gerrity, John Emmett. Oral history interview by Mary McChesney. Smithsonian Archives of American Art, 1965. http://www.aaa.si.edu/collections/oral histories/transcripts/gerrit65.htm.

Gibson, Mary. *A Record of Twenty-Five Years of the California Federation of Women's Clubs, 1900–1925*. San Francisco: The California Federation of Women's Clubs, 1927.

Gioia, Dana. *California Poetry*. Berkeley: Heyday Books, 2004.

Grauman, Sidney. "Twenty Minutes at Coffee Dan's," 1916. Digitized from the Library of Congress Rare Books and Special Collections Division; http://memory.loc.gov/cgi-bin/query/r?ammem/varstg:@field(NUMBER+@band(varsep+s44442)).

Greene, Graham. *The End of the Affair*. London: William Heinemann Ltd., 1951.

Griffith, Ernest S. *A History of American City Government: The Progressive Years and Their Aftermath, 1900–1920*. New York: Praeger Publishers, 1974.

Griswold, Mary Edith. *Western World*, n.d. in Martinez scrapbook no. 4, collection of the Oakland Museum of California.

Hailey, Gene, ed. *California Art Research* 10, first series, San Francisco: Works Progress Administration (1937).

Hakutani, Yoshinobu. *Selected Writings of Yone Noguchi: An East-West Literary Assimilation. Vol. 1: Poetry*. Cranbury: Associated University Presses, 1990.

Harrington, Michael. *Socialism*. New York: Saturday Review Press, 1972.

"Harry Noyes Pratt" Biographical file in archives of the San Francisco Public Library.

Hasselmann, Merv. *The First Unitarian Church of Berkeley: A History*. Berkeley: The First Unitarian Church of Berkeley, 1981.

Hemingway, Andrew. *Artists on the Left: American Artists and the Communist Movement, 1926–1956*. New Haven and London: Yale University Press, 2002.

Herron, Don. *A Guidebook to the Literary World of San Francisco and its Environs*. San Francisco: City Lights Books, 1985.

Hicks, L. D. "A Few Words of Criticism upon the Work of Each Exhibitor, Leveled in a Kindly Spirit by the Editor, with Reproductions of Striking Pictures." *Camera Craft*, January 1902, 121–22.

Higgins, C. A. and Charles A. Keeler. *To California and Back*. New York: Doubleday, Page & Company, 1903.

Hjalmarson, Birgitta. *Artful Players: Artistic Life in Early San Francisco*. Los Angeles: Balcony Press, 1999.

Hodghead, Beverly Lacy. Campaign Speech to the Hillside Club. Undated typescript. Beverly Lacy Hodghead papers, Berkeley: Bancroft Library, University of California.

Hoexter, Mary R. and David F. Hoexter. "The Blochmans of San Francisco, Santa Maria, and Berkeley." Unpublished essay dated January 1979. Berkeley: Berkeley Historical Society biographical files.

Howard, Robert. Oral history interview by Mary McChesney. Smithsonian Archives of American Art, 1964. http://www.aaa.si.edu/collections/oral histories/transcripts/howard64.htm.

Howison, George. "Cooperation of religion and science in uplifting humanity." *Addresses at the thirtieth meeting of the Unitarian Club of California*. San Francisco: C. A. Murdock & Co., 1897.

Hughes, Edan Milton. *Artists in California 1786–1940*. Sacramento: Crocker Art Museum, 2002.

Hume, Samuel. Letters to Witter Bynner, 1920–1922. Department of Dramatic Art Papers, Bancroft Library.

Hunt, Robert. "Editor's Foreword." *Selected Poems by Witter Bynner*. New York: Alfred A. Knopf, 1943.

Indvik, Gail Marie and Dimitri Shipounoff. *Adelaide Hanscom Leeson—Pictorialist Photographer—1876–1932*. Carbondale: Southern Illinois University, 1981.

The Institute of Buddhist Studies. *Letters to the Pacific World, June 1925*. Berkeley: The Institute of Buddhist Studies, 1982.

James, George Wharton. "Charles Keeler—Scientist and Poet." *National Magazine*, November 1911.

Jewett, Masha Zakheim. *Coit Tower, San Francisco: Its History and Art*. San Francisco: Volcano Press, 1983.

Johnson, Drew Heath. *Capturing Light*. Oakland: Oakland Museum of California, 2001.

Jones, Harvey. *Twilight and Reverie: California Tonalist Painting 1890–1930*. Oakland: Oakland Museum of California, 1995.

Jordan, David Starr. "The Conflict of Science." *Addresses at the thirtieth meeting of the Unitarian Club of California*. San Francisco: C. A. Murdock & Co., 1897.

Jury, Florence. "How the City Weathered the Cruelest Depression Year," *Exactly Opposite the Golden Gate: Essays on Berkeley's History, 1845–1945*, Berkeley: Berkeley Historical Society, 1983.

Jury, Florence and Jacomena Maybeck. *The Four-Year Stretch: College Life at U. C. Berkeley, 1923–1927*. Berkeley, 1979.

Kang-hu, Chiang. "Socialism in China." *The Masses*, October 1917. Reprinted online at www.marxists.org.

Keeler, Charles A. *A Light Through the Storm*. San Francisco: William Doxey, 1894.

———. *A Wanderer's Songs of the Sea*. San Francisco: A. M. Robertson, 1902.

———. *An Epitome of Cosmic Religion*. Berkeley: The Sign of the Live-Oak, 1925.

———. "Auto-Suggestion for Prosperity." Unpublished poem. Charles Keeler Collection, Berkeley Historical Society, undated.

———. *Bird Notes Afield*. San Francisco: D. P. Elder & Morgan Shepard, 1899.

———. "Buddha to the Knight." *Songs of the Cosmos*. No. 12, *Bruno Chap Books*. New York: Guido Bruno, 1915–1916.

———. *Enchanted Treasure Island*. Berkeley: Professional Press, 1939.

———. *Evolution of Colors of North American Birds*. San Francisco: California Academy of Sciences, 1893.

———. *Friends Bearing Torches*. Unpublished manuscript at the Berkeley Historical Society, 1934–37.

———. Letter to Dr. L. Esterbrook, September 15, 1929. Charles Keeler Family Papers, Berkeley: Bancroft Library, University of California.

———. *San Francisco and Thereabout*. San Francisco: The California Promotion Committee, 1902.

———. *San Francisco Through Earthquake and Fire*. San Francisco: Paul Elder and Company, 1906.

———. *Sequoia Sonnets*. Berkeley: The Sign of the Live-Oak, 1919.

———. *Hillside Club Suggestions for Berkeley Homes*. Berkeley: Arts and Crafts Press, 1999.

———. *Tahiti The Golden*. San Francisco: Oceanic Steamship Company, 1902.

———. *The Promise of the Ages*. Privately published, 1896.

———. *The Simple Home*. San Francisco: Paul Elder and Company, 1904.

———. *The Simple Home*. Santa Barbara: Peregrine Smith, 1979. (Reprint of the 1904 edition.)

———. *The Triumph of Light*. Berkeley: The Sign of the Live-Oak, 1904.

———. *The Victory*. New York: Laurence J. Gomme, 1916.

———. *A Season's Sowing*. San Francisco: A. M. Robertson, 1899.

———. *Elfin Songs of Sunland*. Berkeley: The Sign of the Live-Oak, 1904.

———. *The Idyls of El Dorado*, San Francisco: A. M. Robertson, 1900.

———. *Southern California*. Los Angeles: Passenger Department, Santa Fe Route, 1898.

———. Music by Chas. H. McCurrie. *Songs of Sunland for Little Children*. Alameda: Alameda Music Co., 1909.

Keeler, Sarah I. Keeler family scrapbook containing newspaper clippings and programs, 1904–1931. Collection of the Berkeley Historical Society.

Keith-McHenry-Pond Papers BANC MSSC-B595. Berkeley: The Bancroft Library, University of California.

Kraft, James. *Who Is Witter Bynner? A Biography*. Albuquerque: University of New Mexico Press, 1995.

LaFrance, Danielle, ed. *Berkeley! A Literary Tribute*. Berkeley: Heyday Books, 1997.

Leeds-Hurwitz, Wendy. *Rolling in Ditches with Shamans: Jaime de Angulo and the Professionalization of American Anthropology*. Lincoln: University of Nebraska Press, 2004.

Lewis, Oscar. *Bay Window Bohemia*. Garden City: Doubleday & Company, 1956.

London, Jack. *Martin Eden*, with an introduction by Andrew Sinclair. New York: Viking Penguin, Inc., 1984.

———. Preface to *War of the Classes*, 1905. Reprinted online at http://london.somona.edu/Writings/WarOfTheClasses/preface.html.

Lozier, Frances Cheney. "My Recollections of Jack London and Becky." Reprinted from *Jack London Echoes*, April 1982. www.jacklondons.net/my_London_recollections1.html.

Mann, Margery. *Women of Photography*. San Francisco: San Francisco Museum of Art, 1975.

Martinez, Elsie Whitaker. San Francisco Bay Area writers and artists/Elsie Whitaker Martinez; an interview conducted by Franklin D. Walker and Willa Klug Baum; with an introduction by Franklin D. Walker. Berkeley: University of California, Bancroft Library, Regional Oral History Office, 1969.

Maurer, Oscar. "A Plea for Recognition." *Camera Craft*, June 1900, 60.

———. Unpublished autobiographical typescript, 1963, 5. Collection of the Oakland Museum of California.

Maybeck, Jacomena. *Maybeck: The Family View*. Berkeley: Berkeley Architectural Heritage Association, 1980.

———. *People and Places: A Memoir*. Berkeley, Stonegarden Press, 1992.

McCardle, Phil, ed. *Exactly Opposite the Golden Gate: essays on Berkeley's History, 1845–1945*. Berkeley: Berkeley Historical Society, 1983.

McCarroll, Stacey. *California Dreamin'—Camera Clubs and the Pictorial Photography Tradition*. Boston: Boston University Art Gallery, 2004.

McDevitt, William. *Jack London as Poet and As Platform Man. Did Jack London Commit Suicide?* San Francisco: Recorder-Sunset Press, 1947.

McElrath Jr., Joseph R. and Jesse S. Crisler. *Frank Norris: a life*. Urbana and Chicago: University of Illinois Press, 2006.

Meltzer, Milton. *Dorothea Lange: a photographer's life*. New York: Farrar, Straus, Giroux, 1978.

———. *Violins and Shovels: The WPA Arts Projects.* New York: Delacorte Press, 1976.

Meyer, Frederick H. "Why an Art School," *Remembering Dr. Meyer.* Oakland: California College of Arts and Crafts Alumni Society, 1961.

Meyer, Laetitia (Babs). Interview by Margaret Pennrose Dhaemers. *California College of Arts and Crafts, 1907–1944.* (MA thesis). Oakland: Mills College, 1967.

Milton J. Wershow Company. "A Maharaja's Palace will be offered at Real Estate Public Auction Tues. Dec. 12, 1967 at 2 PM." Los Angeles: Milton J. Wershow Company, 1967.

Mitutoyo Mfg. Co, Ltd. *The 50-Year History of Mitutoyo.* Tokyo: Mitutoyo Mfg. Co., Ltd., 1986.

National Delegate Convention of Spiritualists of the United States of America. *Proceedings of the National Delegate Convention of Spiritualists of the United States of America, held in Chicago, Illinois, September 27, 28, and 29, 1893: with an alphabetical list of the delegates present at the convention, containing also Cora L. V. Richmond's paper on spiritualism, presented by her to the Parliament of Religions, and an essay on the same subject by J. S. Loveland.* Washington, D.C.: Stormont & Jackson, 1893.

Nelles, Laura Gearns. Letter to Charles Keeler, August 7, 1931. Charles Keeler Family Papers. Berkeley: Bancroft Library, University of California.

Noguchi, Yone. "Childish Play." *Seen and Unseen.* Reprinted in *Selected Writings of Yone Noguchi: An East-West Literary Assimilation. Vol. 1: Poetry.* Edited by Yoshinobu Hakutani. Cranbury: Associated University Presses, 1990.

———. *The Story of Yone Noguchi: Told by Himself.* Philadelphia: George W. Jacobs and Co., 1914.

Norris, Frank. "The Santa Cruz Venetian Carnival," *The Wave,* June 27, 1896. http://www.santacruzpl.org/history/19thc/norris.shtml.

Numata, Ewart (Yehan). Letter to Charles Keeler, September 11, 1925. Charles Keeler Family papers, Bancroft Library.

O'Shaughnessy, Arthur William Edgar. "Ode" (1874). *A Concise Treasury of Great Poems.* New York: Permabooks, 1961.

Ostrander, Gilman Marston. *The Prohibition Movement in California, 1848–1933.* Berkeley: University of California Press, 1957.

"The Overland Monthly." *The Cambridge History of English and American Literature in 18 Volumes* XVII (1907–21) (Later National Literature, Part II.) Reprinted online at http://www.bartleby.com/227/1214.html.

Palache, Charles. "Six weeks in the Saddle: A trip to Stockton,—Hetch-Hetchy,—Yo Semite,—Mts. Dana & Lyell,—Mono Lake,—Mariposa Big Trees,—Livermore and Berkeley. In July and August 1889." Diary published at http://franklin-sterling hill.com/cp/sixweeks.shtml.

Palmquist, Peter E. *Shadowcatchers—A Directory of Women in California Photography Before 1901.* Arcata: Peter E. Palmquist, 1990.

———. *Shadowcatchers II—A Directory of Women in California Photography 1900–1920.* Arcata: Peter E. Palmquist, 1991.

Parker, Cornelia Stratton. *An American Idyll: The Life of Carleton H. Parker.* Boston: The Atlantic Monthly Press, 1919.

Parry, Albert. *Garrets and Pretenders: A History of Bohemianism in America.* Originally published by Covici-Friede, 1933. Republished with additional chapters, New York: Dover Publications, Inc., 1960.

Partridge, Elizabeth. *Restless Spirit: The Life and Work of Dorothea Lange.* New York: Viking Press, 1998.

"The Pasmore Trio and Charles Edward Clarke," 1910. From the University of Iowa Redpath Chautauqua Collection. http://sdrcdata.lib.uiowa.edu/libsdrc/details.jsp?id=/pasmoretce/1.

Pauly, Steve. "William Keith, A Friend of John Muir," *The View From John Muir's Window.* Online newsletter of the John Muir Memorial Association. February 1996, issue 86. Available online at http://www.johnmuir.org/martinez/view/issue_86.html.

Payne, Ninetta Eames. Letters to Charles Keeler. Charles Keeler Family Papers, Berkeley: Bancroft Library, University of California.

Peixotto, Ernest. *Romantic California.* New York: C. Scribner's sons, 1927.

Pescatello, Ann M. *Charles Seeger: A Life in American Music.* Pittsburgh: University of Pittsburgh Press, 1992.

Pettitt, George Albert. *A History of Berkeley.* Alameda County Historical Society, 1976.

Pettitt, Kenneth. *A Berkeley Antebellum.* Berkeley: K. I. Pettitt, 2000.

"Poets and things," *Overland Monthly and Out-West Magazine* LXXXII, no. 10 (October 1924).

Pratt, Harry Noyes. Letters to Ina Coolbrith. May 25, 1923. Harry Noyes Pratt papers, Bancroft Library.

———. Letters to Ina Coolbrith. July 28, 1919. Harry Noyes Pratt papers, Bancroft Library.

Prebish, Charles S. *American Buddhism.* North Scituate: Duxbury Press, 1979.

Quitzow, Charles. *Dance at the Temple of the Wings, the Boynton-Quitzow family in Berkeley.* Oral history interview with Charles Quitzow and Sülgwynn Boynton Quitzow conducted by Suzanne Riess and

Margaretta Mitchell. Berkeley: University of California, Bancroft Library, Regional Oral History Office, 1972.

Raithmell, George. *Realms of Gold: The Colorful Writers of San Francisco, 1850–1950*. Berkeley: Creative Arts Book Company, 1998.

Rhodehamel, Josephine DeWitt and Raymond Francis Wood. *Ina Coolbrith: Librarian and Laureate of California*. Provo: Brigham Young University Press, 1973.

Robbins, Millie. "Millie's Column, Back to Nature For the Boyntons." *San Francisco Chronicle,* Tuesday, September 15, 1959.

Robbins, Tim. *Cradle Will Rock: The Movie and the Moment*. New York: New Market Press, 2000.

Robinson, Madge. "The Hillside Problem." *The House Beautiful* 6, no. 1 (June 1899). Reprinted at http://www.berkeley heritage.com/berkeley_landmarks/ hillside_problem.html.

"San Francisco Illustrators—Curbstone Bohemia." *Overland Monthly,* July 1895.

Schwartz, Stephen. *From West to East: California and the Making of the American Mind*. New York: The Free Press, 1998.

Seeger, Charles. *Reminiscences of an American Musicologist,* oral history transcript: Charles Seeger, interviewed by Adelaide G. Tusler, [1966] and Ann M. Briegleb, [1970 and 1971]. Oral history collection, Department of Special Collections, University Library, University of California, Los Angeles, 1972.

Shipounoff, Dimitri. Introduction to *The Simple Home*, by Charles Keeler. Santa Barbara: Peregrine Smith, Inc., 1979.

Sproul, Ida Amelia. *The President's Wife*. Oral history interview conducted by Suzanne Reiss,1980–81. Berkeley: University of California, Bancroft Library, Regional Oral History Office, 1981.

Starr, Kevin. *Americans and the California Dream, 1850–1915*. New York: Oxford University Press, 1973.

Statz, Clarice. *American Dreamers: The Story of Charmian and Jack London*. New York: St. Martin's Press, 1988.

Stern, Albert. Letters to Witter Bynner, April 5, 1929 and August 30, 1929. Bancroft Library.

Tanaka, Colette M. *John Emmett Gerrity*. Catalogue for an exhibition held at the Art Exchange Gallery and Sculpture Garden, San Francisco, 1998.

Taylor, Judith. *Tangible Memories: Californians and their Gardens, 1800–1950*. Pennsylvania: Xlibris Corp., 2003.

Thompson, Daniella. *First Unitarian Church: 2401 Bancroft Way, Berkeley, CA*. Published at http://www.berkeley heritage.com/berkeley_landmarks/ 1unitarian.html.

Tinniswood, Adrian. *The Arts and Crafts House*. New York: Watson-Guptill Publications, 1999.

Wagner, Harr. *Joaquin Miller and His Other Self*. San Francisco: Harr Wagner Publishing Company, 1929.

Walker, Franklin. *The Seacoast of Bohemia*. Santa Barbara: Peregrine Smith Inc., 1973.

Walker, Richard. "Classy City: Residential Realms of the Bay Region." Online version, October 2004. http://geography .berkeley.edu/PeopleHistory/faculty/ R_Walker/ClassCity.pdf. Previously published as "Landscape and City Life: Four Ecologies of Residence in the San Francisco Bay Area." *Ecumene* 2, no. 1 (1995).

Walton, Eda Lou. Poem from *WB in California*. Reproduced on Gay Bears! Collection of the University Archives. "The Hidden History of the UC Campus." http://sunsite .berkeley.edu/gaybears/.

"Wedding to a Conga Beat: Bizarre Ritual in Berkeley 'Temple,'" *San Francisco Chronicle*, October 5, 1959.

Wessels, Glen. Interview by Margaret Pennrose Dhaemers. *California College of Arts and Crafts, 1907–1944*. (MA thesis). Oakland: Mills College, 1967.

West, S. H. *Life and Times of S. H. West*. Self-published, 1906.

Whitaker, Herman. "Berkeley, The Beautiful." *Sunset Magazine*. December 1906.

Whitney, Deborah. "Childhood Memories of Nut Hill." *Berkeley Historical Society Newsletter*. Summer 1999.

Wilson, J. Stitt. *How I Became a Socialist*. Berkeley: self-published, 1912.

———. "The harlots and the Pharisees, or The Barbary Coast in a barbarous land; also, The Story of a socialist mayor; Letter declining mayoralty nomination." Berkeley: self-published, 1913.

Wilson, Michael. G. and Dennis Reed. *Pictorialism in California*. Malibu: J. Paul Getty Museum, 1994.

Wollenberg, Charles. *Berkeley, A City in History*. Lecture series at the Berkeley Public Library, 2002. Reprinted online at http://berkeleypubliclibrary.org/ system.html.

Works Progress Administration. *Berkeley: The First Seventy-Five Years*. Compiled by workers of the writer's program of the WPA. Berkeley: Gillick Press, 1941.

Young, John P. *Journalism in California, and Pacific Coast and Exposition Biographies*. San Francisco, Chronicle Publishing Co., 1915.

index

SEA
OF DREAMS
The Isle of
Delectable Islands
The Cape of Storms
PAYS DE LA JEVNESSE
o The
Veritas
City of Shams
LISTIA
Vanitas
B O
at
The
ftinc.
Hi